The Divided Therapist

C000153410

This important new book explores the nature of the divided brain and its relevance for contemporary psychotherapy. Citing the latest neuroscientific research, it shows how the relationship between the two hemispheres of the brain is central to our mental health, and examines both the practical and theoretical implications for therapy.

Disconnections, dissociations, and imbalances between our two hemispheres underlie many of our most prevalent forms of mental distress and disturbance. These include issues of addiction, autism, schizophrenia, depression, anorexia, relational trauma, borderline and personality disorders, psychopathy, anxiety, derealisation and devitalisation, and alexithymia. A contemporary understanding of the nature of the divided brain is therefore of importance in engaging with and treating these disturbances.

Featuring contributions from some of the key authors in the field, *The Divided Therapist* suggests that hemispheric integration lies at the heart of the therapeutic process itself, and that a better understanding of the precise mechanisms that underlie and enable this integration will help to transform the practice of psycho-therapy and psychoanalysis in the twenty-first century. The book will be essential reading for any therapeutic practitioner interested in how the architecture of the brain informs and effects their client's issues and challenges.

Rod Tweedy, PhD, is the author of *The God of the Left Hemisphere: Blake, Bolte Taylor and the Myth of Creation* (Routledge, 2013), a study of William Blake's works in the light of contemporary neuroscience, and the editor of *The Political Self: Understanding the Social Context for Mental Illness* (Routledge, 2017). He is also an active supporter of Veterans for Peace UK and the user-led mental health organisation, Mental Fight Club.

"A magnificent achievement."
Professor Jeremy Holmes, psychiatrist and author of *Exploring in Security: Towards an Attachment-Informed Psychoanalytic Psychotherapy* and *The Search for the Secure Base: Attachment Theory and Psychotherapy*

"Fascinating – both lucid and intriguing."
Adam Phillips, psychoanalyst and author of *Becoming Freud: The Making of a Psychoanalyst* and *Attention Seeking*

"Wonderful – a really important book revealing the missing key to understanding psychopathology and psychotherapy."
Dr Phil Mollon, psychoanalyst and author of *Shame and Jealousy: The Hidden Turmoils*; *Psychoanalytic Energy Psychotherapy*; and *The Fragile Self: The Structure of Narcissistic Disturbance*

"This book explores and explicates insights that are fundamentally important to the practice of therapy today. Really fascinating."
Robert Snell, analytic psychotherapist and author of *Uncertainties, Mysteries, Doubts: Romanticism and the Analytic Attitude*

The Divided Therapist

Hemispheric Difference and
Contemporary Psychotherapy

Edited by Rod Tweedy

Routledge
Taylor & Francis Group

LONDON AND NEW YORK

First published 2021
by Routledge
2 Park Square, Milton Park, Abingdon, Oxon OX14 4RN

and by Routledge
52 Vanderbilt Avenue, New York, NY 10017

Routledge is an imprint of the Taylor & Francis Group, an informa business

British Library Cataloguing-in-Publication Data
A catalogue record for this book is available from the British Library

Library of Congress Cataloging-in-Publication Data
A catalog record has been requested for this book

ISBN: 978-0-367-49286-1 (hbk)
ISBN: 978-0-367-50442-7 (pbk)
ISBN: 978-1-003-04987-6 (ebk)

Typeset in Bembo
by Swales & Willis, Exeter, Devon, UK

Contents

Contributors

Bonnie Badenoch, PhD, LMFT, is a marriage and family therapist, supervisor, teacher, and author who is integrating the discoveries of relational neuroscience into the art of therapy. Bonnie currently teaches at Portland State University, and speaks internationally about applying IPNB principles both personally and professionally.

Louis Cozolino is an American clinical psychologist, a Professor of Psychology at Pepperdine University and an Adjunct Professor of Psychiatry at UCLA. He has authored and co-authored articles and book chapters on topics from child abuse and schizophrenia, to language and cognition. He holds degrees in philosophy from the State University of New York at Stony Brook, theology from Harvard University, and a PhD in clinical psychology from UCLA.

Barbara Dowds, PhD, MIACP, MIAHIP, was educated in Trinity College Dublin and was a university lecturer and researcher in molecular genetics until 2002. She now works as a therapist and supervisor in the Dublin area and offers CPD courses and workshops.

Susan P. Gantt, PhD, ABPP, CGP, is a psychologist and Assistant Professor in Psychiatry at Emory University School of Medicine where she coordinates group psychotherapy training. She is the Director of the Systems-Centered Training and Research Institute. She was recently awarded the Alonso Award for Excellence in Psychodynamic Group Psychotherapy by the Group Psychotherapy Foundation for her work with Paul Cox on the special issue of the *International Journal of Group Psychotherapy* on "Neurobiology and Interpersonal Systems: Groups, Couples and Beyond".

Iain McGilchrist is a former Fellow of All Souls College, Oxford, a Fellow of the Royal College of Psychiatrists, a Fellow of the Royal Society of Arts, and former Consultant Psychiatrist and Clinical Director at the Bethlem Royal & Maudsley Hospital, London. He has been a research fellow in neuroimaging at Johns Hopkins Hospital, Baltimore, and has published original articles and research papers in a wide range of publications on topics in literature, philosophy, medicine, and psychiatry.

Russell Meares is Emeritus Professor of Psychiatry at the University of Sydney. He trained in psychiatry at the Bethlem Royal & Maudsley Hospital, London, and collaborated with the late Robert Hobson to develop the Conversational Model of psychotherapy. He is also founder of the academic department of Psychiatry, University of Melbourne, at the Austin Hospital. Professor Meares has established programmes for the treatment of borderline personality disorder which have been taught across Australia.

Clara Mucci is a psychoanalytically oriented psychotherapist practising in Milan and Pescara, Italy. She received a PhD from Emory University, Atlanta, and was a Fellow in 2005–2006 at the Institute of Personality Disorder, New York. The author of several monographies on Shakespeare, Psychoanalysis and Literary Theory, she has taught in Westminster College, London and Hunter College, New York.

Darcia Narvaez, PhD, is Professor of Psychology at the University of Notre Dame specialising in ethical development and moral education. She is a fellow of the American Psychological Association and of the American Educational Research Association and is former editor-in-chief of the *Journal of Moral Education*. Dr Narvaez's research explores questions of species-typical and species-atypical development in terms of wellbeing, morality, and sustainable wisdom.

Vadim S. Rotenberg, MD, PhD, is Senior Lecturer in the Sackler Medical School of Psychiatry at the Tel Aviv University, Tel Aviv, Israel. He was born in Russia and achieved his master's degree in Medicine in the First Moscow Medical Institute, Moscow. Dr Rotenberg specialised in clinical and experimental psychiatry and neurology and was Scientific Chief Coordinator in the Psychiatry and Psychosomatic Medicine Research in Moscow.

Allan N. Schore is on the clinical faculty of the Department of Psychiatry and Biobehavioral Sciences, UCLA David Geffen School of Medicine. His Regulation Theory, grounded in developmental neuroscience and developmental psychoanalysis, focuses on the origin, psychopathogenesis, and psychotherapeutic treatment of the early forming subjective implicit self. His contributions appear in multiple disciplines, including developmental neuroscience, psychiatry, psychoanalysis, developmental psychology, attachment theory, trauma studies, behavioural biology, clinical psychology, and clinical social work.

Alexander Welch Siegel is a graduate of the University of California, Berkeley. He is currently a professional musician working as a performer, composer and producer. He can be contacted at AlexSiegel.com

Daniel J. Siegel is a clinical Professor of Psychiatry at the UCLA School of Medicine and the founding co-director of the Mindful Awareness Research Center at UCLA. An award-winning educator, he is a Distinguished Fellow of the American Psychiatric Association and recipient of several honorary fellowships. Dr Siegel is also the Executive Director of the Mindsight Institute, and serves as the Medical Director of the LifeSpan Learning Institute and on the Advisory Board of the Blue School in New York City, which has built its curriculum around Dr Siegel's Mindsight approach.

Rod Tweedy, PhD, is the author of *The God of the Left Hemisphere: Blake, Bolte Taylor and the Myth of Creation* (Routledge, 2013), a study of William Blake's works in the light of contemporary neuroscience, and the editor of *The Political Self: Understanding the Social Context for Mental Illness* (Routledge, 2017). He is also an active supporter of Veterans for Peace UK and the user-led mental health organisation, Mental Fight Club.

Acknowledgements

The chapter by Allan N. Schore, "The right brain is dominant in psychotherapy", was originally published in the American Psychological Association *Psychotherapy* journal (September 2014), and is reprinted by kind permission of the publisher and the author. The chapter "Social and Emotional Laterality" by Louis Cozolino is from THE NEUROSCIENCE OF HUMAN RELATIONSHIPS: ATTACHMENT AND THE DEVELOPING SOCIAL BRAIN by Louis Cozolino. Copyright © 2006 by Louis Cozolino. Used by permission of W.W. Norton & Company, Inc. "Ways of Attending: How our Divided Brain Constructs the World" by Iain McGilchrist is an edited version of an article that originally appeared in the *Scientific and Medical Network Review* and is reproduced by kind permission of the author and the Scientific and Medical Network (www.scimednet.org). The image of "Drawing Hands" by M.C. Escher is reproduced by permission of the M.C. Escher Company.

I would also like to thank the contributors to this volume for all of their tremendous support, patience, and help with this project, the excellent editorial staff at Routledge for their assistance and care, and Diego Max for his remarkable cover image.

Introduction

Rod Tweedy

This book explores the nature of the divided brain and its relevance for contemporary psychotherapy. It will show how the relationship between the two hemispheres of the brain is central to our well-being and mental health, and will examine both the practical and theoretical implications for therapy that the latest neuroscientific and psychoanalytic research has opened up.

Hemispheric imbalances and disconnections underlie many of our most prevalent forms of mental distress and disturbance, as a number of authors in the present volume suggest. A contemporary understanding of the nature of the divided brain is therefore of importance in engaging with and treating these conditions. As Cozolino observes, "psychotherapy can serve as a means to reintegrate the patient's disconnected hemispheres", noting that "the integration of dissociated processing systems is often a central focus of treatment":

> A primary focus of neural integration in traditional talk psychotherapy is between networks of affect and cognition. Dissociation between the two occurs when high levels of stress inhibit or disrupt the brain's integrative abilities among the left and right cerebral hemispheres as well as among the cortex and limbic regions … Examples from psychiatry and neurology strongly suggest that psychological health is related to the proper balance of activation, inhibition, and integration of systems biased toward the left and right hemispheres.
>
> (Cozolino, 2010, pp. 110–111, 24)

As we'll see, psychotherapy facilitates neural integration between the cortex and limbic regions, as well as between conscious and unconscious processes, and the networks of affect and cognition, thereby restoring coordination among a number of vital systems where these have been disrupted or damaged. *The Divided Therapist* will also show that the hemispheric relationship lies at the heart of the therapeutic process itself, and that a better understanding of the underlying mechanisms that enable integration between the left and right brain will help to transform the practice of psychotherapy and psychoanalysis in the twenty-first century.

Far from being at odds with Freud's original psychological speculations regarding mental processes and functions, many of his theories are finding surprising corroboration in contemporary neuroscience. These are especially evident with regard to his prescient observations concerning the nature of the unconscious, and how unconscious processes map onto what we now know about the structure and function of the right hemisphere. As Schore strikingly notes, there is now widespread agreement that "the right brain is the biological substrate of the unconscious" – a remarkable finding that will have profound implications for our conceptualisation of psychotherapy, and is already transforming both the theoretical and practical aspects of therapeutic practice. Pointing to the increasing recognition of the role of the right hemisphere in particular in our modern understanding of the relational foundation of therapy and the underlying change mechanism of therapy, Schore acutely observes that "right brain processes that are reciprocally activated on both sides of the therapeutic alliance lie at the core of the psychotherapeutic change process" (p. 75).

The present volume brings together a number of the leading authors and researchers in this exciting and rapidly expanding area, to show the relevance of these new discoveries for understanding a whole range of different forms of psychological distress and disorder, from autism, anxiety, depression, and schizophrenia to issues of addiction, anorexia, alexithymia, and trauma, as well as a number of relational and dissociative pathologies including borderline, narcissistic, schizoid and paranoid personality disorders. Indeed, as Schore has compellingly suggested, "deficits in right brain relational processes and resulting affect dysregulation underlie all psychological and psychiatric disorders" (Schore, 2012, p. 13).

Knowledge of the exact role and nature of hemispheric dysfunction and imbalance is therefore seen as being of increasing importance for contemporary therapists, who themselves of course are equally "divided" in terms of hemispheric bilateralisation. Indeed, it is precisely the nature of the relationship between the two hemispheres of the patient, and between the hemispheres of the patient and the therapist, that is central to successful therapeutic outcomes, as a number of the authors in the present volume suggest. As Cozolino notes, the attuned therapist acts as a sort of bridge, or integrator, of these divided worlds, and he compellingly explores the pivotal role of the therapist in being able to access and repair these often rather dissociated and dis-integrated systems:

> Hopefully, the therapist will be better integrated than the client in a therapeutic relationship. This will allow the therapist to react to what is said with emotion, resonate with the client's emotions, and then share thoughts about these emotions with the client. Thus, the therapist's ability to traverse the colossal bridge between his or her own right and left hemispheres serves as a model and guide for the client.
>
> (Cozolino, 2010, pp. 110–111)

Indeed, this new understanding of the therapist as both a mediator and integrator of hemispheric worlds – and of the therapeutic importance of the role of the integrated, attuned, and compassionate therapist (the "undivided therapist") – may I believe provide an important model for all of us in suggesting a radically new approach to attending to and caring for each other in our increasingly divided and divisive world.

The divided brain: two brains, two worlds

"It was Freud's hope", neurologist David A. Scola observed, "that a neural basis for his clinical observations and psychological explanations of the human mind would eventually be established" (Scola, 1984, p. 2). A hundred years after Freud's pioneering work into the nature and structure of the human mind, and perhaps appropriately following in the tradition of his own early interest in neurology and neuropathology, we are finally beginning to glimpse the outlines of this exciting new topography. "Throughout Freud's writings", Solms notes, "again and again he said that he was eagerly looking forward to the day when it would be possible to reunite his observations from the psychological perspective with neuroscientific ones" (Solms, cited in Ayan, 2018). Thanks to recent advances in interpersonal neurobiology, affective neuroscience, developmental neuropsychiatry, and psychoanalytic theory – much of which is presented in this book – we are now near to establishing the "neural basis" – the biological substrate – for the processes and mechanisms of the mind that Freud once dreamed of.

One of the most exciting discoveries has been the uncovering of the nature of the divided human brain, and a new understanding of the precise nature of hemispheric difference. Of particular relevance to therapy has been the discovery of the correlation between the "right hemisphere" of the brain with "unconscious" processes and networks, and the left hemisphere of the brain with the more explicit, verbal "conscious" activities. As Cozolino notes:

> The similarity between hemispheric specialization and Freud's notion of the conscious and unconscious mind has not been lost on psychotherapists. Right hemisphere functions are similar to Freud's model of the unconscious in that they develop first and are emotional, nonverbal, and sensorimotor … This nonlinear mode of processing allows the right hemisphere to contain multiple overlapping realities, similar to Freud's primary process thinking most clearly demonstrated in dreams. The linear processing of conscious thought in the left hemisphere parallels Freud's concept of secondary process, which is bound by time, reality, and social constraints.
>
> (Cozolino, 2010, p. 110)

Indeed, this idea of the right hemisphere being associated or identified with the more implicit or "unconscious" self, and the left hemisphere with the conscious self (the "conscious left brain self system", as Schore puts it), is one of the most consistent and striking findings. There is widespread consensus that the right hemisphere of the brain constitutes the "biological substrate of the human unconscious" (Schore, p. 84). There could hardly be a more succinct or striking endorsement of Freud's initial suppositions regarding the existence of the unconscious, or confirmation of his hope for the discovery of neural correlates for the processes he did so much to unearth and bring to our attention.

In discussions about the brain it is sometimes thought that the notion of a "divided brain" is just a metaphor. It isn't: even a cursory glance shows that it is profoundly, fundamentally, physically, literally, divided. Indeed, its central division is one of its most salient, and in some senses most curious, features. Given that the brain exists almost entirely in order to make connections, and that "the power of the brain consists precisely in the number and complexity of its connections", as McGilchrist observes, to have it so profoundly divided seems on the surface of things a massive waste of "computing power":

> If the whole purpose of the brain is to make connections, and if, as many believe, consciousness arises, in some yet to be specified manner, from the sheer interconnectedness of such a vast array of neurones, why chop it down the middle? It could have evolved as a single mass. But in fact hemisphere divisions go right down the phylogenetic tree. So whatever it is for, it must operate, not just for man, but for animals and birds, too. What is that?
> (Rowson & McGilchrist, 2017, pp. 92–93; McGilchrist, p. 95)

And the questions multiply when we realise that the brain is not simply divided in two, but that there are pervasive and consistent differences *between* the hemispheres, existing at every level. As McGilchrist notes:

> The two hemispheres are different sizes, shapes, and weights (the right hemisphere is bigger and heavier in all social mammals); have expansions in different areas, different gyral conformations on the surface, and in places different architecture of the underlying cells; have different proportions of grey matter to white, different sensitivity to neuroendocrine influences, and rely on different preponderances of neurotransmitters.
> (Rowson & McGilchrist, 2017, p. 92)

The two hemispheres of the brain differ, in other words, in every way we can measure them: they differ in terms of their mass, their structure, their size, their shape, their chemical composition – even on a neuronal level they differ both in the number of neurons as well as the size of individual nerve cells. As Allan Schore remarks, "numerous studies now indicate that the right and left hemispheres differ in macrostructure, ultrastructure, physiology, chemistry, and control of behaviour" (Schore, 2012, p. 7). And these striking differences in form, function, and physiology are directly correlated to and interwoven with each hemisphere's distinct mode of operating. The two hemispheres store different forms of knowledge and mediate qualitatively different forms of cognitive activity. Metaphor itself, for example, is something that only the right hemisphere of the brain recognises and delivers (McGilchrist, 2009, pp. 49–51) – so if you think the divided brain is only a metaphor, that's the right side of the metaphor that is thinking that.

Recent advances in our understanding of the brain have been so spectacular and widely publicised that many ideas about the two hemispheres, and what it means to be "left" or "right" brained, have become commonplace. But unfortunately these popular conceptions are often misleading: it is widely assumed, for example, that the left brain, with its focussed, analytic approach to the world is perhaps a bit dull but generally more accurate and reliable than the right brain's more creative and "emotional" approach. This is not the case at all. It is the right hemisphere – with its more complex and intimate connection with the embodied, relational, and contextual aspects of the world – that consistently provides the more reliable and realistic view of things. The left brain, however skilled at unpacking, dissecting, and manipulating that world, provides a useful, but also more unreal, view of the world:

> A completely false view prevailed that the right hemisphere was somehow airy-fairy and unreliable and simply added some emotional colour to the perceptions of the "intelligent" left hemisphere. But it is in reality the right hemisphere that sees more, that is more in touch with reality, and is more intellectually sophisticated … The left hemisphere does not understand things, so much as process them: it is the right hemisphere that is the basis of understanding. This has an impact on the way we live now: because the left hemisphere is better than the right hemisphere at manipulating both figures and words, but less good than it at understanding their meaning.
> (Rowson & McGilchrist, 2017, p. 96; see also McGilchrist, 2009, p. 92)

The left hemisphere might perhaps in this sense be seen as rather like the "sat nav" in your car – an extremely helpful guide to the terrain, but also a drastically over-simplified and rather "virtualised", self-enclosed guide to the actual land, and one that can often go catastrophically wrong if its connection to the real, embodied world becomes detached or severed.

When it comes to therapy, these hemispheric differences are particularly significant. It might therefore be useful to provide a very brief outline of some of the key differences between the hemispheres, and how they relate to therapy. As psychotherapist Barbara Dowds notes, the two sides of the brain have two very different and distinct ways of relating to the world:

> The left is detached, objectifying, atomistic, abstract, analytical, narrowly-focused and deals with the known, the non-living and impersonal; the right is direct, holistic, intuitive, empathic, broadly-focused and deals with the unknown, the living and personal. The left hemisphere is associated with the conscious mind and the right with the unconscious, and it is through the right cortex and limbic system that we connect to our embodied experience ... We need the left hemisphere for language and the right for nonverbal aspects of communication.
>
> (Dowds, p. 182)

These hemispheric differences, that is, correlate to and underwrite two distinct and consistent ways of knowing or relating to the world. As McGilchrist observes, "our brains are so constructed as to enable us to bring into being and conceive the experiential world in two quite distinct, complementary, but ultimately incompatible, ways". Each of these ways of being, or ways of relating to the world, he notes, are of fundamental importance for us as human beings, and each "is rooted in the bihemispheric structure of the brain" (2009, pp. 94, 3). Each hemisphere therefore delivers and indeed embodies a different reality, a different way of being-in-the-world. *The Divided Therapist* will examine these differences, and show how the practice of therapy is both informed and affected by these "two individually coherent, but incompatible" ways of relating (ibid., p. 94).

Many of the authors in the current volume note the particular importance of the right hemisphere to therapy, and its crucial role in both the therapeutic relationship and the change mechanisms of therapy itself. It is worth noting, for example, its intimate connection to the emotional and affective, attachment-based centres of the limbic system, its greater skill in gestalt or holistic recognition and contextual reality, its primary role in empathy, theory of mind, and the implicit sense of self, its greater involvement in relational and embodied processes than the left hemisphere, its alertness to the new and to all aspects of learning new information, and new ways of seeing and thinking, and its greater facility with free association, metaphor, and pattern recognition. The importance of the right brain to many fundamental aspects of therapeutic work may already be evident from this brief summary. This book will unpack many of those aspects, and show how central the right hemisphere is to the actual process of therapeutic change.

This emphasis on the right hemisphere might come as a bit of a surprise for a profession which is famously known as "the talking cure" – suggesting perhaps that the more verbally skilled, explicit, and "conscious" processes of the left brain might be dominant. While it is undeniably true, as we shall see, that both hemispheres play vital and distinct roles in therapy, there has been a significant shift in recent decades in our understanding of the importance of more implicit, affective, and relational mechanisms in therapeutic healing, and a corresponding recognition of the more limited role of purely cognitive and verbal processes. Clearly some forms of therapy rely much more on left-hemisphere processes and approaches (CBT, for example, or more classical forms of psychoanalysis), and successful treatment can often depend on the therapist recognising which form of approach is best suited both to the patient and to the nature of the distress being treated (Dowds provides a helpful summary of these different approaches in her section "Hemisphere Dominance in different Therapy Orientations", pp. 49–51). Nonetheless, the more we understand about the importance of unconscious, affective, and attachment systems in our bodies, the more we realise that it is the right hemisphere that plays a particularly fundamental role in all aspects of our relational and social lives. As Schore notes, "despite the designation of the verbal left hemisphere as 'dominant' due to its capacities for explicitly processing language functions, it is the emotion processing right hemisphere and its implicit homeostatic-survival and communication functions that is truly dominant in human existence" (Schore, 2011, p. 76). "The right hemisphere is dominant", he observes, "for subjective emotional experiences", "for the nonverbal, implicit, holistic processing of emotional information and social interactions", "for the emotional sense of self", and "dominant for affiliation, while the left supports power motivation" (p. 73).

Schore's reference to the right hemisphere being "dominant" in so many areas of human life is a reminder that for most of the last two centuries, it has in fact been the linguistically adept and analytically powerful left hemisphere that has been considered the dominant hemisphere. In traditional neuroscientific literature up until recently, the left brain was routinely referred to as the "major" hemisphere (and the right as the "nondominant" or "minor" hemisphere) – a sign perhaps of the left-hemispheric nature of the scientific thinking that itself dominated in the post-Enlightenment period, and indeed of the left hemisphere's remarkable skill at self-promotion. As Cozolino observes:

> More than a century ago, the left cortex was dubbed the *dominant* hemisphere because of its leading role in language…. We have learned a great deal about the brain during the past century, and our ideas about the roles of each of the hemispheres and their working relationship with one another have become increasingly sophisticated. Although it remains true that the left hemisphere usually takes the lead in semantic and conscious processing, social and emotional dominance are functions that lean toward the right.
>
> (Cozolino, p. 110)

This growing recognition of the contribution that the right hemisphere plays is part of what has aptly been called a "paradigm shift" that is currently happening in neuroscience, and indeed across the disciplines. Schore drew attention to this radical realignment in our thinking in his landmark 2009 Plenary Address to the APA ("The Paradigm Shift: The Right Brain and the

Relational Unconscious"), which compellingly articulated this shift in con-sciousness, and signalled, as he put it, the transition "from left brain con-scious cognition to right brain unconscious affect" (Schore, 2012, p. 3). It's a paradigm shift that is happening, he notes, across a number of fields, "including developmental psychology, biological psychiatry, affective neuro-science, and psychoanalysis" (ibid., p. 292), which is what makes this par-ticular period of history so exciting, transforming our understanding of both neuroscience and psychoanalysis in the process. "After a century of discon-nection", Schore notes, "psychoanalysis is returning to its psychological *and* biological sources, and this re-integration is generating a palpable surge of energy and revitalization of the field" (Schore, 2017, p. 73).

The nature of attention

It is not therefore simply that there are two different hemispheres, but that there are two different cognitive ways of knowing the world, two different modes of relating to reality, even two different types of self available (Schore, 2011, p. 77). These two different ways of knowing or being are instantiated and incarnated in each hemisphere – as McGilchrist notes, "there are two fundamentally opposed realities" rooted in the bihemispheric structure of the brain (McGilchrist, 2009, p. 3). But why? Why should the brain be so physically, physiologically, and functionally divided, and what are its implications for our mental health?

In trying to answer these questions, classical neuroscience generally con-centrated on the possible differences in *function* between the hemispheres – believing, perhaps understandably, that the reason for the division of the brain must have something to do with what each side of the brain "does". However, they were then perplexed to find that each side of the brain is involved in absolutely everything – even language, with its strong lateralisa-tion to the left (Broca and Wernicke centres), they discovered, is also vitally dependent on networks in the right side of the brain, such as those relating to prosody, affect, and all the non-verbal aspects of communication, which are equally essential for effective communication.

It was McGilchrist's remarkable insight to see that the key difference between the two hemispheres is not *what* they do, but *how* they do it. As he explains:

> The whole problem is that we are obsessed, because of what I argue is our affiliation to left-hemisphere modes of thought, with "what" the brain does – after all, isn't the brain a machine, and like any other machine, the value of it lies in *what it does*? I happen to think this machine model gets us only some of the way; and like a train that drops one in the middle of the night far from one's destination, a train of thought that gets one only some of the way is a liability. The difference,

I shall argue, is not in the "what", but in the "how" – by which I don't mean "the means by which" (machine model again), but "the manner in which", something no one ever asked a machine.

(McGilchrist, 2009, p. 3)

As he acutely notes, in the very assumption that the brain must simply be about "functions", traditional neuroscience was very much following a much wider cultural bias which favoured specifically and recognisably "left hemisphere" ways of seeing and interpreting the world. Classic neuroscience saw the brain, that is, from the point of view of only half the brain – hence its "affiliation to left-hemisphere modes of thought" – and consequently missed fundamental aspects of the object they were apparently studying. This is particularly relevant to psychoanalysis and psychotherapy because in exactly the same way that "our affiliation to left-hemisphere modes of thought" distorted and limited our understanding of the brain in classical neuroscience, so too in classical psychoanalysis, clinicians persistently over-emphasised the cognitive, conscious, functional, and verbal aspects of therapy, while neglecting the crucial non-verbal, implicit, and embodied nature of therapeutic communication and healing. Traditional post-Freudian psychoanalysis focussed on the "talking" side of the talking cure – the cognitive, conscious, explicit aspects – not on the *way in which* the patient was communicating, or indeed the way in which the therapist was listening. Once this blind spot was recognised, and the shift towards the realisation of the crucial role that these implicit, non-verbal, bodily forms of "talking" was taken, a whole wealth of new experience, insight, and information was suddenly opened up and became available to the attuned therapist.

This is particularly interesting, because if we focus on the "way" in which each hemisphere operates and relates to the world, something very striking becomes apparent, which is that each hemisphere has a distinct way of attending to the world. And it is that seemingly innocuous word "attention" that really provides the key to the whole understanding of the divided brain. "Attention may sound a bit boring", notes McGilchrist – who has perhaps done more than anyone to draw our attention to our attention – "but it isn't at all":

Attention is not just another "function" alongside other cognitive functions. Its ontological status is of something prior to functions and even to things. The kind of attention we bring to bear on the world actually alters the nature of the world we attend to … Attention changes *what kind of a thing* comes into being for us: in that way it changes the world.

(McGilchrist, p. 97; McGilchrist, 2009, p. 28)

Attention "changes the world": this recognition of the peculiar nature of attention, and the realisation of the availability of two distinct modes of attention, each bringing into being a different sort of world, is I think the key element in the new understanding of hemispheric difference and its importance to psychotherapy. Therapy is all about relationship, and as McGilchrist notes, attention *underwrites relationship*: it both directs and determines our sense of relationship with the world – to what we pay attention *to*, and therefore to what kind of relationships we find ourselves in. "What we pay attention to and how we pay attention shapes the flow of energy and information within our bodies and relationships", note Siegel and Siegel: "a shift in attention has the ability to radically transform states from chaos or rigidity to integrative functioning, as when sensing the body calms the mind, or naming an emotion tames distress" (p. 144).

And the left and right hemispheres of the brain play such a pivotal role because they mediate and deliver two distinct types or modes of attention. Thus, "the left hemisphere specialises in a sort of piecemeal attention that helps us make use of the world, but in doing so it alters our relationship with it", observes McGilchrist, while "the right hemisphere subserves a broad open attention which enables us to see ourselves connected to – and in the human case, to empathise with – whatever is other than ourselves" (p. 98). Attention, to be clear, is not a "function", it's what *enables* functions – it precedes them: "It is not a 'function' alongside other functions, but the foundation for having a world at all, in which those 'functions' can be exercised" (p. 99). This point is clearly of crucial importance to therapy – which is all about relationship, and indeed all about attention. *How* we pay attention to another both underwrites and realises what sort of relationship we will have with it, and because the kind of attention we bring to bear on the world "actually alters the nature of the world we attend to", we can alter what sort of relationships we have, by altering our mode of attention.

This splitting of the brain into two different and distinct modes of attention has a compelling evolutionary basis, notes McGilchrist. "In order to stay alive", he observes, "birds have to solve a conundrum. They have to be able to feed and watch out for predators at the same time" (p. 98). That is, they have to be able to do two distinct and in some respects incompatible things: focus closely on what is in front of them in order to find their food, and focus widely on everything else, in order to avoid becoming someone else's food. Splitting the brain into two seems to be Nature's way of solving an evolutionary conundrum.

> How are you to focus closely on what you are doing when you are trying to pick out that grain of seed from the grit on which it lies while, at the same time, keeping the broadest possible open attention to whatever may be, in order to avoid being eaten? It's a bit like trying to pat your head and rub your tummy at the same time – only worse, because it's impossible. What we know is that the difference in attention between the hemispheres makes the apparently impossible possible.

Birds pay narrowly focussed attention on what they are eating with their right eye (left hemisphere), while keeping their left eye (right hemisphere) open for predators.

(McGilchrist, p. 98)

This evolutionary need to maintain two distinct and in many ways oppositional and irreconcilable forms of attention simultaneously in operation has resulted in two distinct and in many ways oppositional and irreconcilable modes of being in the world, two distinct ways of *relating to* the world: one, a very focussed, detailed, and directed form of instrumental attention aimed at analysing and manipulating the world in front of it, and the other, a completely different form of broad, open, vigilant, and receptive attention that seeks and invites relationship and is open to the other. All of the hemispheric differences that we have been so far considering – structural, formal, compositional, functional – seem to serve and in a sense underwrite these two very different modes of attention.

This affects therapy, because attention lies at the heart of therapeutic practice and underwrites every therapeutic relationship. Ever since Freud's first analytic sessions at Berggasse 19, Vienna in 1891, attention has been at the centre of the whole psychoanalytic project. Indeed, therapists have to hold these two different and distinct modes of attention as part of their everyday practice: on the one hand, maintaining a close, focussed attention on what the patient is saying ("the task of keeping in mind all the innumerable names, dates, detailed memories and pathological products which each patient communicates in the course of months and years of treatment", as Freud noted; Freud, 1912e, p. 111), and at the same time holding and sustaining a completely opposite kind of attention – one that is "evenly suspended", as Freud famously put it, open-ended, broad, receptive, and alert to whatever the unconscious is trying to "smuggle" through, and which requires a very different mode. These unconscious communications can be apprehended through the particular tone of an expression, or an unexpected image or association, or a shift in body gesture; or even simply through a silence. Holding these two modes of attention simultaneously is the technical secret to the whole therapeutic encounter, as Freud himself realised, and requires in itself a form of sophisticated integration. Therapy, a bit like McGilchrist's impossible "tummy rub", is a way of making the "apparently impossible possible": the impossible therapist.

The "open, vigilant, broad, contextual form of attention" that McGilchrist characterises as the right hemispheric mode is of particular significance to Freudian psychoanalysis, as it is exactly the mode of attention that Freud himself claimed lay at the centre of the practice. As psychotherapist Robert Snell has shown in his fascinating study of this state (*Uncertainties, Mysteries, Doubts*, 2013), "this undirected but somehow actively receptive state of mind" is of "central importance in psychotherapy" and is "generally referred to, conveniently but far too concretely, as the 'analytic attitude'":

> Freud called it "free-floating" or "evenly suspended attention" ... It is a kind of "free" listening, the counterpart to the free association that psychoanalysts encourage in their patients, through which the unconscious, like contraband in the ordinary unchecked stream of thought, might have a chance of declaring itself. It is an emotional orientation in the therapist, a commitment, founded in respect, to maintaining a radically open-minded stance: a suspended state somewhere between passivity and readiness for emotional and verbal activity.
>
> (Snell, 2013, p. 1)

Freud's "evenly suspended attention" correlates with the radically open-minded stance that McGilchrist identifies as the right hemisphere form of attention. As Schore notes:

> Freud's concept of the state of receptive readiness as "evenly suspended attention" can also be identified as a function of the right hemisphere, which uses an expansive broad attention mechanism that focuses on global features (as opposed to the left that narrowly focuses on local detail).
>
> (Schore, 2011, p. 84)

Freud made the recognition of this state central to his technique. Indeed, he calls cultivating this mode of attention "the fundamental rule of psychoanalysis", and in his classic paper "Recommendations to Physicians Practising Psycho-analysis" (Freud, 1912e), he formulates it in terms of the requirement on the analyst's part to maintain exactly this type of "evenly distributed", "suspended", "hovering", "circling" or "free-floating attention":

> The technique ... consists simply in not directing one's notice to anything in particular and in maintaining the same "evenly suspended attention" (as I have called it) in the face of all one hears ... as soon as anyone deliberately concentrates his attention to a certain degree, he begins to select from the material before him; one point will be fixed in his mind with particular clearness and some other will be correspondingly disregarded, and in making this selection he will be following his expectations or inclinations. This, however, is precisely what must not be done. In making the selection, if he follows his expectations he is in danger of never finding anything but what he already knows; and if he follows his inclinations he will certainly falsify what he may perceive.
>
> (Freud, 1912e, pp. 111–112)

Two things are striking about this passage: the first of course is Freud's attention to attention: the way he places it at the very heart of his whole work ("The technique ... consists simply in not directing one's notice to anything in particular and in maintaining the same 'evenly suspended attention' ..."). The second is his registering of two distinct types of attention that can occur – one a selective, fixed, judgemental mode ("as soon as anyone deliberately concentrates his attention to a certain degree, he begins to select from the material before him") and the other a much freer, more expansive mode – one that seems open both to the unconscious and to a much wider and deeper mode of relationship and awareness. He notes that the analyst must encourage the latter mode in order for treatment to be successful, and to strongly discourage the narrower, pre-selective mode, which already knows what it wants to find ("This, however, is precisely what must not be done"). These are the right and the left modes, respectively, and Freud places them at the centre of his practice.

In his "Recommendations to Physicians Practising Psycho-analysis", Freud is talking about the importance of cultivating this openly-directed mode of attention in the analyst. But he also, strikingly, argues that a similar, radically open-minded stance must be encouraged in the patient as well, in order to stimulate the unconscious processes of free association and therapeutic receptivity:

> It will be seen that the rule of giving equal notice to everything is the necessary counterpart to the demand made on the patient that he should communicate everything that occurs to him without criticism or selection. If the doctor behaves otherwise, he is throwing away most of the advantage which results from the patient's obeying the "fundamental rule of psychoanalysis". The rule for the doctor may be expressed: "He should withhold all conscious influences from his capacity to attend, and give himself over completely to his "unconscious memory". Or, to put it purely in terms of technique: "He should simply listen, and not bother about whether he is keeping anything in mind." What is achieved in this manner will be sufficient for all requirements during the treatment.
>
> (Freud, 1912e, p. 112)

Rather remarkably, Freud perceptively saw in 1912 that the secret of psychoanalysis lay in directly engaging what we today recognise as right hemispheric processes, and he also discovered a way to do this – the mechanism of "free association". Freud's formulations were to have an enduring impact on all subsequent psychoanalytic practice, from Ferenczi's understanding of the importance of engaged "witnessing" ("it appears that patients cannot believe that an event took place, or cannot fully believe it, if the analyst, as the sole witness of the events persists in his cool, unemotional and ... purely intellectual attitude", Ferenczi, 1995, p. 24), to Bion's recognition of the importance of "reverie" in the therapeutic alliance, and Grotstein's recent formulations regarding "right-hemispheric listening" and "right hemispheric processing" during the analytic session (Grotstein, 2009, pp. 31, 37), the nature of therapeutic attention is key to unlocking both the unconscious and the transformative mechanisms of therapeutic change. Grotstein remarks that "Freud apparently never realised that he had, in effect, discovered the functioning of the right cerebral hemisphere!", but in fact, both in terms of his cultivation of free association and evenly suspended attention, and through his introduction of the couch as a means to further engage and facilitate these processes, he seems to have been a remarkably perceptive and pioneering practitioner in this. Thus, the origins of the famous analytic couch seems to have been directly linked to facilitating right hemispheric processes: "this 'right-brain' shift in the lying-down position in analysis", notes Grotstein, "would be demonstrated by the nature of the patient's associations, which would be 'free' — that is, optimally disconnected from 'left-brain' editing, censorship, and control — and would instead be organised by the unconscious" (ibid., pp. 13–14). That these "free" associations were emanating from the patient's right hemisphere is further corroborated by the recent research of Grabner, Fink, and Neubauer, who note that "the right hemisphere operates in a more free-associative, primary process manner, typically observed in states such as dreaming or reverie" (Grabner, Fink, & Neubauer, 2007, p. 228) — exactly the sort of state that Freud sought to develop and encourage.

The left brain watchman

Freud also recognised that in doing this (that is, in trying to access the unconscious right hemisphere through the conscious left hemisphere) the analyst faces considerable resistance from the more critical, selective, and judgmental process of the "conscious" self ("he should withhold all conscious influences from his capacity to attend", Freud urges, "he should communicate everything that occurs to him without criticism or selection"). He acutely saw that it was not the fixed, focussed (left hemisphere) mode of attention that provided the necessary insight, or was the more accurate or reliable agent in this, and indeed that left to its own devices it would pre-select and find only what it wanted to find ("if he follows his inclinations he will certainly falsify what he may perceive", Freud, 1912e, p. 112) — a remarkably accurate appraisal of left-hemispheric processes, and what we now know about the "confabulatory" nature of the left brain (McGilchrist, 2009, p. 81).

Freud's observations on the mechanisms of "repression" and "resistance", which emanate from the "conscious" mind, also strikingly correlate with modern neuroscientific insights into how the left hemisphere operates. The structural mechanisms of repression, Freud notes, need to be disengaged and discouraged before the work of the analyst can take hold (Freud, 1916–1917). It was precisely for this reason that Freud developed the deceptively simple method of "free association" in his patients, as a way of bypassing the censorious and selective mechanisms of the conscious mind (deceptive, that is, to the judgmental mechanisms of the left brain). This dynamic – of encouraging the unconscious right brain while stilling or bypassing the censorious left brain – is at the heart of his practice. Freud thus describes the process of "free" association in the following way: "We instruct the patient to put himself into a state of quiet, unreflecting self-observation, and to report to us whatever internal perceptions he is able to make – feelings, thoughts, memories in the order in which they occur to him" (ibid., p. 287). Freud is thereby encouraging his patients to enter into a right-hemisphere state that is open, reflective, and neither self-judgemental nor self-critical: "a state of quiet, unreflecting self-observation". It is precisely the non-judgmentalism of this mode that is key to the success of free association for Freud:

> At the same time we warn him expressly against giving way to any motive which would lead him to make a selection among these associations or to exclude any of them, whether on the ground that it is too *disagreeable* or too *indiscreet* to say, or that it is too *unimportant* or *irrelevant*, or that it is *nonsensical* and need not be said. We urge him always to follow only the surface of his consciousness and to leave aside any criticism of what he finds, whatever shape that criticism may take; and we assure him that the success of the treatment, and above all its duration, depends on the conscientiousness with which he obeys this fundamental technical rule of analysis.
>
> (Freud, 1916-1917, p. 287)

One could of course put this the other way round: it is precisely the maintenance of the critical and judgmental state that maintains the distress and the neuroses in the patient, and that blocks access to both their causes and their treatment. By shifting to the right hemisphere mode (in Schore's terms) the analyst can thereby bypass, or shift their attention, from that critical, repressive mode to a deeper, more receptive, more embodied, more open, more knowing, and more empathic state. That is to say, this isn't a minor point about psychoanalytic treatment for Freud – in a way, it *is* the treatment – the very method of analysis ("this fundamental technical rule of analysis"). The patient is ill – why? – they repress or resist knowledge of what's making them ill – how can the therapist overcome this? By entering and accessing right-hemispheric "free association" states.

Freud makes the further revelatory point that this method not only quietens and disengages the critical, repressive, conscious system but also "leads to the uncovering of the unconscious". In other words, that this relaxed state leads to the revealing of the truth that the "conscious" mind does not want to engage with or admit. Freud's comments clearly place the mechanism of repression not in the "unconscious" but in the selective, analytic, judgmental "conscious" and egoic part of the mind: "what is being mobilized for fighting against the alterations we are striving for are character-traits, attitudes of the ego" (Freud, 1916–1917, p. 291).

> We must above all get rid of the mistaken notion that what we are dealing with in our struggle against resistances is resistance on the part of the *unconscious*. The unconscious – that is to say, the "repressed" – offers no resistance whatever to the efforts of the treatment. Indeed, it itself has no other endeavour than to break through the pressure weighing down on it and force its way either to consciousness or to a discharge through some real action. Resistance during treatment arises from the same higher strata and systems of the mind which originally carried out the repression ... [W]e can say that the patient's resistance arises from his ego.
>
> (Freud, 1920g, pp. 19–20, italics in original)

It is the ego, and the conscious mind, that is preventing the treatment, the therapy from happening – the ego that mobilises against both the patient and the analyst in order to protect the patient from self-knowledge.

This process is particularly fascinating in relation to our current understanding of the left and the right hemispheres. As Mucci notes, this process of repression "has to do with an active removal from consciousness of material or contents that have undergone a process of repression .... As processes controlled by the left brain, they deal with contents that have been consciously learned and maintained" (Mucci, 2016, p. 105) – a point underlined by Schore, who observes that "current neurobiology suggests that repression is a developmentally more advanced left brain defense against affects like anxiety that are represented at the cortical level of the right brain" (Schore, 2003, p. 246). As we have seen, Freud notes that the repression and resistance to treatment occurs because of the filtering, selective, and highly critical nature or personality of the "conscious" self, which is actively engaged in preventing anything disturbing from entering its consciousness. This critical nature of the left hemisphere personality recalls Bolte Taylor's characterisation of its persistently judgmental, critical nature: the left brain, she observes, takes pride "in its ability to categorize, organize, describe, judge, and critically analyze absolutely everything" (Bolte Taylor, 2008a, p. 142). Our left hemisphere, she notes, "places the judgment of good on those things we like and bad on those things we dislike. Through the action of critical judgment and analysis, our left brain constantly compares us with everyone else", and she repeatedly refers to the left hemisphere's "judging and analytical character" (ibid., pp. 33, 49, 135).

It is these immensely powerful forces and activities of the left brain – its vast apparatus of "critical judgment and analysis" that act to repress anything disagreeable to it – which Freud encountered so vividly and consistently in his clinical room day after day. Indeed, he strikingly summed up this aspect of the conscious repressing agency in a very striking image: that of the "Watchman", which, he said, stands on the threshold between "two rooms":

> On the threshold between these two rooms a watchman performs his function: he examines the different mental impulses, acts as a censor, and will not admit them into the drawing-room if they displease him ... It is the same watchman whom we get to know as resistance when we try to lift the repression by means of the analytic treatment.
>
> (Freud, 1916–1917, pp. 295–296)

Freud's hypothesis of the watchman brilliantly captures the nature of the left hemispheric observer who guards access into consciousness, an agency or activity that constantly examines, censors, watches, and "performs his function". It is the watchman, Freud notes, "whom we get to know" as the prime agent of resistance and repression; and it is, contrariwise, the unconscious right hemisphere with its much more open, freer, and less judgmental stance that the therapist must try to engage for successful treatment to occur.

Freud's "watchman" has some fascinating similarities with what Gazzaniga has more recently called the left brain "interpreter" (see Gazzaniga, 2002). "There is a specialised left hemisphere system we have designated as the 'interpreter'", a highly advanced and specialised critical and interpretive structure (hence its name). This left hemispheric interpreter "constructs theories to assimilate perceived information" according to internal, self-consistent theories, and acts to reject any information or experience that might disrupt this. "The left hemisphere's capacity for continual interpretation" observes Gazzaniga, "suggests that it is always looking for order and reason, even where there is none" (Gazzaniga, 2002, pp. 209, 211). It seems to be this watchman or interpreter that acts as both a censor and guard to egoic consciousness. Thus, as Freud notes, "in investigating resistance, we have learnt that it emanates from forces of the ego" – that is, repression does not emanate from the (right brain) unconscious, but from the "conscious", left brain system. The conscious mind is not however aware of doing this, hence the rather curious situation in which the apparently conscious mind generates the (repressed) unconscious due to its own unconsciousness. Bypassing the watchman is both difficult and dangerous: Freud repeatedly notes how immensely fraught this seemingly simple procedure is, and how deeply resistant the conscious, explicit self is to both change and self-knowledge.

Freud's understanding of the peculiarly compelling nature of attention, and how it lies at the heart of therapeutic practice, is one of his most prescient discoveries. "Attention is an unbelievably powerful force", Jordan Peterson observes:

> You see this is psychotherapy, too, because a lot of what you do – and in any reparative relationship – is really pay attention to the other person. Pay attention and *listen*. You would not believe what people will tell you or reveal to you if you watch them *as if you want to know,* instead of watching them so that you'll have your prejudices reinforced.
>
> (Peterson, 2017)

The key to therapy, or indeed to any kind of "reparative relationship", he therefore notes, is "*more* consciousness, it's *more* attention", and this increase in attention operates and acts in therapy both through the analyst and the analysand. The talking cure works not so much because someone is talking, but because somebody is actually, truly, *listening* – truly paying attention to them. And that act, Adam Philips observes, is revelatory: something changes, something *shifts*. "The power of being listened to", he notes, "is extraordinary":

> Being listened to, and being with somebody who takes genuine pleasure in listening, is really powerful. It really has an effect. And it seems to me – and it isn't a "cure", but if it was a "cure" – it's a *listening* cure, not a talking cure. And it's amazing what people will say if they think they're being listened to.
>
> (Phillips, 2015)

This quality of attention is one of the great secrets of psychoanalysis, as indeed it is of all our relationships. We are, sadly, so used to people attending to us in the left brain way – an essentially egoic, self-enclosed, instrumental way (McGilchrist, 2009, pp. 392–393, 403). When someone actually turns on the full force of the right-hemispheric mode of attention – which wants nothing, which simply engages and listens, and cares – then extraordinary things happen.

On a neurological level, the way we direct our attention actually alters the brain, as Siegel and Siegel note in their chapter in the present book: "What we pay attention to and how we pay attention shapes the flow of energy and information within our bodies and relationships", and a shift in attention therefore has the ability to radically transform states:

> Attention is the process that directs this flow of energy and information both within the body and between people … what we pay attention to changes the function and structure of the brain. A shift in attention has the ability to radically transform states from chaos or rigidity to integrative functioning, as when sensing the body calms the mind, or naming

an emotion tames distress. Where attention goes, neural firing flows, and neural connection grows.

(Siegel and Siegel, pp. 143–144, 139)

Where attention goes, neuronal firing flows – this goes to the heart of the power of attention, and to the crucial issue of which mode of attention we choose to employ, and when. The *way* we direct our attention is the underlying change mechanism of both psychoanalysis and mindfulness: as Kabat-Zinn notes: "mindfulness means paying attention in a particular way: on purpose, in the present moment, and nonjudgmentally" (Kabat-Zinn, 1994, p. 4). "This kind of attention nurtures greater awareness, clarity, and acceptance of present-moment reality" (ibid., p. 4).

Many of the chapters in the present book outline the radical and trans-formative changes that altering our mode of attention brings. From Freud's and Ferenczi's observations of its reparative effects in individual therapy, to its central role in modern forms of group therapy and systems-centred therapy (Gantt and Badenoch, Chapter 5), body psychotherapy and relational psychology (Meares, Chapter 9; Mucci, Chapter 7), and gestalt and existential therapy (Dowds, Chapter 6), attention holds a vital and fundamental place, and our ability to shift forms of attention occupies a crucial role in many reparative and reintegrative practices. EMDR therapy, for example, is a particularly striking instance of how shifts in bilateral attention can produce significant cognitive and affective alterations. Encouraging the patient to "just notice" (pay attention to) certain bodily sensations and to shift attention from the left to the right side of the body, can facilitate significant flow and movement within the mind and body: as Mollon notes, "the act of directing attention to the sensation, while continuing the eye movements or other bilateral stimulation, tends to bring about a bodily change, usually in the direction of reduction of physiological agitation" (Mollon, 2005, p. 2).

Perhaps we should not be so surprised at the power of directed attention, or its central role in therapy. Attention, as we have seen, is the very basis of our relationship to the world, and how we are attended to, and how we in turn attend to others, profoundly shapes our experience of that world. That "attention" should play such a prominent role in modern therapy seems apt: as the Jungian analyst James Hillman once observed, the very term *therapeutes* – the origin of our modern word "therapist" – means "one who attends", and in classical times, what the *therapeutes* attended to was both "the Gods" and "the sickness". Indeed, in some senses, he suggests, they are perhaps the same (Hillman, 1975, p. 192).

Right brain-to-right brain therapy

We have seen how the "evenly suspended" right-hemispheric mode of attention of the therapist and the "free associating" right-hemispheric unconscious processes of the patient constitutes both the basis of the therapeutic relationship and the "fundamental rule of psychoanalysis". Freud saw that the therapeutic mechanism lay in the connection between the unconscious of the patient and that of the analyst: as he observed in 1915, "it is a very remarkable thing that the *Ucs.* of one human being can react upon that of another, without passing through the *Cs*" (Freud, 1915, p. 194). Freud's remarkable understanding of this form of unconscious-to-unconscious communication has been confirmed by recent neuroscientific findings, as Schore notes: "Freud's dictum", he remarks, is "neuropsychoanalytically understood as a right brain-to-right brain communication from one relational unconscious to another" (Schore, 2011, p. 84). Indeed, therapy itself is increasingly being seen as primarily a right hemisphere-to-right hemisphere ("RH–RH") process of interaction and integration, again underlining Schore's observation that "the right hemisphere is dominant in psychotherapy" (p. 70).

Freud understood that the therapeutic relationship was forged in the connection between the unconscious of the patient and that of the analyst. The analyst must therefore, he notes, use "his own unconscious like a receptive organ toward the transmitting unconscious of the patient", and in his key 1912 paper, "Recommendations to Physicians Practising Psycho-Analysis", he elaborates on this striking metaphor of transmitting and receiving, suggesting how the unconscious of the one attunes itself to that of the other:

> Just as the patient must relate everything that his self-observation can detect, and keep back all the logical and affective objections that seek to induce him to make a selection from among them, so the doctor must put himself in a position to make use of everything he is told for the purposes of interpretation and of recognizing the concealed unconscious material without substituting a censorship of his own for the selection that the patient has forgone. To put it in a formula: he must turn his own unconscious like a receptive organ towards the transmitting unconscious of the patient. He must adjust himself to the patient as a telephone receiver is adjusted to the transmitting microphone. Just as the receiver converts back into sound waves the electric oscillations in the telephone line which were set up by sound waves, so the doctor's unconscious is able, from the derivatives of the unconscious which are communicated to him, to reconstruct that unconscious, which has determined the patient's free associations.
>
> (Freud, 1912e, pp. 115–116)

What Freud was accessing, and noticing, in these early clinical sessions, was a direct communication or communion between the unconscious or primary process system of one person being implicitly, intuitively, and unconsciously reflected and received by that of another. Schore has developed a compelling and highly sophisticated neuroscientific model of these "*implicit communications* within the therapeutic relationship, whereby right brain-to-right brain transference–countertransference communications represent interactions of the patient's and therapist's unconscious primary process systems":

> In line with current developmental and relational models, I have argued that right brain-to-right brain communications represent interactions of the patient's unconscious primary process system and the therapist's primary process system … and that primary process cognition is the major communicative mechanism of the relational unconscious.
>
> (Schore, 2011, p. 78, italics in original, 2012, p. 86)

These "right brain-to-right brain communications within the therapeutic alliance", he adds, constitute "the change mechanism of longterm psychotherapy" and are both neurologically grounded and transmitted "in the connections between the patient's prefrontal, cortical, and subcortical areas of the right brain" (Schore, 2012, p. 7). The right brain, Schore explains, "nonverbally communicates its unconscious states to other right brains that are tuned to receive these combinations" (Schore, 2012, p. 127), in exactly the manner that Freud talks about with his "telephone receiver" image. This ability to "empathically receive and express bodily based nonverbal communications" (p. 85) is *precisely* what Freud was alluding to in his earlier model of analyst–patient exchange and transmission.

Schore also notes that "the core clinical skills of any effective psychotherapy are right brain implicit capacities", including

> the ability to empathically receive and express bodily based nonverbal communications, the ability to sensitively register very slight changes in another's expression and emotion, an immediate awareness of one's own subjective and intersubjective experience, and the regulation of one's own and the patient's affect.

Indeed such is the salience of these skills and capacities in the change mechanism of therapy that he concludes "that the right hemisphere is dominant in treatment, and that psychotherapy is not the 'talking cure' but the affect communicating and regulating cure" (p. 85; Schore, 2012, pp. 42, 85).

As Schore suggests, empathy is central to these clinical skills, and empathy again is right lateralised: the neurological centres for empathy are located in the right hemisphere, as McGilchrist also notes: "When we put ourselves in others' shoes, we are using the right inferior parietal lobe, and the right lateral prefrontal cortex, which is involved in inhibiting the automatic tendency to espouse one's own point of view" (McGilchrist, 2009, p. 57). Empathy lies at the beating heart of all our relationships: mother and child, lover and beloved, therapist and client. "This empathy is the first thread that restores the violated, vivid, and polysemantic relationships between the client and the world", notes Rotenberg in his compelling chapter (p. 274) – a vital clue to the way in which the act of empathy itself is healing, and an act of resistance against a world all too often posited on a detached, indifferent, and instrumental stance. As McGilchrist pointedly notes, the right hemisphere in this sense contrasts dramatically from the left:

> Above all the right hemisphere is more empathic: its stance towards others is less competitive, and more attuned to compassion and fellow-feeling … it is still the right hemisphere that is better able to understand what is going on in other people's heads, and to empathise, than the left hemisphere, which in these respects is relatively autistic.
>
> (McGilchrist, pp. 101–102)

It is for this reason, he adds, that "the intuitive moral sense is closely bound up with empathy for others and seems to depend on part of the right frontal cortex that is dysfunctional in psychopaths" (p. 102). Empathy has such a vital, and vitalising role, in therapy because it is actually quite an odd thing. Rather as with attention, it is not just a "function", like turning on a tap; it is rooted in a profound "sense" of connection with another being, a profound "going out" of oneself and into another. Being aware that another is not using you, or looking at you instrumentally, is the deep magic here – and as any child knows, it cannot be faked, or forced. It is an extraordinary expansive and liberating act, and perhaps an increasingly rare one in our ever more competitive, polarised, and manipulative world, which is why the therapeutic process can be both so poignant and so powerful.

I say, "as any child knows", because it is in childhood that these deep centres and networks of empathic communion are first formed and stabilised. This mode of non-verbal, non-instrumental attention and empathic care is central to the mother–infant relationship. In neurological terms, this relationship is rooted in specifically right brain-to-right brain forms of communication that are located in the right orbitofrontal cortices of the mother and her child (McGilchrist, 2009, p. 88; Schore, 1994, p. 125). In popular terms it's called "motherese" – a sophisticated and complex process of rapid affective cueing and response that underlies all early developmental and relational regulation. As a number of authors in the current volume note, it is the right hemisphere that is dominant for the first eighteen months of life, a period of significant neuronal, affective, and developmental integration, during which the relational templates and internal working models (IWMs) are laid down in the neural tapestry of our brains. Cozolino deftly explains how these intimate and profound RH–RH connections between the caregiver and child are formed:

The right hemisphere experiences a growth spurt during the first 18 months of life, whereas areas of the left are held back for later-developing abilities ... During these critical 18 months, the child learns hand–eye coordination, crawling, and walking – all while becoming acquainted with the world. Countless early interactions shape right-brain circuitry so we can recognize and react to the people around us, our sense of safety and danger, and our ability to regulate our emotions. Although the social brain is capable of learning throughout life, stable attachment patterns are apparent by the end of the first year.

(Cozolino, p. 111)

Our "social brain", therefore, is profoundly shaped by these early months of our lives: our relationships, our interactions, and the attention we are given, physically develop and restructure our brains. And it does this through a complex dance of sensory coordination – through eyes, and sounds, and minds, and hands, and hearts:

The infant's early maturing right hemisphere, which is dominant for the child's processing of visual emotional information, the infant's recognition of the mother's face, and the perception of arousal-inducing maternal facial expressions, is psychobiologically attuned to the output of the mother's right hemisphere, which is involved in the expression and processing of emotional information and in nonverbal communication.

(Schore, 1994, p. 63)

This "linking up of right hemispheres", Cozolino beautifully notes, is thus accomplished "through eye contact, facial expressions, soothing vocalizations, caresses, and exciting exchanges":

Sensitive caretakers learn to respond to their children's responses and synchronized engagement and disengagement. As children and caretakers move in and out of attunement, the cycle of joining, separating, and reuniting becomes the central aspect of developing psychobiological regulation.

(Cozolino, p. 112)

It is an intimate orchestration of some of the deepest networks and systems of the human body, ones which underlie both our implicit sense of self (who we fundamentally are, before social construction of the "ego" – which is aligned with the more explicit, conscious left hemisphere systems) and our most basic, and most enduring relational dynamics.

The early mother–infant dynamic forms the basis of every subsequent relational pattern, including that between the patient and therapist (see chapters by Mucci, Narvaez and Dowds in this volume). Indeed, in many ways the therapeutic relationship echoes, mirrors, and repeats this earlier care-giver relationship; recognising and responding to the deep emotional patterning and early-forming self-regulation systems of the patient can be crucial for treatment. As Mucci notes, mother–child communications are "fundamental for establishing the pattern of attachment development" and are based on "implicit right hemisphere interactions", a point elaborated on by Schore: "The transfer of affect between mother and child is thus mediated by right-hemisphere-to-right-hemisphere arousal-regulating transactions" before it is then "inscribed in implicit procedural memory in the early developing right hemisphere" (Mucci, p. 204; Schore, 2003, p. 222). A large body of developmental neurobiological research now supports the hypothesis that the central attachment mechanisms are embedded in these early infant–caregiver right brain-to-right brain affective transactions. "The highest centers of this hemisphere", notes Schore, "especially the orbitofrontal cortex, the locus of Bowlby's attachment system, act as the brain's most complex affect and stress regulatory system" (Schore, 2011, p. 80), and he explicitly identifies this attachment system with the right brain: "the control system for attachment", he concludes, "is in the right frontal lobe" (Schore, 2012, p. 232).

Attachment theory "is the most influential theory of early social–emotional development available to science", as Schore expertly explains in his chapter in the present volume, and "the attachment mechanism is embedded in infant–caregiver right brain-to-right brain affective transactions" (pp. 71 and 73). Early attachment bonding is central to all later aspects of human development, and therefore engaging these deep attachment systems is a core part of all relational psychotherapy: "the patient's unconscious internal working model of attachment, whether secure or insecure, is reactivated in right-lateralized implicit–procedural memory and reenacted in the psychotherapeutic relationship" (p. 75).

The relevance of the these early-forming attachment patterns for subsequent therapy, especially in instances of early trauma and working therapeutically with borderline patients, is also spelled out by Mucci in her groundbreaking chapter, which explains how these

> unrepressed but early memories of amygdala encoding … can be reactivated in therapy through the right brain participation of the attuned therapist and, through the mechanism of enactment, projective identification and dissociation itself, can be brought from nonverbal, sub-symbolic form, to symbolic and verbal expression (this is in fact the path of psychotherapy).
>
> (Mucci, p. 215)

Her chapter provides a compelling illustration of the therapeutic significance and clinical implications of these early right-lateralised systems of arousal, regulation, and attachment, for all forms of therapy.

From machinery to prosody: the new model of the brain

Since "talk" is at the heart of "the talking cure", *how* we talk with patients is crucial to the success of the relationship. As we have seen, psychotherapy is in this sense not so much the "talking cure" but "the affect communicating and regulating cure" (Schore, 2012, pp. 42, 85), and the "listening cure" (Phillips, 2015). In recent years there has been some fascinating research done on the ways in which both prosody and the subtle and implicit nonverbal forms of embodied communication and body language profoundly shape and inform therapeutic practice. As Schore acutely remarks, "nonverbal variables such as tone, tempo, rhythm, timbre, prosody, and amplitude of speech as well as body language signals may need to be reexamined as essential aspects of therapeutic technique" (Schore, 2011, p. 82). In fact most of what we communicate, when we do, is nonverbal: recent studies suggest that between 60 percent and an astonishing 90 percent of all human communication is nonverbal (Schore, 2011, p. 82). And as Bessel van der Kolk notes: "according to recent research, up to 90 percent of human communication occurs in the nonverbal, right-hemisphere realm" (van der Kolk, 2014, p. 298).

Attuned therapists are now aware of a whole chorus of implicit communication that is going on, at far greater speeds than the more explicit and semantic left hemisphere systems can consciously register or detect. Forms of non-verbal relating include body language (kinesics); distance and positioning (proxemics); physical appearance (height, weight, clothing, posture, style); gestures; elements of voice (paralanguage – voice quality, rate, pitch, volume, and speaking style, as well as prosodic features such as rhythm, intonation, and stress); touch (haptics); chronemics (the use of time); oculesics (eye contact and the actions of looking while talking and listening); as well as information conveyed through smell (pheromones), and through preconscious modelling (mirror neurones): all of these aspects of communication and relation are embodied and implicit, and can profoundly affect the therapeutic relationship. Together they form what might be termed "the music of the unconscious". As Schore observes, "the intuitive psychobiologically attuned therapist, on a moment-to-moment basis, implicitly tracks and resonates with the patterns of rhythmic crescendos/decrescendos of the patient's regulated and dysregulated states of affective arousal" (Schore, 2011, p. 89).

These implicit elements of dialogue and discourse are amongst the most powerful, but also amongst the most mysterious and difficult to analyse, because they operate implicitly and unconsciously, not explicitly and consciously. The affective potency of these nonverbal elements of communication is largely due to the element of prosody or musicality within language – what Schore has strikingly called "the music behind the words" (p. 77). This "musical" aspect to communication also explains why so many recent researchers, therapists, and neuroscientists are increasingly using metaphors and models drawn from music to describe and capture these highly sophisticated, highly nuanced, fluid, and dynamic processes of constant mutual interaction and reciprocity. Indeed, the word that most therapists and neuroscientists use to describe and denote this intimate form of right hemisphere-to-right hemisphere implicit communication is "attunement": "through sequences of attunement, mis-attunement, and re-attunement", Schore thus notes, "an infant becomes a person" (Schore, 2012, p. 32). This new appreciation of the sense of "attunement" and "resonance" also lies at the heart of current attachment and affect regulation theory (see for example Cozolino, Siegel, Dowds, Gantt and Badenoch, Mucci, and Narvaez in the present volume).

In fact, when you look at contemporary neuroscientific, developmental, neurobiological and psychoanalytic literature it is full of musical references, models, and metaphors. Hence the widespread use and clinical importance of such terms as "limbic resonance", "resonance circuitry", "modulation", "reverberation", "affect synchrony", "vibrational models", "relational synchronising" and "orchestration". This points us to a very remarkable, and fascinating, aspect of contemporary neuroscientific discourse, which is the increasing recognition that the model and metaphor that best captures the deep neurological workings of the social and relational brain is not that of machinery, but rather that of *musical* processes and structures. Thus, as Schore observes,

> during these bodily based affective communications, the attuned mother synchronises the spatiotemporal patterning of her exogenous sensory stimulation with the infant's spontaneous expressions of his endogenous organismic rhythms. … In play episodes of affect synchrony, the pair are in affective resonance, and in such, an amplification of vitality affects and a positive state occurs.
>
> (Schore, 2012, p. 75)

The relationship between the mother and child is not that of one machine interfacing with another, but that of one responsive and attuned system working in a moment-by-moment synchrony with another, and these dynamic communications are effected and transmitted through their respective (right) brains.

Indeed, what McGilchrist aptly calls the "music" of speech — in the sense of prosody, intonation, and all that is not, as he says, "just" the content —

> constitutes the majority of what it is we communicate, when we do. Denotative language is not necessary for I-thou communication. Music is largely right-hemisphere-dependent, and the aspects of speech that enable us truly to understand the meaning of an utterance at a higher level — including intonation, irony, metaphor, and the meaning of an utterance in context — are still served by the right hemisphere.
>
> (McGilchrist, p. 97)

The particular importance of this "music behind the words" for therapy has been compellingly explored by Professor Brett Kahr, who suggests that it lies at the very centre of therapeutic interaction and transformation. In his remarkable chapter in *How Does Psychotherapy Work?*, Kahr observes "that the musicianship of the psychotherapist may well prove to be one of the most transformational ingredients in the clinical encounter". As he explains:

> The patient will be deeply affected by our tone of voice, our accent, the volume of our voice, the pitch of our voice, its cadence, its flow, its pressure, as well as by our sentence structure ... These components of the voice, arguably the most important physical items that we bring into the session – especially if we work with analysands on the couch who cannot see our face – remain among the most shamefully undertheorized and underinvestigated components of psychological work.
>
> (Kahr, 2005, p. 10)

This appreciation of the potency of modulation and affect, and the implicit power of these deep nonverbal systems of communication, recall the very earliest and most life-forming systems of implicit interaction between mother and child. As Kahr rightly notes, these crucial aspects of the "talking cure" have historically been significantly "undertheorized and underinvestigated". Their rediscovery in recent years is one of the most exciting and revelatory aspects of the current research into the role of the right hemisphere in contemporary psychotherapeutic work.

The relevance of music to therapy goes beyond our new understanding of relational attunement, limbic resonance, affect synchrony, and the recognition of "the music behind the words". The brain itself seems to operate in ways that more strongly resemble the dynamic, relational and multilinear aspects of music, than the cruder systems of linearity, duality, and logic that characterise machinery. These subtle processes of attunement and synchronisation seem to run deep, but exactly how deep has only been revealed in the last few years, with new research into how the neurons in our brains actually operate. For it seems that our brains themselves run in nonlinear, implicit, and reverberative ways. As McGilchrist notes, it is often assumed that neurons must operate in sequential, linear ways – that one nerve transmits an impulse to the next, which transmits it in turn to another, and so on. But as it happens, he points out, "the way in which neurons behave is *not* linear, sequential, unidirectional: they behave in a reciprocal, reverberative fashion, and not just in the right hemisphere" (McGilchrist, 2009, p. 194). It is an observation confirmed by Kinsbourne:

> Counter to the traditional image of the brain as a unidirectional information thoroughfare, when cell stations in the brain connect, the traffic is almost always bi-directional. The traffic is not in one direction,

with a little feedback, either. Areas interact equally in both directions, directly reciprocally, or indirectly by looping across several cell stations, so that the neural traffic reverberates through its starting point. The forebrain is overwhelmingly an area of reverberating reciprocal influence.

(Kinsbourne, 2003)

This introduces a new level of understanding into science, and a new metaphor: "reverberation". At the very level at which the brain itself operates, neurons themselves seem to behave in a "reciprocal", not a "linear" way. Thus, in perhaps a striking form of reverberation itself, this new sense of multi-directional, multimodal, and multivalent systems interacting "equally in both directions, directly reciprocally, or indirectly by looping across several cell stations" is both how the brain itself works, and how the right hemisphere understands reality – in a nonlinear, reciprocal, and holistic way. Reverberation captures something of how reality itself emerges into being, out of a form of reciprocity: "The world comes into being between *us* and this something *other* than ourselves", notes McGilchrist, and this "is a reverberative process in which each, as it were, *calls* to the other" (Cleese & McGilchrist, 2018).

These deep patterns of resonance, attunement, and mutual synchronisation, McGilchrist suggests, allowed "a critical evolution of the human brain" by enabling us to imitate, reflect, empathise, imagine, and relate to what was around us, and are themselves the neuronal embodiments and cognitive footprints of all those multiple exchanges, refractions, and affective engagements (McGilchrist, 2009, p. 248). Van der Kolk makes a similar point with regard to this evolutionary process of "attunement", drawing out its relevance to therapy: "Children are intensely social from the start", he observes,

> they are captivated by faces and voices. From birth they are exquisitely sensitive to facial expressions. This inborn capacity for attunement – for being able to match their inner experience with that of those around them – is an evolutionary product essential to the survival of our species.
>
> (van der Kolk, foreword to Frewen & Lanius, 2015, p. xiii)

Our models of the brain have always reflected the society out of which they emerged. During the last couple of centuries, the brain was routinely compared to a machine or a computer, a mechanical and functionalist device – where for example memories were said to be "stored" or "filed", like you would on a computer or filing cabinet. We can now see how limited and rather quaint this model is, with its unilinear modelling and rather static, mechanical, lifeless, representational feel. In the neuroscientific modelling world of the twenty-first century, the brain is now revealed to be a much

more sophisticated and dynamic, and above all alive, entity – an extraordinarily fluid, engaged, nonlinear, responsive, relational form of organisation,
one that is constantly coming into being – like a score – through the sum of
its interactions. It is an interweaving, interconnecting world of mutual resonance and constant reverberation, acting and reacting in response both to
experiences within and without, where the metaphors of resonance, attunement, and reverberation come alive in a dazzling display of mutual action
and interaction – of constant call and response.

In an earlier age, Plato used a very different metaphor for the brain than
the machine model that has dominated Western scientific thinking since the
Enlightenment. In his dialogue *Theaetetus*, which explores the nature of knowledge, Socrates compares our thoughts and memories to birds in an aviary
(Plato, 1988, 196d–200c), perhaps drawing on the "call-and-reply" aspect of
consciousness that modern researchers have again begun to recognise and
appreciate. The aviary model also suggests the intimate association that is felt
between "music" and "memory" – how the "past" also calls to us, reverberates – which is why its resonant patterns and structures are so evocative. With
the rise of more left hemispheric ways of thinking about the world in the
Enlightenment, this organic and dynamic model was replaced by a more rigid,
and much more passive, model of the mind (as simply a "tabula rasa" upon
which things were unilinearly inscribed). This mechanical and materialistic
view of the brain generally prevailed in scientific literature until the late twentieth century. One brief exception was during in the eighteenth century,
when a more dynamic understanding of the brain and body re-emerged with
David Hartley's "Associationist" school of psychology, which focussed on
neural connectivity and explored how various neural "vibrations" and "modu-
lations" in the brain had an impact on both our bodily and mental activity.
This "vibrational" model of the mind was picked up by a number of the leading Romantic writers and thinkers, including Coleridge, Wordsworth, and
Shelley, in their striking "Aeolian Harp" metaphors for consciousness. Shelley's magnificent – and extraordinarily prescient – incorporation of this way of
thinking about consciousness is evident in his *A Defence of Poetry* (1821):
"Man is an instrument over which a series of external and internal impressions
are driven", he notes, "like the alternations of an ever-changing wind over an
Æolian lyre, which move it by their motion to ever-changing melody"
(Reiman & Powers, 1977, p. 480). Interestingly, as we have seen, a rather
similar model has emerged in recent neuroscience, with the concept of
"reverberation", "modulation" and "resonance", in which our brains similarly
render and receive fast influences in rapid multilinear and multivalent ways,
and in which the forebrain itself is now seen as being "overwhelmingly an
area of reverberating reciprocal influence" (Kinsbourne, 2003). At the very
level at which the brain itself operates, matter itself seems to behave in
a "reciprocal", not a "linear", way, in a constant and mutual process of call
and response, rather as Socrates had suggested. As McGilchrist remarks, "it

seems that this reciprocity, this betweenness, goes to the core of our being" (McGilchrist, 2009, p. 194). Plato was right. Our heads, it seems, are full of birdsong.

Integrating the Hemispheres: The clinical implications of the divided brain

Sometimes of course the attunement and the early reverberative music breaks down, and the results can be catastrophic. If there is no appropriate reciprocity or mutual modulation between caregiver and child, or within wider familial relationships, the effects on both our sense of self and our relationship to the outer world can become deeply dysregulated. When these early systems become disturbed and the mutual regulatory systems fail to register the appropriate call and response patterns, it can generate traumatic effects that last lifetimes long, as a number of authors in the present volume poignantly note (Mucci, Schore, Meares).

Our earliest attachment patterns imprint themselves on our being, and form the relational templates and internal working models that we carry with us and apply to every subsequent relationship, including of course that of the therapeutic alliance. Many of the authors in the current volume show how the affectively attuned therapist can engage with these deep, implicit systems of regulation and response, and thereby facilitate reintegration and reparation of these dysregulated and damaged structures. As we'll see, this is a right hemisphere-to-right hemisphere process of mutual engagement and integration. As Schore observes, "internal representations of attachment experiences are imprinted in right-lateralized implicit–procedural memory as an internal working model that encodes nonconscious strategies of affect regulation", and these internal representations and encoded strategies can be accessed and repaired through right brain-to-right brain communication with the therapist. Thus, "the patient's unconscious internal working model of attachment, whether secure or insecure, is reactivated in right-lateralized implicit–procedural memory and reenacted in the psychotherapeutic relationship" (pp. 72 and 75). Psychotherapy regulates these patterns of call and response, these often fractured relationships of dissonance or dissociation, and in so doing it re-writes the brain. As Cozolino succinctly and strikingly notes, "psychotherapy can serve as a means to reintegrate the patient's disconnected hemispheres":

> In the language of neuroscience, we are integrating dissociated systems of memory and processing systems by teaching new strategies for integrating rational and emotional information. These processes aid in the construction of a more inclusive self-narrative, which, in turn, serves as a blueprint for ongoing neural integration.
>
> (Cozolino, 2010, pp. 110–111)

As we've seen, early developmental processes are especially dependent on right hemisphere networks and functions, and therefore later relational and attachment adjustments are focussed there. It follows that damage to these early networks of attachment, affect regulation, and sense of self – all of which are rooted in and delivered by the right hemisphere – can lead to significant patterns of disruption and imbalances between the hemispheres, which are the focus of psychotherapeutic attention. As Schore, one of the pioneers in investigating these systems and their impact on subsequent relational development, notes, "there is now consensus that deficits in right brain relational processes and resulting affect dysregulation underlie all psychological and psychiatric disorders" (p. 74). "Impaired integration", notes Siegel, another major figure in our understanding of the role of hemispheric re-integration in the clinical practice of therapy, "is the root of mental dysfunction" (Siegel & Solomon, 2013, p. 2).

There is growing consensus that many forms of early relational trauma are also rooted in forms of "impaired integration": even the DSM, Siegel observes, has recognised this correlation (Siegel & Solomon, 2013). And as Meares notes in the present volume, "disintegration is perhaps *the* central pathology induced by relational trauma. It manifests a failure to develop a co-ordination among the elements of the brain/mind system necessary to the emergence of self" (p. 242). Because of these powerful and compelling associations between impaired integration, hemispheric disconnection, and mental distress, there is increasing awareness that we need to rethink and reframe our understanding of what we actually mean by "mental disorder". What we currently term "disorders" might in fact be more accurately thought of as "dis-integrations", since so many forms of distress that we encounter are rooted in forms of hemispheric disorganisation and disruption. According to the most recent neuroscientific and psychoanalytic research, disorder is not so much a breakdown in order as a breakdown in integration.

The present volume explores some of the practical implications of our new understanding of left–right hemisphere imbalances and impaired integrations, and suggests the relevance this new research has both for our theoretical understanding and clinical practice of therapy. *The Divided Therapist* will explain how these processes of dis-integration and discordance happen on a neurological level, as well as a psychological one, and suggest that the therapist or analyst has an unusual – indeed, in many ways a unique – role in helping to repair and restore these disrupted and dysregulated systems. Therapeutic reparation and re-integration happens even on a neurological level – indeed, this is precisely what the psychotherapy helps to effect. As Glass notes, "psychotherapy changes brain function and structure", affecting such diverse aspects as "neurotransmitter metabolism, gene expression, and persistent modification in synaptic plasticity" (Glass, 2008, p. 1589). Therapy affects, re-writes, and changes the unconscious through its engagement with right hemispheric processes and networks: as Cozolino observes, "psycho-therapy is a means of creating or restoring coordination among various neural networks", and therefore the integration of dissociated processing systems is often "a central focus of treatment" (Cozolino, 2010, pp. 25, 111).

The story of the self

It is the right brain that is the centre for our earliest sense of self, often referred to as the preverbal or "implicit" self, and early disruption to right hemispheric activities and functioning can have particularly profound and enduring consequences for our very sense of who we are. As Schore notes, "neuroscientists contend that the right hemisphere is centrally involved in maintaining a coherent, continuous and unified sense of self", and that "the survival strategy of pathological dissociation is expressed as a dis-integration of the right brain emotional-corporeal implicit self, the biological substrate of the human unconscious" (Schore, 2011, p. 81).

"Right frontal damage impairs the sense of self over time – self with a narrative, and a continuous flow-like existence", notes McGilchrist (2009, p. 88), and this idea of the self as a sort of "story" that can be continually re-integrated, re-told, and re-examined, suggests not only that the self is inherently a *process* (dynamic, self-creating, and relational, as Dowds suggests; see Dowds, 2014, p. 66), but also points to the importance of narratives, and story-telling, in letting us find out who we are. Narrative power and effective story-telling lie at the very heart of psychoanalysis, as Adam Phillips compellingly suggests:

> I think that the pursuit of narrative – and what people are actually doing with narratives, both defensively and progressively in their lives – is in a sense what psychoanalysis is about. It's partly about storytelling – selves constituted and interrupted through storytelling.
>
> (Phillips, 2000)

Freud himself was "also preoccupied with the struggle to articulate", notes Phillips: "We change ourselves by redescribing ourselves. And we redescribe ourselves in dialogue with someone else" (Phillips, 2019). Stories are themselves a striking product of hemispheric collaboration. Being word-driven, they are clearly an expression of the verbally dextrous left brain, and yet "the understanding of narrative is a right-hemispheric skill", observes McGilchrist: "the left hemisphere cannot follow a narrative" (it follows abstracted sequences, but not contextual, "real-world", temporal worlds that unfold in time; see McGilchrist, 2009, p. 76). Language itself marries both hemispheres, a constant dance and interplay of implicit and explicit, left and right: "language bridges the gap between abstraction and experience" (McGilchrist, 2018) – in that sense, language is itself a sort of corpus callosum, bridging the worlds of left-brain abstraction and right-brain experience. In terms of the central relevance of this to therapy and the talking cure, Cozolino has persuasively shown how these constantly integrative and inter-hemispheric processes lie at the heart of all therapeutic communication and treatment: "Stories also serve as powerful tools for neural network integration", he remarks, noting how our stories are woven not simply with words but with neural networks:

> The combination of a linear story line and visual imagery woven together with verbal and nonverbal expressions of emotion activates circuitry of both cerebral hemispheres, cortical and subcortical networks, the various regions of the frontal lobes, the hippocampus, and the amygdala. This integrative neural processing may also account, in part, for the positive correlations between coherent narratives and secure attachments.
>
> (Cozolino, 2016, p. 23)

The stories that our networks weave connect not only hemispheres, but peoples, communities, histories – even global hemispheres: "Human beings are natural storytellers", Cozolino observes, and "shared stories contain images and ideas that stimulate imagination and link individuals to the group mind". And this "group mind", the basis of our social brains themselves, "coevolved with storytelling". "It is no coincidence that storytelling is a cornerstone of what we call the talking cure", he acutely remarks: "It is very likely that our brains have been able to become as complex as they are precisely because of the power of narratives to integrate both our brains and social groups" (Cozolino, 2016, pp. 22, 23; 2010, pp. 236–237). Cozolino is himself one of psychotherapy's great storytellers.

"Talking works", notes Launer, "because it provides people with a means of creating a coherent narrative from disconnected symptoms, events, memories and thoughts in the context of a relationship with someone compassionate and attentive" (Launer, 2005, p. 466). This process of creating coherence from disconnection is what makes narratives so compelling. Through the talking cure, as Freud discovered, we can be both restored and re-storied.

But it is not as if we can tell ourselves any old story. As David Smail has noted,

> with many "postmodernist" approaches (e.g. "narrative therapy") magical voluntarism reaches its apotheosis: the world is made of words, and if the story you find yourself in causes you distress, tell yourself another one. From any rational, scientific standpoint, this kind of view is completely incoherent – indeed it is psychotic.
>
> (Smail, 2005, p. 7)

Stories must include, and be embedded in, social reality if they are to be compelling – and the new stories of the self, and of psychoanalysis, will have to include the material, social world in them as well, if they are to be therapeutically useful or ontologically meaningful. As Johnson observes, meanings emerge "as structures of organism-environment interactions" (Johnson, 2007, p. xii), not in isolation from the environment and environmental interactions (which is why, until recently, meaningful art told stories about the world, rather than itself). "Art matters because it provides heightened, intensified, and highly integrated experiences of meaning" (Johnson, 2007, p. xiii). Indeed, the way that art spontaneously engages and combines elements of the explicit and the implicit, the unconscious and the conscious, affect and cognition, make it in many ways a strikingly sophisticated model of integrative process, as a number of therapists and clinicians in the present volume note. "Poetry may be seen as the supreme example of this synthesis", observes Dowds, "where language – a left-brain function – and processing of experience is assembled into a new whole that is a reflection of, but greater than, the original experience" (Dowds, 2014 p. 72).

These recent developments in our understanding of the ways in which implicit connections between felt affect and spoken verbalisation may be impaired and non-integrated, and the role of the therapist in finding a way to encourage and allow the patient to "put the affect into words", is an exciting refinement and development of Freud's original analysis of this process over a hundred years ago, and lends significant scientific corroboration to his clinical findings. "Recollection without affect almost invariably produces no result" (Breuer & Freud, 1895d, p. 6). As Cozolino puts it:

> Left–right integration allows us to put feelings into words, consider feelings in conscious awareness, and balance the positive and negative affective biases of the left and right hemispheres … *Left–right* or *right–left integration* involves abilities that require the input of both the left and right cerebral cortex and lateralized limbic regions for optimal functioning. For example, adequate language production requires an integration of the grammatical functions of the left and the emotional functions of the right.
> (Cozolino, 2010, p. 28)

The innovative techniques and methods that Freud developed to do this – the techniques of free association in the patient, evenly suspended attention in the analyst, and of bringing the unconscious into contact with the conscious – forged a new way of integrating and reconciling the patient's often disrupted and damaged limbic and cerebral cortex networks, and constitute one of the most extraordinary and humanitarian techniques in modern psychology. Freud's talking cure is *precisely* a way of integrating what has not hitherto been able to be integrated. Psychoanalysis is a remarkable and potent fusion of both left hemisphere and right hemisphere, detailed attention and global apprehension: the impossible therapist. In many respects, "psycho-analysis" *is* integration – a unique fusion of analysis and synthesis. Psychosynthesis.

It follows that if so many disorders result from hemispheric dis-integration and imbalance, and the work of the therapist and clinician is to help reintegrate and repair these systems and ways of being in the world, then this involves a new understanding of what the therapist actually is, or does. Far from being a "shrink", as the analyst was often seen in classical psychoanalysis, we can now see that the therapist is actually an integrator, a mediator, an *expander*. As Siegel and Solomon acutely note in their book *Healing Moments in Psychotherapy*, "the therapist is an integrator, cultivating the linkage of differentiated elements within the two fundamental domains of mind: the body, and our relationships with each other" (Siegel & Solomon, 2013, pp. 14–15). This idea of "linkage" is unpacked further in the present book (Siegel and Siegel, Chapter 4). And as both Siegel and Cozolino note, in acting as a form of hemispheric "bridge", therapists are themselves intimately involved in the process of integration and healing, are *part* of the left–right brain pattern of integration, in fact living embodiments of it. They are the transitional bridges that cross and unite these dissociated and divided worlds. The book is called "The Divided Therapist" precisely to draw attention to the fact that therapists are not only themselves part of these split worlds, these complementary but contrary ways of being, but to suggest that they also play a powerful and pivotal role in allowing integration between those worlds to occur, "teaching new strategies for integrating rational and emotional information", as Cozolino puts it (Cozolino, 2010, p. 111). Learning how to more effectively engage with and understand these processes of balance, harmony, and re-integration is an aim of the book and I hope may be of use both to practising therapists and to anyone wanting to work towards a more integrated and meaningful world.

The divided world

A number of the authors in the present volume note that much of the distress and dysfunction encountered in the consulting room is often driven or amplified by factors in the social environment (see for example Narvaez, Dowds, McGilchrist). The "divided therapist" is inevitably part of these wider and systemic divisions as well, as indeed is the profession as a whole. One of the most exciting developments in recent years has been the willingness of so many new mental health practitioners and professionals to engage with these wider systems as part of a much bigger work of integration, and indeed of what one might call social therapy.

In our increasingly divisive and dissociated world, therapy can perhaps provide a guide for how we might start to repair these rather dysregulated and dysfunctional wider systems. For, as a number of therapists and clinicians have suggested, from Jung and R. D. Laing to Smail and McGilchrist, our world seems to suffer from curiously similar forms of dysregulation and dissociation that our brains do. Psychotherapy is a way to understand and to bridge those schisms, to both physically and psychologically restore and re-write our currently disorganised and dis-integrated systems. Therapists are perhaps particularly well-equipped for this task, familiar with these deep systems of repair and regulation. "There is indeed a possibility for attributing new meaning to the traumatic events", remarks Mucci affirmatively in her chapter, "restructuring the brain activity in a way that is more balanced and that deactivates the excessive response of the limbic system, while giving more possibility of cortical awareness and explicit verbalization" (p. 220). Deactivating the excessive responses of the limbic system and restructuring our wider systems to enhance greater cortical awareness seems exactly like what the world requires at the moment. As for any patient, healing involves not just cognitively "knowing" that the current way of doing things is damaging and disordered, but actively engaging with and *restructuring* our imaginative and political unconscious, so that the corrupted limbic and affective systems in which it is rooted can finally be restored and healed. "No child can be left at the mercy of a dysregulated limbic system", notes Batmanghelidjh acutely, and a dysregulated limbic system is, sadly, exactly what modern Britain resembles (Batmanghelidjh & Rayment, 2017, p. 64). "In siloed intellectual frames, we chop up human beings into fragmented pieces while deluding ourselves that we're making them whole", she observes: "There is a reticence to cross boundaries in the belief that thought and talking should be separated from the body and that the body should be separated from its social environment" (Batmanghelidjh, 2015, p. 58). This form of profound dislocation and dysfunction, a world of silos and discrete compartments held together by bureaucracy and fear, is the inevitable instan-tiation of a dysfunctional and divided brain, and is what the contemporary welfare system in some ways strikingly resembles, as McGilchrist has also noted ("Divided brain, divided world", Rowson & McGilchrist, 2017). Indeed, the model of holistic, integrative, and socially contextualised child health care that Batmanghelidjh developed at Kids Company was a remarkable glimpse at what an integrated, compassionate, person-centred system of child welfare might resemble, before it was deliberately and reck-lessly disrupted by the dissociated systems of political and media dysfunction that engulfed it (Tweedy, 2017). Psychotherapy works because it can recog-nise and engage with these broken and damaged systems, these disrupted and disconnected lives, and in that it perhaps serves as a wider model for social health and wellbeing. As Cozolino suggests, "applying this model, psy-chotherapy is a means of creating or restoring coordination" among numer-ous different networks (Cozolino, 2010, p. 25).

Perhaps no one has done more to draw attention to the ways in which the divided self, the divided brain, and the divided world are interconnected than Iain McGilchrist, in his comprehensive study of "The Divided Brain and the Making of the Western World", as the subtitle to his landmark *The Master and His Emissary* (2009) suggests:

I believe the battle between the hemispheres (which is only a battle from the left hemisphere's point of view) explains the shape of the history of ideas in the West and may ultimately cast light on the predicament we find ourselves in today: living in what to many seems like an increasingly mechanistic, fragmented, decontextualized world, marked by an unwarranted optimism mixed with a feeling of emptiness, and prone to self-destruction, as its ravaging of the environment and the recent near total collapse of the financial system might suggest.

(McGilchrist, 2013, p. 75)

This modern sense of being fragmented and decontextualised, rooted in a profound "feeling of emptiness" and an excessive form of hyper-rationality, resembles, he observes, a particular psychiatric condition: schizophrenia. "Both schizophrenia and the modern condition, I suggest, deal with the same problem: a free-wheeling left hemisphere" (McGilchrist, p. 403, 332). Drawing our attention to the powerful ways in which the inner and the outer – the psychological and the political – constantly interact and shape each other, McGilchrist poignantly records how in recent decades "urbanisation, globalisation and the destruction of local cultures has led to a rise in the prevalence of mental illness", one that has led to intense feelings of devitalisation, depersonalisation, and derealisation, "a loss of depth of emotion and capacity for empathy", "a fragmentation of the sense of self", depression, and dissociation. "All these features", he notes, "will be recognisable as signs of left hemisphere predominance" (McGilchrist, 2009, pp. 436, 406–407). Multiple personality disorder is, he observes, another dissociative disorder which is characterised by a "relative left hemisphere over-activation", an observation that

> fits with the fact that multiple personality disordered patients exhibit first-rank symptoms of schizophrenia, and describe being the passive victims of a controlling force, since schizophrenia is another condition in which there is a failure to integrate left-hemisphere and right-hemisphere processes, with a dysfunctional right hemisphere and an overactive left hemisphere, giving rise to the sense of alien control.
>
> (McGilchrist, 2009, p. 406)

Indeed, this issue of "dissociation" seems to underlie and underwrite some of the most severe and painful conditions that therapists encounter in the modern world:

> Anorexia nervosa, multiple personality disorder and deliberate self-harm are linked by "dissociation": there is a sense of being cut off – and often a craving to be cut off – from one's feelings, and from embodied existence, a loss of depth of emotion and capacity for empathy, a fragmentation of the

sense of self; and these features also characterise what is known as "border-line" personality disorder. Once again, this may be a condition whose prevalence is increasing ... Here too there is evidence of right-hemisphere dysfunction, with many regions of the right hemisphere appearing underactive.

(McGilchrist, 2009, p. 406)

These possible hemispheric dissociations and dis-integrations therefore touch on the very deepest issues of human existence, and our sense of relationship to the world. In her remarkable chapter in the present volume, Barbara Dowds unpacks some of the more existential aspects of this process of dis-integration, which can lead to such a devastating loss of meaning in many patients. Indeed, the fundamental aim of all psychotherapy, she suggests – even beyond any relational, familial, or attachment issues – is to restore a sense of meaning and connection to what she terms the "ground of being" – to allow the patient to recover this innate and implicit connection (p. 186).

Integrating the hemispheres

Integration does not simply mean finding a "balance" between the hemispheres, as if each were two identical and equal players: "The relationship between the hemispheres", McGilchrist notes, "is not symmetrical. Each needs the other; each has an important role to play. But those roles are not equal – one depends more on the other, and needs to be aware of that fact":

> One hemisphere, the right hemisphere, has precedence, in that it under-writes the knowledge of that the other comes to have, and is alone able to synthesise what *both* know into a usable whole.
>
> (McGilchrist, p. 95; McGilchrist, 2009, p. 176)

The right hemisphere, he notes, has precedence not only in terms of "primacy of experience", but also in terms of "primacy of wholeness", "the primacy of the implicit", "primacy of broad vigilant attention", "primacy of affect", and "primacy of the unconscious will" (McGilchrist, 2009, pp. 176–208). It is the hemisphere that grounds us and sustains us when we start breathing, the hemisphere that underwrites the first eighteen months of our life and our earliest developmental formations, it is the hemisphere that supports and delivers every relationship, attachment, and embodied experience we have (as "the seat of our unconscious, our embodiment and emotional regulation"; Dowds, 2014, p. 70), and it is the hemisphere that empathises with our final breath. The right hemisphere therefore underwrites and "delivers" our experience of the world, which the left brain then "unpacks" and processes, before returning it to the right hemisphere, to be re-integrated into the wider picture. As Dowds notes in her compelling discussion of this process:

> McGilchrist argues – by analogy to the Hegelian triad of thesis, antithesis, and synthesis – that complete and rich processing of experience requires a sequence of transfers between the hemispheres in the following order: right, left, and then right again. This entails: holistic experiencing by the right brain; logical examination and categorisation by the left; and then a return to the right for a final synthesis of the original gestalt with the abstract analysis, so as to generate an integrated and transformed whole that is more than the sum of its parts.
>
> (Dowds, 2014, pp. 71–72)

This is the process that therefore underlies and underwrites integration: right–left–right (R–L–R). It also underwrites the integrative form of "Systems-Centered Therapy" (SCT) developed by Gantt and Badenoch, as they explain in their chapter: "SCT's theory uses a left brain map to access greater right brain knowing and integration, again a flow of R–L–R" (p. 154), thereby facilitating and nurturing "a group mind that supports right brain function and right–left–right hemispheric integration", as indeed the title of their chapter in this volume suggests (p. 149). They call this movement "the ongoing collaboration of right–left–right, which is our brain's natural pattern of development and transformation" (p. 161), and again links it to McGilchrist's work in understanding the relationship between the "master" hemisphere and the "emissary". In other words, first psycho-analysis, and then psycho-synthesis ("the emissary reporting back to the Master, who alone can see the broader picture" – McGilchrist, p. 104).

"The work of the left hemisphere needs to be *integrated* with that of the right hemisphere", notes McGilchrist (2009, p. 131, italics in original). He eloquently argues "that the rationality of the left hemisphere must be resubmitted to, and subject to, the broader contextualising influence of the right hemisphere, with all its emotional complexity" and "that the rational workings of the left hemisphere. should be subject to the intuitive wisdom of the right hemisphere" (ibid., p. 203). What the left hemisphere offers, brilliantly, and uniquely, is "a valuable, but intermediate process, one of 'unpacking' what is there and handing it back to the right hemisphere, where it can once more be integrated into the experiential whole" (p. 104). What the left hemisphere delivers, then, is dissection, analysis, separation. What the right brain delivers is *wholeness*, and in this again it has a peculiar resonance and relationship with therapy. For the whole purpose of therapy is wholeness – the very word "health" (as in "mental health") *means* wholeness (O. E. *hælan*, "to make whole, sound and well"). And wholeness is the result of integration: "healing emerges from integration", note Siegel and Solomon, again pointing to the intimate connections between healing, health, and wholeness (Siegel & Solomon, 2013, p. 7). The result of all this all this talking, then – all this knowing thyself, all these examined and unexamined lives, all this distress and division and dysfunction – is integration.

> It is this integration that emerges within us and between us that frees the mind from its suffering in isolation, its repeated states of chaos and rigidity that emerge from an unintegrated life.
>
> (ibid., Siegel & Solomon, 2013, pp. 8, 268)

How do you know if you're integrated? "The outcome of integration", notes Siegel, "is kindness and compassion". Kindness is a state which is not judgmental, competitive, or instrumental. These are signs and symptoms of an inner disconnection, an obstacle, a dis-organisation or dis-harmony. "From this perspective mental illness results from a disconnection from others and a retreat into selfishness", notes Cozolino (2006, p. 414). And if, as Cozolino strikingly suggests, mental illness is the result of separation from others, from disconnection and lack of integration, then mental health is the emergence into interconnection, into interdependency, into wholeness. Into kindness.

Beyond the talking cure

This process of "R–L–R" integration has special saliency for psychoanalysis. Traditionally, post-Freudian analysis sought to "make the unconscious conscious", but the more we learn about the unconscious and its involvement with right hemisphere networks and processes, and therefore with the more sophisticated and aware aspects of the brain, the more this formulation needs to be revised and updated, and to some extent abandoned. Pioneering figures such as Allan Schore, Mark Solms, Iain McGilchrist, Louis Cozolino, and Dan Siegel are indeed doing exactly that:

> In terms of psychotherapy, change is not so much about increasing the left's reasoned control over emotion, as it is the expansion of affect tolerance and regulation of the right-lateralised "emotional brain" and the human relatedness of the right-lateralised "social brain".
>
> (Schore, 2012, pp. 202–203)

The aim of psychotherapy, in other words, is not to convert the id into the ego, the implicit into the explicit, or the right brain into the left, but rather to restructure and expand the "unconscious" itself (see Schore, Dowds, Narvaez, McGilchrist, this volume).

This involves re-thinking our ideas about exactly what we mean by "consciousness", and even to open up the possibility that what we have previously considered and called the "unconscious" might actually be a far more highly conscious, aware, and functioning system than the explicit, verbalised, slower form of rational, egoic "consciousness", that traditionally therapy and psychoanalysis has focussed on – and one which increasingly seems itself to be "unconscious" in many of its approaches and suppositions about itself. As Solms and Panksepp note, commenting on the exciting new theories regarding the nature and structures of what they strikingly term "the conscious id", it seems to be the core of the brain (that is, the deeper limbic structures in the brain stem and midbrain) that generates consciousness, not the cortex: "when Freud famously proclaimed 'where id was, there shall ego be' as the therapeutic goal of his 'talking cure', he assumed that the ego enlightened the id. It now appears more likely that the opposite happens" (Solms & Panksepp, 2012).

Our recent recognition of the sophistication of the right hemisphere, its crucial role in early developmental regulation and relational attachment systems, its global, multilinear functioning and holistic operating capacities, and its location as the site of our earliest, implicit sense of who we are, has led many commentators to re-evaluate what exactly it is we mean by "conscious" and "unconscious". As McGilchrist remarks, what we formerly considered to be the dominant, conscious system of self (aligned with the left hemisphere), turns out to be a rather peculiar, limited form of consciousness – one whose primary value is to make things explicit, separate them, and verbalise them.

> If what we mean by consciousness is the part of the mind that brings the world into focus, makes it explicit, allows it to be formulated in language, and is aware of its own awareness, it is reasonable to link the conscious mind to activity almost all of which lies ultimately in the left hemisphere.
>
> (McGilchrist, 2009, p. 188)

"This type of consciousness", he notes, "is a minute part of brain activity, and must take place at the highest level of integration of brain function" (ibid., p. 188). The left hemisphere brings the world into focus, and in so doing, it interprets and analyses it: it is, McGilchrist observes,

> the one that does the interpreting, the translation into words … Note the significance of the metaphor. Meaning does not originate with an interpreter – all one can hope for from the interpreter is that in his or her hands the true meaning is not actually lost.
>
> (McGilchrist, 2009, p. 188)

What the left brain does, then, is to "translate" and "interpret" the world apprehended and delivered to it through the right hemisphere – to analysis it, unpack it, take it apart, and bring it "into focus", so it can be more effectively used and manipulated. And it does this interpreting in rather an unusual way: in making explicit and "conscious" whatever it encounters, the left brain alters it – contracts it, limits it, rationalises it, and fixes it. It converts experience so that it becomes a "thing", an object. The left hemisphere mode of attention, notes McGilchrist, "isolates, fixes and makes each thing explicit by bringing it under the spotlight of attention. In doing so it renders things inert, mechanical, lifeless" (p. 103) – in short it makes things, *things*. It converts what is flowing, implicit and process-based, into something static, isolated, and "known". It is also rather unusual in that it does not know that it is doing this: it takes this way of interpreting the world for granted – indeed, it takes this way of interpreting or translating the world as *being* the world. In that sense, as McGilchrist notes, the "conscious" left hemisphere is not, in a sense, "aware". It "does not know what it does not know" (McGilchrist, 2014).

What the left hemisphere excels at is a focussed, explicit, slower mode of cognition, one that filters what it finds, converts it, and thereby alters it. And it's slower for a good reason: this form of explicit-making, interpretive, "working-out" consciousness is "an extremely limited resource", as Solms notes:

> Consciousness ('working memory') is an extremely limited resource, so there is enormous pressure to consolidate and automatise learned solutions to life's problems (for a review see Bargh & Chartrand, 1999, who conclude that only 5% of goal-directed actions are conscious).
>
> (Solms, 2018, p. 5)

Solms's point that perhaps only "5% of goal-directed actions are conscious" suggests how precious, and limited, this mode of processing reality is. Indeed, some estimate that only two per cent of mental activity is consciously experienced (see Eagleman, 2015a), again pointing to how extensive and fundamental what we call "unconscious" activity is.

Since it has traditionally been the verbal, left brain "conscious" system that has done most of the defining of the "unconscious", our understanding of the much faster but more implicit and non-verbal systems of the unconscious have been subject to the left brain's rather self-preferential mode of processing. Indeed, that's partly why we call it the "unconscious" – it is simply not "conscious" to the slower operating speeds of the rather clunky, linear, left brain. In terms of its speed, intuitive skill, and implicit multi-linear processing, the right hemisphere unconscious networks might perhaps best be seen as the sort of superfast "5G" of the brain, allowing it to operate much more rapidly, and over far greater numbers of networks, simultaneously, than the left. As Schore notes, these implicit systems carry *more* information, not less, than the slower semantic processes of the left hemisphere: speaking of the importance of these "rapid communications" in the therapeutic alliance, he remarks that "these implicit clinical dialogues convey much more essential organismic information than left brain explicit, verbal information" (p. 75).

The fact that the right brain has significantly more white matter than the left is what allows this greater communication speed, facilitating faster transfer of information across regions, faster and more accurate identification of emotions, and an increased ability to sustain global attention. As McGilchrist notes, "the right hemisphere has a greater degree of myelination, facilitating swift transfer of information between the cortex and centres below the cortex, and greater connectivity in general" (McGilchrist, 2009, p. 42). The right brain's impressive ratio of white matter to grey is what *allows* it to function and communicate so rapidly, and is also what underwrites the rapid processes of the unconscious brain, which operates at speeds far faster and deeper than the conscious, left-brain networks.

> The more "diffuse" organization of the right hemisphere has the effect that it responds to any stimulus, even speech stimuli, more quickly and, thus earlier. The left hemisphere is activated after this and performs the slower semantic analysis.
>
> (Buklina, 2005, p. 479)

And it carries it far too quickly for the slower, more explicit, left brain to observe or detect – to be "conscious" of: as Schore notes, the right brain's implicit functions operate beneath levels of normal awareness because they are "too rapid to reach consciousness" (Schore, 2012, p. 28). "Current brain research on human decision making", he remarks, "articulates dual-process theories that clearly differentiate reasoning, which is slow, controlled, and effortful, from intuition, which is fast, emotional, effortless, and creative" (Schore, 2011, p. 87).

The unconscious mind not only seems to travel faster than the conscious, but also seems to know what the conscious mind will do even before the conscious mind itself does. In a fascinating series of experiments in the 1980s, Libet suggested that the unconscious will, more closely related to right hemisphere functioning, is indeed "well ahead of anything our explicit verbalizing consciousness can be aware of" (Siegel & Solomon, 2013, p. 81). Libet's famous "readiness potential" experiment indicates that the brain "registers" a decision to make movements *before* a person consciously decides to move. Thus, the "conscious" decision to, say, move one's finger, happens about 0.2 seconds *after* – not before – the relevant activity in the brain, indicating that the unconscious "knew" in advance that it's "owner" was going to make a decision, or carry out an action (McGilchrist, 2009, p. 186). "More complex reasoning without consciousness is continually going on", suggests Jaynes: "our minds work much faster than consciousness can keep up with" (Jaynes, 1976, p. 42) – a point elaborated on by Lakoff and Johnson:

> Conscious thought is the tip of an enormous iceberg. It is the rule of thumb among cognitive scientists that unconscious thought is 95 percent

of all thought – and that may be a serious underestimate. Moreover, the 95 percent below the surface of conscious awareness shapes and constructs all conscious thought. If the cognitive unconscious were not there doing this shaping, there could be no conscious thought.

(Lakoff & Johnson, 1999, p. 13)

Psychoanalysis is of course familiar with this terrain, grounded in Freud's early speculations on the topographical nature and relationship of the conscious and unconscious mind, and his observations about how many of our choices, behaviours, relationships, and indeed slips, are determined by more implicit and unconscious forces, predating the findings of Libet, Jaynes, and McNeill by several decades. What the new research does is to provide therapists with powerful new experimental insights and information regarding how these systems operate within us.

This ability to render and receive right-hemispheric communications also lies behind what is commonly called "clinical intuition", which, as Schore notes, is a major factor in therapeutic effectiveness and "relies more on nonconscious nonverbal right brain than conscious verbal left brain functions" (Schore, 2012, p. 42). If we understand intuition as "direct knowing that seeps into conscious awareness without the conscious mediation of logic or rational process" (Boucouvalas, 1997, p. 7), then this "describes a right and not left brain function":

> Phases of intuitive processing are generated in the subcortical-cortical vertical axis of the therapist's (and patient's) right brain, from the right amygdala, right insula, and right anterior cingulate to the right orbitofrontal system ... The latter, the highest level of the right brain, acts as an "inner compass that accompanies the decoding process of intuition" ...
>
> (Schore, 2011, p. 89)

What we call "intuitions" are really highly sophisticated, implicitly learned, and rapid forms of cognition that are essential both for our relational and social lives, and also for our evolutionary survival (ibid., pp. 87–88).

> Psychological theoreticians now assert that intuition depends on accessing large banks of implicit knowledge formed from unarticulated person–environment exchanges that occur between environmental input and the individual's phenomenological experience ... It operates on a nonverbal level, with little effort, deliberation, or conscious awareness, and is thus characterized as "phenomenally unconscious" ...
>
> (Schore, 2011, p. 78)

All of these processes, Schore notes, "clearly implies right and not left brain processing" (ibid., p. 78).

"The nature of unconscious thought that emerges from contemporary experiments", concludes McGowan, "is radically different from what Freud posited so many years ago: It looks more like a fast, efficient way to process large volumes of data and less like a zone of impulses and fantasies" (McGowan, 2014). This new understanding not only affects our view of the unconscious, but also necessarily alters our concept of what therapy is all about. As Schore has suggested, "the current, expanding body of knowledge of the right hemisphere suggests a major alteration in the conceptualisation of the Freudian unconscious" (Schore, 2003, p. 269). Given that we now know that the right hemisphere is more holistic, more in touch with reality, more emotionally and relationally advanced, and in many ways more aware than the slower, more explicit, left hemispheric system, the classical formulation of making "the unconscious conscious" seems increasingly flawed.

In his famous *New Introductory Lectures* of 1933, Freud influentially described the project of psychoanalysis as being like the draining of a sea, a cultural attempt to make the "unconscious conscious", and to reinforce the conscious, explicit, left brain system. The aim and intention of psychoanalysis, he famously remarked, was

> to strengthen the ego, to make it more independent of the super-ego, to widen its field of perception and enlarge its organization, so that it can appropriate fresh portions of the id. Where id was, there ego shall be. It is a work of culture – not unlike the draining of the Zuider Zee.
>
> (Freud, 1933a, p. 80)

The "intention" of psychoanalysis, in these terms, suggests depletion, drying up, and conversion – turning the unconscious id into the conscious ego. It is presented almost as an act of colonisation, as the Jungian analyst James Hillman suggested in his reference to it as "this imperialistic fantasy" (1975, p. 26): the heroic little ego "appropriating" the dark, inaccessible continent of the "Es" in order to turn it into more of itself, and make it civilised, enlightened, and ordered. "Freud was always a rationalist", notes John Forrester, Professor in the Department of History of Philosophy of Science. "His talking cure is partly based on the idea that putting things into words is a way of putting them into the realm of reason" – a notably Enlightenment stance, in which Freud presents psychoanalysis as a sort of rationalising, "civilising" manoeuvre. "For Jung", on the other hand, Forrester notes, "concentration on Logos, on speech, may be part of the imbalance that is characteristic of neurosis or psychosis" (Forrester, 2012). "The ego represents what may be called reason and common sense", Freud himself once remarked, "in contrast to the id, which contains the passions", and which he portrays as "a chaos, a cauldron full of seething excitations" (Freud, 1923b, p. 25; 1933a, p. 73) – a seething cauldron which needs to be tamed, converted, and civilised by the heroic little ego. Thus, he notes, "psychoanalysis is an instrument to enable the ego to achieve a progressive conquest of the id" (Freud, 1923b, p. 56). This project of cultural "conquest" and "appropriation" clearly has problematic aspects, as Adam Phillips points out:

> Conquest, of course, has troubling associations with both sexuality and empire, as though psychoanalysis had become imperialism by other means. As though Freud was proposing, as a man of his times, the colonisation of the self or the id – as though "Where Id was, There Ego shall be" could be an epigraph for Conrad's *Heart of Darkness* …
>
> (Phillips, 2018)

It is therefore perhaps not surprising that we find Freud, as "a man of his times", frequently referring to the "primitive" nature of the id, or commenting that "the content of the *Ucs.* may be compared with an aboriginal population of the mind" ("The Unconscious", Freud, 1915, p. 195).

This traditional view of the "id" as a rather dumb, dark, brute is sadly familiar. It's also how people used to see the right brain. And surely that's no coincidence, given what we now know about the correlations between the two. It is also not perhaps surprising that the "ego" should regard the "id" in this way – it regards everything it encounters as an "It", as a thing to be defeated, conquered, or controlled. As Marcuse acutely remarked:

> The ego which undertook the rational transformation of the human and natural environment revealed itself as an essentially aggressive, offensive subject, whose thoughts and actions were designed for mastering objects. It was subject *against* an object.
>
> (Marcuse, 1987, p. 109, italics in original)

Marcuse reveals the essentially pathological nature of this entity, rooted in how it sees itself in relation to the world: "It was subject *against* an object" (i.e., this is how the ego sees and defines itself). "Nature (its own as well as the external world) were 'given' to the ego as something that had to be fought, conquered, and even violated – such was the precondition for self-preservation and self-development" (ibid., p. 110). That is, the idea of "conquering" is built into the ego's central program, its self-definition.

It is perhaps no surprise, therefore, that the ego tends to see the "id" as a similar thing to be colonised and converted, and Marcuse expertly relates this rather "aggressive" character or default attitude of the ego to its view of the "Id", and its desire to dominate, demonise, and conquer it as well: "The struggle begins with the perpetual internal conquest of the 'lower' faculties of the individual: his sensory and appetitive faculties." Of "Eros", in fact, in Marcuse's terms. The conquest of these is, he suggests, the essence and mission of civilised "rationality": "Their subjugation is, at least since Plato, regarded as a constitutive element of human reason, which is thus in its very function repressive." The posh term for this subjugation, he remarks, is "Logos" (ibid., pp. 110, 111). Marcus neatly thereby links the colonial project of the rationalising ego not only to the subjugation of external "Nature", and to the mastering of external populations and colonies, but also to the subjugation and repression of the internal world itself, as something to be equally "fought, conquered, and even violated" – converted into itself.

The very word "It" is indicative of this stance – Groddeck's original enigmatic term (*"Es"*) might perhaps be better defined as "the Other", for Groddeck had a far more appreciative – and indeed far more modern – understanding of the "id", and recognised that it was in many ways a remarkably sophisticated and rather mysterious, powerful agency which actually drove the therapeutic work, and that the best he could do as a physician, was to get his ego out of the way:

> I was confronted with the strange fact that I was not treating the patient, but that the patient was treating me; or, to translate it into my language, the It of this fellow being tried so to transform my It, did in fact so transform it, that it came to be useful for its purpose ... The success of the treatment is not determined by what we prescribe, according to our lights, but by what the It of the sick man makes of our prescriptions.
>
> (Groddeck, 1949, pp. 24, 228, 225)

Groddeck's apprehension of the remarkable, fluid, generative, symbol-forming nature of the "id" is strikingly in accord with recent neuroscientific findings regarding its complex, protean and implicate nature (a characterisation also curiously evocative of the similarly mysterious surface of the planet Solaris in Tarkovsky's extraordinary 1972 film: as Groddeck notes, "The It is always in eruption, it bubbles and boils, and casts up now this bit of experience, now that"; Groddeck, 1949, p. 127). Indeed, one of the defining characteristics of the right-hemisphere "unconscious", McGilchrist remarks, is precisely its openness to the "Other", and it is in relation to the Other, he observes, that the hemispheres essentially differ:

> I believe the essential difference between the right hemisphere and the left hemisphere is that the right hemisphere pays attention to the Other, whatever it is that exists apart from ourselves, with which it sees itself in profound relation.
>
> (McGilchrist, 2009, p. 93)

The ego, on the other hand – the conscious, left hemispheric system – exists largely in relation to itself – as a sort of "hall of mirrors", McGilchrist notes: "There is a reflexivity to the process, as if trapped in a hall of mirrors: it only discovers more of what it already knows, and it only does more of what it is doing" (2009, p. 86). It is the *ego*, therefore, that is in this sense the real "It", the objectifying and rather disembodied "it-making" factory (see also Laing, 1960, pp. 22, 69), and what makes its misunderstanding of itself and its relation to the unconscious so tragic is that it seems utterly unaware that what it calls the unconscious is actually far more in touch with "reality", far more emotionally and socially intelligent, and far more attuned to others, than it is itself. "The left hemisphere's world is ultimately narcissistic", McGilchrist observes, "in the sense that it sees the world 'out there' as no more than a reflection of itself" (2009, p. 438). Indeed, it was precisely for this reason that Freud encouraged therapists and physicians to try and bypass the rather self-involved processes of the "conscious" ego when trying to access the patient's unconscious mind (Freud, 1912e, pp. 111–112).

McGilchrist also notes that the left hemisphere's world is a relentlessly "explicit" one. "The attentional 'spotlight'", he observes, "is a function of the left hemisphere" (2009, pp. 224, 335), and this spotlight can both illuminate and blind. Not everything benefits from having a spotlight shone on it constantly, as he perceptively notes: "All artistic and spiritual experience – perhaps everything truly important – can be implicit only; language, in making things explicit, reduces everything to the same worn coinage, and, as Nietzsche said, makes the uncommon common". There are dangers, therefore, in altering reality to make everything implicit explicit – whether that is psychoanalysis, literary criticism, or any other form of interpretive activity:

> The whole process of literary criticism seemed inevitably to involve making explicit what had to remain implicit (if it was not to be seriously disrupted) … We cerebralised what had to remain the "betweenness" of two living things. The result was a sort of superior knowingness that traduced the innocence of the work. Something often of undeniable interest emerged, but it nonetheless, subtly, missed the point altogether.
> (McGilchrist, p. 94)

Twentieth-century hermeneutics, just like twentieth century philosophy and twentieth century literary criticism, he observes, with their pronounced analytical "left-hemisphere" bent, inevitably altered and indeed "disrupted" what it was that they were purportedly analysing, deracinating their subjects and submitting them to the full glare of the left-hemispheric, detached and detaching gaze:

> Philosophers spend a good deal of time inspecting and analysing processes that are usually – and perhaps must remain – implicit, unconscious, intuitive; in other words, examining the life of the right hemisphere from the standpoint of the left. It is perhaps then not surprising that the glue begins to disintegrate, and there is a nasty cracking noise as the otherwise normally robust sense of the self comes apart,

possibly revealing more about the merits (or otherwise) of the process, than the self under scrutiny.

(McGilchrist, 2009, p. 89)

"Examining the life of the right hemisphere from the standpoint of the left" is in a sense what the project of traditional psychoanalysis was all about. But this project itself needs to be scrutinised, as McGilchrist suggests, since not everything benefits from being made self-conscious. In a riposte to Socrates' much-quoted aphorism that "the unexamined life is not worth living", Dennett reminds us that "the over-examined life is nothing much to write home about either" (Dennett, 1984, p. 278).

Poems petrify under the dissecting stare of the literary critic, philosophy becomes a circular and self-enclosed system of signified and signifiers, and psychoanalysis becomes a rather relentless operation of making everything conscious and explicit. As Dowds acutely notes, the "raylike gaze" of the left hemisphere's "sharply and narrowly focussed" gaze, can itself amplify detachment and dissociation, further separating the patient from their embodied and relational, implicit world (p. 181). In all such cases, "there is a nasty cracking noise as the otherwise normally robust sense of self comes apart", as McGilchrist starkly observes. This is obviously particularly problematic for psychoanalysis, which is meant to be about developing a sense of self, not pulling it apart and ungluing it. As both Ferenczi and Laing have suggested, the very method of detached, instrumental observation, and the deliberate use of a depersonalising "technical vocabulary" is in some ways itself an alienating and rather schizophrenic one. Laing, for example, perceptively notes how the very "words one has to use are specifically designed to isolate and circumscribe the meaning of the patient's life to a particular clinical entity" (1960, pp. 18, 33). Indeed, Laing sees rather beautiful symmetries in the mutual reflection of the schizoid "patient" in the "doctor" – how the language of the one constantly constructs the other:

> If we look at his [the patient's] actions as "signs" of a "disease", we are already imposing our categories of thought on to the patient, in a manner analogous to the way we may regard him as treating us; and we shall be doing the same if we imagine that we can "explain" his present as a mechanical resultant of an immutable "past".
>
> (Laing, 1960, pp. 18, 33)

It is perhaps significant in this respect that both schizophrenia and classical psychoanalysis are characterised by what Norman Brown calls "an overvaluation of words": "Orthodox psychoanalytical therapy", he notes, "with its emphasis on the role of verbalization in consciousness and its de-emphasis of the relation of consciousness to external reality, cultivates word-consciousness", and he suggests that we can see the results of this rather schizoid technical detachment in the "chatter" and "verbal gymnastics" of so many clinical textbooks, which he compares to the chatter of schizophrenics (Brown, 1959, p. 151). An "excess of consciousness", and an "over-explicitness", or "over-verbalisation", has tended to characterise, Brown notes, "orthodox psychoanalytical therapy". And this detaching process also requires separating the patient's head from their body, and their body from their social living context:

> If one had to sum up these features of modernism they could probably be reduced to these: an excess of consciousness and an over-explicitness in relation to what needs to remain intuitive and implicit; depersonalisation and alienation from the body and empathic feeling; disruption of context; fragmentation of experience; and the loss of "betweenness" … They are aspects of a single world: not just the world of the schizophrenic, but, as may by now be clear, the world according to the left hemisphere.
>
> (McGilchrist, 2009, p. 397)

In this sense, as indeed a number of recent therapists and clinicians have suggested, a purely analytic approach *might itself* result in the disintegration and ungluing of the patient's sense of self. As Dowds compellingly argues:

> Classical psychoanalysis claims to work with the unconscious of the client, but it is usually the left brain of the therapist analysing the products (dreams, images, impulses, fantasies) of the client's right brain and translating them into a LH [left hemisphere] interpretation: "where id was there ego shall be". The client's feelings and experiences or their reaching out towards relationship are subjected to the cold, detached and dissecting left hemisphere of the analyst in a way that can only be damaging. Even when the interpretation is correct and the client feels understood, their own self-discovery has been hijacked.
>
> (Dowds, p. 195)

This recalls Ferenczi's earlier astute criticism of the detached, "intellectual attitude" of the analyst:

> It appears that patients cannot believe that an event really took place, or cannot fully believe it, if the analyst, as the sole witness of the events, persists in his cool, unemotional and, as patients are fond of stating, purely intellectual attitude.
>
> (Ferenczi, 1995, p. 24)

Ferenczi recognised that the form of attention the therapist deploys can profoundly affect the treatment, and that a "cool, unemotional and … purely intellectual attitude" is often not a means to therapeutic healing and integration, but an obstacle to it. "The objectifying gaze also kills the target through depersonalising the other in relationship … we need right-brain empathy, embodiment and emotional intelligence to facilitate relationship with other humans and sentient beings" (Dowds, 2014, p. 56).

The "cold, detached and dissecting left hemisphere" can undoubtedly be useful in certain situations and contexts – sometimes we do need to stand back, to take things apart, and to apply a very focussed, verbal, analytical approach. But we need to recognise that when we do this we transform whatever it is we are taking apart, or analysing, into an object, into a "thing" (Laing strikingly compares this feat of *objectification* and depersonalisation to the "Medusa's head", 1960, p. 76). As McGilchrist suggests, the central problem with the old "make it explicit" model is not that it analyses, unpacks, and focuses, but that it analyses, unpacks, and focuses without repacking it and returning or reintegrating it back into the implicate and implicit, into the "unconscious". It's rather like the case with professional athletes, or concert pianists, he notes – the point is to *forget* all the explicit, "conscious" learning and insight, and to allow all that interpretation and analysis to become spontaneous again, lived, intuitive (McGilchrist, p. 104; see also Grotstein, 2009, p. 29, and Schore, p. 85).

> What the left hemisphere offers is then a valuable, but intermediate process, one of "unpacking" what is there and handing it back to the right hemisphere, where it can once more be integrated into the experiential whole; much as the painstaking fragmentation and analysis of the sonata in practice is reintegrated by the pianist in performance at a level where he must no longer be aware of it.
>
> That, at any rate, is how the two should work together: the emissary reporting back to the Master, who alone can see the broader picture.
>
> (McGilchrist, p. 104)

So, the point of therapy is not just to leave the patient in an explicit, "there ego shall be", drained, objectifying conscious state, but to help return the patient, together with all of the new therapeutic insights gleaned and gained from the mutual process of shared cognitive, affective, and verbal "witnessing" (as Ferenczi terms it), back to their "unconscious" – back to her or his relational embodied, implicit, and contextual life, to be integrated – to be *lived*. Where LH was, there RH shall be.

Coming to psychotherapy is therefore not about "explaining" a symptom, or indeed a person, as if the analyst was a literary critic taking apart or explaining a play – indeed, it is not "about" anything, as Adam Phillips acutely notes:

> The problem is living in a culture that's hypnotised by explanation. And the risk is that these things become formulations – and in a way this is

the risk of psychoanalysis – that formulations are made as though they replace the original text. The risk is that we believe plays are "about" something. "Aboutness" is what everything is about. And that's very reductive.

(Phillips, 2000)

Focussing on the "aboutness" of everything is very much part of the left hemisphere's take on the world: and trying to find out what something is "about" usually means, taking it apart, separating it from its context, and making everything explicit and translated into abstract, analytic concepts. Psychoanalysis, Phillips suggests, is something far more enjoyable, and disruptive, than that.

Coda

We have seen how "the current, expanding body of knowledge of the right hemisphere suggests a major alteration in the conceptualisation of the Freudian unconscious, the internal structural system that processes information at non-conscious levels" (Schore, 2003, p. 269). This has also required an alteration in how we view therapy itself, and the change mechanism of therapeutic transformation and healing: not simply one of making the unconscious conscious, but of expanding and restructuring the unconscious itself via therapy (Schore, 2011, p. 94). Psychotherapy alters the neurological mechanisms in the right hemisphere, accessing the deep and implicit systems of self, attachment, and affective regulation. As Schore notes, "the regulation of stressful and disorganizing high or low levels of affective-autonomic arousal facilitates the repair and reorganization of the right brain, the biological substrate of the human unconscious" (Schore, 2011, p. 90). Psychotherapy can restructure, repair and reintegrate these damaged and dysregulated hemispheres – and only psychotherapy: neither medical drugs nor intrusive surgery can engage these deep networks of self-formation and relational patterning; psychoanalysis deals with the unconscious, and is the science of the unconscious.

Twenty-first century psychotherapy therefore aims not at converting the unconscious into the conscious, the id into the ego, but at "the expansion of the right brain human unconscious" itself:

> In terms of psychotherapy, change is not so much about increasing the left's reasoned control over emotion, as it is the expansion of affect tolerance and regulation of the right-lateralised "emotional brain" and the human relatedness of the right-lateralised "social brain".
>
> (Schore, 2012, pp. 202–203)

Psychotherapy – the repair and healing of the psyche – is thus a process of *reorganising, re-regulation, and repair* of the unconscious itself. "Regulation theory describes not just making the unconscious, conscious but restructuring the unconscious, allowing for further maturation of the right brain unconscious system":

> At the most fundamental level, regulation theory offers a clinically relevant theory of the structural and functional development of the unconscious over the life span. This evidence-based model suggests that the therapeutic social–emotional change mechanisms of relational, emotionally focused psychodynamic psychotherapy occurs in the right brain, the biological substrate of the human unconscious, and that effective treatment can facilitate the growth and thereby complexity of the unconscious itself.
>
> (Schore, 2015, p. 546)

Therapy repairs the brain. And this new raft of neuroscientific, affective, and relational research beautifully develops and confirms Rycroft's earlier speculations regarding the aim of analysis. In his brilliant, pioneering paper "Beyond the Reality Principle" (1962) Rycroft remarked that

> If the hypothesis presented here is correct, the aim of psycho-analytical treatment is not primarily to make the unconscious conscious, nor to widen or strengthen the ego, but to re-establish the connexion between dissociated psychic functions, so that the patient ceases to feel that there is an inherent antagonism between his imaginative and adaptive capacities.
>
> (Rycroft, 1968, p. 113)

This is an exquisite formulation of our current understanding of how therapy works: not through "strengthening the ego", not through "making the unconscious conscious", but in actually *extending the unconscious,* re-integrating the conscious systems with the deeper, unconscious processes of the right brain.

"It is commonly believed", note Solms and Panksepp, "that consciousness is a higher brain function". But as their recent work suggests, the latest research indicates that it is actually the "lower brain affective phenomenal experiences" which generate consciousness (Solms & Panksepp, 2012). This seems to confirm earlier suggestions (made by Freud himself in his later years) that what we call the "ego", or the conscious, explicit self, is not the origin of consciousness or thinking, but is – as Bion also intuited – a secondary mode of consciousness, a form of "after-thinking": "Thinking itself is, according to Bion, essentially unconscious. What we normally call 'thinking' might better be called 'after-thinking' or 'secondary thinking', and what we call 'thoughts' might better be called 'after-thoughts' or 'secondary thoughts'" (Grotstein, 2007, p. 47). Primary thinking, and awareness, seem to arise from the implicit systems of the so-called unconscious: or what Solms and Panksepp have now reformulated as "the conscious id":

> Our major conclusion may be stated thus: the core self, synonymous with Freud's "id", is the font of all consciousness; the declarative self, synonymous with Freud's "ego", is unconscious in itself. However, because the ego stabilizes the core consciousness generated by the id, by transforming affects into object representations, and more particularly verbal object re-representations, we ordinarily think of ourselves as being conscious in the latter sense.
>
> (Solms & Panksepp, 2012)

What the so-called "conscious" self does, then, is to "stabilize" – select, fix, and "re-present" – the information it receives from the core "unconscious" or super-conscious networks. This is entirely, of course, in line with what we have seen concerning the explicit, slower, semantic left brain system of interpretation and filtering.

> The dumb id, in short, knows more than it can admit. Small wonder, therefore, that it is so regularly overlooked in contemporary cognitive science. But the id, unlike the ego, is only dumb in the glossopharyngeal sense. It constitutes the primary stuff from which minds are made; and cognitive science ignores it at its peril. We may safely say, without fear of contradiction, that were it not for the constant presence of affective feeling, conscious perceiving and thinking would either not exist or would gradually decay. This is just as well, because a mind unmotivated (and unguided) by feelings would be a hapless zombie, incapable of managing the basic tasks of life.
>
> (Solms & Panksepp, 2012)

Rather than draining, converting, or conquering the id through verbalisation and "consciousness" (putting affect into words), Solms and Janksepp note that reflexive "talking" is in fact "apt to dampen and constrain core consciousness". This is not to bypass or dismiss talking, but to recognise its limits – indeed, to recognise that its purpose, and prime function, is itself to limit consciousness, to put a horizon on thought. To "re-present" it, as Solms and Panksepp put it ("by transforming affects into object representations"). "The realization that Freud's id is intrinsically conscious", they note,

> has massive implications for psychoanalysis, biological psychiatry, and our understanding of the nature of mind. This turn of events could be profound, not least because when Freud famously proclaimed "where id was, there shall ego be" as the therapeutic goal of his "talking cure", he

assumed that the ego enlightened the id. It now appears more likely that the opposite happens ...

As the cognitive science of the late twentieth century is complemented by the affective neuroscience of the present, we are breaking through to a truly mental neuroscience, and finally understanding that the brain is not merely an information-processing device but also a sentient, intentional being. Our animal behaviors are not "just" behaviors; in their primal affective forms they embody ancient mental processes that we share, at the very least, with all other mammals.

(Solms & Panksepp, 2012)

These new discoveries about "the conscious id" may be as revolutionary in their way as Freud's original speculations about the nature of the "unconscious", a hundred years ago.

About the chapters

This book brings together a number of leading authors and researchers to show the relevance of these new discoveries concerning hemispheric difference and integration for the understanding and treatment of a range of different forms of psychological distress and disorder, from addiction, autism, and schizophrenia to relational trauma, borderline and personality disorders, anorexia, anxiety, and depression. They show how hemispheric processes lie at the heart of a number of different therapeutic approaches and modalities, from group and systems-centred therapy, to classical psychoanalysis, EMDR, embodied psychotherapy, and various gestalt and existential forms of engagement and treatment. This new understanding of the neuroscientific nature of mental processing is dramatically reshaping the cultural landscape of twenty-first century therapy, and these clinicians, theoreticians and therapists are remarkable pioneers of this rapidly expanding world.

Allan N. Schore is one of the most prominent and prescient of those pioneers. His ground-breaking work has compellingly demonstrated the importance of hemispheric lateralisation and its relevance for all therapeutic work. In his chapter he examines how recent studies of the right brain, which as he demonstrates is dominant for the implicit, nonverbal, intuitive, and holistic processing of emotional information and social interactions, can elucidate the neurobiological mechanisms that underlie and underwrite the relational foundations of psychotherapy. "Internal representations of attachment experiences", he observes, "are imprinted in right-lateralized implicit–procedural memory as an internal working model that encodes nonconscious strategies of affect regulation". Utilising the interpersonal neurobiological perspective of regulation theory, he describes the fundamental role of the early developing right brain in all relational processes, throughout the life span. He also presents interdisciplinary evidence documenting right brain functions in early attachment processes, in emotional communications within the therapeutic alliance, in mutual therapeutic enactments, and in the therapeutic change mechanism itself. As his work powerfully suggests, the current emphasis on relational and affective processes is transforming both psychology and neuroscience, with important consequences for clinical psychological models of psychotherapeutic change.

The significance of McGilchrist's remarkable work in drawing our attention to attention has already been noted, and his chapter ("Ways of Attending") compellingly unpacks the importance of this issue and suggests its relevance to the problems we experience in an increasingly instrumental and "free-wheeling left hemisphere" world (McGilchrist, 2009, p. 403). His chapter reveals that the key difference between the hemispheres lies not in what they do, but in how they do it, and in doing so he reminds us that the human brain is not a machine, nor indeed a collection of "functions" – it is what we are, a lived subjectivity, and "a living person". When we talk about the divided brain, we are therefore talking about our own deepest processes, our own dual nature, the locus of our sense of immediate, lived, embodied, affective, intellectual, and even spiritual relationship with the world. Due in part perhaps to over-familiarity with everything "neuro" these days, and indeed the tendency of the left hemisphere to explain reality in terms of machinery, things, and functions (its own rather narcissistic operating mode), it is sometimes easy to lose sight of what we are dealing with in talking about the brain: McGilchrist's work is a timely reminder of the unique and powerful nature of our own embodiment, and how deep this all goes. His work is already having a significant impact not only in the world of therapy, but also in contemporary discussions of education, politics, contemporary philosophy, spirituality, and art. Above all, his discussion of the nature of the divided brain, the two modes of attention available to us, and their impact on culture reminds us that we have a *choice*: as therapists, as parents, as educators, and as citizens.

Indeed, the "social" aspect to our brains is the theme of Louis Cozolino's masterful elaboration of laterality in terms of our social and affective engagement with the world. For the brain itself is a "social organ", he notes: a remarkable network of constant exchange between the inside and outside world, a complex adaptation built through innumerable interactions with others. "To write the story of this journey", he notes, "we must begin our guidebook with the understanding that *there are no single human brains – brains only exist within networks of other brains*" (p. 109). His pioneering concept of "social synapses" – inter-relational spaces that are filled with implicit meaning and communication – is both striking and profound in its implications. The consulting room is one such synapse: the therapeutic space through which the transmission and reception of right-hemisphere messages between therapist and client are received and communicated, as indeed Freud himself recognised in his telephonic metaphor of therapeutic exchange. But our whole world is filled with such spaces, as we are only just beginning to glimpse, and they constitute the relational gravity within which we exist: our "betweenness", to use McGilchrist's evocative term for this vital inter-subjective field. Cozolino is also eloquent in demonstrating how these early social relationships and interactions actually alter and develop the brain, noting the impact of the early years in founding and forming these relational structures, and showing how the self itself "emerges" from these myriad interactions. When we interact, he observes, "we are impacting each other's internal biological state and influencing the long-term construction of each other's brains". Dependency is therefore built into the fabric of who we are as social and biological beings, hardwired into our mainframe: it is "how love becomes flesh", in Cozolino's striking phrase. His very moving case history of "Dylan" is in many ways what this whole book is all about: the extraordinary power of attention, attunement, and empathy, and a sense of both the profound and precarious distance and closeness contained within our betweennesses, our social synapses. Therapy is revealed as a shared moment, as something that emerges out of deeply integrative practice, allowing us to play again.

This process of integration forms the focus of Alex and Dan Siegel's chapter, showing how integration involves "linkages", not merging: what they call "distinct linking". Indeed, their idea of distinct linking is rather beautifully present in the joint authorship – a reminder of how collabora-tive our acts are. And as they note, on another meta level, every word, sentence, and paragraph we encounter is the result of this same process: "Each word you read is a unique combination of linked, differentiated let-ters." These fundamental processes of merging and emerging, dividing and individuating, are constantly happening all around us, they remind us – even as you read this thought. Effective therapeutic integration requires the combination and collaboration of discrete parts in order to produce harmony and balance: metaphors of music flow powerfully through their chapter, illustrating the importance of this model for our new dynamic apprehension of the reverberative quality of the integrated brain. "The music arises", they observe, "not from the sameness of its constituent elements, but from their unique and often surprising differentiation and linkages": "each individual musician plays a unique and differentiated part within the group, yet it is the ways in which these parts are linked that gives rise to the music" (p. 129). Just as the hemispheres themselves need to be kept apart in order to be able to deliver their distinct takes on the world, so too integration does not mean abandoning either subjectivity or objectivity, but holding both, simultaneously, together. The result of suc-cessful integration, they suggest, is "flow", and they compellingly draw out the importance of this for therapy, where the presenting issues are often ones of being stuck, of being fixed, or being too rigid (or alternatively, they note, of being too merged and chaotic – "interestingly, every symptom of every syndrome in the DSM-5 can be understood as chaos, rigidity, or both"). Here again the relevance and resonance of the musical metaphor becomes evident. Integration is also, they note, the root of healing, remarking that the process of "wellbeing" itself is grounded in these ideas of integration, linkage, balance, wholeness, health – "the outcome of *bilateral integration*" (p. 133). This process of integration applies both individually and socially, and of course has to in order for integration to be meaningful: "integration within and between us", in their great phrase. "Our hope", they remark,

> is to broaden the discussion of bilaterality to the larger issue of integration in the cultivation of well-being ... promoting integration is essential as we honor differences and cultivate compassionate linkages. An integrated society would be one in which compassion, connection and kindness thrive.
>
> (Siegel & Siegel, pp. 131 and 146)

Indeed, the relevance of bilaterality to group states is the subject of Gantt and Badenoch's exploration in this volume of systems-centred group psychotherapy, developing a group mind that "supports right brain function and right–left–right hemispheric integration", as the subtitle for their chapter indicates. SCT is a striking example of how hemispheric lateralisation is being developed and thought about in contemporary therapy situations, in exciting new ways. Like Siegel and Siegel, Gantt and Badenoch note the importance of integration, and of recognising where this doesn't happen in groups, and why – using a right hemisphere/left hemisphere framework in order to explore how holistic versus narrowly-focussed and more individualistic (or atomised) modes of attention play out in larger dynamics. And it is a matter of dynamics – they compelling reveal how each hemisphere exerts a sort of gravitational pull in group settings. In our rather left-hemispheric, individualised, societies, they note, which constantly privilege autonomous, detached positions and undermine collaborative thinking, "this dominant cultural shift to the left pulls on us constantly". This pull is felt as a tendency to control – to control the situation, the group – rather than to emphasise connection and multimodality within groups. The same "cultural shift to the left", they suggest, is also evident in the dominance of individual, one-to-one, forms of therapy and psychoanalysis, and they note how most therapy, in our culture, favours "cognitive", verbal approaches, rather than group or relational (RH) therapy forms. As they remark, "psychotherapy groups are under-utilized in our culture in spite of the research showing equivalent outcomes for patients in group therapy when compared to individual therapy" (p. 152). Applying left/right modes of attention, and recognising when group states need to shift from a more right-dominant state to a more left-dominant one, and vice versa, can produce startling results, as their work shows. Their chapter compellingly illustrates how SCT groups work to develop right-brain attending and better integration between right and left brain function. "Group psychotherapy", they observe, "may be ideal for creating secure contexts which support for right-centric ways of attending to others and enhancing our social brain function, especially important in the context of our left-dominated culture."

Our "left-dominated culture", with its emphasis on deracination, decontextualisation, and depersonalisation, profoundly affects both how we think of ourselves, the meaning of our lives, and how we engage with others, as Dowds powerfully and poignantly suggests in her chapter on connection and emergent meaning in life and in therapy. Meaning emerges out of context, and so once this is removed (as "context" is hard for the left brain to quantify, isolate, and measure), an increasingly left-dominated culture is an increasingly meaningless one. "Despair and meaninglessness are products of living in a LH world", she observes, noting that meaning cannot be willed – it has to be "emergent" (as Rotenberg also notes in his concluding chapter). The relevance for these intimate issues of connection and meaning for therapy are clear. "The underlying, but largely implicit, agenda in psychotherapy", observes Dowds, "is the creation of meaning. This emerges, as I contend, from connection – to self, other and the world". And only the right hemisphere can apprehend and deliver this sense of living and lived connection – which is why damage to the right brain (such as in strokes) can be so much more devastating to the individual than damage to the left. The right hemisphere, Dowds notes, is in touch with the "ground of being" – with the very sources of connection and meaning, and our sense of relationship with the world, she notes, must remain implicit, embodied, and emergent – away from the left brain's relentless isolating spotlight: its "sharply and narrowly focused, raylike gaze". In her summary of the different hemispheric approaches of various therapeutic modalities, she notes how some more left-hemispheric therapies can simply echo and enforce the wider detachments and disconnections of our culture, a sort of cold and rather mocking detached stance (over-analytic, over-verbal, and over-egoic, as we've already seen). "The experience of doing in the absence of a secure sense of being", Dowds remarks, "degenerates into a meaningless succession of mere activities (as in the obsessional's meaningless repetition of the same thought, word or act), not performed for their own proper purpose but as a futile effort to 'keep oneself in being', to manufacture a sense of 'being' one does not possess" – hence the striking title for her piece, a reference to Samuel Beckett's classic study of obsessional repetition in his novel *Molloy*. "The self-referentiality of the more or less cut-off left brain is inherently meaningless", she notes, pointing to the dangerously echo-chamber nature of the left brain, for all its skill at manipulation and technical analysis. The results have been catastrophic for our sense of self, for our sense of being-in-the-world. Depression is now the condition that is most treated by the NHS, and cases of addiction and suicides are accelerating – perhaps unsurprisingly so in "an era when meaning is being drained from experience by the technological, bureaucratic and instrumentalising forces of late modernity" (Fisher, 2009, p. 19; McGilchrist, 2009, p. 87; Dowds, p. 188; Potter similarly notes that "suicide among adolescents has tripled since the 1950s and today it is the third leading cause of death among teens, behind accidents and homicide", 2013, p. 3). And as McGilchrist has observed, "it is not just mental health, but physical health that suffers when we are not socially integrated. 'Social connectedness' predicts lower rates of colds, heart attacks, strokes, cancer, depression, and premature death of all sorts" (2009, p. 436). In other words, this issue of meaning and connectedness is not just a matter for therapists, or clients, but for politics and politicians – for all of us. Relatedness thus has an ethical or political aspect, as Dowds powerfully suggests – in fact, is always a political aspect of our lives: "How we view and engage with the world and the other is always an ethical and political question – in other words a question about relatedness."

Denial, disconnection and dissociation may be hallmarks of our era, but as Clara Mucci poignantly reminds us, they are also at the heart of some of the most debilitating and distressing clinical conditions. Her analysis of the vital distinction between processes of *dissociation* and those of *repression* in borderline and other severe psychopathologies of early traumatic origin has done much to establish our modern understanding of those traumatic self-pathologies as "right-brain disorders" – that is, to do with early disruptions to right-hemisphere systems that the patient has subsequently dissociated from (these experiences, she notes, are formed too early for them to be consciously "repressed" as in the case of the neuroses that Freud treated). Her chapter is a powerful testament to the importance of those first early months for all our relationships, all our sense of connection – to our caregivers, to the world around us, and to ourselves. These patterns are burned into our limbic systems, and our affective neurobiology, and help make us who we are, for better or worse. Her analysis of how these early experiences are imprinted and encoded in our emotional systems, attachment networks, self formations, and early limbic structures is invaluable for anyone working therapeutically in this field, as the therapeutic relationship is often rooted in these early attachment configurations (RH–RH). As she suggests, the therapist is trying to access and repair (integrate) some of these very deep, early relational and identity dissociations (as Ferenczi posited *contra* Freud), through the use of enactment, projective identification, implicit attunement, and affect regulation, in order to try and reach and to adjust these vital encodings and relational patterns. Her remarkable research provides "a new psychoanalytic theoretical model of psychopathology", one that outlines a "clear divide in psychopathologies between those based on the structure of dissociation deriving from early relational trauma (as attachment studies and neuroscientific research have consistently indicated) and those psychopathologies rooted in repression, as indicated by Freud". Thanks to the discovery of these underlying neurological mechanisms, therapists can now be much more nuanced and attuned in their approach to and treatment of these conditions. As she notes, "psychotherapy that is fine-tuned between patient and therapist through the right brain allows dissociative moments, enactments, and projective identification to return in the right hemispheric exchanges of the therapy". In this way, "the unrepressed but early memories of amygdala encoding can be reactivated in therapy through the right brain participation of the attuned therapist and, through the mechanism of enactment, projective identification and dissociation itself, can be brought from nonverbal, sub-symbolic form, to symbolic and verbal expression" (p. 215). It is both a remarkable confirmation, and significant updating, of Freud's early theories regarding trauma, dissociation, and the unconscious, whereby, as Mucci notes, "we have now arrived at an intersubjective, relational unconscious that is right-brain based".

One of the most striking forms of dissociation that has become evident in the last few years is our increasing disconnection from the planet itself, from the environment understood in its broadest, most global (right hemispheric) sense, as Narvaez compellingly suggests in the chapter on "Growing, Living and Being Rightly". As both McGilchrist and Dowds also note, our divided hemispheres allow us distinct and different ways of attending, different ways of relating, and different ways of being in the world – distinct ways of living. Our current civilisation seems to be marked by a profound imbalance in favour of one hemisphere, the left, and its piecemeal, siloed, compartmentalised, and fragmented take on the world is finally beginning to reach the limits of the world it has so efficiently manipulated and mechanised. Narvaez is one of a number of therapists who are increasingly engaged with these wider aspects of the therapeutic project, and she movingly cites Bolte Taylor's direct experience of the right-hemispheric apprehension of reality, with its very different ontological "take" on the world, which she vividly experienced following the massive haemorrhage that exploded in the left side of her brain in 1996, and soon wiped out most of the left hemisphere skills and functions associated with that area. "To the right mind", Bolte Taylor observes,

> no time exists other than the present moment, and each moment is vibrant with sensation ... the moment of *now* is timeless and abundant ... The present moment is a time when everything and everyone are connected together as *one*. As a result, our right mind perceives each of us as equal members of the human family.
>
> (cited in Narvaez, p. 230)

Empathy is a necessary corollary of this interconnected state, not some add-on or cognitive luxury. "Our ability to be empathic, to walk in the shoes of another and feel their feelings, is a product of our right frontal cortex".

Hence also our "relationally attuned morality" – what Narvaez calls "an *engagement mindset*", one which "is receptive to the other as an equal, as a partner in co-constructing the present encounter". Narvaez's chapter eloquently reminds us of the value of this "bigger picture" recognition – that it's not just a recognition, it's a deep *sense* of inter-involvement with reality. It's when we stop playing games with words, and cleverness, and denial, and actually address the world we have and are generating, the world that we are bringing into being through our *acts*, not our wishes. Integrating our neural hemispheres means integrating our global hemispheres, and Narvaez acutely links this discussion with the political and social aspects of living in a left-dominated world: "integrated Right Hemisphere living is different from what we see around us in civilized societies", she observes:

> Engagement ethics are more obviously present among foraging communities, representative of the majority of humanity's history ... Flourishing societies live within a balanced biodiversity. A flourishing society is one that lives with the earth where non humans are considered partners, not adversaries, where relational responsibility to all Life is fundamental.
>
> (Narvaez, p. 232)

It is a far cry from the world that has been built up from the hyper-rationalising left brain logic of competition, self-importance, and conquest. "The Western world", she notes, "has suppressed the wisdom of the right hemisphere and instead is governed by the bureaucratic/scientific mode of the left hemisphere (which prefers static dead things and absolute control)" (p. 233). Absolute control over a static world seems like an uncanny prediction of the brave new virtual worlds the left hemisphere seems intent on incarnating, but Narvaez powerfully reminds us that here again we have a choice: that there are *ways* of attending, and there is therefore another way of thinking, and of living.

Correctly reflecting the reality of the world, Meares suggests, is in itself a key aspect of hemispheric functioning, and in his chapter on "The Therapeutic Purpose of Right Hemisphere Language" he compellingly examines how this process of mirroring and reflecting is captured and held in language itself. Meares explores the mirroring aspect of language, and how in cases of early trauma this can severely disrupt and damage these natural processes of reflecting and mutual self-recognition. As he says, "this chapter is about the therapeutic significance of the *form* of language, of the way in which words are put together so as to create expressive patterns which 'fit' similar patterns presented by the patient" – the essential processes of attunement, resonance, and patterning that we have seen are so vital in early development and which are largely handled through the right hemisphere. The divided brain allows us distinct ways of doing things, and when it comes to language it is no different: Meares compellingly investigates the "duplex" forms of language available to us, each with their different worlds and ways of understanding reality (analogical vs. propositional, symbolising vs. syntactical). He shows how different forms of language are linked to different ideas of "self", and how in instances of early relational trauma these intimate affective lexicons can become literally incoherent, depriving the infant of a sense of internal integrity and self-image. As he notes, "the right side is particularly vulnerable" in this, being the locus not only of the implicit self, but also of the early relational structures: "The effects of the traumatic impacts are evident in language and deficiencies of right hemispheric function. The outstanding pathology is one of disintegration. The chief clinical problem is a stunted experience of self." In many ways, as he acutely points out, integration *is* self: what we call "identity" is both the result and cause of this emergent process of self-organisation. But self is also, as we've seen, double: Meares brings in the classic pioneering work of Hughlings Jacksons, Vygotsky, Roman Jakobson, and William James, to show how "doubleness is a feature of self": we are formed in relationship with another, and we can then internalise this doubleness and look "at" ourselves, as selves ("reflective awareness"). We exist in each other's eyes – again pointing to the vital role of attention in our early development. As Meares suggests, "self" is therefore not a fixed "thing" but a dynamic *process*: the generation of self is "understood as a dynamism, a process, arising in conversation as a third thing, *between* people". In early trauma this emergence fails to fully happen, he notes, and so the therapist must find a way to engage with these "duplex" structures and find ways of reintegrating, cohering, them. Meares's pioneering development of the "conversational model" of psychotherapy (together with English psychiatrist Robert Hobson) was exactly this – a theory "based around the idea that the central task of psychotherapy is to potentate the emergence and amplification of that dualistic form of consciousness that William James called self", through recognising the structures of relatedness which underpin it (Meares, 2000, p. 2). This relational, duplex, aspect to the self is of course central to the "talking cure", in itself an early form of "conversational model". "In this space 'conversations' occur between two people that range from the earliest communications between mother and newborn to the most intimate (simultaneously self-revealing and self-creating) experiences of adults (which are to a large extent mediated by language)" (Meares, 2000, p. x). Through our conversations we are constantly born, and re-born, and through the therapeutic conversations our selves can be recreated and restored.

Just as Meares explores the hemispheric distinction between "analogical" and "prepositional" language, and Gantt and Badenoch note the difference between "apprehensive" and "comprehensive" states, so Rotenberg examines the crucial difference between "polysemantic" and "monosemantic" language, and its relevance to therapeutic communication. "The main task of psychotherapy", he notes, "is the restoration of the patient's right frontal lobe skills, the polysemantic way of thinking". By this he means the patient's "holistic grasping of numerous interrelationships", echoing Dowds' argument regarding the "kind of broad, diffuse and holistic attention that is characteristic of the right hemisphere" and which "is destroyed by the intense focus and analytic atomisation of the left". Rotenberg emphasises that this right brain sense of interrelationship and integrative ability is also manifested in the way it responds to words and communication – in a "polysemantic" way, he notes, rather than the more linear, simplified, unambiguous and "logical" manner of the left hemisphere's "monosemantic" mode. "Polysemantic" simply means "on many semantic planes simultaneously", and as examples of this mode he gives the richly condensed formations of dreaming, poetry, and art. "The common function of all of the structures of the right hemisphere", he notes, "is to apprehend and deliver the holistic approach to the world". Each hemisphere has a distinct semantic style, therefore, and this is related to their distinct sense of self: the left hemisphere is discrete, conscious, differentiated (Rotenberg calls this "self-concept"); the right hemisphere is more relational, more implicit and less conscious; more embodied ("self-image"), and these dual aspects manifest themselves in various psycho-physiologies. Rotenberg beautifully links the early maturational movement from the right hemisphere (which as we have seen is dominant for the first eighteen months) to the left, with the development of much wider historical and cultural shifts. His startling reinterpretation of the story of Adam and Eve as symbolising exactly such a transition (from right-hemisphere oceanic "oneness", to a necessary fall into separation and discreteness – and then a final return to reintegration or "paradise regained") is a striking example of the deeper aspects of this discussion. We continually fall in and out of paradise, in that sense, he suggests: there is a constant dynamic of merging and separation, giving and receiving, holistic awareness and analytic self-consciousness. Too often, he notes, the patient remains stuck in a monosemantic world, and he suggests that in such instances the task of the therapist is "the reintegration of the subject in the polydimensional world", to help the patient to a more fully integrated and alive state, on a deeper level. Therapy is in that sense a way of restoring on a new level that "pre-reflective state", a deeper and more interconnected world of neurological maturation and integration – a restored and regained "Eden", in Rotenberg's powerful and evocative metaphor of this process of necessary separation and synthesis (pp. 270–271). Thus, the aim "is not to make the unconscious conscious", notes Rotenberg, so much as "the reintegration of the subject in the polydimensional world" (p. 274) – the restoration of an "I/Thou" sense of relationship with reality, rather than an objectifying and instrumental "I/It" one, in Buber's terms (Buber, 2008). Therapy helps to heal that sense of rupture (of subject-object, inner-outer, mind-body), through the difficult process of *tikkun olam* that so many practices and traditions have sought to recapture, a deep longing for reconnection and re-union. The world's literature has always been about recovery, about reintegration – an enduring recognition of the need to recover these forgotten or mis-remembered worlds, these dis-membered gods, these broken shards of meaning: integration regained.

Bibliography

Allman, J. M., Watson, K. K., Tetreault, N. A., & Hakeem, A. Y. (2005). Intuition and autism: A possible role for Von Economo neurons. *Trends in Cognitive Sciences, 9*, 367–373.

Alvarez, A. (2006). Some questions concerning states of fragmentation: Unintegration, under-integration, disintegration, and the nature of early integrations. *Journal of Child Psychotherapy, 32*, 158–180.

Ayan, S. (2018). The Brain's Autopilot Mechanism Steers Consciousness. *Scientific American*, December 19, 2018. www.scientificamerican.com/article/the-brains-auto pilot-mechanism-steers-consciousness [last accessed 31.7.19].

Bargh, J., & Chartrand, T. (1999). The unbearable automaticity of being. *American Psychologist, 54*, 462–479.

Batmanghelidjh, C. (2015). Clinical snobbery—get me out of here! New clinical paradigms for children with complex disturbances. In T. Warnecke (Ed.), *The Psyche in the Modern World: Psychotherapy and Society*. London: Karnac.

Batmanghelidjh, C., & Rayment, T. (2017). *Kids: Child Protection in Britain: The Truth*. London: Biteback Publishing.

Beckett, S. (1955). *Molloy*. London: Olympia Press.

Bollas, C. (2015). Interview with Matt Olien. *Prairie Plus*. www.youtube.com/watch?v=Qy9LAyhwNZo [last accessed 26.6.16].

Bolte Taylor, J. (2008a). *My Stroke of Insight*. London: Hodder & Stoughton.

Bolte Taylor, J. (2008b). "Jill Bolte Taylor's stroke of insight", February 2008. TED podcast. www.ted.com/talks/jill_bolte_taylor_s_powerful_stroke_of_insight. html [last accessed 19.6.2012].

Bolte Taylor, J. (2009). http://podcast.cbc.ca/mp3/tapestry_20091206_ 24,061.mp3 [last accessed 6.12.2009].

Boucouvalas, M. (1997). Intuition: The concept and the experience. In R. D. Floyd & P. S. Arvidson (Eds.), *Intuition: The inside Story* (pp. 39–56). New York, NY: Routledge.

Breuer, J., & Freud, S. (1895d). *Studies on Hysteria. S.E., 2*. London: Hogarth Press.

Brown, N. O. (1959). *Life against Death: The Psychoanalytic Meaning of History*. Middletown, CT: Wesleyan University Press.

Buber, M. (2008). *I and Thou*. New York: Simon & Schuster.

Buklina, S. B. (2005). The corpus callosum, interhemispheric interactions, and the function of the right hemisphere of the brain. *Neuroscience and Behavioral Physiology, 35*, 473–480.

Centre for Social Justice & Eastman, A. (2014). *Enough Is Enough: A Report on Child Protection and Mental Health Services for Children and Young People*. London: Centre for Social Justice.

Cleese, J. & McGilchrist, I. (2018). "John Cleese and Iain McGilchrist (Second Night)". The Harper's Podcast. *Harper's Magazine*. https://harpers.org/blog/2018/12/john-cleese-and-iain-mcgilchrist/ [last accessed 13.12.18].

Corballis, M. C. (1991). *The Lopsided Ape: Evolution of the Generative Mind*. Oxford: Oxford University Press.

Corballis, M. C., & Beale, I. L. (1976). *The Psychology of Left and Right*. London: Wiley.

Cozolino, L. (2006). *The Neuroscience of Human Relationships: Attachment and the Developing Social Brain* (2nd ed.). New York: W. W. Norton.

Cozolino, L. (2010). *The Neuroscience of Psychotherapy: Healing the Social Brain* (2nd ed.). New York: W. W. Norton.

Cozolino, L. (2016). *Why Therapy Works: Using Our Minds to Change Our Brains.* New York: W. W. Norton.

Craparo, G., & Mucci, C. (Eds.). (2017). *Unrepressed Unconscious, Implicit Memory, and Clinical Work.* London: Karnac.

Dalal, F. (1988). Jung: A racist. *British Journal of Psychotherapy, 4*(3), 263–279.

Dennett, D. C. (1984). *Elbow Room: The Varieties of Free Will Worth Wanting.* Oxford: Clarendon Press.

Dowds, B. (2014). *Beyond the Frustrated Self: Overcoming Avoidant Patterns and Opening to Life.* London: Karnac.

Eagleman, D. (2015a). *The Brain. The Story of You.* New York: Pantheon.

Eagleman, D. (2015b). The Brain with David Eagleman: Part 5, Why Do I Need You. www.youtube.com/watch?v=6VwIQq9aOkQ [last accessed 11.6.16].

Edinger, E. F. (1972, reprinted 1992). *Ego & Archetype: Individuation and the Religious Function of the Psyche.* Boston, MA: Shambhala.

Edinger, E. F. (1999). *Archetype of the Apocalypse: Divine Vengeance, Terrorism, and the End of the World.* Chicago, IL: Open Court.

Ferenczi, S. (1995). *The Clinical Diary of Sándor Ferenczi.* (Edited by Judith Dupont). Cambridge, MA: Harvard University Press.

Fisher, M. (2009). *Capitalist Realism: Is There No Alternative?* Alresford: Zero Books.

Forrester, J. (2012). "Freud vs Jung". *BBC Radio 4.* www.bbc.co.uk/programmes/b019qj15 [last accessed 31.7.19].

Freud, A. (1936). *The Ego and the Mechanisms of Defence.* London: Hogarth Press.

Freud, S. (1905e). *Fragment of an Analysis of a Case of Hysteria. S.E., 7: 1–123.* London: Hogarth Press.

Freud, S. (1912e). 'Recommendations to Physicians Practising Psycho-analysis', *S.E., 12.* London: Hogarth Press.

Freud, S. (1915). *The UnconsciouS. S.E., 14.* London: Hogarth Press.

Freud, S. (1916-1917). *Introductory Lectures on Psycho-Analysis. S.E., 15–16.* London: Hogarth Press.

Freud, S. (1920g). *Beyond the Pleasure Principle. S.E., 18.* London: Hogarth Press.

Freud, S. (1923b). *The Ego and the Id. S.E., 19.* London: Hogarth Press.

Freud, S. (1933a). *New Introductory Lectures on Psycho-Analysis. S.E., 22.* London: Hogarth Press.

Frewen, P., & Lanius, R. (2015). *Healing the Traumatized Self: Consciousness, Neuroscience, and Treatment.* New York: W.W. Norton & Co.

Gazzaniga, M. S. (2002). Brain and Conscious Experience. In *Foundations in Social Neuroscience* (pp. 203–213). Cambridge, MA: MIT Press.

Gazzaniga, M. S., Ivry, R. B., & Mangun, G. R. (2009). *Cognitive Neuroscience: The Biology of the Mind* (3rd ed.). New York: Norton.

Glass, R. M. (2008). Psychodynamic psychotherapy and research evidence: Bambi survives Godzilla? *Jama, 300*(13), 1587–1589.

Ginot, E. (2007). Intersubjectivity and neuroscience. Understanding enactments and their therapeutic significance within emerging paradigms. *Psychoanalytic Psychology, 24,* 317–332.

Grabner, R. H., Fink, A., & Neubauer, A. C. (2007). Brain correlates of self-related originality of ideas: Evidence from event-related power and phase–locking changes in the EEG. *Behavioral Neuroscience, 121,* 224–230.

Groddeck, G. (1949). *The Book Of The It.* London: Vision Press.

Grotstein, J. S. (2007). *A Beam of Intense Darkness: Wilfred Bion's Legacy to Psychoanalysis.* London: Karnac.

Grotstein, J. S. (2009). *But at the Same Time and on Another Level: Volume 2: Clinical Applications in the Kleinian/Bionian Mode.* London: Karnac.

Hallam, R. (2015). "The therapy relationship: A special kind of friendship", in *Karnacology.* https://karnacology.com/2015/10/19/the-therapy-relationship-a-special-kind-of-friendship-by-richard-hallam/ [last accessed 19.10.15].

Hillman, J. (1975). *Re-Visioning Psychology.* New York: HarperCollins.

Jaynes, J. (1976). *The Origin of Consciousness in the Breakdown of the Bicameral Mind.* Boston, MA: Houghton Mifflin.

Johnson, M. (2007). *The Meaning of the Body: Aesthetics of Human Understanding.* Chicago, IL: The University of Chicago Press.

Jørgensen, C. R. (2019). *The Psychotherapeutic Stance.* New York: Springer International Publishing.

Jung, C. G. (1957). *The Collected Works of Carl Jung, Bollingen Series XX* (Vol. 13). Princeton, NJ: Princeton University Press.

Jung, C. G. (1964). *Man and His Symbols.* London: Aldus Books.

Kabat-Zinn, J. (1994). *Wherever You Go, There You Are: Mindfulness Meditation in Everyday Life.* New York: Hyperion.

Kahr, B. (2005). The fifteen key ingredients of good psychotherapy. In J. Ryan (Ed.), *How Does Psychotherapy Work?* London: Karnac.

Kinsbourne, M. (2003). The Multimodal Mind: How the senses combine in the brain. https://semioticon.com/virtuals/multimodality/kinsbourne.pdf [last accessed 31.7.19].

Laing, R. D. (1960). *The Divided Self: An Existential Study in Sanity and Madness.* London: Penguin Books Ltd.

Lakoff, G., & Johnson, M. (1999). *Philosophy in the Flesh: The Embodied Mind and Its Challenge to Western Thought.* New York: Basic Books.

Launer, J. (2005, June). Anna O and the "talking cure". *QJM: An International Journal of Medicine, 98*(6), 465–466.

Lieberman, M. D. (2000). Intuition: A social neuroscience approach. *Psychological Bulletin, 126,* 109–137.

Lucini, F. A., Del Ferraro, G., Sigman, M., & Makse, H. A. (2019, July 15). How the brain transitions from conscious to subliminal perception. *Neuroscience, 411,* 280–290.

Lyons-Ruth, K. (2000). "I sense that you sense that I sense …": Sander's recognition process and the emergence of new forms of relational organization. *Infant Mental Health Journal, 21,* 85–98.

Marcuse, H. (1987). *Eros and Civilization: A Philosophical Inquiry into Freud.* London: Routledge & Kegan Paul Ltd.

McGilchrist, I. (2009). *The Master and His Emissary: The Divided Brain and the Making of the Western World.* New Haven, CT: Yale University Press.

McGilchrist, I. (2010). The Divided Brain and the Making of the Western World [RSA event, online]. Available at: https://www.youtube.com/watch?v=SbUHx C4wiWk.

McGilchrist, I. (2013). Hemisphere Difference and Their Relevance to Psychotherapy. In D. J. Siegel & M. Solomon (Eds.), *Healing Moments in Psychotherapy*. New York: W.W. Norton & Co.

McGilchrist, I. (2014). Anyone with half a brain can see that! Iain McGilchrist at TEDxGhent. https://www.youtube.com/watch?v=DiPrM0DNI8w [last accessed 29.7.19].

McGilchrist, I. (2018). An Evolutionary Account of Brain Laterality: Dr Iain McGilchrist. Address given at the Second Symposium of the Evolutionary Psychiatry Special Interest Group of the Royal College of Psychiatrists. https://www.youtube.com/watch?v=TdNe5guQapk [last accessed 31.7.19].

McGowan, K. (2014). "The Second Coming of Sigmund Freud". *Discover Magazine, March 06*, 2014. http://discovermagazine.com/2014/april/14-the-second-coming-of-sigmund-freud [last accessed 31.7.19].

Meares, R. (2000). *Intimacy and Alienation: Memory, Trauma and Personal Being*. New York: Routledge.

Mollon, P. (2005). *EMDR and the Energy Therapies: Psychoanalytic Perspectives*. London: Karnac.

Mollon, P. (2008). *Psychoanalytic Energy Psychotherapy: Inspired by Thought Field Therapy, EFT, TAT, and Seemorg Matrix*. London: Karnac.

Mucci, C. (2013). *Beyond Individual and Collective Trauma: Healing and Psychoanalytic Treatment, Intergenerational Transmission of Trauma and the Dynamics of Forgiveness*. London: Karnac.

Mucci, C. (2016). Implicit memory, unrepressed unconscious and trauma theory: The turn of the screw between contemporary Psychoanalysis and Neuroscience. In G. Craparo & C. Mucci (Eds.), *Unrepressed Unconscious, Implicit Memory, and Clinical Work* (pp. 99–130). London: Karnac.

Peterson, J. (2017). Biblical Series III: God and the Hierarchy of Authority Transcript. www.jordanbpeterson.com/transcripts/biblical-series-iii/ [last accessed 31.7.19].

Phillips, A. (2019). *Attention Seeking*. London: Penguin Books Ltd.

Phillips, A. (2000). Psychoanalysis and Literature - In Our Time: Culture - Podcast. *BBC Radio 4*. www.bbc.co.uk/programmes/p00546y5 [last accessed 31.7.19].

Phillips, A. (2015). Adam Phillips in conversation with psychoanalyst James Mann. www.youtube.com/watch?v=lbJOuxpe1q8 [Last accessed 28.7.19].

Phillips, A. (2018). The Cure for Psychoanalysis. Confer. www.conferevents.org/phillips.html [last accessed 31.7.19].

Plato. (1988). *Theaetetus*, D. Bostock (Trans.). Oxford: Clarendon Press.

Potter, B. (2013). *Elements of Self-Destruction*. London: Karnac.

Quinodoz, J. (2004, reprinted 2005). *Reading Freud: A Chronological Exploration of Freud's Writings*. D. Alcorn (Trans.). London: Routledge.

Reiman, D. H., & Powers, S. B. (Eds.). (1977). *Shelley's Poetry and Prose: A Norton Critical Edition*. Norton: New York and London.

Rowson, J., & McGilchrist, I. (2017). Divided brain, divided world. In R. Tweedy (Ed.), *The Political Self: Understanding the Social Context for Mental Illness*. London: Karnac.

Rushkoff, D. (2019). "Evolution Is Not the Cause of Selfish Capitalism". In *Medium*, 14.1.19. https://medium.com/s/douglas-rushkoff/no-evolution-did-not-make-us-into-selfish-capitalists-95cb9f1402d6 [Last accessed 19.7.19].

Rycroft, C. (1962). Beyond the reality principle. *International Journal of Psycho-Analysis*, *43*, 388–394.

Rycroft, C. (1968, reprinted 1987). *Imagination and Reality: Psycho-Analytical Essays 1951–1961*. London: Maresfield Library.

Sarup, M. (1992). *Jacques Lacan*. New York: Harvester Wheatsheaf.

Sass, L. (1994). *The Paradoxes of Delusion: Wittgenstein, Schreber, and the Schizophrenic Mind*. Ithaca NY: Cornell University Press.

Schore, A. N. (1994). *Affect Regulation and the Origin of the Self: The Neurobiology of Emotional Development*. Hillsdale, NJ: Lawrence Erlbaum.

Schore, A. N. (2003). *Affect Regulation and the Repair of the Self*. New York: W. W. Norton.

Schore, A. N. (2011). The right brain implicit self lies at the core of psychoanalysis. *Psychoanalytic Dialogues*, *21*(1), 75–100.

Schore, A. N. (2012). *The Science of the Art of Psychotherapy*. New York: W. W. Norton.

Schore, A. N. (2013). Regulation theory and the early assessment of attachment and autistic spectrum disorders: A response to Voran's clinical case. *Journal of Infant, Child, and Adolescent Psychotherapy*, *12*(3), 164–189.

Schore, A. N. (2015). Review of The emotional life of your brain. [Review of the book *The emotional life of your brain*. R. J. Davidson & S. Begley]. *Psychoanalytic Psychology*, *32*(3), 539–547.

Schore, A. N. (2017). The right brain implicit self: A central mechanism of the psychotherapy change process. In G. Craparo & C. Mucci (Eds.), *Unrepressed Unconscious, Implicit Memory, and Clinical Work*. London: Karnac.

Scola, D. A. (1984). The hemispheric specialization of the human brain and its application to psychoanalytic principles. *Jefferson Journal of Psychiatry*, *2*(1), 5.

Sédat, J. (2005). *Freud*. (Trans. Susan Fairfield). New York: Other Press.

Siegel, D. J., & Solomon, M. (Eds.). (2013). *Healing Moments in Psychotherapy*. New York: W.W. Norton & Co.

Smail, D. (2005). *Power, Interest and Psychology: Elements of a Social Materialist Understanding of Distress*. Ross-on-Wye, UK: PCCS.

Snell, R. (2013). *Uncertainties, Mysteries, Doubts: Romanticism and the Analytic Attitude*. London and New York: Routledge.

Solms, M. (2018). The scientific standing of psychoanalysis. *BJPsych International*, *15* (1), 5–8.

Solms, M., & Panksepp, J. (2012). The "Id" knows more than the "Ego" admits: Neuropsychoanalytic and primal consciousness perspectives on the interface between affective and cognitive neuroscience. *Brain Sciences*, *2*(2). www.mdpi.com/192076-3425/2/2/147/htm [last accessed 31.7.19].

Tweedy, R. (2018). Was there a conspiracy against Kids Company? https://thehumandivine.org/2018/08/16/was-there-a-conspiracy-against-kids-company/ [last accessed 31.7.19].

Tweedy, R. (Ed.). (2017). *The Political Self: Understanding the Social Context for Mental Illness*. London: Karnac.

van der Kolk, B. (2014). *The Body Keeps the Score: Mind, Brain and Body in the Transformation of Trauma*. London: Penguin Books Ltd.

Warnecke, T. (Ed.). (2015). *The Psyche in the Modern World: Psychotherapy and Society*. London: Karnac.

Chapter 1

The right brain is dominant in psychotherapy

Allan N. Schore

In 2009, the American Psychological Association invited me to offer a plenary address, "The Paradigm Shift: The Right Brain and the Relational Unconscious." In fact, that was the first time an APA plenary address was given by a member in independent practice, and by a clinician who was also psychoanalytically informed. Citing 15 years of my interdisciplinary research, I argued that a paradigm shift was occurring not only within psychology but also across disciplines, and that psychology now needed to enter into a more intense dialogue with its neighboring biological and medical sciences. I emphasized the relevance of developmental and affective neuroscience (more so than cognitive neuroscience) for clinical and abnormal psychology. And so I reported that both clinicians and researchers were now shifting focus from left brain explicit conscious cognition to right brain implicit unconscious emotional and relational functions (Schore, 2009). Only a few years before, the APA explicitly articulated its new found emphasis on the relational foundations of psychotherapy. In 2006, the APA Presidential Task Force on Evidence-Based Practice boldly stated:

> Central to clinical expertise is interpersonal skill, which is manifested in forming a therapeutic relationship, encoding and decoding verbal and nonverbal responses, creating realistic but positive expectations, and responding empathically to the patient's explicit and implicit experiences and concerns.
>
> (p. 277)

This relational trend in psychotherapy had largely evolved from seminal contributions of psychodynamic clinicians, including Sullivan (1953), Kohut (1971), Mitchell (1988), and more recently, Bromberg (2011).

Over this same time, in parallel with psychological advances in psychotherapy, the paradigm shift to a relational "two-person psychology" had also progressed within neuroscience, especially in the discipline of interpersonal neurobiology. In this chapter, I briefly summarize my work in that field, utilizing the relational perspective of regulation theory (Schore, 1994, 2003a, 2003b, 2012) to model the development, psychopathogenesis, and treatment of the implicit subjective self. This interdisciplinary work integrates psychology and biology to more deeply understand precisely how relational experiences, for better or worse, impact the early development of psychic structure and the emergent subjective self, and how these structures are expressed at all later stages of the life span, especially in psychotherapeutic contexts. My studies continue to describe the fundamental role of the early developing right brain in relational processes. In the following, I present interpersonal neurobiological models of attachment in early development, in the therapeutic alliance, in mutual therapeutic enactments, and in the therapeutic change processes. This work highlights the fact that the current emphasis on nonconscious relational processes is shared by, cross-fertilizing, and indeed transforming both psychology and neuroscience, with important consequences for clinical psychological models of psychotherapeutic change.

A major purpose of regulation theory is to construct more complex theoretical models that can generate both heuristic experimental research and clinically relevant models of human social–emotional development. My studies in attachment neurobiology indicate that mother–infant relational communications operate rapidly, beneath levels of conscious awareness, while my research in developmental neuropsychoanalysis describes the early evolution of a "relational unconscious" and a right lateralized "social brain" that represents the biological substrate of the human unconscious. A large body of brain laterality studies now confirms the principle that "The left side is involved with conscious response and the right with the unconscious mind" (Mlot, 1998, p. 1006). Regulation theory thus strongly supports currently evolving psychodynamic models of psychotherapy, especially in the treatment of early forming attachment trauma. (Throughout, for the purposes of this chapter, the term "psychodynamic" can be equated with "psychoanalytic," and "psychotherapist" with "analyst".)

Interpersonal neurobiology of attachment: interactive regulation and the maturation of the right brain

A major contributor to the current relational trend derives from recent advances in attachment theory, now the most influential theory of early social–emotional development available to science. Following John Bowlby's (1969) seminal contributions, over the past two decades I have utilized an interdisciplinary relational perspective to describe and integrate the developmental psychological and biological processes that underlie the formation of an attachment bond of emotional communication between the infant and primary caregiver (Schore, 1994, 2003a, 2003b, 2012). The organizing principle of this work dictates that "the self-organization of the developing brain occurs in the context of a relationship with another self, another brain"

(Schore, 1996, p. 60). At the core of the model is the relational, interactive regulation of affects, which in turn impacts and shapes the maturation of the early developing right brain.

Modern attachment theory (J. Schore & A. Schore, 2008) is essentially a theory of the development of affect regulation, and thus emotional development. During attachment episodes of right-lateralized visual–facial, auditory–prosodic, and tactile–gestural nonverbal communications, the primary caregiver regulates the infant's burgeoning positive and negative bodily based affective states. The theory posits that the hard wiring of the infant's developing right brain, which is dominant for the emotional sense of self, is influenced by implicit (nonconscious), right brain-to-right brain affect communicating and regulating transactions with the mother. In this manner, the evolutionary mechanism of early attachment bonding is central to all later aspects of human development, especially adaptive right brain social–emotional functions essential for survival (Schore, 1994, 2003a, 2003b, 2012).

At the most fundamental level, the right brain attachment mechanism is expressed as interactive regulation of affective–autonomic arousal, and thereby the interpersonal regulation of biological synchronicity between and within organisms. During dyadic attachment transactions, the sensitive primary caregiver implicitly attends to, perceives (recognizes), appraises, and regulates nonverbal expressions of the infant's more and more intense states of positive and negative affective arousal. Via these communications, the mother regulates the infant's postnatally developing central and autonomic nervous systems. In this cocreated dialogue, the "good enough" mother and her infant coconstruct multiple cycles of both "affect synchrony" that up-regulates positive affect (e.g., joy–elation, interest–excitement) and "rupture and repair" that down-regulates negative affect (e.g., fear–terror, sadness–depression, shame). Internal representations of attachment experiences are imprinted in right-lateralized implicit–procedural memory as an internal working model that encodes nonconscious strategies of affect regulation.

Emotional states are initially regulated by others, but over the course of infancy it increasingly becomes self-regulated as a result of neurophysiological development and actual lived experience. These adaptive capacities are central to the emergence of self-regulation, the ability to flexibly regulate an expanding array of positive and negative affectively charged psychobiological states in different relational contexts, thereby allowing for the assimilation of various adaptive emotional–motivational states into a dynamic, coherent, and integrated self-system. Optimal attachment experiences that engender a secure attachment with the primary caregiver thus facilitate both types of self-regulation: interactive regulation of emotions accessed while subjectively engaged with other humans in interconnected contexts, and autoregulation of emotions activated while subjectively disengaged from other humans in autonomous contexts. Regulation theory defines emotional well-being as non-conscious yet efficient and resilient switching between these two modes (interconnectedness and autonomy), depending on the relational context. Internal working models of attachment encode both of these modes of coping strategies of affect regulation. Recall that Bowlby (1969) asserted that these internal representations of attachment operate at levels beneath conscious awareness.

As the securely attached infant enters toddlerhood, his or her interactively regulated right brain visual–facial, auditory–prosodic, and tactile–gestural attachment experiences become more holistically integrated, allowing for the emergence of a coherent implicit (unconscious) emotional and corporeal sense of self (Schore, 1994). Developmental neurobiological research supports the hypothesis that the attachment mechanism is embedded in infant–caregiver right brain-to-right brain affective transactions. Neuroscientific studies with adults now clearly indicate that right (and not left) lateralized prefrontal systems are responsible for the highest level regulation of affect and stress in the brain (see Schore, 2013; Schore, 2012 for references). They also document that in adulthood the right hemisphere continues to be dominant for affiliation, while the left supports power motivation (Kuhl & Kazen, 2008; Quirin et al., 2013b).

Furthermore, my work in developmental neuropsychoanalysis models the early development of the unconscious (vs. the later-forming conscious) mind. These studies echo a basic premise of classical developmental psychoanalysis, that the first relational contact is between the unconscious of the mother and the unconscious of the infant (Palombo, Bendicsen, & Koch, 2009; J. Schore, 2012a). Throughout the life span, implicit psychobiological regulation, operating at nonconscious levels, supports the survival functions of the right brain, the biological substrate of the human unconscious (Joseph, 1992; Schore, 1994, 2003b, 2012). Consonant with this proposal, the neuropsychologist Don Tucker has asserted, "The right hemisphere's specialization for emotional communication through nonverbal channels seems to suggest a domain of the mind that is close to the motivationally charged psychoanalytic unconscious" (2007, p. 91). Indeed, a growing body of studies document that unconscious processing of emotional information is mainly subsumed by a right hemisphere subcortical route (Gainotti, 2012), that unconscious emotional memories are stored in the right hemisphere (Gainotti, 2006), and that this hemisphere is centrally involved in maintaining a coherent, continuous, and unified sense of self (Devinsky, 2000; McGilchrist, 2009). From infancy throughout all later stages of the life span, right-lateralized spontaneous, rapidly acting emotional processes are centrally involved in enabling the organism to cope with stresses and challenges, and thus in emotional resilience and well-being.

Right brain attachment communications within the therapeutic alliance

Regulation theory dictates that early social–emotional experiences may be either predominantly regulated or dysregulated, imprinting secure or insecure attachments. Developmental neuroscience now clearly demonstrates that all children are not "resilient" but "malleable," for better or worse (Schore, 2012). In marked contrast to the earlier described optimal growth-facilitating attachment scenario, in a relational growth-inhibiting early environment of attachment trauma (abuse and/or neglect), the primary caregiver of an insecure disorganized–disoriented infant induces traumatic states of enduring negative affect in the child (Schore, 2001, 2003a). This caregiver is too frequently emotionally inaccessible and reacts to her infant's expressions of stressful affects inconsistently and inappropriately (massive intrusiveness or massive disengagement), and therefore shows minimal or unpredictable participation in the relational arousal-regulating processes. Instead of modulating, she induces extreme levels of stressful stimulation and arousal, very high in abuse and/or very low in neglect. Because she provides little interactive repair, the infant's intense negative affective states are long lasting.

A large body of research now highlights the central role of insecure attachments in the psychoneuropathogenesis of all psychiatric disorders (Schore, 1996, 2003a, 2012, 2013). Watt (2003) observes, "If children grow up with dominant experiences of separation, distress, fear, and rage, then they will go down a bad pathogenic developmental pathway, and it's not just a bad psychological pathway but a bad neurological pathway" (p. 109). More specifically, during early critical periods, frequent dysregulated and unrepaired organized and disorganized–disoriented insecure attachment histories are "affectively burnt in" the infant's early developing right brain. Not only traumatic experiences but also the defense against overwhelming trauma, dissociation, is stored in implicit–procedural memory. In this manner, attachment trauma ("relational trauma," Schore, 2001) is imprinted into right cortical–subcortical systems, encoding disorganized–disoriented insecure internal working models that are nonconsciously accessed at later points of interpersonal emotional stress. These insecure working models are a central focus of affectively focused psychotherapy of early forming self-pathologies and personality disorders. There is now consensus that deficits in right brain relational processes and resulting affect dysregulation underlie all psychological and psychiatric disorders. All models of therapeutic intervention across a span of psychopathologies share a common goal of attempting to improve emotional self-regulatory processes. Neurobiologically informed relational infant, child, adolescent, and adult psychotherapy can thus potentially facilitate the intrinsic plasticity of the right brain.

Recall, Bowlby (1988), a psychoanalyst, asserted that the reassessment of *nonconscious* internal working models of attachment is a primary goal of any psychotherapy. These interactive representations of early attachment experiences encode strategies of affect regulation, and contain coping mechanisms for maintaining basic regulation and positive affect in the face of stressful environmental challenge. Acting at levels beneath conscious awareness, this internal working model is accessed to perceive, appraise, and regulate social–emotional information and guide action in familiar and especially novel interpersonal environments. Regulation theory dictates that in "heightened affective moments" (Schore, 2003b), the patient's unconscious internal working model of attachment, whether secure or insecure, is reactivated in right-lateralized implicit–procedural memory and reenacted in the psycho-therapeutic relationship.

In light of the commonality of nonverbal, intersubjective, implicit right brain-to-right brain emotion transacting and regulating mechanisms in the caregiver–infant and the therapist–patient relationship, developmental attachment studies have direct relevance to the treatment process. From the first point of intersubjective contact, the psychobiologically attuned clinician tracks not just the verbal content but the nonverbal moment-to-moment rhythmic structures of the patient's internal states, and is flexibly and fluidly modifying his or her own behavior to synchronize with that structure, thereby cocreating with the patient a growth-facilitating context for the organization of the therapeutic alliance. Decety and Chaminade's (2003) characterization of higher functions of the right brain is directly applicable to the psychotherapeutic relational context: "Mental states that are in essence private to the self may be shared between individuals ... self-awareness, empathy, identification with others, and more generally intersubjective processes, are largely dependent upon ... right hemisphere resources, which are the first to develop" (p. 591). As the right hemisphere is dominant for subjective emotional experiences (Wittling & Roschmann, 1993), the communication of affective states between the right brains of the patient–therapist dyad is thus best described as "intersubjectivity."

In accord with a relational model of psychotherapy, right brain processes that are reciprocally activated on both sides of the therapeutic alliance lie at the core of the psychotherapeutic change process. These implicit clinical dialogues convey much more essential organismic information than left brain explicit, verbal information. Rather, right brain interactions "beneath the words" nonverbally communicate essential nonconscious bodily based affective relational information about the inner world of the patient (and therapist). Rapid communications between the right-lateralized "emotional brain" of each member of the therapeutic alliance allow for moment-to-moment "self-state sharing," a cocreated, organized, dynamically changing dialogue of mutual influence. Bromberg (2011) notes, "Self-states are highly individualized modules of being, each configured by its own organization of cognitions, beliefs, dominant affect, and mood, access to memory, skills, behaviors, values, action, and regulatory physiology" (p. 73). In this relational matrix, both partners match the dynamic contours of different emotional–motivational self-states, and simultaneously adjust their social attention, stimulation, and accelerating/decelerating arousal in response to the partner's signals.

Regulation theory models the mutual psychobiological mechanisms that underlie any clinical encounter, whatever the verbal content. Lyons-Ruth (2000) characterizes the affective exchanges that communicate "implicit relational knowledge" within the therapeutic alliance. She observes that most relational transactions rely on a substrate of affective cues that give an evaluative valence or direction to each relational communication. These occur at an implicit level of cueing and response that occurs too rapidly for verbal transaction and conscious reflection. In the clinical literature, Scaer (2005) describes essential implicit communication patterns embedded within the therapist–client relationship:

> Many features of social interaction are nonverbal, consisting of subtle variations of facial expression that set the tone for the content of the interaction. Body postures and movement patterns of the therapist ... also may reflect emotions such as disapproval, support, humor, and fear. Tone and volume of voice, patterns and speed of verbal communication, and eye contact also contain elements of subliminal communication and contribute to the unconscious establishment of a safe, healing environment.
>
> (pp. 167–168)

These implicit right brain/mind/body nonverbal communications are bidirectional and intersubjective, and thereby potentially valuable to the clinician. Meares (2005) observes:

> Not only is the therapist being unconsciously influenced by a series of slight and, in some cases, subliminal signals, so also is the patient. Details of the therapist's posture, gaze, tone of voice, even respiration, are recorded and processed. A sophisticated therapist may use this processing in a beneficial way, potentiating a change in the patient's state without, or in addition to, the use of words.
>
> (p. 124)

Neuroscience characterizes the role of the right brain in these nonverbal communications. At all stages of the life span, "The neural substrates of the perception of voices, faces, gestures, smells and pheromones, as evidenced by modern neuroimaging techniques, are characterized by a general pattern of right-hemispheric functional asymmetry" (Brancucci, Lucci, Mazzatenta, & Tommasi, 2009, p. 895). More so than conscious left brain verbalizations, right brain-to-right brain visual facial, auditory—prosodic, and tactile—gestural subliminal communications reveal the deeper aspects of the personality of the patient, as well as the personality of the therapist (see Schore, 2003b for a right brain-to-right brain model of projective identification, a fundamental process of implicit communication between the relational unconscious systems of patient and therapist).

To receive and monitor the patient's nonverbal bodily based attachment communications, the affectively attuned clinician must shift from constricted left hemispheric attention that focuses on local detail to more widely expanded right hemispheric attention that focuses on global detail (Derryberry & Tucker, 1994), a characterization that fits with Freud's (1912) description of the importance of the clinician's "evenly suspended attention." In the session, the empathic therapist is consciously, explicitly attending to the patient's verbalizations to objectively diagnose and rationalize the patient's dysregulating symptomatology. However, she is also listening and interacting at another level, an experience-near subjective level, one that implicitly processes moment-to-moment attachment communications and self-states at levels beneath awareness. Bucci (2002) observes, "We recognize changes in emotional states of others based on perception of subtle shifts in their facial expression or posture, and recognize changes in our own states based on somatic or kinesthetic experience" (p. 194).

Writing on therapeutic "nonverbal implicit communications" Chused (2007) asserts,

It is not that the information they contain cannot be verbalized, only that sometimes only a nonverbal approach can deliver the information in a way it can be used, particularly when there is no conscious awareness of the underlying concerns involved.

(p. 879)

These nonverbal communications are examples of "primary process communication." According to Dorpat (2001), "The primary process system analyzes, regulates, and communicates an individual's relations with the environment" (p. 449). He observes, "Affective and object-relational information is transmitted predominantly by primary process communication. Nonverbal communication includes body movements (kinesics), posture, gesture, facial expression, voice inflection, and the sequence, rhythm, and pitch of the spoken words" (p. 451). The right brain thus processes "the music behind the words."

The organizing principle of working with unconscious primary process communications dictates that just as the left brain communicates its states to other left brains via conscious linguistic behaviors, so the right nonverbally communicates its other states to other right brains that are tuned to receive these communications. Bromberg (2011) concludes,

Allan Schore writes about a right brain-to-right brain channel of affective communication—a channel that he sees as "an organized dialogue" comprised of "dynamically fluctuating moment-to-moment state sharing." I believe it to be this process of state sharing that … allows … "a good psychoanalytic match".

(p. 169)

Writing in the psychiatry literature, Meares (2012) describes "a form of therapeutic conversation that can be conceived … as a dynamic interplay between two right hemispheres" (for other clinical examples of right brain-to-right brain tracking see Chapman, 2014; Marks-Tarlow, 2012; Montgomery, 2013; Schore, 2012).

On the matter of the verbal content, the words in psychotherapy, it has long been assumed in the psychotherapeutic literature that all forms of language reflect left hemispheric functioning of the conscious mind. Current neuroscience now indicates this is incorrect. In an overarching review Ross and Monnot conclude, "Thus, the traditional concept that language is a dominant and lateralized function of the left hemisphere is no longer tenable" (2008, p. 51).

> Over the last three decades, there has been growing realization that the right hemisphere is essential for language and communication competency and psychological well-being through its ability to modulate affective prosody and gestural behavior, decode connotative (nonstandard) word meanings, make thematic inferences, and process metaphor, complex linguistic relationships and nonliteral (idiomatic) types of expressions.
>
> (p. 51)

Other studies reveal that the right hemisphere is dominant for the processing of, specifically, emotional words (Kuchinke et al., 2006), especially attachment words associated with positive interpersonal relationships (Mohr, Rowe, & Crawford, 2008). These data suggest that the early responding right brain, which is more "physiological" than the later responding left, is involved in rapid bodily based intersubjective communications within the therapeutic alliance.

Intersubjectivity is more than a communication or match of explicit verbal cognitions or overt behaviors. Regulated and dysregulated bodily based affects are communicated within an energy-transmitting intersubjective field co-constructed by two individuals that includes not just two minds but two bodies (Schore, 2012). At the psychobiological core of the co-constructed intersubjective field is the attachment bond of emotional communication and interactive regulation. Implicit intersubjective communications express bodily based emotional self-states, not just conscious cognitive "mental" states. The essential biological function of attachment communications in all human interactions, including those embedded in the therapeutic alliance, is the regulation of right brain/mind/body states. Intersubjective, relational, affect-focused psychotherapy is not the "talking cure," but the "affect communicating cure."

Transference–countertransference communications within mutual enactments

Regulation theory's relational perspective allows for a deeper understanding of the critical intersubjective brain/mind/body mechanisms that operate at implicit levels of the therapeutic alliance, beneath the exchanges of language and explicit cognitions. One such essential mechanism is the bidirectional transference–countertransference relationship. There is now a growing consensus that despite the existence of a number of distinct theoretical perspectives in clinical work, Freud's concepts of transference and countertransference have now been expanded and (re-)incorporated into all forms of psychotherapy. Transference–countertransference affective transactions are currently seen as an essential relational element in the treatment of all patients, but especially the early forming severe psychopathologies.

In such cases, implicit right brain-to-right brain nonverbal communications (facial expressions, prosody–tone of voice, gesture) convey unconscious transference–countertransference affective transactions, which revive earlier attachment memories, especially of intensely dysregulated affective states. Gainotti (2006) observes, "the right hemisphere may be crucially involved in those emotional memories which must be reactivated and reworked during the psychoanalytical treatment" (p. 167). In discussing the role of the right hemisphere as "the seat of implicit memory," Mancia (2006) notes: "The discovery of the implicit memory has extended the concept of the unconscious and supports the hypothesis that this is where the emotional and affective—sometimes traumatic—presymbolic and preverbal experiences of the primary mother-infant relations are stored" (p. 83). Transference has been described as an expression of the patient's implicit memories. These memories are expressed in "heightened affective moments" as transferential right brain-to-right brain nonverbal communications of fast acting, automatic, dysregulated bodily based states of intensely stressful emotional arousal (e.g., fear–terror, aggression–rage, depression—hopeless despair, shame, disgust). Right-lateralized implicit–procedural emotional memory also encodes the dissociative defense against re-experiencing relational trauma and thereby generates dissociated (unconscious) affects.

Recent psychodynamic models of transference now contend, "no appreciation of transference can do without emotion" (Pincus, Freeman, & Modell, 2007, p. 634). Clinical theoreticians describe transference as "an established pattern of relating and emotional responding that is cued by something in the present, but oftentimes calls up both an affective state and thoughts that may have more to do with past experience than present ones" (Maroda, 2005, p. 134). This conception is echoed in neuroscience, where Shuren and Grafman (2002) assert:

> The right hemisphere holds representations of the emotional states associated with events experienced by the individual. When that individual encounters a familiar scenario, representations of past emotional experiences are retrieved by the right hemisphere and are incorporated into the reasoning process.
>
> (p. 918)

Research now indicates that the right hemisphere is fundamentally involved in autobiographical memory (Markowitsch, Reinkemeier, Kessler, Koyuncu, & Heiss, 2000).

Recall Racker's (1968) classical dictum, "Every transference situation provokes a countertransference situation." Translating this into modern neuropsychoanalytic terms, transference–countertransference transactions are expressions of bidirectional nonconscious, nonverbal right brain–mind–body stressful communications between patient and therapist. These reciprocal psychoneurobiological exchanges reflect activities of both the central and autonomic nervous systems. Behaviorally, the patient's transferential communications are expressed in nonverbal, visual, auditory, and gestural affective cues that are spontaneously and quickly expressed from the face, voice, and body of the patient. Countertransference is similarly defined in nonverbal implicit terms as the therapist's autonomic responses that are reactions on an unconscious level to nonverbal messages. In my first book, I stated:

> Countertransferential processes are currently understood to be manifest in the capacity to recognize and utilize the sensory (visual, auditory, tactile, kinesthetic, and olfactory) and affective qualities of imagery which the patient generates in the psychotherapist ... countertransference dynamics are appraised by the therapist's observations of his own visceral reactions to the patient's material.
>
> (Schore, 1994, p. 451)

As the empathic clinician implicitly monitors the patient's nonverbal transferential communications, her psychobiologically attuned right brain, which is dominant for emotional arousal (MacNeilage, Rogers, & Vallortigara, 2009), tracks, at a preconscious level, the patterns of arousal rhythms and flows of the patient's affective states. Clinicians are now asserting "transference is distinctive in that it depends on early patterns of emotional attachment with caregivers" (Pincus et al., 2007, p. 636) and describing the clinical importance of "making conscious the organizing patterns of affect" (Mohaupt, Holgersen, Binder, & Nielsen, 2006, p. 243). Converging evidence from neuroscience now indicates, "Simply stated, the left hemisphere specializes in analyzing sequences, while the right hemisphere gives evidence of superiority in processing patterns" (van Lancker & Cummings, 1999, p. 95). Even more specifically, "Pattern recognition and comprehension of several types of stimuli, such as faces, chords, complex pitch, graphic images, and voices, has been described as superior in the normal right hemisphere" (van Lancker Sidtis, 2006, p. 233).

But in addition, the therapist is implicitly tracking her own countertransferential responses to the patient's transferential communications, patterns of her own somatic countertransferential, interoceptive, bodily based affective responses to the patient's right brain implicit facial, prosodic, and gestural communications. Via these right brain mechanisms, the intuitive psychobio-logically attuned therapist, on a moment-to-moment basis, nonconsciously focuses her right brain countertransferential broad attentional processes (Der-ryberry & Tucker, 1994) on patterns of rhythmic crescendos/decrescendos of the patient's regulated and dysregulated states of affective autonomic arousal. Freud's dictum, "It is a very remarkable thing that the *Ucs.* of one human being can react upon that of another, without passing through the *Cs.*" (1915, p. 194) is thus neuropsychoanalytically understood as a right brain-to-right brain communication from one relational unconscious to another. In this manner, "The right hemisphere, in fact, truly interprets the mental state not only of its own brain, but the brains (and minds) of others" (Keenan, Rubio, Racioppi, Johnson, & Barnacz, 2005, p. 702).

Right brain-to-right brain transferential—countertransferential uncon-scious communications between the patient's and therapist's "internal worlds" represent an essential relational matrix for the therapeutic expression of dissociated affects associated with early attachment trauma and thereby "subjectively unconscious danger" (Carretié, Hinojosa, Mercado, & Tapia, 2005) and "unconscious emotion" (Sato & Aoki, 2006). These affective communications of traumatized self states were neither intersubjectively shared nor interactively regulated by the original attachment object in the historical context, but now the patient has the possibility of a reparative rela-tional experience. According to Borgogno and Vigna-Taglianti (2008):

> In patients whose psychic suffering originates in … preverbal trauma … transference occurs mostly at a more primitive level of expression that involves in an unconscious way … not only the patient but also the ana-lyst … These more archaic forms of the transference-countertransference issue—which frequently set aside verbal contents—take shape in the analyt-ical setting through actual mutual enactments.
>
> (p. 314)

Right brain bodily based dialogues between the relational unconscious of the patient and the relational unconscious of the affectively sensitive empathic therapist are activated and enhanced in the "heightened affective moments" of reenactments of early relational trauma. Enactments are now seen as powerful manifestations of the intersubjective process and expressions of complex, though largely unconscious, self-states and relational patterns (see Schore, 2012 for an extensive interpersonal neurobiological model of working in clinical enactments).

The relational mechanism of mutual enactments represents an interaction between the patient's emotional vulnerability and the clinician's emotional avail-ability (the ability to "take" the transference). It is most fully operational during (inevitable) ruptures of the therapeutic alliance, described by Aspland, Llewelyn, Hardy, Barkham, and Stiles (2008) as "points of emotional disconnections between client and therapist that create a negative shift in the quality of the alliance" (p. 699), that act as "episodes of covert or overt behavior that trap both participants in negative complementary interactions" (p. 700). Although such ruptures of the alliance are the most stressful moments of the treatment, these "collisions" of the therapist's and patient's subjectivities also represent an intersubjective context of potential "collaboration" between their subjectivities, and thereby a context of interactive repair, a fundamental mechanism of therapeutic change. This co-created emergent relational structure within the therapeutic alliance contains a more efficient feedback communication system of not only right brain communications but also right brain interactive regulations of intensely dysregulated affective states associated with early relational trauma.

Indeed, the essential biological homeostatic functions of affective, bodily based, intersubjective attachment communications in all human interactions, including those embedded in the psychobiological core of the therapeutic alliance, are involved in the regulation of right brain/mind/body states. Aron observes,

> Patient and analyst mutually regulate each other's behaviors, enactments, and states of consciousness such that each gets under the other's skin, each reaches into the other's guts, each is breathed in and absorbed by the other ... the analyst must be attuned to the nonverbal, the affective ... to his or her bodily responses.
>
> (Aron, 1998, p. 26)

The importance of this right limbic–autonomic connection is stressed by Whitehead:

> Every time we make therapeutic contact with our patients we are engaging profound processes that tap into essential life forces in our selves and in those we work with ... *Emotions are deepened in intensity and sustained in time when they are intersubjectively shared.* This occurs at moments of *deep contact.*
>
> (Whitehead, 2006, p. 624, author's italics)

At moments of deep contact, intersubjective psychobiological resonance between the patient's and clinician's relational unconscious generates an interactively regulated amplification of arousal and affect, and so unconscious affects are deepened in intensity and sustained in time. This increase of emotional intensity (energetic arousal) allows dissociated affects beneath levels of awareness to emerge into consciousness in both members of the therapeutic dyad.

"Heightened affective moments" of the treatment afford opportunities for right brain interactive affect regulation, the core of the attachment process. Ogden concludes:

> Interactive psychobiological regulation … provides the relational context under which the client can safely contact, describe and eventually regulate inner experience … It is the patient's experience of empowering action in the context of safety provided by a background of the empathic clinician's psychobiologically attuned interactive affect regulation that helps effect … change.
>
> (Ogden, Pain, Minton, & Fisher, 2005, p. 22)

In a seminal article in the clinical psychology literature, Greenberg (2007) describes a "self-control" form of emotion regulation involving higher levels of cognitive executive function that allows individuals "to change the way they feel by consciously changing the way they think" (p. 415). He proposes that this explicit form of affect regulation is performed by the verbal left hemisphere, and unconscious bodily based emotion is usually not addressed. This regulatory mechanism is at the core of verbal–analytic understanding and controlled reasoning, and is heavily emphasized in models of cognitive–behavioral therapy. In contrast to this conscious emotion regulation system, Greenberg describes a second, more fundamental implicit affect regulatory process performed by the right hemisphere that rapidly and automatically processes facial expression, vocal quality, and eye contact in a relational context. This type of therapy attempts not control but the "acceptance or facilitation of particular emotions," including "previously avoided emotion," to allow the patient to tolerate and transform them into "adaptive emotions." Citing my work he asserts, "it is the building of implicit or automatic emotion regulation capacities that is important for enduring change, especially for highly fragile personality-disordered clients" (2007, p. 416).

Right brain relational mechanisms of therapeutic change

In cases of early attachment maturational failures, especially histories of relational trauma, deep emotional contact and implicit interactive affect regulation are central mechanisms of right brain psychotherapy change processes. Recall, the hallmark of trauma is damage to the relational life (Herman, 1992). The repair and resolution of relational trauma therefore must occur in a therapeutic relational context. In this challenging work, more so than cognitive understanding, relational factors lie at the core of the change mechanism. The clinical work involved in traumatic reenactments involves a profound commitment by both participants in the therapeutic dyad and a deep emotional involvement on the part of the therapist. These types of cases, difficult as they may be, represent valuable learning experiences for the therapist, and they call for expert skills (Schore, 2012). Ultimately, effective psychotherapeutic treatment of early evolving self pathologies (including personality disorders) can facilitate neuroplastic changes in the right brain, which is dominant for attachment functions throughout the life span. This interpersonal neurobiological mechanism allows optimal longer term treatment to potentially transform disorganized–disoriented attachments into "earned secure" attachments.

That said, the developing right brain system ("right mind," Ornstein, 1997) is relationally impacted in all attachment histories, including insecure organized and secure attachments. Regulation theory's transtheoretical clinical perspective that describes the basic psychoneurobiological processes of therapeutic action applies to all patients, insecure and secure, and to all forms of psychotherapy. In a recent neuroimaging study Tschacher, Schildt, and Sander (2010) contend, "psychotherapy research is no longer concerned with efficacy but rather with how effective change occurs" (p. 578). Changes mediated by affectively focused, relationally oriented psychotherapy are imprinted into the right brain, which is dominant for the nonverbal, implicit, holistic processing of emotional information and social interactions (Decety & Lamm, 2007; Hecht, 2014; Schore, 2012; Semrud-Clikeman, Fine, & Zhu, 2011). The right brain is centrally involved in implicit (vs. explicit) affectivity, defined as "individual differences in the automatic activation of cognitive representations of emotions that do not result from self-reflection" (Quirin, Kazen, Rohrmann, & Kuhl, 2009, pp. 401–402). It also predominates over the left for coping with and assimilating novel situations but also for emotional resilience (see Schore, 2012). These adaptive functions are mobilized in the change processes of psychotherapy.

Long-term treatment allows for the evolution of more complex psychic structure, which in turn can process more complex right brain functions (e.g., intersubjectivity, empathy, affect tolerance, stress regulation, humor, mutual love, and intimacy). The growth-facilitating relational environment of a deeper therapeutic exploration of the relational–emotional unconscious mind can induce plasticity in both the cortical and subcortical systems of the patient's right brain. This increased connectivity in turn generates more complex development of the right-lateralized biological substrate of the human unconscious, including alterations of the patient's nonconscious internal working model that encodes more effective coping strategies of implicit affect regulation and thereby adaptive, flexible switching of self-states in different relational contexts. This interpersonal neurobiological mechanism underlies Jordan's assertion that "people grow through and toward relationships throughout the life span" (Jordan, 2000, p. 1007).

The intrinsically relational aspect of regulation theory also models the reciprocal changes in the clinician's right brain that result from working repeatedly with therapeutic processes (Schore, 2012). Recall the APA's characterization of clinical expertise as "interpersonal skill," expressed in "encoding and decoding verbal and nonverbal responses" and "responding empathically to the patient's explicit and implicit experiences." With clinical experience (the proverbial "10,000 hours"), psychotherapists of all schools can potentially become expert in nonverbal intersubjective processes and *implicit relational knowledge*, which enhance therapeutic effectiveness. The professional growth of the clinician reflects progressions in right brain relational processes that underlie clinical skills, including affective empathy (Decety & Chaminade, 2003; Schore, 1994), the ability to tolerate and interactively regulate a broader array of negative and positive affective self-states (Schore, 2003b, 2012), implicit openness to experience (DeYoung, Graziopiene, & Peterson, 2012), clinical intuition (Marks-Tarlow, 2012; Schore, 2012), and creativity (Asari et al., 2008; Mihov, Denzler, & Forster, 2010). In a comprehensive overview of laterality research, Hecht (2014) states:

> Mounting evidence suggests that the right hemisphere has a relative advantage over the left hemisphere in mediating social intelligence— identifying social stimuli, understanding the intentions of other people, awareness of the dynamics in social relationships, and successful handling of social interactions.
>
> (p. 1)

I would argue that clinical experience enhances the therapist's right brain "social intelligence."

Regulation theory proposes that the core clinical skills of any effective psychotherapy are right brain implicit capacities, including the ability to empathically receive and express bodily based nonverbal communications, the ability to sensitively register very slight changes in another's expression and emotion, an immediate awareness of one's own subjective and intersubjective experience, and the regulation of one's own and the patient's affect. All techniques sit atop this relational substratum. As Valentine and Gabbard (2014) have eloquently stated, "Technique, in general, should be invisible. The therapist should be viewed by the patient as engaging in a natural conversational dialog growing out of the patient's concerns; the therapist should not be perceived as applying a stilted, formal technique" (p. 60). Over the course of the treatment, in an array of emotionally charged clinical exchanges, the empathic therapist is flexibly accessing a storehouse of affective experiences gained over the course of his or her career. A relational perspective of professional development dictates that the continuously evolving psychotherapist frequently reflects on the subjective experiences of *being with* patients, including not only *the patients'* unique personalities, but also *their own* conscious and especially unconscious intersubjective co-participation in the therapeutic process.

To be optimally effective in treating the regulatory and relational deficits of both psychiatric and personality disorders, the expert clinician learns how to fluidly access not only the patient's left-lateralized conscious mind and explicit self, but even more importantly the patient's right-lateralized unconscious mind and implicit, bodily based self. This principle applies to clinical psychology's models of both assessment and treatment. Interestingly, as opposed to verbal questionnaires that measure explicit functions, projective tests, such as the Rorschach and Thematic Apperception Test, directly tap into right brain implicit functions (Asari et al., 2008; Hiraishi et al., 2012). Indeed Finn (2012) is now applying regulation theory to Rorschach assessments of right brain attachment failures (see also the use of the Adult Attachment Projective Picture System by Finn, 2011; and the Operant Motive Test by Quirin, Gruber, Kuhl, & Dusing, 2013a).

In addition, the *explicit knowledge* the psychologist acquires from studying the rapidly expanding amount of clinically relevant interdisciplinary research is essential to professional growth. My ongoing studies indicate that the current explosion of information on early social–emotional development, attachment, relational trauma, unconscious processes, and developing brain functions is directly relevant to clinical models of psychotherapeutic change. The expanding knowledge of the biological and medical disciplines that border psychology needs to be incorporated into and thereby update our professional curriculum, training, and internship programs, where it can promote more effective relational and therapeutic skills.

The practice of psychotherapy is not just explicitly teaching the patient coping skills. Rather, it is fundamentally relational: the therapeutic alliance, the major vector of change is, in essence, a two-person system for (implicit) self exploration and relational healing. At all points in the life span, this emotional growth of the self that supports emotional well-being is facilitated in relational contexts, as described above. The importance of "context" is currently highlighted by all scientific and clinical disciplines. For most of the past century, science equated context with the organism's physical surround; this has now shifted to the social, relational environment. All human interactions, including those between therapist and patient as well as researcher and experimental subject, occur within a relational context, in which essential nonverbal communications are transmitted at levels beneath conscious awareness, thereby activating/deactivating basic homeostatic processes in both members of an intersubjective dyad. This reciprocal communication between the relational unconscious of both members of the therapeutic alliance is described by Casement (1985): "It is usual for therapists to see themselves as trying to understand the unconscious of the patient. What is not always acknowledged is that the patient also reads the unconscious of the therapist, knowingly or unknowingly" (p. 3). The ubiquitous expression of the relational unconscious in the therapeutic alliance strongly supports psychodynamic, interpersonal models of psychotherapy, as well as amplifying Sigmund Freud's call for paradigm shifting scientific explorations of the unconscious in everyday life.

At the beginning of this work I suggested that a paradigm shift is now occurring across a number of disciplines, from left brain conscious cognition to right brain unconscious, relational, emotional functions. Writing in the neuropsychoanalytic literature on "Emotions, unconscious processes, and the right hemisphere" Gainotti (2005) concludes:

> [T]he right hemisphere subserves the lower "schematic" level (where emotions are automatically generated and experienced as "true emotions") whereas the left hemisphere the higher "conceptual" level (where emotions are consciously analyzed and submitted to intentional control).
>
> (p. 71)

In his masterly review of brain laterality research, Iain McGilchrist (2009) asserts:

> If what one means by consciousness is the part of the mind that brings the world into focus, makes it explicit, allows it to be formulated in language, and is aware of its own awareness, it is reasonable to link the conscious mind to activity almost all of which lies ultimately in the left hemisphere.
>
> (p. 188)

On the other hand:

> The right hemisphere, by contrast, yields a world of individual, changing, evolving, interconnected, implicit, incarnate, living beings within the context of the lived world, but in the nature of things never fully graspable, always imperfectly known—and to this world it exists in a relationship of care.
>
> (McGilchrist, 2009, p. 174)

Psychotherapy, "a relationship of care," can alter more than the left-lateralized conscious mind; it also can influence the growth and development of the unconscious "right mind." It is undoubtedly true that both brain hemispheres contribute to effective therapeutic treatment, but in light of the current relational trend that emphasizes "the primacy of affect," the right brain, the "social," "emotional" brain is dominant in all forms of psychotherapy.

References

APA Presidential Task Force on Evidence-Based Practice. (2006). Evidence-based practice in psychology. *American Psychologist, 61*, 271–285. doi:10.1037/0003-066X.61.4.271

Aron, L. (1998). The clinical body and the reflexive mind. In L. Aron & F. Sommer Anderson (Eds.), *Relational perspectives on the body* (pp. 3–37). Hillsdale, NJ: The Analytic Press.

Asari, T., Konishi, S., Jimura, K., Chikazoe, J., Nakamura, N., & Miyashita, Y. (2008). Right temporopolar activation associated with unique perception. *Neuroimage, 41*, 145–152. doi:10.1016/j.neuroimage.2008.01.059

Aspland, H., Llewelyn, S., Hardy, G. E., Barkham, M., & Stiles, W. (2008). Alliance rupture resolution in cognitive-behavior therapy: A preliminary task analysis. *Psychotherapy Research, 18*, 699–710. doi:10.1080/10503300802291463

Borgogno, F., & Vigna-Taglianti, M. (2008). Role-reversal: A somewhat neglected mirror of heritages of the past. *The American Journal of Psychoanalysis, 68*, 313–324. doi:10.1057/ajp.2008.31

Bowlby, J. (1969). *Attachment and loss. Vol. 1: Attachment.* New York, NY: Basic Books.

Bowlby, J. (1988). *A secure base* (2nd ed.). New York, NY: Basic Books.

Brancucci, A., Lucci, G., Mazzatenta, A., & Tommasi, L. (2009). Asymmetries of the human social brain in the visual, auditory and chemical modalities. *Philosophical Transactions of the Royal Society of London.* Series B, Biological Sciences, *364*, 895–914. doi:10.1098/rstb.2008.0279

Bromberg, P. M. (2011). *The shadow of the tsunami and the growth of the relational mind.* New York, NY: Routledge.

Bucci, W. (2002). The referential process, consciousness, and the sense of self. *Psychoanalytic Inquiry, 22*, 766–793. doi:10.1080/07351692209349017

Carretié, L., Hinojosa, J. A., Mercado, F., & Tapia, M. (2005). Cortical response to subjectively unconscious danger. *Neuroimage, 24*, 615–623. doi:10.1016/j.neuroimage.2004.09.009

Casement, P. (1985). *Learning from the patient.* New York, NY: Guilford Press.

Chapman, L. (2014). *Neurobiologically informed trauma therapy with children and adolescents. Understanding mechanisms of change.* New York, NY: Norton.

Chused, J. F. (2007). Nonverbal communication in psychoanalysis: Commentary on Harrison and Tronick. *Journal of the American Psychoanalytic Association, 55*, 875–882. doi:10.1177/00030651070550030401

Decety, J., & Chaminade, T. (2003). When the self represents the other: A new cognitive neuroscience view on psychological identification. *Consciousness and Cognition, 12*, 577–596. doi:10.1016/S1053-8100(03)00076-X

Decety, J., & Lamm, C. (2007). The role of the right temporoparietal junction in social interaction: How low-level computational processes contribute to meta-cognition. *The Neuroscientist, 13*, 580–593. doi:10.1177/1073858407304654

Derryberry, D., & Tucker, D. M. (1994). Motivating the focus of attention. In P. M. Niedentahl & S. Kiyayama (Eds.), *The heart's eye: Emotional influences in perception and attention* (pp. 167–196). San Diego, CA: Academic Press. doi:10.1016/B978-0-12-410560-7.50014-4

Devinsky, O. (2000). Right cerebral hemisphere dominance for a sense of corporeal and emotional self. *Epilepsy and Behavior, 1*, 60–73. doi:10.1006/ebeh.2000.0025

DeYoung, C. G., Graziopiene, R. G., & Peterson, J. B. (2012). From madness to genius: The openness/Intellect trait domain as a paradoxical simplex. *Journal of Research in Personality, 46*, 63–78. doi:10.1016/j.jrp.2011.12.003

Dorpat, T. L. (2001). Primary process communication. *Psychoanalytic Inquiry, 21*, 448–463. doi:10.1080/07351692109348946

Finn, S. E. (2011). Use of the Adult Attachment Projective Picture System (AAP) in the middle of long-term psychotherapy. *Journal of Personality Assessment, 93*, 427–433. doi:10.1080/00223891.2011.595744

Finn, S. E. (2012). 2011 Bruno Klopfer Distinguished Contribution Award. Implications of recent research in neurobiology for psychological assessment. *Journal of Personality Assessment, 5*, 440–449.

Freud, S. (1912). *Recommendations to physicians practicing psychoanalysis* (Standard Edition, Vol. 12) London: Hogarth Press, 1957.

Freud, S. (1915). *The unconscious* (Standard Edition, Vol. 14). London: Hogarth Press, 1957.

Gainotti, G. (2005). Emotions, unconscious processes, and the right hemisphere. *Neuro-psychoanalysis, 7*, 71–81.

Gainotti, G. (2006). Unconscious emotional memories and the right hemisphere. In M. Mancia (Ed.), *Psychoanalysis and neuroscience* (pp. 151–173). Milan: Springer Milan. doi:10.1007/88-470-0550-7_6

Gainotti, G. (2012). Unconscious processing of emotions and the right hemisphere. *Neuropsychologia, 50*, 205–218. doi:10.1016/j.neuropsychologia.2011.12.005

Greenberg, L. S. (2007). Emotion coming of age. *Clinical Psychology Science and Practice, 14*, 414–421. doi:10.1111/j.1468-2850.2007.00101.x

Hecht, D. (2014). Cerebral lateralization of pro- and anti-social tendencies. *Experimental Neurobiology, 23*, 1–27.

Herman, J. L. (1992). *Trauma and recovery*. New York, NY: Basic Books.

Hiraishi, H., Haida, M., Matsumoto, M., Hayakawa, N., Inomata, S., & Matsumoto, H. (2012). Differences of prefrontal cortex activity between picture-based personality tests: A near-infrared spectroscopy study. *Journal of Personality Assessment, 94*, 366–371. doi:10.1080/00223891.2012.666597

Jordan, J. V. (2000). The role of mutual empathy in relational/cultural therapy. *Journal of Clinical Psychology, 56*, 1005–1016. doi:10.1002/1097-4679(200008)56:8_1005:: AID-JCLP2_3.0.CO;2-L

Joseph, R. (1992). *The right brain and the unconscious*. New York, NY: Plenum Press. doi:10.1007/978-1-4899-5996-6

Keenan, J. P., Rubio, J., Racioppi, C., Johnson, A., & Barnacz, A. (2005). The right hemisphere and the dark side of consciousness. *Cortex, 41*, 695–704. doi:10.1016/S0010-9452(08)70286-7

Kohut, H. (1971). *The analysis of the self*. New York, NY: International Universities Press.

Kuchinke, L., Jacobs, A. M., Vo, M. L. H., Conrad, M., Grubich, C., & Herrmann, M. (2006). Modulation of prefrontal cortex by emotional words in recognition memory. *Neuroreport, 17*, 1037–1041. doi:10.1097/01.wnr.0000221838.27879.fe

Kuhl, J., & Kazen, M. (2008). Motivation, affect, and hemispheric asymmetry: Power versus affiliation. *Journal of Personality and Social Psychology, 95*, 456–469. doi:10.1037/0022-3514.95.2.456

Lyons-Ruth, K. (2000). "I sense that you sense that I sense…": Sander's recognition process and the specificity of relational moves in the psychotherapeutic setting. *Infant Mental Health Journal, 21*, 85–98. doi:10.1002/(SICI)1097-0355(200001/04)21:1/2_85::AID-IMHJ10_3.0.CO;2-F

MacNeilage, P. F., Rogers, L., & Vallortigara, G. (2009). Origins of the left and right brain. *Scientific American, 301*, 60–67. doi:10.1038/scientificamerican0709-60

Mancia, M. (2006). Implicit memory and early unrepressed unconscious: Their role in the therapeutic process (How the neurosciences can contribute to psychoanalysis). *The International Journal of Psychoanalysis, 87*, 83–103.

Markowitsch, H. J., Reinkemeier, A., Kessler, J., Koyuncu, A., & Heiss, W. D. (2000). Right amygdalar and temperofrontal activation during autobiographical, but not fictitious memory retrieval. *Behavioral Neurology, 12*, 181–190. doi:10.1155/2000/303651

Marks-Tarlow, T. (2012). *Clinical intuition in psychotherapy: The neurobiology of embodied response.* New York, NY: Norton.

Maroda, K. J. (2005). Show some emotion: Completing the cycle of affective communication. In L. Aron & A. Harris (Eds.), *Revolutionary connections. Relational psychoanalysis. vol. II. Innovation and expansion* (pp. 121–142). Hillsdale, NJ: Analytic Press.

McGilchrist, I. (2009). *The master and his emissary.* New Haven, CT: Yale University Press.

Meares, R. (2005). *The metaphor of play: Origin and breakdown of personal being* (3rd ed.). London: Routledge.

Meares, R. (2012). *A dissociation model of borderline personality disorder.* New York, NY: Norton.

Mihov, K. M., Denzler, M., & Forster, J. (2010). Hemispheric specialization and creative thinking: A meta-analytic review of lateralization of creativity. *Brain and Cognition, 72*, 442–448. doi:10.1016/j.bandc.2009.12.007

Mitchell, S. A. (1988). *Relational concepts in psychoanalysis.* Cambridge, MA: Harvard University Press.

Mlot, C. (1998). Probing the biology of emotion. *Science, 280*, 1005–1007. doi:10.1126/science.280.5366.1005

Mohaupt, H., Holgersen, H., Binder, P.-E., & Nielsen, G. H. (2006). Affect consciousness or mentalization? A comparison of two concepts with regard to affect development and affect regulation. *Scandinavian Journal of Psychology, 47*, 237–244. doi:10.1111/j.1467-9450.2006.00513.x

Mohr, C., Rowe, A. C., & Crawford, M. T. (2008). Hemispheric differences in the processing of attachment words. *Journal of Clinical and Experimental Neuropsychology, 301*, 1–480.

Montgomery, A. (2013). *Neurobiology essentials for clinicians: What every therapist needs to know.* New York, NY: Norton.

Ogden, P., Pain, C., Minton, K., & Fisher, J. (2005). Including the body in mainstream psychotherapy for traumatized individuals. *Psychologist Psychoanalyst, 25*, 19–24.

Ornstein, R. O. (1997). *The right mind. Making sense of the hemispheres.* New York, NY: Harcourt Brace.

Palombo, J., Bendicsen, H. K., & Koch, B. J. (2009). *Guide to psychoanalytic developmental theories.* New York, NY: Springer.

Pincus, D., Freeman, W., & Modell, A. (2007). A neurobiological model of perception: Considerations for transference. *Psychoanalytic Psychology, 24*, 623–640. doi:10.1037/0736-9735.24.4.623

Quirin, M., Gruber, T., Kuhl, J., & Dusing, R. (2013a). Is love right? Prefrontal resting brain asymmetry is related to the affiliation motive. *Frontiers in Human Neuroscience, 7*, 1–11.

Quirin, M., Kazen, M., Rohrmann, S., & Kuhl, J. (2009). Implicit but not explicit affectivity predicts circadian and reactive cortisol: Using the implicit positive and negative affect test. *Journal of Personality, 77*, 401–426. doi:10.1111/j.1467-6494.2008.00552.x

Quirin, M., Meyer, F., Heise, N., Kuhl, J., Kustermann, E., Struber, D., & Cacioppo, J. T. (2013b). Neural correlates of social motivation: An fMRI study on power versus affiliation. *International Journal of Psychophysiology, 88*, 289–295. doi:10.1016/j.ijpsycho.2012.07.003

Racker, H. (1968). *Transference and countertransference.* New York, NY: International Universities Press.

Ross, E. D., & Monnot, M. (2008). Neurology of affective prosody and its functional-anatomic organization in right hemisphere. *Brain and Language, 104*, 51–74. doi:10.1016/j.bandl.2007.04.007

Sato, W., & Aoki, S. (2006). Right hemisphere dominance in processing unconscious emotion. *Brain and Cognition, 62*, 261–266. doi:10.1016/j.bandc.2006.06.006

Scaer, R. (2005). *The trauma spectrum: Hidden wounds and human resiliency.* New York, NY: Norton.

Schore, A. N. (1994). *Affect regulation and the origin of the self.* Mahweh, NJ: Erlbaum.

Schore, A. N. (1996). The experience-dependent maturation of a regulatory system in the orbital prefrontal cortex and the origin of developmental psychopathology. *Development and Psychopathology, 8*, 59–87. doi:10.1017/S0954579400006970

Schore, A. N. (2001). The effects of relational trauma on right brain development, affect regulation, and infant mental health. *Infant Mental Health Journal, 22*, 201–269. doi:10.1002/1097-0355(200101/04)22:1_201::AID-IMHJ8_3.0.CO;2-9

Schore, A. N. (2003a). *Affect dysregulation and disorders of the self.* New York, NY: Norton.

Schore, A. N. (2003b). *Affect regulation and the repair of the self.* New York, NY: Norton.

Schore, A. N. (2009, August 8). The paradigm shift: The right brain and the relational unconscious. Invited plenary address to the American Psychological Association 2009 Convention, Toronto, Canada. Retrieved from www.allanschore.com/pdf/SchoreAPAPlenaryFinal09.pdf

Schore, A. N. (2012). *The science of the art of psychotherapy.* New York, NY: Norton.

Schore, A. N. (2013). Regulation theory and the early assessment of attachment and autistic spectrum disorders: A response to Voran's clinical case. *Journal of Infant, Child, and Adolescent Psychotherapy, 12*, 164–189. doi:10.1080/15289168.2013.822741

Schore, J. R. (2012a). Using concepts from interpersonal neurobiology in revisiting psychodynamic theory. *Smith College Studies in Social Work, 82*, 90–111. doi:10.1080/00377317.2012.644494

Schore, J. R., & Schore, A. N. (2008). Modern attachment theory: The central role of affect regulation in development and treatment. *Clinical Social Work Journal, 36*, 9–20. doi:10.1007/s10615-007-0111-7

Semrud-Clikeman, M., Fine, J. G., & Zhu, D. C. (2011). The role of the right hemisphere for processing of social interactions in normal adults using functional magnetic resonance imaging. *Neuropsychobiology, 64*, 47–51. doi:10.1159/000325075

Shuren, J. E., & Grafman, J. (2002). The neurology of reasoning. *Archives of Neurology, 59*, 916–919. doi:10.1001/archneur.59.6.916

Sullivan, H. S. (1953). *The interpersonal theory of psychiatry*. New York, NY: WW Norton.

Tschacher, W., Schildt, M., & Sander, K. (2010). Brain connectivity in listening to affective stimuli: A functional magnetic resonance imaging (fMRI) study and implications for psychotherapy. *Psychotherapy Research, 20*, 576–588. doi:10.1080/10503307.2010.493538

Tucker, D. M., & Moller, L. (2007). The metamorphosis. Individuation of the adolescent brain. In D. Romer & E. F. Walker (Eds.), *Adolescent psychopathology and the developing brain* (pp. 85–102). Oxford: Oxford University Press. doi:10.1093/acprof:oso/9780195306255.003.0004

Valentine, L., & Gabbard, G. O. (2014). Can the use of humor in psychotherapy be taught? *Academic Psychiatry, 38*, 75–81. doi:10.1007/s40596-013-0018-2

van Lancker, D., & Cummings, J. L. (1999). Expletives: Neurolinguistic and neurobehavioral perspectives on swearing. *Brain Research Reviews, 31*, 83–104. doi:10.1016/S0165-0173(99)00060-0

van Lancker Sidtis, D. (2006). Where in the brain is nonliteral language? *Metaphor and Symbol, 21*, 213–244.

Watt, D. F. (2003). Psychotherapy in an age of neuroscience: Bridges to affective neuroscience. In J. Corrigal & H. Wilkinson (Eds.), *Revolutionary connections: Psychotherapy and neuroscience* (pp. 79–115). London: Karnac.

Whitehead, C. C. (2006). Neo-psychoanalysis: A paradigm for the 21st century. *Journal of the Academy of Psychoanalysis and Dynamic Psychiatry, 34*, 603–627. doi:10.1521/jaap.2006.34.4.603

Wittling, W., & Roschmann, R. (1993). Emotion-related hemisphere asymmetry: Subjective emotional responses to laterally presented films. *Cortex, 29*, 431–448. doi:10.1016/S0010-9452(13)80252-3

Ways of attending

How our divided brain constructs the world

Iain McGilchrist

Introduction

There's a story somewhere in Nietzsche that goes something like this. There was once a wise spiritual master, who was the ruler of a small but prosperous domain, and who was known for his selfless devotion to his people. As his people flourished and grew in number, the bounds of this small domain spread, and with it the need to trust implicitly the emissaries he sent to ensure the safety of its ever more distant parts. It was not just that it was impossible for him to order all that needed to be dealt with personally: as he wisely saw, he *needed* to keep his distance from, and even to remain ignorant of, such concerns. And so he nurtured and trained his emissaries carefully, in order that they could be trusted. Eventually, however, his cleverest and most ambitious vizier, the one he most trusted to do his work, began to see himself as the master and used his position to advance his own wealth and influence. He saw his master's temperance and forbearance as weakness, not wisdom, and on his missions on the master's behalf adopted his mantle as his own: the emissary became contemptuous of his master. And so it came about that the master was usurped, the people were duped, the domain became a tyranny, and eventually it collapsed in ruins.

This story is as old as humanity, and I think it tells us something important about what is going on inside ourselves, in our very brains. It is being played out in the world around us right now, and, since the consequences are grave indeed, we need to understand what it is.

The master and his emissary

The story of the relationship between the structure of the brain and its influence on Western culture was the subject of my 2009 book, *The Master and his Emissary: The Divided Brain and the Making of the Western World*. I will try here to give an idea of how this book came about, since it may be of interest to those outside the world of neuroscience.

The idea of writing it goes back to the time before I even started training in medicine, more than 25 years ago. I had been troubled by problems of the academic study of literature, which was my business at the time: why was it that the things we prized about the work of a great poet, for example, turned to a handful of dust when one tried to inspect them more closely? On analysis and explicit discussion, the uniqueness of the work, which lay in these very same much-valued qualities, seemed to consist only of imperfections. I began to think less well of perfection. The whole process of literary criticism seemed inevitably to involve making explicit what had to remain implicit (if it was not to be seriously disrupted), substituting general words and thoughts that one might have got almost anywhere else for the irreducible uniqueness of the work of art and replacing the incarnate being before us with a series of abstractions – a coded message of which the author was unaware. We cerebralised what had to remain the "betweenness" of two living things. The result was a sort of superior knowingness that traduced the innocence of the work. Something often of undeniable interest emerged, but it nonetheless, subtly, missed the point altogether.

The crux seemed to be a misunderstanding of what is *embodied*, both in us and in the work of art, in the world we bring about for ourselves. I studied what was then thought of as the "mind–body problem" but found the philosophers too disembodied in their approach. (I had not yet come across the European philosophers – particularly Merleau-Ponty – who were aware of this difficulty and made it the centre of their work; such philosophers were ignorantly ignored in Oxford in those days.) I decided to train in medicine and get, as far as was possible, first-hand *experience* of how the brain and the body actually affect the mind, and how the mind affects the brain and the body.

After my training I went to the Maudsley, where, in 1990, I had the good fortune to hear John Cutting lecture on the right hemisphere of the brain, a subject on which he could fairly be said to be a world authority and on which he had just published an important book (Cutting, 1990). I was amazed. I had been taught that – as one leading neuroscientist put it – the right hemisphere was about as gifted as a chimpanzee. But it turned out, on the basis, not of speculation, but of painstaking observation of what happened to people when something went wrong with the right hemisphere, that it was crucial to just about everything we are and do – which is why the prospects for subjects with right-hemisphere damage are worse than for those with left-hemisphere damage, even though for most people loss of left-hemisphere function affects their speech and the use of their primary hand. It also turned out that the right hemisphere had a capacity the left hemisphere lacked for understanding the implicit, for appreciating uniqueness, for the embodied rather than the purely conceptual, for the ambiguous rather than the certain. There was even evidence that the left hemisphere had a more confident, superior attitude to whatever formed its "subject" than the right. Might this have some bearing on my dissatisfaction with the process of literary criticism? I set about gathering information.

The difference between the hemispheres

Some of you may already be thinking: not the old chestnut about the hemispheres again, surely? Despite frequent acknowledgment by many leading neuroscientists that there do seem to be fundamental differences between the hemispheres, and despite some tantalising glimpses, scientists have largely given up trying to put their finger on what these might be, piece after piece of information showing that every conceivable activity – language, visual imagery, and all the things we thought in the past distinguished right from left – is served by *both* hemispheres, not just one. The problem is that we generally look at the brain as having "functions", and if you do that, sure enough, those functions are shared by both hemispheres. But if you look, not at what the brain does, as if it were just a machine, but at how – in the sense of "in what manner" – it does it, as if it were part of a living person, some very important differences start to emerge, and a picture begins to take shape that tells us some astonishing things about ourselves and our world. My view is that the relationship between the hemispheres, like that of the master and his emissary in the story, is not symmetrical. Each needs the other; each has an important role to play.

But those roles are not equal – one depends more on the other and needs to be aware of that fact. So I am not going to argue anything as facile as that the left hemisphere is "mistaken" in what it sees or what it values. It is not: but its vision is necessarily limited. The problem comes with its unawareness of that fact.

The first question has to be: why is the brain divided at all? If the whole purpose of the brain is to make connections, and if, as many believe, consciousness arises, in some yet to be specified manner, from the sheer interconnectedness of such a vast array of neurones, why chop it down the middle? It could have evolved as a single mass. But, in fact, hemisphere divisions go right down the phylogenetic tree. So whatever it is for, it must operate, not just for man, but also for animals and birds. What is that?

And, taking a closer look at the brain, why is it that the human brain is asymmetrical? There is a bump on the left side towards the back, which has traditionally been associated with the development of language. What is less well known is that there is a bump at the front on the right, too, as if the brain had been given a fairly sharp tweak clockwise from below. What on earth is that about?

Well, the bump on the left is already more of a puzzle than it seems. In the first place, it can't just be that in man language needed to be all in one place and, having to be *somewhere*, just happened to set up residence in the left hemisphere, where it caused the cortex to expand. For a start, as neuroscience has explained to us, everything – and that includes language – goes on in both hemispheres. Important aspects of language are served by the right hemisphere, too, so it can't be a matter of keeping it all "under one roof". In any case, it turns out that chimps and the great apes in general also have this bump on the left, even though they lack language in the human sense. And examination of the skulls of humans from long before language developed also show it. So it must be for something else. What was that?

You may say, "it's not about anything – it's just one of those things". But that would be a very odd finding. In nature structure and function go hand in hand. A good example is that in songbirds the left hemisphere (their "speech" centre) expands during the mating season and then contracts again when they stop singing once it is over. And the right hippocampus, where we store what we know about visuospatial exploration of the environment, grows larger in London cabbies when they take "the Knowledge". So we should assume that structure has meaning in terms of function.

Perhaps it has to do with handedness, then. But why do we have handedness at all? Skill acquisition is not like putting books on a shelf: that the more are put on one end, the more they will fall off the other. No, we could have had two equally skilful hands. And once again, while apes do have the left-sided bump, they don't exhibit handedness in the same way as we do – so it cannot be that, either. The plot thickens when you realise that the relative advantage of the left hemisphere/right hand is not, after all, the result of an overall increase in function in the left hemisphere, but of a *deliberate handicapping* of the right. There are several strands of research that demonstrate that quite clearly. It looks as if our conventional explanations just don't stand up.

Equally clearly, language and dominance of the right hand, now that we have them, are remarkably closely associated in the left hemisphere, and they have a great deal in common. For example, we use them both to *grasp* things, as we say. They must play a part in the story: it's just that they cannot be the cause. That must lie elsewhere, and language and handedness must be the "symptoms", rather than the explanation, of hemisphere differences.

The divided brain and the evolution of language

If we come to look at the evolution of language, we find further puzzles. Why do we have language at all? Surely, in order to communicate. And if not that, then at least to think. But neither of these propositions is true.

The fact that humans can speak is dependent on the evolution, not just of the brain, but of the articulating apparatus – the larynx, the tongue and so on – and of respiratory control. That is why birds can imitate human speech, whereas apes, our nearest relatives, cannot: birds have the necessary equipment, in order to be able to sing. Through some fascinating detective work we can tell from looking at human skeletons when it was that the necessary developments in control of the tongue and larynx, and of the muscles of respiration, developed. That turns out to be from a time long before – from other evidence – we believe we developed language. So what were these developments for?

The answer, according to many anthropologists, appears to have been: in order to sing. That might sound odd, because we are used to thinking of music as a bit peripheral. But in fact the "music" of speech – in the sense of the intonation and all that is not "just" the content, coupled with other forms of non-verbal communication – constitutes the majority of what it is we communicate, when we do. Denotative language is not necessary for I–thou communication. Music is largely right-hemisphere-dependent, and the aspects of speech that enable us truly to understand the meaning of an utterance at a higher level – including intonation, irony, metaphor, and the meaning of an utterance in context – are still served by the right hemisphere. Denotative language becomes necessary when we have projects: when we need to communicate about a third party, or about things that are not present at the time. It expands immeasurably our capacity for manipulation – what one might call "I–it" communication. It is therefore, necessary, not for communication in itself, but for a certain *kind* of communication. Equally, there is a mass of evidence that we do not need language to think, even to conceptualise. One rather wonderful example is that, believe it or not, pigeons can distinguish between a Picasso and a Monet, without having any language in which to do it (Cerella, 1980; Matsukawa, Inoue, & Jitsumori, 2004; Watanabe, Sakamoto, & Wakita, 1995). But we also know that tribes that do not have numbers above "three" can calculate perfectly well to much larger numbers and have a grasp of concepts they cannot put into words. Language is not necessary for thinking, just for certain *kinds* of thinking. What was it for, then?

My view is that language and the hand have a certain common agenda – that is, they enable us to *grasp* things: to pin them down and make them useful. And we cannot deny that they have done that in spades. They have helped us to use the world and, by doing so, to develop many of the things of which we are most justly proud, the fruits of civilisation. But there is a price for this kind of approach to the world, and that brings us back to the question why the hemispheres are separated.

The nature of attention

Let's go back to birds and what we call the lower animals. What do we know about hemisphere differences there? The first thing one can say is that they seem to underwrite different kinds of attention. Attention may sound a bit boring, but it isn't at all. It is not just another "cognitive function" – it is actually nothing less than the way in which we relate to the world. And it doesn't just dictate the *kind* of relationship we have with whatever it is: it dictates *what it is that we come to have a relationship with.*

In order to stay alive, birds have to solve a conundrum: they need to be able to feed and watch out for predators simultaneously. How are you to focus closely on what you are doing when you are trying to pick out that grain of seed from the grit on which it lies while, at the same time, keeping the broadest possible open attention to whatever may be, in order to avoid being eaten? It's a bit like trying to pat your head while rubbing your stomach at the same time – only worse, because it is impossible. What we know is that the difference in attention between the hemispheres makes the apparently impossible possible. Birds pay narrowly focused attention with their right eye (left hemisphere) to what they are eating, while keeping their left eye (right hemisphere) open for predators. At the same time, birds and animals use their left eye (right hemisphere) in forming bonds with others of their kind. And this difference is preserved as we evolve. In fact, it seems that the left hemisphere specialises in a sort of piecemeal attention that helps us to make use of the world, but in doing so it alters our relationship with it. Equally, the right hemisphere subserves a broad, open attention that enables us to see ourselves connected to – and, in the human case, to empathise with – whatever is other than ourselves.

These kinds of attention are mutually incompatible, though we need to be able to employ both simultaneously. In humans, because of the development of the frontal lobes, which enable us to stand back from the world, the need for specialisation becomes greater. As we stand back, we can see the world either as separate from ourselves, as something we can *use*, or as quite the opposite – as connected to ourselves more deeply: we can see others, for the first time, as beings like ourselves, the ground of empathy. Being able to represent the world artificially – to map it conceptually, substituting tokens for things, like the general's map at army HQ – enables us to have an overall strategy; and this is what language achieves. But it inhibits us from being *there*, in the experiential world. It places us at one remove from things. So for humans the need to have both ways of understanding the world, and yet keeping them apart, is paramount. And it turns out that in humans the corpus callosum, the band of tissue that connects the hemispheres, while it does both connect and inhibit, is more involved with the process of inhibition, with keeping things separate.

What is the left-hemisphere expansion in apes for, then? It has to do with their capacity to form concepts, in order the better to manipulate the world. And so it is in humans, where it is also related to our capacity for language and, literally, to manipulation with the right hand. And the bump at the front on the right in humans, and in some apes, is associated with a whole array of "functions" that distinguish us from other animals and relate to our capacity for empathy: in intimate connection with the right hemisphere as a whole, it plays a significant part in imagination, creativity, the capacity for religious awe, music, dance, poetry, art, love of nature, a moral sense, a sense of humour and the ability to change our minds. The ways in which hemisphere differences affect what each hemisphere "does" are profound.

Unfortunately, though the hemispheres need to cooperate, they find themselves in competition, simply because the left hemisphere's take on things is such that it thinks it knows it all, while it *cannot* be aware of what the right hemisphere knows. Each needs the other, but the left hemisphere is more dependent on the right than the right is on the left. Yet it thinks exactly the opposite and believes that it can "go it alone". I believe the battle between the hemispheres (which is only a battle from the left hemisphere's point of view) explains the shape of the history of ideas in the West and explains the predicament we find ourselves in today.

How our divided brain constructs the world

Let's return to attention. As has been noted, attention is the basis of our experience of the world. It is not a "function" alongside other functions, but the foundation for having a world at all in which those "functions" can be exercised. And although it is true that what it is we are attending to determines the type of attention we pay to it, it is also importantly true that the type of attention we pay determines *what it is we see*. The way reality comes into being for us is like the famous picture by M. C. Escher of hands that draw hands.

So what has the exponential growth in brain research over recent years actually revealed about hemisphere differences? And what sort of a world does each create for us? Here I am going to have to summarise in almost telegraphically compressed form what we know. All I can say is that the evidence is, in my view, both extensive and convincing, and those who are interested will find the relevant research given in detail in *The Master and his Emissary*.

As if to confirm that there is something quite distinct about the ways the hemispheres work, we might just note that there are differences in their structure and function at the most basic level. The right hemisphere is longer, wider, and generally larger as well as heavier than the left: a finding that applies to all social mammals.

The hemispheres also differ in their sensitivity to particular neurotransmitters and neurohormones, as well as in neuronal architecture and organisation, in ways that make sense in terms of their neuropsychological differences.

In the first place, the nature of right-hemisphere attention means that whatever we experience comes to us first – it "presences" to us in unpreconceived freshness – in the right hemisphere. New experience of all kinds – whether it be music, words, imaginary constructs, objects in the environment, even skills – comes to us first from the right hemisphere and is dealt with by the left hemisphere only later, once it becomes familiar. The

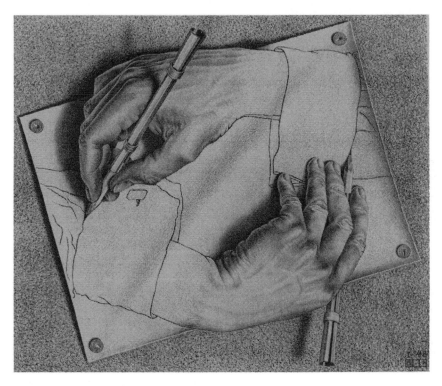

Figure 2.1 "Drawing Hands" by M. C. Escher.
Reproduced by permission of the M. C. Escher Company

right hemisphere is better at making connections between things: it tends to see things whole, whereas the left hemisphere sees the parts. This has further consequences. The left hemisphere tends to see things more in the abstract, the right hemisphere sees them more embedded in the real-world context in which they occur. As a corollary, the right hemisphere seems better able to appreciate actually existing things in all their uniqueness, while the left hemisphere schematises and generalises things into categories. But since much of what matters in experience depends ultimately on not being snatched from the context in which alone it has meaning, this is a vastly significant difference. All artistic and spiritual experience – perhaps everything truly important – can only be implicit; language, in making things explicit, reduces everything to the same worn coinage and, as Nietzsche said, makes the uncommon common.

There is a mass of evidence that the left hemisphere is better attuned to tools and to whatever is inanimate, mechanical, machine-like, and which it itself has made: such things are understandable in their own terms, because they were put together by it, piece by piece, and they are ideally suited to this kind of understanding. In contrast, the right hemisphere is adapted to dealing with living things, which are flexible, organic, constantly changing, and which it has not made. The right hemisphere alone appears to be able to appreciate the organic wholeness of a flowing structure that changes over time, as in fact all living things are; and, indeed, almost all aspects of the appreciation of time are in the right hemisphere. By contrast, the left hemisphere sees time as a succession of points and sees flow as a succession of static moments, rather like the still frames of a ciné film. Everything, including living wholes, is put together from bits; and if there are no clear bits, it will invent them.

It is therefore not surprising that the right hemisphere is far more important than the left for the appreciation of music – which is organic, which flows, which needs to be appreciated as a whole, and which exists almost entirely in "betweenness". The left hemisphere can appreciate rhythm, as long as it is simple, but little else: melody, timbre, and, especially, harmony are all largely right-hemisphere-dependent, as are complex rhythms, with cross-beats and syncopations. (Professional musicians are an exception to this right-hemisphere dependency, for a number of possible reasons that are interesting in themselves – see *The Master and his Emissary*, McGilchrist, 2009, p. 75.)

The visual equivalent of harmony could be said to be depth of the visual field; the sense of depth is also largely right-hemisphere-dependent, in keeping with the right hemisphere's world as one from which we are not isolated, but with which we stand in an important relationship. The left hemisphere, on the other hand, tends to see things as flat, detached from us, as though projected onto a screen.

While both hemispheres are involved in the expression and appreciation of emotion, the majority of our emotional life depends on the right hemisphere. The one emotion that is robustly demonstrated to be more associated with the left hemisphere is anger, though emotions that are superficial, conscious or willed may be subserved by the left hemisphere. We express more with the left side of the face, which is governed by the right hemisphere; the left hemisphere cannot read emotional facial expression or understand or remember emotional material as well as the right. In fact, the recognition of faces, discriminating their uniqueness, interpreting their expressions, are all largely dependent on the right hemisphere. Above all, the right hemisphere is more empathetic: its stance towards others is less competitive and more attuned to compassion and fellow feeling. Although it can deal well with the entire range of emotions, it is far better attuned to sadness than the left hemisphere. The close relatedness between empathy and the capacity for sadness has indeed been confirmed by studies in children.

The right hemisphere is more interested in what has personal relevance "for me", the left hemisphere in what is impersonal. But it is still the right hemisphere that is better able to understand what is going on in other people's heads, and to empathise, than the left hemisphere, which in these respects is relatively autistic. Our sense of our self is complex, but again the sense of ourselves as beings with a past and a future, as single beings with an enduring story over time, is dependent on the right hemisphere. (Narrative is appreciated by the right hemisphere, whereas the left hemisphere sees a mass of discrete episodes, which it often gets out of sequence.) The sense of ourselves as identified with our conscious will may be more subserved by the left hemisphere.

That our embodied nature enters into everything we do – not just our actions, or even our feelings, but our ability to reason, philosophise or engage in science – is something of which we have become more aware in the last hundred years. The hemispheres have different ways of understanding the body. Only the right hemisphere has a whole-body image; the left hemisphere sees the body as an assemblage of parts and as if it were an object in space alongside other objects, rather than a mode of existence. For the right hemisphere, we live the body; for the left, we live *in* it, rather as we drive a car. Reasoning is by no means confined to the left hemisphere, though sequential analysis largely is. Deductive reasoning, many kinds of mathematical procedures and problem-solving, and the phenomenon of sudden insight into the nature of a complex construct seem to be underwritten by the right hemisphere – in fact, by areas that cognitive science tells us are also involved in the "processing" of emotion.

The intuitive moral sense is closely bound up with empathy for others and seems to depend on part of the right frontal cortex that is dysfunctional in psychopaths. Above all, the left hemisphere is over-optimistic and unrealistically positive in its self-appraisal; it is in denial about its short-comings, unreasonably certain that it understands things of which it has little knowledge, and disinclined to change its mind. By contrast, the right hemisphere sees more but is far more inclined to self-doubt, is more uncertain of what it knows – and it has no voice, since the motor speech centre (though, importantly, not all of language) lies in the left hemisphere.

If one had to characterise the difference overall, it is something like this. Experience is forever in motion, ramifying and unpredictable. In order for us to *know* anything at all, that thing must have enduring properties. If all things flow and one can never step into the same river twice – Heraclitus's phrase is, I believe, a brilliant evocation of the core reality of the right hemisphere's world – one will always be taken unawares by experience: since nothing is ever being repeated, nothing can ever be known. We have to find a way of fixing it as it flies, stepping back from the immediacy of experience, stepping outside the flow. Hence the brain has to attend to the world in two completely different ways, and in so doing to bring two different worlds into being. In the one, that of the right hemisphere, we *experience* the live, complex, embodied world of individual, always unique, beings, forever in flux, a net of interdependencies, forming and reforming wholes, a world with which we are deeply connected. In the other, that of the left hemisphere, we "experience" our experience in a special way: a "re-presented" version of it, containing now static, separable, bounded, but essentially fragmented entities, grouped into classes on which predictions can be based. This kind of attention isolates, fixes and makes each thing explicit by bringing it under the spotlight of attention. In doing so it renders things inert, mechanical, lifeless. But it also enables us for the first time to know, and consequently to learn and to make things. This gives us power.

These two aspects of the world are not symmetrically opposed. They are not equivalent, for example, to the "subjective" and "objective" points of view, concepts that are themselves a product of, and already reflect, one particular way of being in the world – which, in fact, importantly, already reflect a "view" of the world, such as only the left hemisphere can take. The distinction I am trying to make is between, on the one hand, the way in which we experience the world pre-reflectively, before we have had a chance to "view" it at all or to divide it up into bits – a world in which what has later come to be thought of as subjective and objective are held in a suspension that embraces each potential "pole" and their togetherness, together – and, on the other, the world we are more used to thinking of, in which subjective and objective appear as separate poles. At its simplest, a world where there is "betweenness", and one where there is not. These are not different ways of *thinking about* the world: they are different ways of *being in* the world. And their difference is not symmetrical, but fundamentally asymmetrical.

Above I suggested that we have developed language not for communication, not even for thinking, but to enable a certain type of functional manipulation of the world. Language is like the general's map at HQ: a *representation* of the world. It is no longer present, but literally "re-presented" after the fact. What it delivers is a useful fiction.

I believe the essential difference between the right hemisphere and the left hemisphere is that the right hemisphere pays attention to the Other: to whatever it is that exists apart from ourselves, with which it sees itself in profound relation. It is deeply attracted to, and given life by, the relationship, the betweenness, that exists with this Other. By contrast, the left hemisphere pays attention to the virtual world that it has created, which is self-consistent but self-contained, ultimately disconnected from the Other, making it powerful – but also curiously impotent, because it is ultimately only able to operate on, and to know, itself.

The primacy of the right hemisphere

You might say: OK, here are two different ways of conceiving the world: but how do you know that they are not equally valid? I say that they are both very important – both, in fact, essential for our ability to lead civilised lives – but not equally valid. And there are many reasons for this.

In the first place, it is interesting that, in the late nineteenth and the twentieth centuries, both mathematics and physics (for example, Cantor, Boltzmann, Gödel, Bohr) and philosophy (I am here thinking particularly of the American pragmatists, Dewey and James, and the European phenomenologists, Husserl, Heidegger, Scheler, Merleau-Ponty and the later Wittgenstein), though starting absolutely from the premise of the left hemisphere that sequential analysis will lead us to the truth, have ended up with results that approximate far more closely – and in fact confirm the validity of – the right hemisphere's way of understanding the world, *not* that of the left. That is in itself a remarkable fact, since generally speaking the preconceptions with which you start will determine where you end.

But there are other indications. Broad vigilant attention must come before we can focus on one part of the field. We see the whole before we see the parts, rather than putting the whole together from the parts. We experience everything at first with the right hemisphere, not with the left. Language originates in the body and is implicit: it does not function at the abstract level, as something explicit. Affect is primary, not the result of calculation based on cognitive evaluation of the parts. As Libet (1985) has demonstrated, the unconscious will, more closely related to right-hemisphere functioning, is well ahead of anything our explicit verbalising consciousness can be aware of (Kornhuber & Decke, 1965). Careful analysis of the relationship between speech and gesture shows that both thought and its expression actually originate in the right hemisphere, not in the left. Re-presentation necessarily relies on earlier "presencing". And even the mode of functioning of the nervous system itself is more right-hemisphere-congruent than left-hemisphere-congruent.

What the left hemisphere offers is, then, a valuable but intermediate process, one of "unpacking" what is there and handing it back to the right hemisphere, where it can once again be integrated into the experiential whole, much as the painstaking fragmentation and analysis of a sonata in practice is reintegrated by the pianist in performance at a level where he or she must no longer be aware of it.

That, at any rate, is how the two should work together: the emissary reporting back to the master, who alone can see the broader picture. But the self-consistent rationalism of the left hemisphere has convinced it that it does not need to concern itself with what the right hemisphere knows: it believes it has the whole story itself. And it has three great advantages. First, it has control of the voice and the means of argument: the three Ls – language, logic and linearity – are all ultimately under left-hemisphere control. It is like being the Berlusconi of the brain: a political heavyweight who has control of the media. Of course we tend to listen more to what it has to say. Second, the self-consistent world of pure theory and ideas is like a hall of mirrors: all attempts to escape are deflected back within. The main paths that might have led us to something beyond the intuitive wisdom embodied in tradition, the experience of the natural world, arts, the body and religion are all emptied of force by the abstracting, rationalising, ironising impact of the world of self-consistent re-presentations that is yielded by the left hemisphere. The living presence is no longer accessible. And, third, there is a tendency for positive feedback to come into play: instead of redressing the balance, we just get more of the same.

Which brings me to the reason we cannot just view this as of academic interest. For I believe the world in which we live has come increasingly to reflect the view of the left hemisphere alone.

The triumph of the left hemisphere

In the second part of *The Master and his Emissary* ("How the Brain Has Shaped Our World"), I look at the evolution of Western culture, beginning in the ancient world with the extraordinary efflorescence of culture in sixth-century BC Athens, where, it seems to me, the two hemispheres worked in harmony as never before or since; then at the decline associated with the rise of the left hemisphere in the late Roman empire; and then, in turn, at the seismic shifts that we call the Renaissance, the Reformation, the Enlightenment, Romanticism, the Industrial Revolution, Modernism and Postmodernism. I believe that they represent a power struggle between these two ways of experiencing the world, and that we have ended up prisoners of just one – that of the left hemisphere alone.

Let's do a thought experiment. What would it look like if the left hemisphere came to be the sole purveyor of our reality?

First of all, the whole picture would be unattainable: the world would become a heap of bits. Its only meaning would come through its capacity to be used. More narrowly focused attention would lead to an increasing specialisation and technicalising of knowledge. This, in turn, would promote the substitution of information, and information gathering, for knowledge, which comes through experience. Knowledge, in its turn, would seem more "real" than what one might call wisdom, which would seem too nebulous, something never to be grasped. Knowledge that has come through experience, and the practical acquisition of embodied skill, would become suspect, appearing either a threat or simply incomprehensible. It would be replaced by tokens or representations – formal systems, to be evidenced by paper qualifications.

There would be a simultaneous increase in both abstraction and reification, whereby the human body itself, and we ourselves, as well as the material world and the works of art we have created to understand it, would both become more conceptual and yet be seen as mere things. The world as a whole would become more virtualised and our experience of it would be increasingly through meta-representations of one kind or another; fewer people would find themselves doing work involving contact with anything in the real, "lived" world, rather than with plans, strategies, paperwork, management and bureaucratic procedures.

There would be a complete loss of the sense of uniqueness. Increasingly, the living would be modelled on the mechanical. This would also have an effect on the way bureaucracies would deal with human situations and with society at large. "Either/or" would tend to be substituted for matters of degree, and a certain inflexibility would result.

There would be a derogation of higher values and a cynicism about their status. Morality would come to be judged at best on the basis of utilitarian calculation, at worst on the basis of enlightened self-interest.

The impersonal would come to replace the personal. There would be a focus on material things at the expense of the living. Social cohesion and the bonds between person and person – and, just as importantly, between person and place, the context in which each person belongs – would be neglected, perhaps actively disrupted, as both inconvenient and incomprehensible to the left hemisphere acting on its own. There would be a depersonalisation of the relationships between members of society, and in society's relationship with its members. Exploitation rather than cooperation would, explicitly or not, be the default relationship between human individuals and between humanity and the rest of the world. Resentment would lead to an emphasis on uniformity and equality, not as just one desirable to be balanced with others, but as the ultimate desirable, transcending all others.

The left hemisphere cannot trust and is prone to paranoia. It needs to feel in control. We would expect government to become obsessed with issues of security above all else, and to seek total control.

Reasonableness would be replaced by rationality, and perhaps the very concept of reasonableness might become unintelligible. There would be a complete failure of common sense, since it is intuitive and relies on both hemispheres working together. One would expect a loss of insight, coupled with an unwillingness to take responsibility, and this would reinforce the left hemisphere's tendency to a perhaps dangerously unwarranted optimism. There would be a rise in intolerance and inflexibility, an unwillingness to change track or to change one's mind.

We would expect there to be a resentment of – and a deliberate under-cutting of – the sense of awe or wonder: Weber's "disenchanted" world. Religion would seem to be mere fantasy. Art would be conceptualised, cerebralised; beauty would be ironised out of existence.

As a culture, we would come to discard tacit forms of knowing altogether. There would be a remarkable difficulty in understanding non-explicit meaning and a downgrading of non-verbal, non-explicit communication. Concomitant with this would be a rise in explicitness, backed up by ever-increasing legislation – what de Tocqueville predicted as a "network of small complicated rules" that would eventually strangle democracy (de Toc-queville, 2003, pp. 723–724). As it became less possible to rely on a shared and intuitive moral sense or on implicit contracts between individuals, such rules would grow ever more burdensome. There would be less tolerance for and appreciation of the value of ambiguity. We would tend to be over-explicit in the language we use to approach art and religion, accompanied by a loss in their vital, implicit, metaphorical power.

Does that ring any bells? In terms of the fable with which I began, the emissary, insightless as ever, appears to believe it can see everything, do everything, alone. But it cannot: on its own it is like a zombie, a sleepwalker ambling straight towards the abyss, whistling a happy tune.

References

Cerella, J. (1980). The pigeon's analysis of pictures. *Pattern Recognition, 12* (1): 1–6.

Cutting, J. (1990). *The Right Cerebral Hemisphere and Psychiatric Disorders.* Oxford: Oxford University Press.

de Tocqueville, A. (2003). *Democracy in America,* trans. H. Reeve & E. W. Plaag. New York: Barnes & Noble.

Kornhuber, H. H., & Decke, L. (1965). Hirnpotentialänderun-gen bei Willkürbewe-gungen und passiven Bewegungen des Menschen: Bereitschaftspotential und reaffer-ente Potentiale. *Pflügers Archiv European Journal of Physiology, 284*: 1–17.

Libet, B. (1985). Unconscious cerebral initiative and the role of the conscious will in voluntary action. *Behavioural and Brain Sciences, 8* (4): 529–539.

Matsukawa, A., Inoue, S., & Jitsumori, M. (2004). Pigeon's recognition of cartoons: Effects of fragmentation, scrambling, and deletion of elements. *Behavioural Processes, 65* (1): 25–34.

McGilchrist, I. (2009). *The Master and His Emissary: The Divided Brain and the Making of the Western World.* New Haven, CT: Yale University Press.

Needleman, J. (2009). *What Is God?* New York: Penguin.

Rose-Stockwell, T. (2017). This is how your fear and outrage are being sold for profit: The story of how one metric has changed the way you see the world. *The Mission,* 15 July. https://medium.com/the-mission/the-enemy-in-our-feeds-e86511488de

Watanabe, S., Sakamoto, J., & Wakita, M. (1995). Pigeons' discrimination of paintings by Monet and Picasso. *Journal of the Experimental Analysis of Behaviour, 63* (2): 165–174.

Chapter 3

Social and emotional laterality

Louis Cozolino

Introduction: the discovery of the brain

Honestly, when was the last time you thought about your brain? Except for the occasional headache that feels like it is in the brain, we don't even remember we have brains. In essence, a well-functioning brain is invisible, which may account for why, at this point in our history, we know more about the movement of the planets than the workings of our brains. In fact, not too long ago, anatomists and physicians thought that the seat of consciousness resided in the heart, with the brain serving as the body's air conditioner, cooling the blood as it passed through.

The brain's deeper significance is infinitely more complex than anything scientists have ever encountered. Studying the brain is like exploring a vast and ancient country with diverse landscapes, cultures, and customs. Our brains defy reduction to simple cause-and-effect relationships and anatomical boundaries. Like complex cultures, many of the interactions are subtle to the point of invisibility. To understand a culture, you need to be immersed in it and stay alert for small clues that may carry deep significance. Even a subtle diversion of gaze in the town square can tell the story of two people or two nations. Adding to this complexity is the fact that each of our brains is a unique interplay of our convoluted evolutionary history and the millions of personal experiences that shape it throughout life.

Our brains are built in the enigmatic interface between experience and genetics, where nature and nurture become one (Crabbe & Phillips, 2003; LeDoux, 2003). At first, genes serve as a template to organize the brain and trigger critical and sensitive periods; later, they orchestrate the ongoing transcription of experience into genetic material. Through the biochemical alchemy of template and transcription genetics, experience becomes flesh, attachment takes material form, and culture is passed through a group and carried forward through time.

Like every living system – from single neurons to complex ecosystems – the brain depends on interactions with others for survival. Each brain is dependent on the scaffolding of caretakers and loved ones for its growth and well-being. So we begin with what we know: *The brain is a social organ of adaptation built through interactions with others.* To write the story of this journey, we must begin our guidebook with the understanding that *there are no single human brains – brains only exist within networks of other brains.*

Scientists have had to expand their thinking to grasp the idea that individual *neurons or single human brains do not exist in nature.* Without mutually stimulating interactions, people and neurons wither and die. In neurons this process is called apoptosis; in humans it is called depression, grief, and suicide. From birth until death, each of us needs others who seek us out, show interest in discovering who we are, and help us feel safe. Thus, understanding the brain requires knowledge of the healthy, living brain embedded within a community of other brains: *Relationships are our natural habitat.* Because therapists, teachers, and parents intuitively grasp this profound reality, just as laboratory scientists often do not, we decidedly "non-science" types who teach preschool, do psychotherapy, or study group behaviour have a great deal to offer neuroscience. We are in a position to help research scientists know where to look as they explore how the brain grows, learns, and thrives throughout life.

The fact that the brain is such a highly specialized social organ of adaptation is both good news and bad news. The good news is that if unexpected challenges emerge, our brains have a greater chance to adapt and survive. When good-enough parenting combines with good-enough genetic programming, our brains are shaped in ways that benefit us throughout life. And the bad news? We are just as capable of adapting to *unhealthy* environments and *pathological* caretakers. The resulting adaptations may help us to survive a traumatic childhood but impede healthy development later in life. The family is the primary environment to which our young brains adapt, and our parents' unconscious minds are our first reality. Because the first few years of life are a period of exuberant brain development, early experience has a disproportionate impact on the development of neural systems. In this way, early negative interpersonal experiences become a primary source of the symptoms for which people seek relief in psychotherapy.

Social and emotional laterality

Parents, educators, and therapists – those of us who should be most concerned with shaping minds – have traditionally paid little attention to the brain. I have heard therapists say that psychotherapy is an art and that the brain is irrelevant to their work. I would respond, as with any art, that a thorough knowledge of our materials and methods can only enhance our skills and capabilities. The brain is a treasure trove of information about where we have come from, what we are capable of, and why we act as we do. It holds many secrets about how we can know ourselves better and improve the way we do psychotherapy, teach, and parent our children.

More than a century ago, the left cortex was dubbed the *dominant* hemisphere because of its leading role in language. Damage to an area in the left frontal lobe (called *Broca's area*) resulted in a consistent disturbance in language. It was this successful brain–behaviour connection upon which the fledgling field of neurology staked its first claim. It was also the first solid piece of evidence that specific functions might exist in distinct areas, lending support to what was then called the *localizationist* theory of brain functioning. We have learned a great deal about the brain during the past century, and our ideas about the roles of each of the hemispheres and their working relationship with one another have become increasingly sophisticated. Although it remains true that the left hemisphere usually takes the lead in semantic and conscious processing, social and emotional dominance are functions that lean toward the right.

As the story of the brain has expanded, we have discovered that mammals are characterized by right-hemisphere control of emotion, bodily experience, and autonomic processes. This asymmetry is found not just in the cerebral cortex but in subcortical and brainstem structures as well. The right cortex is also far more densely connected with subcortical regions than is the left (Shapiro et al., 1997; Stuss & Alexander, 1999). For example, the social engagement system utilizes a network of autonomic and emotional control in the right cortex, the right central nucleus of the amygdala, and the right-sided nuclei of the hypothalamus (Porges, 2011). Because the right brain is grounded in bodily and emotional experience, it serves as the infrastructure of many primitive components of social brain functioning. The experience of a personal emotional self, as opposed to the social self, also appears to be primarily organized in the right hemisphere (Keenan et al., 2000).

Right-brain functions often appear to parallel Freud's notion of the unconscious. They develop earlier and are guided by emotional and bodily reactions, and their nonlinear mode of processing allows for multiple overlapping realities. These and other characteristics make right-brain functioning similar to Freud's conception of the primary process thinking during childhood and later in the logic, or illogic, of dreams. Perhaps most significant, the right brain responds to negative emotional stimuli prior to conscious awareness. Thus unconscious emotional processing based on past experiences invisibly guides our thoughts, feelings, and behaviours (Kimura et al., 2004). The phenomena of projection and transference – central to Freud's case for the existence and influence of the unconscious – are generated within these same neural networks. Because the right brain develops first, it organizes and stores many early social and emotional experiences that can emerge in later relationships, especially when we are under stress.

The bias against left-handedness across many cultures reflects an intuitive understanding of the relationship of the left hand (right brain) to the more primitive, uncivilized, and dark aspects of our nature. Some of these biases date back to prehistory, when the left hemisphere may have exerted less control over the right, leading that side of us to be less "polite" and more dangerous. By offering the right hand in greeting, early humans may have been more likely to speak and behave in a "civil" manner, and less likely to act out their primitive and dangerous impulses. Five-thousand-year-old cave drawings depicting right-handed Hunters suggest that the bias toward right-handedness existed even then (Coren & Porac, 1977).

Although we can only speculate about the reasons for the evolution of hemispheric specialization, it obviously provides increased neural "real estate" for the development of new skills and abilities, instead of having redundant networks performing identical functions. The dominance of the right hemisphere for bodily and emotional functioning and its ability to process this information reflexively and unconsciously have freed the left cortex to attend more to the environment and to engage in abstract reasoning. Meanwhile, the increasing ability of the left hemisphere to filter and inhibit input from the right has enhanced the dissociation between the cognitive and emotional processing of the left and right sides of the brain.

While the increasing inhibitory ability of the left hemisphere has led to greater cognitive abilities, it also resulted in a capacity to separate mind, body, and emotions. Experiencing the world from high atop the left hemisphere led Descartes to equate human existence with thinking, much to the detriment of psychology and neurology. Thus we have found that with specialization and increasingly complex functioning, the "healthy" brain has become vulnerable to the types of dissociation we see in psychological disturbances.

Development

Just as the hemispheres grew increasingly different from each other during primate evolution, their developmental time lines have taken divergent paths. The right hemisphere experiences a growth spurt during the first 18 months of life, whereas areas of the left are held back for later-developing abilities (Chiron et al., 1997; Gould, 1977). During these critical 18 months, the child learns hand-eye coordination, crawling, and walking – all while becoming acquainted with the world. Countless early interactions shape right-brain circuitry so we can recognize and react to the people around us, our sense of safety and danger, and our ability to regulate our emotions. Although the social brain is capable of learning throughout life, stable attachment patterns are apparent by the end of the first year (Ainsworth et al., 1978).

The orbital medial prefrontal cortex (OMPFC), along with the anterior cingulate and insula cortices, are the first regions of the cortex to develop and are all larger in the right hemisphere. Richly connected with subcortical networks of learning, memory, and emotion, these right-biased structures are densely connected with the body, modulating vagal tone and HPA functioning (Barbas, 1995; Price, 1999; Porges, 2003; Sullivan & Gratton, 2002).

These connections reflect the role of the OMPFC as the executive centre of the right-hemispheric networks of attachment, social relationships, affect regulation, and higher-level input into bodily homeostasis. These systems are shaped during childhood in an experience-dependent manner through the attunement and connections of the right hemispheres of parent and child.

The linking up of right hemispheres is accomplished through eye contact, facial expressions, soothing vocalizations, caresses, and exciting exchanges. Sensitive caretakers learn to respond to their children's responses and synchronized engagement and disengagement. As children and caretakers move in and out of attunement, the cycle of joining, separating, and reuniting becomes the central aspect of developing psychobiological regulation. Caretakers intuitively slacken their scaffolding as their children's self-regulatory capacities increase. Through these separations and reunions, children slowly learn that they can survive on their own, that caretakers return, and that they (children) have some ability to regulate their bodily and emotional states.

Damage to the right hemisphere compromises our ability to interpret the significance of facial expressions, hand gestures, and tone of voice (Blonder et al., 1991; Searleman, 1977). Right-OMPFC lesions result in difficulties in reading and reacting to the expressions of others (Zald & Kim, 2001). Deprivation of visual input to the right hemisphere during infancy results in deficits in the ability to identify faces, whereas the same lack of input to the left hemisphere results in no such deficit (Le Grand et al., 2003).

Integration

As the brain grows over the first years of life, so does the experience of self. Soon after birth, the insula and cingulate cortices begin to organize the early sense of the body and the ability to differentiate self from others. As the parietal lobes develop, an integrated sense of the self as a whole within the environment gradually takes shape. All the while, the networks of the OMPFC, cingulate, insula, amygdala, and related structures are building networks of attachment and affect regulation. In the years to come, autobiographical memory will rely on these somatic, emotional, and physical sensations to construct the stories of the self that will come to shape our conscious identities.

As the fibres of the connecting corpus callosum mature, they facilitate increased communication and integration between the two sides of the brain. The right and left hemispheres gradually come to cooperate in an analysis of both the global (right) and specific (left) aspects of our surroundings (Fink et al., 1996; Rossion et al., 2000). Thus, our emerging experience of self results from the coordination and synchrony of circuits in the right and left hemispheres. Although some circuits organize aspects of conscious awareness, most serve as the background "glue" of our experience, an interwoven network of sensory, motor, and affective circuitry. When conditions are right, all these networks integrate to provide us with the experience of a safe, coherent, and liveable inner world.

Our physical experience provides us with patterns of bodily movements, relationships between objects, and a sense of ourselves in space – a kind of sensory, motor, visceral grid – that serves as the infrastructure of our developing thought (Johnson, 1987). As children, we might repeatedly put blocks into a pail and then dump them back out. We may experience the acts of eating and drinking as putting something into our body, only to have it come back out again. We may experience ourselves disappearing into bed each night and then reappearing each morning. These repeated patterns of physical containment are used to organize and understand more abstract notions, such as when we "come out" of hiding during a game of hide and seek, when we manage to "get out" of trouble, or when we "fall in" love. Our experience and understanding of these abstract concepts are grounded in our physical experiences related to containment (Johnson, 1987). Abstract notions are tied to our bodies through metaphor, thus connecting our minds to the world through the experience of our bodies.

Countless learning experiences are organized and stored in right-hemisphere networks; these stored experiences give rise to what we call "gut feelings". Patients with OMPFC or somatosensory cortex damage have difficulty drawing upon past experiences when making decisions. They may be able to understand the points for or against a choice but lack a "feel" for the right choice that would allow them to "pull the trigger" and make a decision. It can be assumed that this final step (more visceral and emotional than cognitive) requires a "sense" of certainty that comes more from the body than from thought. This perspective has led to the idea of "somatic markers" as a kind of visceral-emotional shorthand providing unconscious input into our conscious choices (Damasio, 1994). In this sense we see that emotions derive ultimately from the physical self, we learn to access our bodily grid to locate ourselves within the world, and we ground the idea of our unique self within it.

Emotions

Whereas more primitive organisms use touch or smell to make approach/avoidance decisions, we use reflexive bodily activation and our emotions to discern whether something is positive or negative (Damasio et al., 2000; Schulkin et al., 2003). Positive emotions orient us to stay on course and explore the environment, whereas negative emotions lead us to make adjustments to our situation (Cacioppo & Gardner, 1999). Emotions are our conscious experiences and interpretations of our bodily states, involving many of the brain's neural networks (Calder et al., 2001). Because our thoughts and emotions are so interconnected, it is difficult to know if they are distinct from one another or just different aspects of the same neural processes (Damasio, 1995; Panksepp, 2003).

Still, hemispheric bias does exist with regard to emotions: The left hemisphere appears biased toward positive (approach) emotions, whereas the right seems biased toward negative (withdrawal) emotions (Canli et al., 1998; Davidson, 1992; Davidson et al., 1990; Paradiso et al., 1999). A history of depression or current depressed affect correlates with decreased left frontal activation (Henriques & Davidson, 1990, 1991). States of stress, anxiety, fear, trauma, and pain all result in heightened activation in right-sided structures (Baker & Kim, 2004; Hari et al., 1997; Rauch et al., 1996; Spivak et al., 1998; Wittling, 1997).

In response to playing a competitive game, the right amygdala is activated by losing, the left by winning (Zalla et al., 2000). Even when we watch movies, greater left frontal activation is correlated with more intense positive affect during the film and a better review afterward (Wheeler et al., 1993). Infants who tend to cry in response to maternal separation show higher right-frontal EEG activation when compared with infants who do not cry (Davidson & Fox, 1989). This same pattern of activation occurs in children of depressed mothers during the expression of negative (but not positive) emotions (Dawson et al., 1997a; Dawson et al., 1997b).

What we experience as negative emotions – those that lead us to fight, flee, or distance ourselves from something or someone – are evolutionarily more primitive than positive emotions. Positive feelings related to humour, social affiliation, and aesthetic responses have arisen as a function of an expanded neocortex (Paradiso et al., 1999; Wild et al., 2003). An unfortunate artefact of the evolution of laterality may be that the right hemisphere, biased toward negative emotions, develops first and serves as the core of self-awareness and identity (Keenan et al., 1999). To be human may be to have vulnerability toward shame, guilt, and depression. So although both sides of the brain are involved in emotion, the dominant role of the right hemisphere in defensive and negative emotions gives it emotional veto power over the left. Just as the left hemisphere can block emotional and visceral input from the right, the right hemisphere can override normal states of consciousness in reaction to threat.

Pedro – something is just not right

Pedro and I met while we were both working at a veterans' hospital. He was an engineer responsible for keeping the buildings functioning, whereas my job was to tame the chaos within. We would often chat on a shaded bench about sports, politics, or our favourite topic: the illogic of the VA (Veterans Administration) system. Once, after Pedro had been absent for a few days, I heard that he had been in a car accident. I was told that it was nothing too serious – he was just taking some time off and would be back in a week or two. When Pedro returned, we met at our usual spot. He told me that his car had been hit broadside while going through an intersection and his head had bounced off the side glass. He was still a bit black and blue, and I noticed that the left side of his face looked stiff and still, refusing to participate in the normal flux of expressions displayed on the right. "Some nerve that goes to my face is pinched or damaged," he told me. "I can't feel the left side of my face." The doctors told him it would probably clear up when the inflamed nerve settled down.

As the months went by, the left side of Pedro's face remained still. He slowly learned to adapt to chewing on the right side and wearing a cap that covered part of his face. He was a private man and wasn't comfortable sharing his struggles about his new disability. I used my interest in neurology as a way to coax him into giving me details of his experience. He appeared willing to talk as long as it was for "medical purposes". Many months after the accident, he said:

> You know, there is something about my accident that I thought you would be interested in. Ever since it happened, being sad feels different. When I feel sad or cry, or when I look at my baby and get that strong feeling of love for her, it doesn't feel the same. It's like, without my face moving, my feelings can't come all the way out, all the way to the surface.

I wondered if a lack of facial expressions on the left side of his face kept Pedro's right hemisphere from getting the feedback from facial muscles, leaving him with a sense of an incomplete experience of his emotions. Put in a slightly different way, Pedro's right brain and the left side of his face constituted a functional system for the experience and expression of emotion. With his current handicap, this system became less active and emotionally less satisfying. Fortunately, the doctors were right, and the feeling on the left side of his face gradually returned. He described it as similar to the feeling you get a few hours after having dental work done, when the anaesthesia begins to wear off. With the return of physical sensations came a fuller experience of his emotions. But what is it like for people who never have these feelings?

Alexithymia as hemispheric disconnection

The term *alexithymia* was initially used to describe the inability to put words to feelings in a group of patients with somatization disorder (Sifneos, 1975). They also seemed to have difficulties with attaining a conscious awareness of bodily experiences or internal emotional states. These individuals could sometimes recognize emotions in others but were unable to find them within themselves. It was thought that their conscious dissociation from their bodies and emotions may have been related to their many physical complaints (Apfel & Sifneos, 1979). This process paralleled what Freud and other pioneers of psychosomatic medicine thought to be the "conversion" of unexpressed negative emotions into physical symptoms.

Over the years, the definition of alexithymia expanded from being an aspect of psychosomatic illnesses to a personality style that came to include a concrete and externally oriented cognitive style, a restricted imagination, and difficulty coping with emotionally stressful situations (Bagby & Taylor, 1997; Parker et al., 2003; Salminen et al., 2006; Silberman & Weingartner, 1986; Verissimo et al., 2000; Zimmermann et al., 2005). Because this pattern of deficits is consistent with what had been seen in neurology patients with either right-hemisphere damage or a cut-off of input from the right to the left hemisphere, alexithymia has been hypothesized to be the result of an "interhemispheric transfer deficit".

The general theory rests on a dissociation of the somatic and emotional networks biased toward the right hemisphere from those primarily responsible for organizing self-awareness and language biased toward the left (Habib et al., 2003; Papciak et al., 1985; Taylor, 2000; Zeitlin et al., 1989). In line with their tendency toward greater functional lateralization, men have been found to suffer with more alexithymia and impairments in emotional understanding and imagination than have women (Bausch et al., 2011; Levant et al., 2009).

Like individuals who suffer from right hemisphere damage, people with alexithymia have difficulty describing the emotional qualities of music, remembering their dreams, and recalling emotionally laden words (Goerlich et al., 2011; Luminet et al., 2006; Meltzer & Nielsen, 2010; Parker et al., 2000; Spalletta et al., 2001). Because they tend to process social information in the left hemisphere, alexithymic individuals are often handicapped in their ability to read social-emotional information via facial expressions and tone of voice (Jessimer & Markham, 1997; Kano et al., 2003; Karlsson et al., 2008; Lane et al., 1996; McDonald & Prkachin, 1990).

Given that understanding the emotions of others depends in large part on our ability to experience and be aware of our own feelings, alexithymics have impairment in perspective taking and empathy. Consistent with the role of the basal forebrain in these abilities, they demonstrate decreased volume and activation of the right anterior cingulate cortex and decreased activation in the medial prefrontal cortex, both of which are required for conscious awareness of the physical and emotional experiences of self and others (Gundel et al., 2004; Karlsson et al., 2008; Moriguchi et al., 2005; Sturm & Levenson, 2011). Females suffering with alexithymia have been shown to have decreased gray matter volume in the key social brain regions such as the anterior cingulate, anterior insula, orbital medial prefrontal cortex, and superior temporal sulcus (Borsci et al., 2009). In addition, deficits in amygdala activation in relation to the detection of social information lead them to not remember social information and to take what they do remember less seriously (Miyaki et al., 2012).

Beneath their dispassionate surface, it appears that alexithymics are actually hypersensitive to pain, as demonstrated by higher levels of right-insula activation when they witness the pain of others (Kano et al., 2007; Moriguchi et al., 2007; Nyklíček & Vingerhoets, 2000) and higher cortisol levels in response to emotionally negative stimuli (de Timary et al., 2008; Stone & Nielson, 2001). This activation pattern within the basal forebrain of the two lower structures (amygdala and insula) being hyperactive to pain and the two higher structures (anterior cingulate cortex and orbital medial prefrontal cortex) being hypoactive in response to pain is consistent with a dissociation of bodily experience from conscious awareness (Bermond et al., 2006). Thus, it appears that the neural "disconnections" in alexithymia may include both a lateral (left–right) and vertical (top–down) component.

It has been proposed that the emotional and cognitive deficits seen in alexithymia are related to preconscious stages of sensory processing where the experience of emotions in the self and others are detoured away from conscious awareness (Pollatos & Gramann, 2011). It is possible that very early activation of the amygdala inhibits the anterior cingulate cortex (ACC) and OMPFC, blocking the somatic and emotional input provided by the insula (Aftanas et al., 2003). This would keep somatic and emotional experiences out of conscious awareness as well as increase vulnerability to physical illnesses through the inhibition of immunological functioning via high resting levels of cortisol.

Alexithymia highlights the importance of the collaboration of networks of cognitive, somatic, and emotional functioning for optimal executive functioning. In fact, alexithymic individuals have been shown to perform worse across multiple domains of executive functioning, including behavioural initiation, response inhibition, cognitive flexibility, self-monitoring, working memory, error recognition, and the ability to organize and plan for the future (Bermond et al., 2010; Koven & Thomas, 2010; Zhang et al., 2011).

From a psychological perspective, alexithymia is associated with depression, emotional exhaustion, and depersonalization (Bratis et al., 2009; Todarello et al., 1995). Depression and exhaustion would be expected consequences of an emotional disconnection. Depersonalization is often the result of chronic high levels of anxiety that can find no expression or relief. If strong negative emotions processed in the right hemisphere are unable to be integrated with conscious and semantic networks of the left, they cannot be adequately discharged or appropriately inhibited. Consistent with this formulation is the finding that children with more emotional complaints report more internalization of fear and less expressive discharge of anger (Rieffe et al., 2004).

Anger and aggression are social emotions that tend to be more aligned with the left hemisphere despite the fact that we tend to think of them as negative. It appears that while prosocial emotions are biased toward the right hemisphere, a more general idea is that the left is involved with approach interactions, including anger and aggression. This may also be why assertiveness training is often the most successful treatment for individuals with somatization and conversion disorders.

We are capable of inhibiting right anterior insula activation through the use of biofeedback, demonstrating that a psychological need to avoid bodily awareness can be physiologically established (Caria et al., 2007). The alternative route for these emotions may be a redirection into the body (internalization) and manifest as psychosomatic disorders. Compared with healthy control populations, subjects suffering from a somatoform condition are significantly more likely to show moderate to severe levels of alexithymia (De Gucht & Heiser, 2003).

The brain abnormalities found in alexithymia could be an adaptation to trauma, and higher levels of alexithymia are correlated with a history of repeated trauma (Kosten et al., 1992; Krystal, 1988; Zeitlin et al., 1993). Individuals with PTSD and alexithymia demonstrate decreased bilateral activation of the anterior cingulate cortex (ACC), anterior insular cortex (AI), and right OMPFC and increased levels of activation in right posterior cingulate and insular cortices in keeping with the increased sensory reactivity to reminders of the traumatic event (Frewen et al., 2008). On the other hand, pre-existing deficits in these central social networks could also make us more vulnerable to dangerous others due to deficits in reading social cues.

Alexithymia has been found to correlate with an avoidant attachment style, a lack of family support, less paternal care, and paternal overprotection (Bratis et al., 2009; De Rick & Vanheule, 2006; Fukunishi et al., 1997; Modestin et al., 2002; Thorberg et al., 2011). Oxytocin administration has been found to assist alexithymics in reading facial expressions (Luminet et al., 2011). The combination of overprotection and less support may result in a lack of individuation and a deficit in the development of a sense of self. The dynamics of some families may even make it dangerous to experience one's own feelings. Attending to and articulating feelings are learned abilities that require the involvement, support, and encouragement of those around us.

This may have cross-cultural implications when comparing people from more communal societies who don't necessary think of themselves as separate from significant others. These issues bring into question whether the diagnosis of alexithymia should be modified or discarded when working with individuals from specific cultures (Dion, 1996). On the other hand, while cultural and gender differences were found in alexithymia, parental emotional socialization mediated the relations between culture, gender, and alexithymia (Le et al., 2002).

The emerging picture from this research is one of right-hemisphere and subcortical dominance in the bottom-up processing of social and emotional information. More recent research is shifting our focus closer to the center of our brains as we explore the right-left biases of the medial structures of the basal forebrain. Our ability to form and sustain relationships relies on the participation and integration of right-hemispheric networks with those biased toward the left. Optimal parenting appears to result in maximal integration of right and left systems as well as a smooth balance between cortical and subcortical systems on both sides. Although our exploration of the social brain leads us to discuss many systems that are biased toward the right hemisphere, it must be kept in mind that they can function to their full potential only in dynamic balance with all other systems.

Dylan – learning to say goodbye

A few years ago Shelly called me about Dylan, her 3-year-old son. His preschool teacher had reported that Dylan had become violent toward her and some of the other children. Dylan's father, Chet, had been diagnosed with an aggressive form of cancer a year earlier and was close to death. Shelly had watched with sorrow as her husband grew sicker and pushed Dylan away. At first she had thought Chet's declining physical condition had something to do with his harsh dismissal of Dylan, but she now knew it was Chet's way of dealing with leaving his family behind. Chet told Shelly, "It will be easier for Dylan if he learns not to love me." Shelly was silent for a while before quietly adding, "That just broke my heart." She went on to tell me that over the past few months Dylan had seemed to be regressing. He was wetting his bed and having frequent nightmares and bouts of inconsolable crying. "We haven't told him what's happening to his dad," she continued, "but he knows that something is terribly wrong." We ended our first conversation by making an appointment for the following week.

At the time of our appointment, I entered the playroom to find Dylan crouching behind a chair. I observed him as he watched his mother fill out forms with my co-therapist. From time to time, he would pop up from his hiding place, shoot at his mother with an imaginary gun, and dip down again behind the chair. After introducing myself to Shelly and talking with her for a few minutes, I sat on the floor next to two toy chests. Thinking of Dylan and what toys he might like to play with, I began rummaging through the chests. As the women left for the observation room, Dylan stared at me intently from behind his chair. If he caught me looking back at him, he would huddle down and hide his eyes.

After a few unsuccessful attempts to engage him by asking questions or inviting him to play, I decided to play on my own. I wondered if, perhaps, he was showing me how it felt to be rejected and have to play alone. I tried to remember all those times in my life when I had felt rejected. If I could get into that state of mind, it might help me to connect with Dylan. He watched closely as I pulled out a toy, played with it for a while, and replaced it with another. I finally came upon a wooden train set. Putting together a few pieces of track, I began to slowly push the train forward while doing my best steam engine sound: "Choo, choo, choo, choo." Instead of getting the next piece out of the toy chest as I approached the end of the track, I said, "Choo, choo, choo. Oh, no, I'm running out of track! What am I going to do? Choo, choo, choo."

Dylan darted from his hiding place, ran to the toy chest, picked out a piece of track, attached it to the existing track, and shot back behind his chair. "Whooo, that was a close one!" I said as I continued to move the train forward. "Choo, choo, choo ..." Halfway through the new length of track, I repeated, "Oh, no!" Dylan popped out of his hiding place to repeat his heroics. This time, he smacked me on the back as he ran by.

We repeated this scenario a few more times. Dylan's smack gradually evolved into longer and longer touches as he passed. He no longer retreated behind the chair but would stand near the train waiting to add the next piece of the track. Then, as if maintaining "electricity" with home base in a game of tag, he kept one hand on my shoulder as he reached out with the other to grab new track. Finally, he planted himself in my lap and added track from there. He slowly began to giggle and squeal with delight. We spent the second half of the session like that, Dylan sitting in my lap, look-ing at the tracks he had set up, telling me stories of the other kids at pre-school, talking about his favourite toys – and, to my surprise, explaining to me what was happening at home.

Because working with young children involves symbolic play and the imagination of both therapist and child, you can never be certain of exactly what may happen in therapy. Dylan seemed angry at his mother for what I imagine was her failure to protect him from the pain and confusion he was experiencing. Through his initial actions with me, Dylan posed many ques-tions: "Am I important to you? Am I needed? Am I wanted? Am I safe? Will I survive?" For a child his age, and perhaps all of us, these questions are one and the same.

By playing by myself, I gave Dylan an opportunity to evaluate me in this strange situation. Allowing him to save the train gave Dylan the chance to demonstrate his competence and value. He found he could smack me with-out retaliation and then move closer, testing my safety and acceptance of him. Our play became a dance of bonding, trust building, and attachment. When he finally felt safe, he wanted sustained physical and verbal contact. He showed me what he had lost and what he needed from his father. Des-pite his regressive behaviours – or maybe because of them – Dylan had become very receptive to an open heart.

However, Dylan's struggle was only one element of the breakdown in his family. Besides connecting with Dylan, I wanted to help Chet say goodbye to his wife and son. I also suspected that Dylan and Shelly would need some help adjusting to their future life without Chet. Shelly was encouraged by the connection I was able to forge with Dylan and was eager to have me talk with Chet. This would be a challenge. Not only was Chet unable to leave his bed, but he wanted no part of sympathetic relatives, well-meaning rabbis, or, most especially, a touchy-feely therapist. Still, Shelly and I set up a time for me to visit with Chet, knowing that he would probably refuse to speak with me.

As I walked into his room, Chet did everything but pull the covers up over his face to avoid me. He shot a glare or two in my direction and remained silent. I felt like I was once again with Dylan in the playroom, only this time there were no toy trains to help us bond. Certain that Chet had already heard all the clichés, platitudes, and comforting remarks from others, I was careful to avoid my impulse to say them. After sitting quietly for a few minutes, I began telling him about my sessions with Dylan and how fond I had become of him. I also told him what I thought was going on in his son's heart and what Dylan needed from him.

Chet began crying softly, but his sadness quickly changed to anger. He was angry at death, at his friends, his wife, his doctors, and God. He even admitted being angry at Dylan for his youth, health, and the many years ahead of him. He stared at the paper cup in his hand, slowly crushing it, the water running out through his fingers and onto the blanket. "I know it's no one's fault, just bad luck; I'm just so pissed off!" Inexplicably, I reacted to his anger with sadness. I felt my eyes grow moist. Seeing my tears, Chet, too, began to cry again. I thought of my own death and of Dylan having to say goodbye to his father for the last time. We cried together for a while, and then, as we sat in the growing darkness, Chet began to speak. He told me about meeting his wife, their courtship and marriage, and his experience of Dylan's birth.

In the few sessions I had with Chet before his death, I discovered that it was his anger that kept him silent. I gave him opportunities to be angry, but he soon realized that what he really needed to do was to say goodbye to his family, his friends, and Dylan. From that point forward, he would muster up some of his failing energy each day – to play with Dylan, to reminisce with his wife, and to talk about their future without him. If a tragic, young death can be considered good, such was Chet's.

My social brain was in overdrive while working with Dylan and Chet. I watched their movements, facial expressions, and gaze and listened to the tones and cadences of their voices. I was the wooden body of the cello and they were the strings as I resonated with their feelings and emotions, both expressed and held within. I imagined how I would feel in each of their situations in order to help myself establish an empathic attunement with them. With both of them, I blended observations, ideas, and my own emotions to try and discern what was in their hearts. Memories of my own childhood emerged, helping me to interact with Dylan at his level of development and understanding. My paternal instincts also led me to want to comfort and soothe Dylan's distress – I felt my body relax as he was increasingly safe with me. In an entirely different way, being with Chet required me to face my own mortality and the cruelty of fate. Together, we shared the fundamental human experience of inhabiting an incomprehensible and often frightening universe.

These complex, magical, and sometimes scary things we call relationships are all around us. How the connections occur, what impact they have on us, and how relationships change the architecture and functioning of the brain are the essential questions of interpersonal neurobiology. Far from detaching ourselves from felt experience, as is routinely accepted as the operative mode of science, our work *requires* the inclusion of our experience. Our personal experiences are no less important than the empirical evidence found in the laboratory.

Thinking of Dylan's experience with his parents, the quality and nature of their attachments, and what will happen after his father's death, we naturally wonder how all these experiences will shape Dylan's brain. How will biochemical changes affect his ability to handle stress and the functioning of his immune system? How will his implicit memories affect his ability to bond with, and attach to, others as he grows into adulthood? What kind of friend, husband, and father will he become?

Will Dylan come to therapy years from now with symptoms and coping strategies that cause him problems? Will he panic at any sign of rejection? Will he spend his life searching for a father figure in a coach, teacher, or boss through whom he may hope to symbolically reconnect with Chet? What if, years from now, Dylan comes to you for therapy? How will you bridge the social synapse, how will you establish trust, and what will you do to activate the neuroplastic processes in Dylan's brain to help him alter patterns of implicit memory, behaviour, and feelings? What will happen in your own psychotherapy to help you know yourself well enough to help Dylan? This is the stuff of interpersonal neurobiology: from the inside out, from the laboratory to the consulting room, from neurons to neighbourhoods, from one human being to another.

Interpersonal neurobiology is the study of how we attach, grow, and interconnect throughout life. It is our story: yours, mine, Chet's, and Dylan's. It is the story of how we become dysregulated and unhealthy and how we regain our emotional balance and mental health. It is also the story of how genes and environments interact to produce who we are and how we create each other through relationships, the stories we tell, and the imaginary worlds we fashion, inhabit, and explore.

References

Aftanas, L. I., Varlamov, A. A., Reva, N. V., & Pavlov, S. V. (2003). Disruption of early event-related theta synchronisation of human EEG in alexithymics viewing affective pictures. *Neuroscience Letters, 340*, 57–60.

Ainsworth, M. D. S., Blehar, M. C., Waters, E., & Wall, S. (1978). *Patterns of attachment: A psychological study of the strange situation*. Hillsdale, NJ: Erlbaum.

Apfel, R. J., & Sifneos, P. E. (1979). Alexithymia: Concept and measurement. *Psychotherapy and Psychosomatics, 32*, 180–190.

Bagby, R. M., & Taylor, G. J. (1997). Affect dysregulation and alexithymia. In G. J. Taylor, R. M. Bagby, & J. D. A. Parker (Eds.), *Disorders of affect regulation: Alexithymia in medical and psychiatric illness* (pp. 26–45). New York: Cambridge University Press.

Baker, K. B., & Kim, J. J. (2004). Amygdalar lateralization in fear conditioning: Evidence for greater involvement of the right amygdala. *Behavioral Neuroscience, 118*, 15–23.

Barbas, H. (1995). Anatomic basis of cognitive-emotional interactions in the primate prefrontal cortex. *Neuroscience and Biobehavioral Reviews, 19*, 499–510.

Bausch, S., Stingl, M., Hartmann, L. C., Leibing, E., Leichsenring, F., Kruse, J., & Leweke, F. (2011). Alexithymia and script-driven emotional imagery in healthy female subjects: No support for deficiencies in imagination. *Scandinavian Journal of Psychology, 52*, 179–184.

Bermond, B., Bierman, D. J., Cladder, M. A., Moormann, P. P., & Vorst, H. C. M. (2010). The cognitive and affective alexithymia dimensions in the regulations of sympathetic responses. *International Journal of Psychophysiology, 75*, 227–233.

Bermond, B., Vorst, H. C. M., & Moormann, P. P. (2006). Cognitive neuropsychology of alexithymia: Implications for personality typology. *Cognitive Neuropsychiatry, 11(3)*, 332–360.

Blonder, L. X., Bowers, D., & Heilman, K. M. (1991). The role of the right hemisphere in emotional communication. *Brain, 114*, 1115–1127.

Borsci, G., Boccardi, M., Rossi, R., Rossi, G., Perez, J., Bonetti, M., & Frisoni, G. B. (2009). Alexithymia in healthy women: A brain morphology study. *Journal of Affective Disorders, 114*, 208–215.

Bratis, D., Tselebis, A., Sikaras, C., Moulou, A., Giotakis, K., Zoumakis, E., & Ilias, I. (2009). Alexithymia and its association with burnout, depression and family support among Greek nursing staff. *Human Resources for Health, 7(1)*, 72–77.

Cacioppo, J. T., & Gardner, W. L. (1999). Emotion. *Annual Review of Psychology, 50*, 191–214.

Calder, A. J., Lawrence, A., & Young, A. W. (2001). Neuropsychology of fear and loathing. *Nature Reviews Neuroscience, 2*, 352–363.

Canli, T., Desmond, J. E., Zhao, Z., Glover, G., & Gabrieli, J. D. E. (1998). Hemispheric asymmetry for emotional stimuli detected with fMRI. *NeuroReport, 9*, 3233–3239.

Caria, A., Veit, R., Sitaram, R., Lotze, M., Weiskopf, N., Grodd, W., & Birbaumer, N. (2007). Regulation of anterior insular cortex activity using real-time fMRI. *Neuroimage, 35*, 1238–1246.

Chiron, C., Jambaque, I., Nabbout, R., Lounes, R., Syrota, A., & Dulac, O. (1997). The right brain hemisphere is dominant in human infants. *Brain, 120*, 1057–1065.

Coren, S., & Porac, C. (1977). Fifty centuries of right-handedness: The historical record. *Science, 198*, 631–632.

Cozolino, L. J. (2010). *The neuroscience of psychotherapy: Healing the social brain.* New York, NY: W. W. Norton.

Crabbe, J. C., & Phillips, T. J. (2003). Mother nature meets mother nurture. *Nature Neuroscience, 6*, 440–442.

Damasio, A. R. (1994). *Descartes' error: Emotion, rationality and the human brain.* New York: Putnam and Sons.

Damasio, A. R. (1995). Toward a neurobiology of emotion and feeling: Operational concepts and hypotheses. *The Neuroscientist, 1*, 19–25.

Damasio, A. R., Grabowski, T. J., Bechara, A., Damasio, H., Ponto, L. L. B., Parvizi, J., & Hichwa, R. D. (2000). Subcortical and cortical brain activity during the feeling of self-generated emotions. *Nature Neuroscience, 3*, 1049–1056.

Davidson, R. J. (1992). Emotion and affective style: Hemispheric substrates. *Psychological Science, 3*, 39–43.

Davidson, R. J., Ekman, P., Saron, C. D., Senulis, J. A., & Friesen, W. V. (1990). Approach-withdrawal and cerebral asymmetry: Emotional expression and brain physiology I. *Journal of Personality and Social Psychology, 58*, 330–341.

Davidson, R. J., & Fox, N. A. (1989). Frontal brain asymmetry predicts infants' response to maternal separation. *Journal of Abnormal Psychology, 98*, 127–131.

Dawson, G., Frey, K., Panagiotides, H., Osterling, J., & Hessel, D. (1997a). Infants of depressed mothers exhibit atypical frontal brain activity: A replication and extension of previous findings. *Journal of Child Psychology and Psychiatry, 38*, 178–186.

Dawson, G., Panagiotides, H., Klinger, L. G., & Spieker, S. (1997b). Infants of depressed and nondepressed mothers exhibit differences in frontal brain electrical activity during the expressions of negative emotions. *Developmental Psychology, 33*, 650–656.

De Gucht, V., & Heiser, W. (2003). Alexithymia and somatization: A qualitative review of the literature. *Journal of Psychosomatic Research, 54*, 425–434.

De Rick, A., & Vanheule, S. (2006). The relationship between perceived parenting, adult attachment style and alexithymia in alcoholic inpatients. *Addictive Behaviors, 31*, 1265–1270.

de Timary, P., Roy, E., Luminet, O., Fillée, C., & Mikolajczak, M. (2008). Relationship between alexithymia, alexithymia factors and salivary cortisol in men exposed to a social stress test. *Psychoneuroendocrinology, 33*, 1160–1164.

Dion, K. L. (1996). Ethnolinguistic correlates of alexithymia: Toward a cultural perspective. *Journal of Psychosomatic Research, 41(6)*, 531–539.

Fink, G. R., Halligan, P. W., Marshall, J. C., Frith, C. D., Frackowiak, R. S. J., & Dolan, R. J. (1996). Where in the brain does visual attention select the forest from the trees? *Nature, 382*, 626–628.

Frewen, P. A., Lanius, R. A., Dozois, D. J. A., Neufeld, R. W. J., Pain, C., Hopper, J. W., & Stevens, T. K. (2008). Clinical and neural correlates of alexithymia in posttraumatic stress disorder. *Journal of Abnormal Psychology, 117(1)*, 171–181.

Fukunishi, I., Kawamura, N., Ishikawa, T., Ago, Y., Sei, H., Morita, Y., & Rahe, R. H. (1997). Mothers' low care in the development of alexithymia: A preliminary study in Japanese college students. *Psychological Reports, 80*, 143–146.

Goerlich, K. S., Witteman, J., Aleman, A., & Martens, S. (2011). Hearing feelings: Affective categorization of music and speech in alexithymia, an ERP study. *PLoS ONE, 6(5)*, 1–11.

Gould, S. J. (1977). *Ontogeny and phylogeny*. Cambridge: Belknap Press of Harvard University.

Gundel, H., Lopez-Sala, A., Ceballos-Baumann, A. O., Deus, J., Cardoner, N., & Martin-Mittage, B. (2004). Alexithymia correlates with the size of the right anterior cingulate. *Psychosomatic Medicine, 66*, 132–140.

Habib, M., Daquin, G., Pelletier, J., Montreuil, M., & Robichon, F. (2003). Alexithymia as a consequence of impaired callosal function: Evidence from multiple sclerosis patients and normal individuals. In E. Zaidel & M. Iacaboni (Eds.), *The parallel brain* (pp. 415–422). Cambridge, MA: MIT Press.

Hari, R., Portin, K., Kettenmann, B., Jousmäki, V., & Kobal, G. (1997). Right-hemisphere preponderance of responses to painful CO_2 stimulation of the human nasal mucosa. *Pain, 72*, 145–151.

Henriques, J. B., & Davidson, R. J. (1990). Regional brain electrical asymmetries discriminate between previously depressed and healthy control subjects. *Journal of Abnormal Psychology, 99*, 22–31.

Henriques, J. B., & Davidson, R. J. (1991). Left frontal hypoactivation in depression. *Journal of Abnormal Psychology, 100*, 535–545.

Jessimer, M., & Markham, R. (1997). Alexithymia: A right hemisphere dysfunction specific to recognition of certain facial expressions? *Brain and Cognition, 34*, 246–258.

Johnson, M. (1987). *The body in the mind.* Chicago: University of Chicago Press.

Kano, M., Fukudo, S., Gyoba, J., Kamachi, M., Tagawa, M., Mochizuki, H., & Yanai, K. (2003). Specific brain processing of facial expressions in people with alexithymia: An H_2 ^{15}O-PET study. *Brain, 126*, 1474–1484.

Kano, M., Hamaguchi, T., Itoh, M., Yanai, K., & Fukudo, S. (2007). Correlation between alexithymia and hypersensitivity to visceral stimulation in human. *Pain, 132*, 252–263.

Karlsson, H., Naatanen, P., & Stenman, H. (2008). Cortical activation in alexithymia as a response to emotional stimuli. *The British Journal of Psychiatry, 192*, 32–38.

Keenan, J. P., McCutcheon, B., Freund, S., Gallup, G. G., Jr., Sanders, G., & Pascual-Leone, A. (1999). Left hand advantage in a self-face recognition task. *Neuropsychologia, 37*, 1421–1425.

Keenan, J. P., Wheeler, M. A., Gallup, G. G., Jr., & Pascual-Leone, A. (2000). Self-recognition and the right prefrontal cortex. *Trends in Cognitive Sciences, 4*, 338–344.

Kimura, I., Kubota, M., Hirose, H., Yumoto, M., & Sakakihara, Y. (2004). Children are sensitive to averted eyes at the earliest stage of gaze processing. *NeuroReport, 15*, 1345–1348.

Kosten, T. R., Kyrstal, J. H., Giller, E. L., Frank, J., & Dan, E. (1992). Alexithymia as a predictor of treatment response in post-traumatic stress disorder. *Journal of Traumatic Stress, 5*, 563–573.

Koven, N. S., & Thomas, W. (2010). Mapping faces of alexithymia to executive dysfunction in daily life. *Personality and Individual Differences, 49*, 24–28.

Krystal, H. (1988). *Integration and self healing: Affect, trauma, and alexithymia.* Hillsdale, NJ: Analytic Press.

Lane, R. D., Sechrest, L., Reidel, R., Weldon, V., Kaszniak, A., & Schwartz, G. E. (1996). Impaired verbal and nonverbal emotion recognition in alexithymia. *Psychosomatic Medicine, 58*, 203–210.

Le Grand, R., Mondloch, C. J., Maurer, D., & Brent, H. P. (2003). Expert face processing requires visual input to the right hemisphere during infancy. *Nature Neuroscience, 6*, 1108–1112.

Le, H., Berenbaum, H., & Raghavan, C. (2002). Culture and alexithymia: Mean levels, correlates, and the role of parental socialisation of emotions. *Emotion, 2(4)*, 341–360.

LeDoux, J. E. (2003). The self: Clues from the brain. *Annals of the New York Academy of Sciences, 1001,* 295–304.

Levant, R. F., Hall, R. J., Williams, C. M., & Hasan, N. T. (2009). Gender differences in alexithymia. *Psychology of Men & Masculinity, 10(3),* 190–203.

Luminet, O., Grynberg, D., Ruzette, N., & Mikolajczak, M. (2011). Personality-dependent effects of oxytocin: Greater social benefits for high alexithymia scorers. *Biological Psychology, 87,* 401–406.

Luminet, O., Vermeeulen, N., Demaret, C., Taylor, G. J., & Bagby, R. M. (2006). Alexithymia and levels of processing: Evidence for an overall deficit in remembering emotion words. *Journal of Research in Personality, 40,* 713–733.

McDonald, P. W., & Prkachin, K. M. (1990). The expression and perception of facial emotion in alexithymia: A Pilot Study. *Psychosomatic Medicine, 52,* 199–210.

Meltzer, M. A., & Nielsen, K. A. (2010). Memory for emotionally provocative words in alexithymia: A role for stimulus relevance. *Consciousness and Cognition, 19,* 1062–1068.

Miyaki, Y., Okamoto, Y., Onoda, K., Shirao, N., Okamoto, Y., & Tamawaki, S. (2012). Brain activation during the perception of stressful word stimuli concerning interpersonal relationships in anorexia nervosa patients with high degrees of alexithymia in an fMRI paradigm. *Psychiatry Research: Neuroimaging, 201,* 111–119.

Modestin, J., Lötscher, K., & Erni, T. (2002). Dissociative experiences and their correlates in young non-patients. *Psychology and Psychotherapy: Theory, Research, and Practice, 75,* 53–64.

Moriguchi, Y., Decety, J., Ohnishi, T., Maeda, M., Mori, T., Nemoto, K., & Komati, G. (2007). Empathy and judging other's pain: An fMRI study of alexithymia. *Cerebral Cortex, 17(9),* 2223–2234.

Moriguchi, Y., Ohnishi, T., Kawachi, T., Mori, T., Hirakata, M., Yamada, M., & Komaki, G. (2005). Specific brain activation in Japanese and Caucasian people to fearful faces. *Brain Imaging, 16(2),* 133–136.

Nyklíček, I., & Vingerhoets, J. J. M. (2000). Alexithymia is associated with low tolerance to experimental painful stimulation. *Pain, 85(3),* 471–475.

Panksepp, J. (2003). At the interface of the affective, behavioural, and cognitive neurosciences: Decoding the emotional feelings of the brain. *Brain and Cognition, 52,* 4–14.

Papciak, A. S., Feuerstein, M., & Spiegel, J. A. (1985). Stress reactivity in alexithymia: Decoupling of physiological and cognitive responses. *Journal of Human Stress, 11,* 135–142.

Paradiso, S., Johnson, D. L., Andreasen, N. C., O'Leary, D. S., Watkins, G. L., Ponto, L. L. B., & Hichwa, R. D. (1999). Cerebral blood flow changes associated with attribution of emotional valence to pleasant, unpleasant, and neutral visual stimuli in a PET study of normal subjects. *America Journal of Psychiatry, 156,* 1618–1629.

Parker, J. D. A., Bauermann, T. M., & Smith, C. T. (2000). Alexithymia and impoverished dream content: Evidence from rapid eye movement sleep awakenings. *Psychosomatic Medicine, 62,* 486–491.

Parker, J. D. A., Taylor, G. J., & Bagby, R. M. (2003). The 20-item Toronto alexithymia scale III. Reliability and factorial validity in a community population. *Journal of Psychosomatic Research, 55,* 269–275.

Pollatos, O., & Gramann, K. (2011). Electrophysiological evidence of early processing deficits in alexithymia. *Biological Psychiatry, 87*, 113–121.

Porges, S. W. (2003). Social engagement and attachment: A phylogenetic perspective. *Annals of the New York Academy of Sciences, 1008*, 31–47.

Porges, S. W. (2011). *The polyvagal theory: Neurophysiological foundations of emotions, attachment, communication, and self-regulation.* New York, NY: W. W. Norton.

Price, J. L. (1999). Prefrontal cortical networks related to visceral function and mood. *Annals of the New York Academy of Sciences, 877*, 383–396.

Rauch, S. L., van der Kolk, B. A., Fisler, R. E., Alpert, N. M., Orr, S. P., Savage, C. R., & Pitman, R. K. (1996). A symptom provocation study of posttraumatic stress disorder using positron emission tomography and script-driven imagery. *Archive of General Psychiatry, 53*, 38–387.

Rieffe, C., Terwogt, M. M., & Bosch, J. D. (2004). Emotion understanding in children with frequent somatic complaints. *European Journal of Developmental Psychology, 1(1)*, 31–47.

Rossion, B., Dricot, L., Devolder, A., Bodart, J. M., Crommelinck, M., de Gelder, B., & Zoontjes, R. (2000). Hemispheric asymmetries for whole-based and part-based face processing in the human fusiform gyrus. *Journal of Cognitive Neuroscience, 12*, 793–802.

Salminen, J. K., Saarijärvi, S., Toikka, T., Kauhanen, J., & Äärelä, E. (2006). Alexithymia behaves as a personality trait over a 5-year period in Finnish general population. *Journal of Psychosomatic Research, 61*, 275–278.

Schulkin, J., Thompson, B. L., & Rosen, J. B. (2003). Demythologizing the emotions: Adaptation, cognition, and visceral representations of emotion in the nervous system. *Brain and Cognition, 52*, 15–23.

Searleman, A. (1977). A review of right hemisphere linguistic capabilities. *Psychological Bulletin, 84*, 503–528.

Shapiro, D., Jamner, L. D., & Spence, S. (1997). Cerebral laterality, repressive coping, autonomic arousal, and human bonding. *Acta Physiologica Scandanavica, 640*, 60–64.

Sifneos, P. E. (1975). problems of psychotherapy of patients with alexithymic characteristics and physical disease. *Psychotherapy and Psychosomatics, 26(2)*, 65–70.

Silberman, E. K., & Weingartner, H. (1986). Hemispheric lateralization of functions related to emotion. *Brain and Cognition, 5*, 322–353.

Spalletta, G., Pasinin, A., Costa, A., De Angelis, D., Ramundo, N., Paolucci, S., & Caltagirone, C. (2001). Alexithymic features in stroke: Effects of laterality and gender. *Psychosomatic Medicine, 63*, 944–950.

Spivak, B., Segal, M., Mester, R., & Weizman, A. (1998). Lateral preference in post-traumatic stress disorder. *Psychological Medicine, 28*, 229–232.

Stone, L. A., & Nielson, K. A. (2001). Intact physiological response to arousal with impaired emotional recognition in alexithymia. *Psychotherapy and Psychosomatics, 70*, 92–102.

Sturm, V. E., & Levenson, R. W. (2011). Alexithymia in neurodegenerative disease. *NeuroCase, 17(3)*, 242–250.

Stuss, D. T., & Alexander, M. P. (1999). Affectively burnt in: A proposed role of the right frontal lobe. In E. Tulving (Ed.), *Memory, consciousness, and the brain: The Tallinn conference* (pp. 215–227). Philadelphia, PA: Psychology Press.

Sullivan, R. M., & Gratton, A. (2002). Prefrontal cortical regulation of hypothalamic–pituitary–adrenal function in the rat and implications for psychopathology: Side matters. *Psychoneuroendocrinology, 27,* 99–114.

Taylor, G. J. (2000). Recent developments in alexithymia theory and research. *Canadian Journal of Psychiatry, 45,* 134–142.

Thorberg, F. A., Young, R. M., Sullivan, K. A., & Lyvers, M. (2011). Parental bonding and alexithymia: A meta-analysis. *European Psychiatry, 26,* 187–193.

Todarello, O., Taylor, G. J., Parker, J. D. A., & Franelli, M. (1995). Alexithymia in essential hypertensive and psychiatric outpatients: A comparative study. *Journal of Psychosomatic Research, 39(8),* 987–994.

Verissimo, R., Taylor, G. J., & Bagby, R. M. (2000). relationship between alexithymia and locus of control. *New Trends in Experimental and Clinical Psychiatry, 16(1),* 11–16.

Wheeler, R. E., Davidson, R. J., & Tomarken, A. J. (1993). Frontal brain asymmetry and emotional reactivity: A biological substrate of affective style. *Psychophysiology, 30,* 82–89.

Wild, B., Rodden, F. A., Grodd, W., & Ruch, W. (2003). Neural correlates of laughter and humor. *Brain, 126,* 2121–2138.

Wittling, W. (1997). The right hemisphere and the human stress response. *Acta Physiologica Scandinavia, 640(Suppl.),* 55–59.

Zald, D. H., & Kim, S. W. (2001). The orbitofrontal cortex. In S. P. Salloway, P. F. Malloy, & J. D. Duffy (Eds.), *The frontal lobes and neuropsychiatric illness* (pp. 33–70). Washington, DC: American Psychiatric Press.

Zalla, T., Koechlin, E., Pietrini, P., Basso, G., Aquino, P., Sirigu, A., & Grafman, J. (2000). Differential amygdala response to winning and losing: A functional magnetic resonance imaging study in humans. *European Journal of Neuroscience, 12,* 1764–1770.

Zeitlin, S. B., Lane, R. D., O'Leary, D. S., & Schrift, M. J. (1989). Interhemispheric transer deficit and alexithymia. *American Journal of Psychiatry, 146,* 1434–1439.

Zeitlin, S. B., McNally, R. J., & Cassiday, K. L. (1993). Alexithymia in victims of sexual assault: An effect of repeated traumatisation? *American Journal of Psychiatry, 150,* 661–663.

Zhang, L., Zhu, C., Zhaolun, R. Y., Tian, Y., Yang, P., Hu, P., & Wang, K. (2011). Impairment of conflict processing in alexithymic individuals. *Neuroscience Letters, 504,* 261–264.

Zimmermann, G., Rossier, J., de Stadelhofen, F. M., & Galliard, F. (2005). Alexithymia assessment and relations with dimensions of personality. *European Journal of Psychological Assessment, 21(1),* 23–33.

Chapter 4

Distinct but linked

Wellbeing and the multimodal mind

Alexander Welch Siegel and Daniel J. Siegel

Introduction

Divisions in the functions between the left and right hemispheres, first identified in neurology and later cognitive neuroscience, have both captured the public imagination and become the cause of scientific debate. This chapter aims to move our understanding beyond controversies concerning anatomical location and illuminate the deeper processes involved in the differentiation and linkage of mental functions. The linking of distinct elements of a system is how complex systems achieve their emergent property of optimal self-organization. The defining features of a complex system are openness, chaos-capability, and non-linearity. Openness refers to the condition of being influenced by factors outside of the system. Chaos-capability indicates the capacity to achieve what appear to be random states. Non-linearity means that small inputs to a system lead to large and difficult to predict outcomes. All of these features can help explain how human experience is a part of a complex system.

For example, during a group musical improvisation commonly known as a "jam session", each individual musician plays a unique and differentiated part within the group, yet it is the ways in which these parts are linked that gives rise to the music. While each individual part is distinct from the others and can be heard on its own, each part intimately complements the others and is a part of an integrated whole. That this process of differentiation and linkage occurs spontaneously, often with no premeditated plan or strategy when the musicians begin playing, is a fascinating example of the tendency of complex systems to move towards integration as they self-organize, even while preserving the unique voice of distinct parts that may sound radically different from one another when heard independently from the whole. In other words, the music arises not from the sameness of its constituent elements, but from their unique and often surprising differentiation and linkages. This reveals how integration – the linkage of differentiated parts – helps explain why and how the whole is greater than the sum of its parts.

As in music, the left and right hemispheres have distinct locations, anatomical connections, and neural processes whose interconnections give rise to integrated functions. *Both* the left and right sides of the brain contribute to a wide range of mental processes such as emotion, thought and memory. The upper and lower regions of the brain also have distinct locations, structural connections and functions whose linkages support our mental lives. The brain itself is connected to the rest of the nervous system extending throughout the body and is inextricably linked to the other various bodily systems, such as the immune, cardiovascular, neuromuscular, and gastrointestinal systems. Further, the brain is constantly in communication with the physical and social world outside of the body.

As part of the nervous system, the brain has its embryonic origins in the ectoderm of the foetus, with this outer layer of skin invaginating to become the neural tube. As these specialized skin cells, the neurons, then accumulate in the head, the brain is formed. From an ontological point of view, this raises the point that just as the skin's major function is to be the interface of the inner and outer world, so too does the nervous system, including the head's brain, function to link the differentiated inner and outer worlds. We can see part of this linkage of inner and outer through the process of communication, a way we connect our inner selves to the world around us.

What is communication? To return to our musical example, each musician in the "jam session" plays a unique part that is different from and complimentary to the others. This is enabled by the selective focus of attention on the individual parts and a simultaneous, broader awareness of the music as a whole. The combination of these different types of attention allows the music to emerge through the musicians' sharing of *patterns of energy*: what they see, what they hear, and what they feel in their bodies. Communication can be defined as the sharing of energy. The left and right hemispheres of the brain communicate with each other, systems of the body communicate with each other, and individuals communicate with each other. While each individual part can be separated out and analysed, the music emerges from this communication and connection.

Attention is the process that directs energy flow. Iain McGilchrist's view (2009) of bilaterality suggests that the left hemisphere is dominant for narrowly focused attention, and the right hemisphere specializes in broader, open attention. When attention is coupled with consciousness it is called focal attention and thus the experience of consciousness in the left and right hemispheres may be distinct because of these differences in attention. However, many aspects of human consciousness involve both sides of the brain and both forms of attention. In listening to music, for example, perceiving melody involves the integration of various cortical processes whereas rhythm involves the linkage of these higher brain regions with the body as a whole (Levitin, 2006). Similarly, the playing of improvisational music links widely distributed areas of the nervous system (Limb & Braun, 2008) and as individual musicians play together, their brains become synchronized (Müller et al., 2013). Such neural coupling of differentiated individual brain processes may be seen more broadly in other forms of human communication, such as the sharing of stories (Hasson et al., 2012).

This chapter will highlight a range of distinct processes, both internal and interpersonal, whose linkages may form the basis of mental health. By identifying these differentiated functions and the ways in which their connections give rise to optimal functioning, our hope is to broaden the discussion of bilaterality to the larger issue of integration in the cultivation of well-being.

Distinct but linked

Each word you read is a unique combination of linked, differentiated letters. Each word in turn is a differentiated contribution to a sentence. Each sentence is a part of a paragraph, which is in turn part of a section. This is a spatial and temporal distribution of the fundamental elements of a chapter; we move from letters, spaces and punctuation marks to meaning. Through attention to sequence in reading, the meaning of the whole emerges from connecting its component parts.

The relationships between these parts have a range of characteristics that are integral to the creation of integration. For example, some of these distinct parts or processes may be complimentary in nature in differing ways. Different types of attention may be distinct from one another, as an intense focus on detail is quite different from attention to broader context. To enable these distinct forms of attention to function well, they need to be separate and differentiable. This may be the reason that these functionally distinct forms of attention are anatomically distributed in the brain. Function follows structure in the brain, and keeping functions anatomically separated can facilitate their optimal activation by enabling specialized differentiation and avoiding competing inhibition. In some situations, as in the musical example given above, distinct functions can be engaged simultaneously so that their distinct natures are maintained while they are both activated at the same time. These processes are *temporally compatible* even if they are necessarily functionally distinct. This reveals how integration is more like a fruit salad than a smoothie; it results not in homogenization or blending but in the maintenance of differentiated elements as they become linked into an integrated whole.

In contrast, some processes cannot be simultaneously activated. Walking, for example, involves the differentiated processes of leaning and lifting the leg. The leaning and lifting cannot occur at the same time for the same leg. For a given leg at a given moment, leaning and lifting are *temporally conflictual*. Walking involves the alternating of leaning and lifting in each leg so that when the left lifts, the right leans. If you don't alternate right and left in this way, you will be playing hopscotch instead of walking. In this case, integration involves linkages that take place across time, the term we use to indicate change. Differentiated functions that are temporally conflictual can still be integrated because they can be engaged in an alternating sequence.

Integration of temporally conflictual elements is a key ingredient of interpersonal communication. In conversation, for example, one person speaks while the other listens, ultimately allowing both people to speak and be heard. This exchange requires that each individual engage a sequence of alternating processes, as speaking is activated and then it is inhibited so that listening can be activated. Conversation is the linkage between these differentiated processes in each individual, and their synchronization between individuals in a temporally integrated manner.

When integration is present, optimal self-organization arises to create harmonious functioning. *FACES* is an acronym that summarizes the qualities of an integrated state: *flexible, adaptive, coherent, energized,* and *stable.* When a system is not integrated, it moves towards one of two extremes away from FACES. One extreme is chaos, where the system becomes unpredictable, flooded, and hyper-activated. The other extreme is rigidity, where the system is excessively predictable, restricted, and hypo-activated. Both extremes reveal a dysfunctional system. Interestingly, every symptom of every syndrome in the DSM-5 can be understood as chaos, rigidity, or both. To date, brain studies carried out on individuals with a range of diagnoses have all revealed impaired integration in the brain (see Siegel, 2012, 2017).

What follows are a sample of differentiable processes that have been identified by various researchers that helps to illuminate a set of functions that have unique and independent characteristics. In science, the term *dissociable* is used to refer to component functions that contribute to larger processes. This is the research background that supports the notion that smaller components become linked to form the integrated whole.

Differentiable processes

Neurological studies for nearly a century have pointed to distinct aspects of the processing of language. As in conversation, there is language reception and language production. Our linguistic communication with each other also involves the dissociable functions of language content and prosody. As we write these words to you, you are receiving content without tone of voice. This can lead to some humorous or disastrous misunderstandings as frequently occur in texts or emails. In addition, you are not receiving non-verbal signals such as our facial expressions, eye contact, posture, gestures, and the timing and intensity of our signals. These, along with tone of voice, are likely mediated primarily in the right hemisphere (McGilchrist, 2009). In contrast, there is dominance in the left hemisphere for interpreting the pure content of language. We will refer to this as the verbal content of linguistic communication. Nielson and colleagues' study of functional connectivity highlights this lateralization of language:

> Our data is broadly consistent with previous studies regarding the spatial distribution of lateralization of functional connectivity … We find that

brain regions showing consistently strong left-lateralization include classical language regions (Broca Area, Wernicke Area, lateral premotor, and anterior supplementary motor areas) … Other left-lateralized hubs include core regions of the default mode network (posterior cingulate, medial prefrontal, temporo-parietal junction) … In contrast, hubs of right-lateralized functional connectivity correspond well to canonical regions of the dorsal and ventral attention networks and the cingulo-insular or salience network. This network is more active during tasks requiring attention to external stimuli or assessment of stimulus salience or novelty.

(Nielson et al., 2013, p. 7)

Harmonious communication between two people requires a balance of the verbal and non-verbal aspects of language, where attention is paid not only to the pure content of speech but its non-verbal context. While the interpretation and production of these different aspects of language have distinct neural origins in the left or right hemispheres, both are combined in effective communication. Healthy states likely involve the integration of both sides of the brain. In unresolved traumatic states, one hemisphere or the other may be inhibited. In speechless terror, for example, Bessel van der Kolk (2014) found that the left hemisphere shuts down during a flashback experience during which word production becomes inhibited. In studies of voluntary emotion regulation, individuals can name an emotion and activate their left hemispheres to inhibit their right-dominant emotional centres (Lieberman et al., 2007). Healthy regulation involves the coordination and balance of the two hemispheres, the outcome of *bilateral integration*.

The non-verbal and verbal aspects of language are temporally compatible and ideal communication involves both occurring in the same transaction. There is a connection between non-verbal aspects of communication and the context – the larger meaning – of an interaction. Context includes sensing the mental state of another person, including the ABCDE of meaning: *associations, beliefs, cognitions, developmental phase*, and *emotions*. Without sensing these components of context, communication between people is reduced to the transfer of content without taking into account personal meaning. Whether the dissociable elements of linguistic communication (non-verbal and verbal) are ultimately originating from one hemisphere of the brain or the other is less important for promoting well-being than simply identifying the importance of both and the ways in which they can become disintegrated.

Another fundamental set of differentiable functions includes "top-down" and "bottom-up" processing. Sometimes these terms are used to refer to the anatomical origins of a direction of neural flow: top-down originating in the cortex and bottom-up originating in the brainstem. Here we will be using these terms instead to indicate neural processing that is derived from either prior experience (top-down) or novel events (bottom-up). For example, if you are walking on a beach and soaking in the sensations of the wind and the sun, you are in a bottom-up "mode" of processing. You are experiencing the sensations with a beginner's mind as best you can. If along your walk you begin to compare your experience to memories of other beaches on other days, you will be activating your top-down mode. Bottom-up is filled with sensation while top-down can be filled with narration. Studies suggest that these two modes are mutually inhibitory (Farb et al., 2007). This suggests that they may be temporally conflictual. Yet both are necessary for a wide array of functions integral to well-being.

Preliminary studies have shown that bottom-up processing of sensation occurs on both sides of the brain in the side regions, whereas top-down narration occurs in the midline regions (Farb et al., 2007). The key is to balance these two modes and not become stuck in one extreme or the other. Mindfulness training may be effective for creating well-being because it enhances an individual's capacity to differentiate and link these two modes and avoid becoming trapped in either alone.

This raises the question of whether these processes exist in binary opposition or as a continuum of functions. It is difficult to avoid creating artificial separations when describing aspects of reality using language. In other words, are the differences we identify due to often unavoidable linguistic artefacts, or are they a part of actual reality?

For example, Table 4.1 highlights some popularly held divisions of functions. The modes in the left column are typically and perhaps inaccurately attributed to the left hemisphere, and those in the right column to the right hemisphere.

However, conscious processes in which mental representations are held within awareness involve both the left and the right hemispheres. Nonconscious processes, sometimes called "unconscious", "subconscious", or "preconscious", also arise from activity in both hemispheres. In this way,

Table 4.1 Popularly held divisions of functions

Left hemisphere	Right hemisphere
Conscious	Unconscious
Explicit	Implicit
Voluntary	Automatic
Top-down	Bottom-up
Logical	Intuitive
Rational	Emotional
Narrow	Broad
Mathematical	Theory of mind

calling the right hemisphere the seat of the unconscious and the left the seat of consciousness may be scientifically inaccurate.

Similarly, explicit and implicit processes emerge from neural firing on both sides of the brain. For example, explicit autobiographical memory involves right-hemisphere activation, and implicit priming of linguistic memory recollection involves the left hemisphere. Attempting to distribute these differentiable aspects of implicit and explicit processing into the anatomical locations of right and left is not consistent with the scientific data.

Voluntary processes involving emotion regulation also rely on both sides of the brain, as do automatic aspects of emotion regulation (Jackson et al., 2003). We can find no evidence that top-down and bottom-up processes are lateralized, or that reasoning and emotions emanate from *only* one side of the brain or the other. Both left and right contribute significant neural activity to reasoning and emotional experience.

In contrast, empirical support exists for the left-lateralization of mathematical systems thinking, as well as for a narrow focus of attention. Empirical data also suggests that theory of mind or mentalization as well as a broad focus of attention may have a right-hemisphere dominance. These research findings highlight the specificity of modes and their potential lateralization. As Nielson and colleagues state, "lateralization of brain connections appears to be a local rather than global property of brain networks" (Nielson et al., 2013, p. 1). The particular mode or process in question must be examined specifically, while global statements about the general predominance of left- or right-hemisphere circuitry in a given person's life should be used cautiously, if at all.

Nielson and colleagues state:

> In popular reports, "left-brained" and "right-brained" have become terms associated with both personality traits and cognitive strategies, with a "left-brained" individual or cognitive style typically associated with a logical, methodical approach and "right-brained" with a more creative, fluid, and intuitive approach. Based on the brain regions we identified as hubs in the broader left-dominant and right-dominant connectivity networks, a more consistent schema might include left-dominant connections associated with language and perception of internal stimuli, and right-dominant connections associated with attention to external stimuli. Yet our analyses suggest that an individual brain is not "left-brained" or "right-brained" as a global property, but that asymmetric lateralization is a property of individual nodes or local subnetworks, and that different aspects of the left-dominant network and right-dominant network may show relatively greater or lesser lateralization within an individual. If a connection involving one of the left hubs is strongly left-lateralized in an individual, then other connections in the left-dominant network also involving this hub may also be more

strongly left-lateralized, but this did not translate to a significantly gener-
alized lateralization of the left-dominant network or right-dominant
network.

(Nielson et al., 2013, p. 8)

That the left and right hemispheres have distinct anatomies and specialization
of function is empirically supported and has existed for hundreds of millions of
years in vertebrates (Duboc et al., 2015). In a section entitled "Advantage of
Functional Lateralization of the Brain", Duboc and colleagues assert,

> the fact that brain lateralization has been either conserved or independ-
> ently acquired during evolution suggests it somehow provides an advan-
> tage and, thus, its loss is detrimental. Furthermore, variation in the
> development of brain asymmetry is suspected to contribute to various
> neuropathologies in humans. Indeed, disorders such as autism and dys-
> lexia are associated with atypical patterns of functional and structural
> asymmetries ... Above all, brain lateralization is assumed to provide cog-
> nitive advantages. This is supported by quantitative functional MRI
> studies that correlate the strength of functional lateralization with the
> level of cognitive ability in humans. Brain lateralization might provide
> benefits by allowing hemispheres to perform parallel tasks.

(Duboc et al., 2015, p. 651)

Some modes may be lateralized and utilize distinct circuits only on one side
of the brain. Other modes may rely primarily on one hemisphere but use
both, while others may involve active participation of both sides of the brain
simultaneously.

A clinically and educationally useful way, in English at least, of summarizing
these broad modes is this. The left mode, dominant on the left side of the
brain, is later to develop, linguistic, logical (syllogistic reasoning that seeks
cause-effect relationships among events), linear (a leads to b which leads to c),
literal, list-making. In contrast, the right is earlier to develop, non-verbal (eye
contact, facial expressions, tone of voice, posture, gestures, timing and intensity of response), holistic (sees context and interconnections), and is dominant
also for autobiographical memory and registering signals of the interior of the
body – called interoception. In the end, the identification of these distinct
modes gives them a differentiated importance, whichever side or sides they
involve. Learning to harness the power of these distinct modes of information
processing can lead to a fuller and more flexible life.

Developmental experience and modes of processing

While recent studies confirm that there are different degrees of neural integration in the left and right hemispheres, it is clear that the various circuits

have relative independence so that saying someone is "left-brained" or "right-brained" overall is not supported by contemporary studies of functional connectivity (Nielson et al., 2013). However, a given individual may have certain modes of processing that predominate in their lives. It may be that certain patterns of modes dominant in one hemisphere may become overdeveloped. As one example, we will discuss the twenty percent of the general population who have a "dismissing" state of mind with respect to attachment (Main, 1995; Main et al., 2008). The adult attachment interview used to determine this state reveals impairments in autobiographical recollection and an insistence that past relationships do not matter. Observation of these individuals reveals that linguistic content may be used without much non-verbal expression, and that perception of the meaning of non-verbal communication is limited. This results in a diminished ability to grasp the wider context of a given interaction.

One way to understand the development of such a profile is that during childhood, this individual had a paucity of emotionally attuned communication and affection (see Schiller, 2017). Neural plasticity is the way the brain grows in response to experience. Early experiences in childhood can lead to both direct and indirect effects on synaptic growth in the brain. Direct effects include how energy flow that comprises an "experience" stimulates neuronal firing and therefore gene activation, protein production, and synaptic growth. Indirect effects include how the individual's attempt to adapt to an experience leads to secondary neural growth to compensate for what has occurred or for the absence of something that ought to have occurred. In the case of dismissing adult attachment, the likely childhood avoidant attachment would mean an absence of stimulation of emotional closeness and reflections on the inner nature of mental experience, such as feelings, thoughts, or memories. The direct effect might be under-stimulation of the circuits underlying these modes of mental processing. An indirect effect would be to reduce self-reflection and emotional awareness so that the longing for connection would not flood the individual's consciousness and disable their functioning.

The combination of both direct and indirect effects would help explain the impediments to non-verbal attunement, autobiographical recollection, and appreciation for the importance of relationships in life. Interestingly, each of these modes may have predominance in the right hemisphere. As Allan Schore has written about extensively (Schore, 1994, 2003), the right hemisphere is dominant in its growth during the important early years of attachment. A period of rapid growth is both a period of opportunity and of vulnerability. Experience-expectant synaptic growth involves the genetically programmed development of neural connections that are established on their own but are dependent on experience to be maintained. Experience-dependent synaptic growth involves the development of neural connections only in response to novel experiences the child encounters. In either case, the experience of an avoidant attachment relationship may lead to impover-ished growth of the right hemisphere circuitry responsible for non-verbal communication, autobiographical memory, and the salience or importance of relationships. This may also reveal the reason that avoidantly attached children are viewed by their peers as controlling (Sroufe et al., 2005).

Recent studies showed that "the left hemisphere is dominant not only for lan-guage but also for problem solving, logical interpretations, and viewing details, whereas the right hemisphere is specialized for global viewing" (Duboc et al., 2015, p. 649). Individuals whose early attachment experiences have impaired the development of right-hemisphere circuitry may experience the overdevelopment of the contralateral side of the brain as compensation. For example, logical inter-pretations may predominate over emotional sensitivity to oneself or others. It is possible that these distinct modes are temporally conflictual and mutually inhibi-tory. Interactions with an adult who exhibits these imbalances can feel discon-nected and dismissive. Rather than having a feeling of presence and openness, the experience is one of pre-existing notions being imposed on the interaction. A lack of receptivity may be related to a hyper-focus on details and the absence of a broader attention to emotional context, a specialty of the right hemisphere. By contrast, communication that involves active attention to the "global view" and emotional context results in feeling felt by the other person, and forms the basis of a sense of closeness and connection.

Energy in formation

The human mind can be viewed as an emergent property of energy flow (see Siegel, 2017). Energy is defined as the movement from possibility to actuality. As neural firing shapes the movement of energy in the brain, neural represen-tations "re-present" sensations, perceptions, memories, and thoughts to create the content of mental life. The mind can either be a *conduit* for this energy flow, as when sensations are experienced in a bottom–up mode, or as a *constructor*, as when memories or thoughts are generated in a top–down mode. Both conduit and constructor are broad modes of energy and informa-tion flow that takes place in the brain, body, our inner mental activities, and even our relationships.

When energy patterns represent something other than themselves, we call them *information*. Information, then, is a pattern of energy with symbolic value. For example, the word "Alcatraz" is a symbol for the island in the San Francisco Bay. Although the term "information" is a noun, it also func-tions as a verb. When the word "Alcatraz" is communicated, it triggers a cascade of associations such as prison, Al Capone, and a recent visit to an art exhibit by Ai Weiwei about freedom. These all enter consciousness as "energy in formation". There is also energy in the form of information that is flowing beneath awareness that we call non-conscious information pro-cessing. We can see that mental life includes (1) information processing with or without consciousness; (2) consciousness; and (3) subjective experience – the felt texture of life that is known through consciousness. A fourth aspect of the mind is the "emergent self-organizing embodied and relational process that regulates the flow of energy and information" (Siegel, 2017).

The mind coordinates and balances this flow of energy and information in an optimal way through the process of integration, the linkage of differentiated parts. A way of understanding the energy flow called information processing is that it involves differentiated forms of information that become linked in various degrees of complexity. For example, perceptual input from the eyes becomes assembled in the back of the neocortex to form visual representations in the occipital lobe. When these visual streams are coordinated with auditory input through the temporal lobes, auditory representations are linked with visual representations to create a more complex, integrated picture of reality. The key to the complexity of this picture is that the perceptual streams are differentiated and then linked in the brain.

Attention is the process that directs this flow of energy and information both within the body and between people. Attention does not have to involve consciousness, and when it doesn't we call it non-focal attention. Focal attention, which streams energy and information into conscious awareness, has a more limited capacity than non-focal attention. However, with or without consciousness, what we pay attention to changes the function and structure of the brain. Where attention goes, neural firing flows, and neural connection grows. When neurons are firing repeatedly, their genes are activated, proteins are produced, and new neural connections established. This is called neuroplasticity.

When the parts of a system are differentiated and then linked, the system can become more efficient at processing information. This could explain why the right and left hemispheres of the brain have had differentiated functions for hundreds of millions of years. For example, an organism may need a simultaneous narrow focus of attention to find food in a specific location, and a wide focus of attention to watch for predators. Narrow and broad attention can occur at the same time, as long as their functions are anatomically separated in the brain. The brain makes this process efficient by creating modes.

As Stephen Kosslyn and G. Wayne Miller suggest, "The Theory of Cognitive Modes rests on a principle universally accepted today: Different regions of the brain carry out different specialized functions. In neuroanatomical terms, highly specialized brain functions are *localized*, not *holistic*" (2015, p. 109). A mode is the way the brain becomes more efficient with information processing. Because information triggers memory and meaning in the mind, it gives rise to more information processing in a domino effect. As energy unfolds in this way, the modes of the mind help form energy in particular patterns. For example, narrow attention looks for the seed in a defined region of sand; broad attention looks for the hawk in the wide sky. Attention drives energy through a particular mode.

Tucker, Luu, and Pribram write,

> In the human brain, hemispheric specialization appears to have led to asymmetric elaborations of dorsal and ventral pathways. Understanding the inherent asymmetries of corticolimbic architecture may be important in interpreting the increasing evidence that the left and right frontal lobes contribute differently to normal and pathological forms of self-regulation.
>
> (Tucker, Luu, & Pribram, 1995, pp. 233–234)

Due to these asymmetric corticolimbic pathways, the right and left hemispheres may give rise to different modes of information processing, forms of attention, patterns of communication, and the pictures of reality they create in our mental lives.

While modes such as narrow and broad focus of attention can be activated simultaneously because of their distinct anatomical origins, some modes inhibit each other, just as the same leg cannot lean and lift at the same time. Sensing and observing appear to be temporally conflictual and mutually inhibitory. In clinical work, if an individual is obsessed with thought, guiding them to sense the body's signals can be an effective pathway to reducing their ruminations. In other words, when a person is lost in the "OWN" mode, observing-witnessing-narrating, they can shift from this excessively differentiated self-referential *constructor mode* of the mind to the *conduit mode* by focusing attention on bodily sensations, thus activating the inhibitory sensing stream of this bottom-up conduit flow and calming their thoughts. This is how a clinician can creatively utilize an understanding of the constructor and the conduit modes as temporally conflictual and mutually inhibitory to allow an individual to become unstuck from states of mental life that are either chaotic or rigid.

Modes, states, and traits

A mode allows the mind to use the circuitry of the brain in an efficient way. In this section we will identify several modes that are independent of the right–left distinction, but ones that may be relevant for clinical work. In a given moment, an individual may harness several modes as well as other features of the mind such as emotion, memory, and perceptual bias to create a *state of mind*. A state of mind is a cluster of modes and other mental processes that can become activated simultaneously to enable complex functions to be achieved. A person's tendency to activate certain states over time can become a *trait* of that individual.

For example, Ruth Baer and colleagues (2006) have identified several "mindfulness traits" which include present moment awareness, non-reactivity, non-judgment, linguistic labelling, and self-observation. These are groupings of states of mind that are exhibited in a person's life as a characteristic way of being for that individual. One goal of mindfulness training is to intentionally create a specific state of mind during the practice period so that over time what was a deliberate creation of a given state becomes an automatic tendency, and the state becomes a trait. A range of studies reveals how mindfulness training increases self-regulation and the integration of the brain (Creswell et al., 2016). These studies also reveal that both hemispheres of the brain, and the corpus callosum linking them to each other, are stimulated and grow from mindfulness practice.

Another interesting finding suggested by Simon Baron-Cohen (2008) is the notion that the mode of attending to mathematical systems tends to be inversely correlated with the capacity for empathic "theory of mind" functions. Whether this is an inherent trait of these individuals or evidence of mutually inhibitory modes is unclear. However, in our own experience, an analytical state can inhibit the activation of an emotionally attuned state. In hyper-focusing on the logical relations of facts, an individual may miss the emotional context, as when a eulogizer coldly recounts the milestones and achievements of a person's life without affective expression.

Upon hearing such a eulogy someone might say, "that speaker was very left-brained!" However, the anatomical location of this state is less significant to our understanding of this person's thought and behaviour than simply recognizing that it finds expression through the dominance of a certain mode. Naturally, a mode will be created utilizing distinct neural circuits. In the case of this analytical and emotionally detached mode, is there evidence that the neural circuitry is left-hemisphere-dominant?

A relevant finding from laterality research is that the *dorsal* corticolimbic stream, dominant in the right hemisphere, incorporates information from the body itself, which makes it "well suited to evaluate stimuli for their motivational significance in relation to internal states" (Tucker et al., 1995, p. 223). This is in contrast to the *ventral* pathway dominant on the left side, which creates a motivational bias towards specific details of objects and involves a feedback system in which there is tight monitoring of present perceptions outside of the body. This feedback process is especially important in analytic processing, which may "be especially involved in object memory and the fine-tuning of the neocortical representation of objects whether the objects are conceptual or perceptual" (Tucker et al., 1995, p. 222). When coupled with contemporary views of the neurobiology of empathy, these findings suggest that modes that incorporate awareness of bodily signals will be associated with insight and empathy (Iacaboni, 2008). In a paper entitled "Right cerebral hemisphere dominance for a sense of corporeal and emotional self", neurologist Orin Devinsky (2000) identifies these body-based and affectively aware modes as being mediated predominantly by the right side of the brain. This supports the idea that the emotionally detached eulogizer from the example above was operating in a left-dominant state favouring object memory and concepts as left-dominant modes rather than body based feelings that are more right-dominant modes that might give rise to empathy and emotional meaning.

The work of Walter Freeman illuminates how the various regions of each hemisphere are primed to work together. Freeman writes,

> Recent findings obtained by recording EEGs from the scalps of volunteers ... indicate that cooperation between the modules of each hemisphere ... shows that sensory and limbic areas of each hemisphere can rapidly enter into a cooperative state, which persists on the order of a tenth of a second before dissolving to make way for the next state. The cooperation depends on the entry of the entire hemisphere into a global chaotic attractor.
>
> (Freeman, 2000, pp. 229–230)

This supports the idea that mental states arise from neural circuits that are dominant in their activity in either the left or the right hemisphere. This may be an adaptive strategy to prevent awareness from being flooded by other mental functions or emotions that can inhibit the task at hand, for example delivering a eulogy.

Walter Freeman's hypothesis is that

> a global spatiotemporal pattern in each hemisphere is the principal correlate of awareness. The interactive populations of the brain are continually creating new local patterns of chaotic activity that are transmitted widely and that influence the trajectory of the global state. That is how the content of meaning emerges and grows in richness, range, and complexity ... So the whole hemisphere, in achieving unity from its myriad shifting parts, can sustain only one global spatiotemporal pattern at a time, but that unified pattern jumps continually, producing the chaotic but purposeful stream of consciousness.
>
> (Freeman, 2000, p. 232)

While it may be reductionist to call a person "right-brained" or "left-brained" as a whole, perhaps it is useful to recognize that a person can operate at certain times in states that favour "right-mode" or "left-mode" dominant processes.

We must be careful not to oversimplify, as states are dynamic entities that influence our awareness moment by moment. Additionally, modes and the more complex states in which they often are activated that we have identified as being either left or right hemisphere dominant may also involve activity on the opposite side of the brain in surprising and useful ways. For example, the work of Richard Davidson supports the view that both sides of the brain are important in emotion and emotion regulation (Davidson, 2003; Davidson & Begley, 2012). Davidson has demonstrated that areas of the left frontal lobe are important in approaching challenges, whereas the homologous areas in the right mediate withdrawal from challenges. His work has also shown that mindfulness meditation increases left frontal activation at baseline and in response to a challenge, considered a neurosignature of resilience. This "left shift" is directly correlated to the improvement of immune function following mindfulness training (Davidson et al., 2003). Interestingly, David Creswell and colleagues (2016) have found that after three days of a mindfulness retreat, inhibitory fibres from the left dorsolateral prefrontal cortex grew to the left posterior cingulate, an important part of the "default mode network" that mediates the OWN modes. This, along with studies of the role of the right hemisphere in emotion regulation, suggests the importance of left hemisphere regulation of obsessive thinking, as well as the cooperation of both hemispheres in facilitating self-regulation.

The idea that there are independent modes that work well together is also suggested by Davidson's theory addressing the central importance of four distinct circuits. These include those circuits mediating emotion regulation, joy creation, the focus of attention, and generosity. Davidson's findings support the general notion that having differentiated modes and linking them together creates wellbeing as they integrate in an individual's life (Davidson & Begley, 2012).

Stephen Kosslyn has built a model for understanding cognitive modes. In his view, higher and lower parts of the cortex – "top brain" and "bottom brain" – are involved in different modes, wherein

> the top brain formulates plans and puts them into motion, and the bottom brain classifies and interprets incoming information about the world … the two parts of the brain always work together; for instance, the top brain uses information from the bottom brain to formulate its plans (and to reformulate them, as they unfold over time). The two parts of the brain are a single system.
> (Kosslyn & Miller, 2015, p. 2; see also Borst et al., 2011)

This reinforces the idea that optimal functioning and complexity is achieved with the differentiation of modes and their linkage, supporting the proposal that integration is the basis of health and wellbeing. Linking different functional modes in the brain would be carried out through anatomic structural linkages of differentiated regions. Recent studies of the brain reveal that the best predictor of well-being across a wide range of measures is how interconnected the connectome is, or how linked the differentiated regions of the brain are (Smith et al., 2015).

Transforming traits: attention, awareness, choice, and change

What we pay attention to and how we pay attention shapes the flow of energy and information within our bodies and relationships. As we have seen, a shift in attention has the ability to radically transform states from chaos or rigidity to integrative functioning, as when sensing the body calms the mind, or naming an emotion tames distress. Though the various modes and states may shape our mental life, consciousness provides the opportunity for choice and change. How does this happen?

Through focal attention, we can bring automatic processes into awareness and transform them, enabling us to shape our own mental life and transform states from chaos or rigidity, the outcome of impaired integration, to the FACES flow of integration by linking differentiated functions. As we activate different modes and create different states with repeated practice, we are able to go beyond shifting in the moment to transforming our traits in the long run. Consciousness is essential for this growth, as the direction of focal attention with intention to aspects of mental life creates the possibility for change. When such conscious processing is intentionally catalysing integration, the automatic pilot states of chaos or rigidity can be transformed into the harmony and resilience of integration. For example, by distinguishing two components of consciousness from each other, differentiating the experience of knowing from the knowns of awareness, it is possible to create freedom. A useful acronym for this process is YODA – *you observe and decouple automaticity.*

Awareness has two essential components: the sense of *knowing* and that which is *known*. For example, as I type at the computer I am aware of the sound of my fingers on the keyboard and of the light emanating from the screen; these are the *knowns* of awareness. Simultaneously, I know I am aware of these objects of perception, which is my sense of *knowing*. Differentiating these aspects of awareness from each other, and strengthening the sense of knowing, creates the possibility of choice when a known arises, such as an impulse or habitual response pattern. When knowing is strengthened in this differentiating way, the capacity to hold even uncomfortable emotions and memories within the space of awareness is expanded and the tendency to identify with them as the totality of one's identity is reduced, allowing an individual to select an alternative path rather than enact the usual pattern of behaviour.

Automaticity, or autopilot, is when a trait of activating certain states and modes dominates in response to changing external or internal stimuli. This autopilot is without reflection or flexibility, not allowing an individual to choose how to act. When these traits are maladaptive, they can imprison a person's life. For example, if someone has a trait of avoiding awareness of emotions by reverting to an analytic mode, they may feel disconnected from others and even themselves. Such a trait may have developed to avoid painful emotions such as loneliness, sadness, or fear, but unavoidably all emotions have become blocked with such a strategy of adaptation. Emotions can be allowed to return as knowns of awareness by increasing the differentiation of the sense of knowing, so that a person can tolerate and even thrive in the presence of the bodily and emotional signals that before were intolerable. Knowing that a known is simply a known and not the totality of who one is creates the experience of being able to tolerate what before was intolerable. Over time, this can transform the trait of the propensity to be analytic when emotions arise into a more resilient and integrated trait of being open to whatever arises and flexible in responding. This is how the integration of consciousness moves an individual toward well-being and resilience.

How do you increase knowing? One way is mindfulness training, which builds *internal attunement* as attention is focused on the internal world. Such attunement can involve differentiating knowing from known, and differentiating conduit of sensation from the construction of thought and memory. Within this integrated consciousness, these various mental activities can then be linked. Another way is group therapy, which builds *interpersonal attunement*. The experience of emotional availability and support, as well as the feeling of being accepted as a differentiated individual by the group, can help strengthen a person's ability to hold within awareness previously intolerable emotions and memories, and begin to transform their lives. Belonging in a group is a form of interpersonal integration.

The role of linking distinct functions in psychotherapy and healing

In summary, the mind can be seen as having subjective experience, consciousness, information processing, and a self-organizing facet. This latter aspect of mind can be defined as the emergent property of a complex system of both embodied and relational energy and information flow. With this definition of one facet of the mind as self-organizing, we can see how integration – the linkage of differentiated functions – moves the complex system of energy flow in our bodies and relationships toward flexibility, adaptability, coherence, energy, and stability, the FACES flow of optimal self-organization. When such integration is impaired, chaos or rigidity result; when integration is facilitated, optimal functioning ensues.

For millions of years, the left and right sides of the brain have had distinct anatomical configurations and functional processes. While some popular interpretations of these distinct functions may be overly simplistic, such as the right is creative and the left is logical, science does in fact support the evolutionary reality of asymmetry of function and structure. Psychotherapists can utilize these scientifically sound findings to help promote integration in the lives of those who enter the psychotherapeutic journey with them. This journey is not just about the brain, or one or another side of the brain. The mind is both fully embodied and relational. As "psychotherapists" – therapists of the soul, the spirit, the intellect, and the mind – knowing that mind is more than brain can help place the mind in a broader and more accurate context. The mind is fully embodied – and so focusing on energy and information flow in the body as a whole, including its brain, is essential. Focusing on the energy and information flow between the individual and other people, and the larger cultural and ecological worlds in which they live, is vital for focusing on our relational minds.

In this embodied and relational way, energy and information flow. When freed to create its natural drive toward integration as an embodied and relational, self-organizing process, the mind can create well-being. But sometimes factors get in the way, and impairments to integration arise leading instead to chaos and rigidity in a person's life. One example of such impaired integration would be the lack of differentiation and linkage of left and right dominant modes of energy flow, as we've discussed in this chapter. But many other impediments to integration exist, including higher and lower neural regions, memory functions, meaning-making narrative integration, and impaired relational integration. In our personal relationships, honouring differences and promoting respectful, compassionate communication is essential to create the integration of our social lives at the heart of well-being. In our larger society as well, promoting integration is essential as we honour differences and cultivate compassionate linkages. An integrated society would be one in which compassion, connection and kindness thrive. Psychotherapists are in an important position to be specialists in the care of the mind and cultivate integration – left and right, up and down, inner and outer – at the heart of well-being in our individual and collective lives.

References

Baer, R. A., Smith, G. T., Hopkins, J., Krietemeyer, J., & Toney, L. (2006). Using self-report assessment methods to explore facets of mindfulness. *Assessment*, 13(I), 27–45.

Baron-Cohen, S. (2008). Theories of the autistic mind. *The Psychologist*, 21(2), 112–116.

Borst, G., Thompson, W. L., & Kosslyn, S. M. (2011). Understanding the dorsal and ventral systems of the human cerebral cortex: Beyond dichotomies. *American Psychologist*, 66(7), 624–632.

Creswell, J. D., Taren, A. A., Lindsay, E. K., Greco, C. M., Gianaros, P. J., Fairgrieve, A., & Ferris, J. L. (2016). Alterations in resting-state functional connectivity link mindfulness meditation with reduced interleukin-6: A randomized control trial. *Biological Psychiatry*. doi:10.1016/j.biopsych.2016.01.008

Davidson, R. J. (2003). Affective neuroscience and psychophysiology: Toward a synthesis. *Psychophysiology*, 40(5), 655–665.

Davidson, R. J., & Begley, S. (2012). *The emotional life of your brain*. London: Hodder & Stoughton.

Davidson, R. J., Kabat-Zinn, J., Schumacher, J., Rosenkranz, M., Muller, D., Santorelli, S. F., et al. (2003). Alterations in brain and immune function produced by mindfulness meditation. *Psychomatic Medicine*, 65(4), 564–570.

Devinsky, O. (2000). Right cerebral hemisphere dominance for a sense of corporeal and emotional self. *Epilepsy & Behavior*, 1(1), 60–73.

Duboc, V., Dufourcq, P., Blader, P., & Roussigné, M. (2015). Asymmetry of the brain: Development and implications. *Annual Review of Genetics*, 49, 647–672.

Farb, N. A. S., Segal, Z. V., Mayberg, H., Bean, J., McKeon, D., Fatima, Z., & Anderson, A. T. (2007). Attending to the present: Mindfulness meditation reveals distinct neural modes of self-reference. *Social Cognitive and Affective Neuroscience*, 2(4), 313–322.

Freeman, W. J. (2000). Emotion is essential to all intentional behaviors. In M. D. Lewis & I. Granic (Eds.), *Emotion, development, and self-organization: Dynamic systems approaches to emotional development* (pp. 209–235). Cambridge, UK: Cambridge University Press.

Hasson, U., Ghazanfar, A. A., Galantucci, B., Garrod, S., & Keysers, C. (2012). Brain-to-Brain coupling: A mechanism for creating and sharing a social world. *Trends in Cognitive Sciences*, 16(2), 114–121. doi:10.1016/j.tics.2011.12.007

Iacaboni, M. (2008). *Mirroring people: The new science of how we connect to others*. New York: Farrar, Straus, & Giroux.

Jackson, D. C., Mueller, C. J., Dolski, I., Dalton, K. M., Nitschke, J. B., Urry, H. L., & Davidson, R. J. (2003). Now you feel it, now you don't: frontal brain electrical asymmetry and individual differences in emotional regulation. *Psychological Science*, 14(6), 612–617.

Kosslyn, S. M., & Miller, G. W. (2015). *Top brain bottom brain: Harnessing the power of the four cognitive modes*. New York: Simon & Schuster Paperbacks.

Levitin, D. J. (2006). *This is your brain on music: The science of a human obsession*. New York: Dutton.

Lieberman, M. D., Eisenberger, N. I., Crockett, M. J., Tom, S. M., Pfeifer, J. H., & Way, B. M. (2007). Putting feelings into words: Affect labeling disrupts amygdala activity in response to affective stimuli. *Psychological Science*, 18(5), 421–428.

Limb, C. J., & Braun, A. R. (2008). Neural substrates of spontaneous musical performance: An fMRI study of Jazz improvisation. *PLoS ONE*, 3(2), e1679. doi:10.1371/journal.pone.0001679

Main, M. (1995). Attachment: Overview, with implications for clinical work. In S. Goldberg, R. Muir, & J. Kerr (Eds.), *Attachment theory: Social, developmental, and clinical perspectives* (pp. 407–474). Hillsdale, NJ: Analytic Press.

Main, M., Hesse, E., & Goldwyn, R. (2008). Studying difference in language usage in recounting attachment history: An introduction to the AAI. In H. Steele & M. Steele (Eds.), *Clinical applications of the adult attachment interview* (pp. 31–68). New York: The Guilford Press.

McGilchrist, I. (2009). *The master and his emissary: The divided brain and the making of the western world*. New Haven, CT: Yale University Press.

Müller, V., Sänger, J., & Lindenberger, U. (2013). Intra- and inter-brain synchronization during musical improvisation on the guitar. *PLoS ONE*, 8(9), e73852. doi:10.1371/journal.pone.0073852

Nielson, J. A., Zielinski, B. A., Ferguson, M. A., Lainhart, J. E., & Anderson, J. S. (2013). An evaluation of the left-brain vs. right-brain hypothesis with resting state functional connectivity magnetic resonance imaging. *PLoS ONE*, 8(8), e71275.

Schiller, V. (2017). *The attachment bond: Affectional ties across the lifespan.* Lanham, MD: Lexington.

Schore, A. N. (1994). *Affect regulation and the origin of the self: The neurobiology of emotional development.* Hillsdale, NJ: Erlbaum.

Schore, A. N. (2003). *Affect dysregulation and disorders of the self.* New York: W.W. Norton & Company, Inc.

Siegel, D. J. (2012). *The developing mind: How relationships and the brain interact to shape who we are, Second Edition.* New York: The Guilford Press.

Siegel, D. J. (2017). *Mind: A journey to the heart of being human.* New York: W.W. Nortan & Company, Inc.

Smith, S. M., Nichols, T. E., Vidaurre, D., Winkler, A. M., Behrens, T. E. J., Glasser, M. F., & Miller, K. L. (2015). A positive-negative mode of population co-variation links brain connectivity, demographics, and behavior. *Nature Neuroscience*, 18(11), 1567–1571.

Sroufe, L. A., Egeland, B., Carlson, E., & Collins, A. (2005). *The development of the person: The Minnesota study of risk and adaptation from birth to adulthood.* New York: The Guilford Press.

Tucker, D. M., Luu, P., & Pribram, K. H. (1995). Social and emotional self-regulation. *Annals of the New York Academy of Sciences*, 769, 213–239.

van der Kolk, B. (2014). *The body keeps the score: Brain, mind, and body in the healing of trauma.* New York: Viking.

Chapter 5

Systems-centred group psychotherapy

Developing a group mind that supports right brain function and right–left–right hemispheric integration

Susan P. Gantt and Bonnie Badenoch

In a recent educational case conference, a patient was interviewed and observed by six faculty discussants, including Susan, and about 30 psychiatry residents where the primary goal was training for the residents and secondarily making suggestions for the patient's continuing treatment. The stance of "observation" defined by the case conference context and its norms set the tone and likely influenced the group dynamics that developed as the attendees interacted about their recommendations for the patient after watching the interview between the patient and one of the faculty discussants. In this discussion after the interview, some of the faculty wanted to require the patient to do active physical exercises with a trainer and make his therapy sessions contingent on his completing his workouts. From the perspective of systems-centred therapy (SCT), they formed one subgroup within the larger group of the case conference-as-a-whole. Listening, I could feel myself pulled by the energy in this "let's shape him up" subgroup. Another group of faculty members (what SCT calls a second subgroup) wanted the patient to consider group therapy, which as a group therapist made sense to me immediately. I also liked the supportive rather than dictatorial stance of this suggestion. Clearly, I felt both subgroups in myself just as both subgroups were apparent in the whole group. (This similarity between the person, the subgroup and the group-as-a-whole is an example of isomorphy in SCT.)

During the interview, I was struck by the relative absence of feelings in the patient. As I listened, I had very little emotional experience in me of him. I was also curious about the strength in the subgroup wanting to take control of the patient, given that I (and others) experienced a push toward "making the patient do something", an uncommon role for me to take, yet clearly elicited in me and others in this context. SCT would consider how this lack of visible emotion in the patient and lack of feeling in me as I listened might have contributed to the energy that was aroused to take control. More specifically, this lack of emotional engagement which relates to our social brain may have contributed to the strength of the "taking control" subgroup.

This leads us to considering how an understanding of our divided brains may help us get an additional sense of what unfolded in this group process. Iain McGilchrist's (2009) unique synthesis of research concerning the two hemispheres is a good place to begin. Rather than each hemisphere *doing* something different, he speaks about how each *attends differently*, literally both seeing and creating a different world. From an SCT view, we can think of these as two different subgroups in our person system. Our right hemispheres focus broadly on the space between and what is emerging in this present moment. Supported by and supporting the primacy of our social nature (Cozolino, 2014; Siegel, 2012), this way of attending fosters collaboration because we have a felt sense of being in connection with each other. Stephen Porges (1995) recognized that the autonomic nervous system circuits of social engagement lateralize right, indicating that right-centric attending also supports safety in relationship. At the same time, people also feel seen and heard more easily because appreciation of uniqueness and individuality is characteristic of right-centric attending when we are secure. On the other hand, this way of seeing can also be uncomfortable because it notices the tentative and unpredictable nature of each emerging moment and is particularly sensitive to suffering and alert for differences that could be threatening.

Our left hemispheres have a different, and equally important, agenda. The left is concerned with what has already been experienced. It is skilled at making static what was flowing in the right so it can be taken apart and reorganized into systems. It creates algorithms, reducing individuality while extracting predictability and generalizations from many pieces of similar data. It makes organizing-maps out of many individual and unique journeys. It is goal-oriented, seeks control, tends toward either/or judgments (a driving force when immediate decisions are needed), and is more oriented to solving problems by putting pieces together than to a felt sense of relationship.

When left hemisphere ways of attending are split off from the right, we lose our sense of the context along with our experience of resonance and connectedness with people so that we feel alone even in the midst of others. This lack of connectedness leaves us wary and fosters some level of sympathetic arousal. SCT often says: "Words without a connection to feeling have no meaning" (Y. M. Agazarian, personal communication, 10 April 2015). When right hemisphere attending is not integrated with left brain function, we lose our ability to observe and reality-test our right brain sense. We need our left brain function to put language to what we sense in our right brain and to generalize from it. Neither way of attending is sufficient unto itself. As McGilchrist says:

> The right hemisphere, the one that believes, but does not know, has to depend on the other, the left hemisphere, that knows, but doesn't believe. It is as though a power that has an infinite, and therefore

intrinsically uncertain, potential Being needs nonetheless to submit to be delimited – needs stasis, certainty, fixity – in order to Be.

(McGilchrist, 2009, p. 428)

The right brain's way of attending provides the relational vision and felt sense experience that the left brain can make manifest by organizing systems in which relatedness can thrive, or, as McGilchrist suggests, the right is the Master and the left the faithful emissary. When our left hemisphere has been fuelled by our right hemisphere way of attending, we can provide solid support for collaborative groups of all kinds.

In our culture today, rather than this collaborative relationship where we can integrate the resources between our two brains, about 75% of us now live in left hemisphere dominance (Fredrickson et al., 2013), far from the complementary relationship of the Master and emissary that McGilchrist has proposed. When our right hemispheres become flooded with too much information or we become frightened because of past implicit experience, we may adaptively shift into left dominance for the temporary security and relief from discomfort this offers. Similarly, SCT sees this as a retreat to left-centric explanations when frightened or flooded by our implicit right-centric experience rather than learning to titrate our experience at the edge of the unknown. In left dominance, we let go of our sense of connection with others and are no longer able to draw on the resources of our social brain. Instead, we begin to focus on the task of controlling the situation, as happened in the subgroup in the case conference. Because our brains do resonate so much with one another, this dominant cultural shift to the left pulls on us constantly. This may partially account for what I was experiencing in the case conference when the patient appeared cut off from his own emotional experience. The interview did not provide a relational context in which he felt secure, so he adapted as we all do by using what SCT calls a past adaptive survival role where his early implicit right brain experience and adaptation dominated his right brain circuitry. It seemed to take the form of him withdrawing when he was not seen, so I (and others) could not "feel" him and both the patient and the listeners were left without our social brain sense of connection. The patient and interviewer were unable to socially engage in emotional resonance leaving the conference itself with little emotional richness or empathy. The interview itself appeared to induce left brain responses in part of the conference group (likely also related to past adaptive survival roles in the attendees), spawning a subgroup that wanted to set consequences for non-compliance.

Fortunately, my experience in SCT, which fosters hemispheric cooperation and integration and emphasizes how group norms govern group behaviour, allowed me to recognize this induction rather than joining the strong pull toward left-centric responding. Instead, I voiced my frustration about not having an emotional sense of the patient. With strong feeling,

I brought in my recognition of the group dynamic to control the patient that had been aroused in many of us in the conference. Like in the case conference, our social brain resonance makes this kind of arousal and induction inevitable when left-centric processes are dominant. Yet there has been little focus on understanding group processes and group norms in settings like case conferences nor on the pull to left-centric processing in group psychotherapy. Awareness of the power of hemispheric location could support group leaders to influence norms that foster social brain development in such groups to increase our capacity to relate more fully with patients and with one another during these consultations in a way that significantly shapes the help we offer our patients.

It is also important to notice that psychotherapy groups are underutilized in our culture in spite of the research showing equivalent outcomes for patients in group therapy when compared to individual therapy (Burlingame, Strauss, & Joyce, 2013). This lack of emphasis on group psychotherapy may be a reflection of the more left brain cultural focus on symptoms and remediation of them as well as a kind of devaluing of our relational/social brains leading to undervaluing collaborative groups in general. Consequently, psychotherapy is often one-on-one with cognitive behavioural approaches, which are more easily measured in left brain research and exclude emphasis on developing the range of relational capacities that group psychotherapy potentially offers. Group psychotherapy may be ideal for creating secure contexts which support right-centric ways of attending to others and enhancing our social brain function, especially important in the context of our left-dominated culture. More specifically, and as we will discuss in the remainder of this chapter, SCT groups and their method of functional subgrouping emphasize developing norms that potentiate greater integration of right and left modes of attending that fosters our overall development and relational lives.

Comprehension and apprehension in systems-centred group therapy

Systems-centred therapy (SCT) and its theory of living human systems has emphasized group psychotherapy and long conceptualized human knowing as being both "apprehensive" and "comprehensive" (Agazarian, 1997). Apprehensive knowing is more right-centric and relates to implicit knowing, including awareness of sensory experience, emotional knowing, sensitivity to nonverbal cues, and attention to bodily sensations. In this mode, we know without words, or we know in metaphors or images. From an apprehensive connection with ourselves, it is natural to look around a group with a broad focus and to more easily see the context and the interconnections between what is happening in the group and between us and others. We are more likely to see the bigger picture and to stay curious about the unknown.

Comprehensive processing comes from left brain attending which creates generalities from data gathered through individual experiences, and uses words to know the world, to grasp things, to pin things down and to translate our apprehensive knowing into simplified maps. When we look around our world in this way, our focus is more narrow and oriented to what we already know, important when steadiness is needed. We are more interested in creating systems to make things work, and less interested in what is happening relationally in the moment, attenuating development of our social here–and–now systems in favour of manipulating the world and abstracting.

One goal of systems–centred therapy is making the boundary appropriately permeable between apprehensive and comprehensive, similar to the right–centric and left–centric ways of attending. Beginning with our nonverbal knowing, we can then translate our experience into words that help us map our experience and the world well enough that we feel more oriented and settled. We can then use our maps to guide our experience back to the right hemisphere for deeper exploration of our emerging apprehensive, nonverbal, contextual knowing, that when translated into words is often in the right–centric language of metaphors. McGilchrist (2009) speaks about this right–left–right (R-L-R) process as the pathway to progressively deepening integration of our experience that leads to greater resilience. In SCT terms, patients seeking group therapy often have boundaries that are too open or too closed to either apprehensive or comprehensive processing. These patients have adapted to conditions earlier in their lives without having the interpersonal support to develop sufficient neural integration to build a collaborative relationship between the two kinds of attending (which SCT sees as internal subgroups) and to develop boundaries that are appropriately permeable to both. Instead, one hemisphere seems to dominate at the expense of the other. Interestingly, McGilchrist points out that many of the connections between the right and left hemispheres are inhibitory, which SCT would see as potentially in the service of appropriate boundary permeability. For example, SCT encourages inhibiting our human tendency to "explain" (left-centric) in order to make space for "exploring" (more right-centric) when the goal is discovering what we do not yet know. On the other hand, inhibiting our right-centric focus when our moment-to-moment experience is faster than we can integrate can also be an important driving force for slowing us down to better integrate new information. Learning to titrate this boundary helps us develop the collaborative relationship between the two.

Systems-centred therapy and its theory of living human systems

SCT was developed by applying a theory of living human systems (Agazarian, 1997, 2012) which defines a hierarchy of isomorphic systems that are energy-organizing, goal-directing, and self-correcting. A living human system can be as small as a person, a couple, family, or group, or as large as a nation or a world. Perhaps not surprisingly, the development of the SCT theoretical map was fuelled by right hemisphere knowing or apprehension and the R–L–R movement McGilchrist has identified. Yvonne Agazarian wrote about her process in developing SCT theory:

> I woke up one night with a wave of excitement and a symbol in my head (like, but not like, the three rings that advertise a beer). I had no idea what it meant, but I knew it was important. I got up and drew it on the back of the nearest piece of paper (a bill). Then I took it into the other room and pondered. My feelings were very mixed – the symbol reminded me of fragments of symbols that I had experienced before; a bright curve, a brush stroke of light, an "s" which was not an "s". I "knew" that each one was important, had no idea of how they were important and had been left to contain them, as a series of tantaliz-ing images which never quite left and which might never reveal their meaning – if they had a meaning. Some of my dread was that this was more of the same. Some of my excitement was that this time, the symbol was not a fragment but a coherent whole. What the symbol gave me was a structure in which I could compare and contrast the levels of abstractions that I was trying to integrate between the individ-ual and the group. It also gave me a frame from which I was later able to develop a theory of living human systems.
>
> (Agazarian & Gantt, 2000, p. 99)

> I have no doubt that for me theory does not come from my comprehen-sive brain. Rather, it comes from some subterranean force that has a rhythm of its own. A rhythm that I sometimes experience with such pressure that it is difficult to contain, and no amount of pacing reduces it. At other times it flows sweetly onto paper and I feel like a cipher rather than author, and often do not comprehend what I have written until after I read it. So this [theory] … contains both the reasoned arguments and also the flow that demands apprehension before comprehension.
>
> (Agazarian & Gantt, 2000, p. 221)

Hierarchy

Just as Yvonne Agazarian's right brain attending fuelled the SCT theory map, applying SCT's theory uses a left brain map to access greater right brain knowing and integration, again a flow of right–left–right. The map broadens our attention beyond our personal reactions to support our ability to see the bigger context, which increases our apprehensive attending. For example, SCT operationally defines its theoretical construct of hierarchy as each system existing in the context of the system above it and being the context for the system below it. Applying this theoretical construct means that a person is never in isolation but always in a context where there is continually emerging mutual influence between the systems in the defined hierarchy. Guided by this theoretical map, SCT leaders actively influence a group norm of undoing our human tendency to take ourselves just person-ally, and often say to a group: "Who we can be has as much, if not more, to do with the group than with just ourselves." Learning to see oneself in context enables group members not to take their own experience or reac-tions as just personal about themselves and instead to see their experience as a group voice.

This first picture (Figure 5.1) illustrates the hierarchy with the person system as the centre circle that provides the energy (the life force energy and exploratory drive) to the whole hierarchy. The member system has the goal of development. This system, in turn, exists in the context of the system-as-a-whole with its goal of transformation. In SCT therapy groups, partici-pants learn to connect to their life force energy and exploratory drive, to connect to others as members, and to see their experience as not only a voice for themselves (person system) but also as a member voice for the group-as-a-whole. As a member, we can contribute with other members to influence the group-as-a-whole norms. Group norms in turn influence member and person system development.

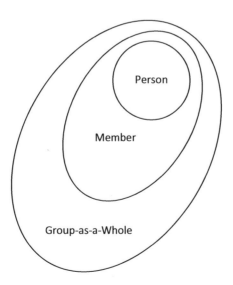

Figure 5.1 Person system, member system, and group-as-a-whole system.

Isomorphy

SCT theory defines isomorphy as similarity in structure and function for systems in a defined hierarchy. As we mentioned, this means that whatever we know at one system level applies to the other levels. Returning to Figure 5.1, there will be a similarity between the structure and function of the person, member, and group-as-a-whole systems. Structure is defined as boundaries that open or close to energy/information. Function defines that all living human systems survive, develop, and transform through the process of discriminating and integrating differences, differences in the apparently similar and similarities in the apparently different. Applying this has led to SCT's functional subgrouping, a conflict resolution method that enables groups to more easily integrate differences by joining first on similarities with differences being explored in a different subgroup.

In a recent SCT training, two groups came together to work as one large group. Initially, members voiced anxiety over the large group of 50. Two subgroups emerged, both of which contained important information for the group. As the first subgroup worked together, they joined each other on their present similarity of feeling anxious. Coming together in this way activates the social brain resources that increase security. In this greater security of the subgroup, they then undid their anxiety together, and their anxiety subsided. Another subgroup then began exploring their experience of seeing the group-as-a-whole, noting their vision broadened, became blurry, not so sharply focused, all language of right-centric apprehensive experience. The SCT "map" of the whole group had guided their exploration of seeing and being part of the whole and subgrouping about this experience where each built on the one before, leading to the experience of feeling part of the whole. This enabled more and more of the individual differences to flow into the group as group voices.

Person-as-a-system

Seeing people as not only *embedded* in living human systems but also *as* living human systems enables still another view. Again thinking in terms of a hierarchy of systems, picture the person system as three nested systems (see Figure 5.2): the inner-person (containing our primary life force energy and our exploratory drive and the past adaptive survival roles we have developed to protect our life force and adapt to our care-givers and socializers), the inter-person (where we develop present adaptive roles as explorer, member, subgroup member, and researcher), and the person-as-a-whole (where we transform and influence norms in ourselves and our contexts) (Agazarian, 2015c).

Roles in
Our Person-as-a-System

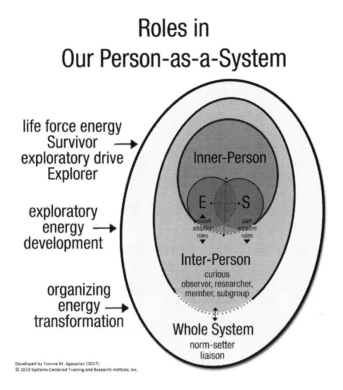

life force energy
Survivor →
exploratory drive
Explorer

exploratory
energy →
development

organizing
energy →
transformation

Inner-Person

E   S

recent   past
adaptive   adaptive
roles   roles

Inter-Person
curious
observer, researcher,
member, subgroup

Whole System
norm-setter
liaison

Developed by Yvonne M. Agazarian (2017).
© 2019 Systems-Centered Training and Research Institute, Inc.

Figure 5.2 Person-as-a-system: the inner-person, inter-person, and person-as-a whole.

SCT group leaders hold SCT's theoretical map both implicitly/apprehensively (through training that focuses on group experience – right-centric) and explicitly/comprehensively (through learning the intricacies of the map – left-centric), enabling them to guide the group in its development.

Group mind

Siegel (2012) defined "mind" as an embodied process that regulates the flow of energy and information. Building on this, SCT has also introduced the idea of the group mind as a bridge between SCT's theory of living human systems (Gantt & Agazarian, 2013) and interpersonal neurobiology. Apprehensively attending to our SCT groups led us to see the group-as-a-whole like a group brain with differential subgroup resources, guiding us to our understanding of the "group mind" as we envision it in SCT. This image emerged while watching a group work and seeing first the right "hemisphere" pulsating (in SCT terms, one subgroup deepening their apprehensive exploration with images and sensations) and then as the first subgroup paused, the left hemisphere (subgroup) translating the exploration of the first subgroup from short words and images into sentences that organized what had happened. This apprehensive image led us to what we have called the group mind (Gantt & Agazarian, 2010): where the group system in its sub-grouping process contains the implicit right-centric emergence which then enables translation into words (more left-centric), which then guides more implicit exploration, elaboration, reality-testing and integration. Seeing it as isomorphic, this process of containing, exploring, and integrating occurs at all levels of the group system: the person, the member, and the group-as-a-whole system. Not surprisingly, this process reflects the internal integration between the hemispheres that a person-as-a-whole experiences when the master and emissary are collaborating.

Similar to Siegel's definition of "mind", SCT conceptualizes living human systems as regulating the flow of energy and information within and between systems in the triadic hierarchy. Thus, "we can conceptual-ize the group mind as the interdependent processes within and between the systems of person, member, subgroup, and group-as-a-whole that regulate the flow of [apprehensive and comprehensive] energy and infor-mation within the system of the psychotherapy group" (Gantt & Agazar-ian, 2013, p. 80). This mind-regulating process is different within each level of the system and interdependent between the different systems in the system hierarchy.

Returning again to SCT's map of the person-as-a-system (Figure 5.2), in the inner-person system, regulation comes from centring into one's primary life force, activating curiosity and one's explorer role, or repeating past adaptive sur-vival roles. Past adaptive roles relate to early implicit memory and attachment solutions, heavily right lateralized in implicit memory. SCT calls these "survival roles" as they relate to past adaptations that ensured adaptive survival for the inner-person system and its connection to its care-givers. Within these survival roles, the boundaries are often impermeable or overly permeable between com-prehensive and apprehensive processing. Our perceptions from within our sur-vivor role selectively attune to the similarities in the present that remind us of the past and we are less aware of the differences between the past and the pre-sent. When we are in a past adaptive role, our here-and-now emotional experi-ence (where the potential for new development lies) is limited as awareness focuses more on these past perceptions due to activation of Hebbian (1949) neural connections (circuits that fire together, wire together) in implicit memory. When survivor roles are activated, broadly focused attention is often restricted and the boundaries of the role orient to staying with the past with little or no capacity for new apprehensive discoveries.

An over-reliance on either apprehensive or comprehensive processing disrupts adaptive here-and-now exploration. SCT groups introduce func-tional subgrouping, an inter-person present adaptive role, for exploring the here-and-now experience which creates a secure relational context in which to explore the survivor roles which then influences the inner-person and the person-as-a-whole. This is compatible with Ecker, Ticic, and Hulley (2012) whose work suggests that pairing activated implicit survival roles with emerging reparative disconfirming experiences can change the felt sense quality of implicit memories, leading to permanent shifts in how we relate with others. SCT's functional subgrouping develops the secure relational contact by joining on resonant similarities and then providing new and different experiences that can be integrated into the familiar implicit.

SCT and the social brain

The SCT method of functional subgrouping (which develops an inter-person role) introduces a group norm of first joining on similarities. This enables boundaries to open in the inter-person system where we can use our social brain resources of empathy, attunement, and resonance to regulate with others. Joining on similarities usually sets in motion the social engagement branch of our autonomic nervous system (Porges, 2011) where members connect and build a here-and-now adaptive system together that discriminates and integrates energy and information as it emerges in functional subgrouping. At times, members react to differences or the unknown and get drawn into re-enacting old adaptations and inducing or being induced into role locks with others as the awakening of one person's implicit memory touches old patterns in another member. The functional subgrouping process provides a secure context for exploring these roles and role locks, giving the members who are experiencing them the felt sense of being understood and joined. This enables their curiosity and exploratory drive to open to new energy and information in the here-and-now. In this way, SCT with its functional subgrouping fosters development of the inherent resources of our social brains.

Cozolino has this to say about the social brain:

> Relationships are the environment of the social brain in much the same way as a barn is the environment of a mouse. As the location of food sources change, so does the mouse's brain, developing new neurons and new neural connections in areas involved with foraging, retrieval, and spatial mapping. Similarly, the social group is the human environment, with the brain adapting to an ever-changing stream of interpersonal information and constellations of relationships.
>
> (Cozolino, 2014, p. 15)

Beckes and Coan (2011), in their work on social baseline theory, state that "the primary ecology to which human beings are adapted is one that is rich with other humans" (p. 976). Integrating findings from both animal and human research, they suggest that the presence of others, especially those with whom we are close, lowers the impact of stress on us and enables us to solve problems more easily and economically than when we are on our own.

Siegel (2012) stresses that dyadic regulation shapes self-regulation, especially in our early development, and that the neural circuits responsible for emotional processing also link our internal and interpersonal relating. He also notes that thanks to neuroplasticity, if there were deficits in co-regulation in early life, safe experiences with others can build the circuitry throughout our lifespan.

Similarly, SCT emphasizes the inter-person system as the most influential system throughout our life for social and emotional processing. Changes in the inter-person system also most easily influence the contiguous systems of inner-person and system-as-a-whole. Thus it is through our inter-person connections with others that our inner-person and whole system character are shaped and reshaped throughout our lives. For this reason, SCT groups begin by building the inter-person system within the group, through functional subgrouping, so that both the neural connections in the right hemispheres of members are developed and the left-centric reality-testing is strengthened. This paves the way for emergence of the group mind.

The development of the group mind as an emergent and regulating process is central in the ongoing experience of any group. Building on Schore's (2010, 2012) landmark work, it is at the level of implicit experiential learning (Greenberg, 2007) that group psychotherapy is particularly effective. SCT group therapy supports access to right brain implicit functioning in the group therapy context which "includes a dysregulating affective experience that is communicated to an empathic other ... with an opportunity for interactive affect regulation, the core of the attachment process" (Schore, 2010, p. 194).

The group mind, as an ongoing embodied process of regulating the flow of energy and information, can support such changes in old patterns or become dominated by survival roles like flight, fight, or dissociation (Gantt & Agazarian, 2013). When survival roles are stimulated, the focus shifts to past survival goals at the expense of development. The example of the case conference earlier in this chapter illustrates a group mind organized by survival patterns, which likely began before the group even convened as part of the initial structure. Only by listening from our more broadly focused, emotional/social right brain, supported by the resources of left-centric awareness of how these processes unfold, can we feel, hear, and understand this kind of implicit and inductive communication. Listening from this collaborative right–left–right perspective is an essential step in supporting movement toward development.

Many group leaders have not had access to training in working with the kind of group processes described in the case conference above.

When the implicit group dynamics are unrecognized and cannot be explored, they can easily derail the group and stimulate group members into past adaptive survival roles originally developed in their earlier attachment relationships or in their socialization processes (Agazarian, 2015a, 2015b; Gantt & Agazarian, 2017). For example, in our case conference, the role induction for many of us was to join in dominance and left-shifted control which could easily develop into a scapegoating pattern. The patient's treatment planning would then be fuelled by scapegoating energy and that in turn would trigger other members in the conference into past adaptive survival roles.

The remainder of this chapter highlights aspects of SCT with groups, emphasizing the ways in which SCT strengthens our right lateralized social brain functioning and both supports and is supported by integration of left-centric resources in the ongoing collaboration of right–left–right, which is our brain's natural pattern of development and transformation (McGilchrist, 2009). We conclude with a brief discussion of the kind of extensive training in which SCT therapists engage in order to internalize both right-centric embodied knowledge of the process and clarity about the left-centric maps that guide what emerges in the group, both supporting and containing the group's experience. A more detailed overview of SCT with groups can be found in Agazarian (1997).

Systems-centred group therapy

We discussed earlier the central idea in SCT that all living human systems survive, develop, and transform from simpler to more complex by discriminating and integrating differences. Applied to a person system, the more we discriminate and integrate our left- and right-centric functions, the more resources we have to survive, develop, and transform from simpler to more complex. We need the relational, contextual knowing of our right brain function with the flow of information unfolding from moment to moment, and the resources of our social brains supporting our interactions with ourselves and with others. Equally important, we need the narrower focus of our left brain function to help us grasp details, generalize, organize, reality-test, and provide stability for our ongoing experience. Developing the capacity to integrate both our left and right brain function in a way that each resource supports the other is at the core of integrating differences. In group therapy, this challenge expands to not only the human differences within us but also between us and others, which is the heart of the work of an SCT group.

When we relate with others who we experience as "too" different from us, our vigilance system, a network that is amygdala-centric and right lateralized, activates to warn us of potential danger. This network draws on circuitry deeper in our midbrain where the roots of our social-emotional experience reside. Panksepp describes a midbrain FEAR system that awakens when we become disconnected from others, a feeling that perceived differences can stimulate (Panksepp & Biven, 2012). Our autonomic nervous system responds to this perceived threat by activating adaptive processes that lead to withdrawal (flight), arguing (fight), or the possibility of dissociation (collapse) if the differences become too overwhelming (Porges, 2011). As this fear process unfolds, activation of past adaptive survival roles in the inner-person can lead to role locks with others in the inter-person system as one person's implicit memory touches and awakens the implicit memories of others. Or at the system-as-a-whole level, groups may establish norms to keep differences out as fear mounts. This is happening currently in many countries with political parties becoming polarized as they respond to the sense of threat that is strong right now, and then appealing to the broader fear in the community to gain the possibility of taking control to extinguish the fear activation. Trying to intervene in this process of escalating fear in individuals or countries with left-oriented facts or control has little to no possibility of promoting the interpersonal connections on which our human systems depend in order to activate the essential resources of our social brains enabling us to interact with much less fear activation (Beckes & Coan, 2011; Porges, 2011; Siegel, 2012).

Being aware of these dynamics, SCT groups establish several important norms that seek to provide an interpersonal environment in which differences can be explored and integrated rather than bringing on a cascade of fear and implicit activation. First, all SCT groups begin with centring, which supports access to right brain apprehensive knowing. In addition, as we have noted, SCT groups use functional subgrouping to provide interpersonal support as differences emerge. This makes it less likely that the members' FEAR systems, amygdala networks, and autonomic nervous systems will activate each other in response to differences and dominate the group process. Even if such activation does occur, functional subgrouping provides a way toward interpersonal joining with others who also feel activated, almost always activating our social engagement system and leading to a calming experience when there is a felt sense of not being alone with our distress.

Centring in an SCT group

Beginning with centring immediately enables SCT groups to shift from comprehension to apprehension and to bring their centred energy into member role (inter-person system) in the group context, as paraphrased below from Agazarian:

> Centering begins by connecting through our feet to the ground, tuning into bodily sensation in our feet as we focus on our contact with the ground. Then we expand our focus to feel the support of the earth under our feet and the support of the chair under the bones in our

pelvis that we sit on, our "sit bones". As we tune into the support of our breathing, we feel our expansion into and contact with the universe on our in-breath and the settling into our physical center on our out-breath, connecting us to our physical center and where we know without words. From this centered connection with ourselves, we bring ourselves into member role and look around and make brief, roving eye contact with the members of the group and let the group know when we are present.

(Agazarian, 2011, p. 8)

The steps in this process also provide the opportunity to interrupt habitual survival roles that as human beings we often import into any unfamiliar interpersonal context. Our social brains are extremely sensitive to gestures, tone of voice, level of eye gaze, and other nonverbal cues, so that individuals who arrive in group in past adaptive survival roles can touch implicit experience in others in ways that draw the whole group into recreating that past experience. Instead, centring and coming into roving eye contact cues us into the eye gaze that is inherently human and can begin to activate the right lateralized social engagement system (Porges, 2011) for here-and-now interaction rather than past implicit neural networks from past adaptive roles. This process provides a here-and-now alternative for regulating the potential activation of a new and unknown context.

In contrast, for example, Tina arrived late to a recent group and so missed the centring process. Her face was "blank" and immobile. In SCT theory, her blank face was a system output that signalled she was in an old survival role adaptation, perhaps stimulated by something outside of group or even the experience of arriving late itself. Tina's blank face likely related to the activation of the dorsal branch of the autonomic nervous system (Porges, 2011), as a protection. We do not know exactly what may have led her to sense a similarity between arriving late to an already-connected group and something in her early history; however, we have the evidence of her face's immobility to attest to the depth of her fear and disconnection.

As is often the case, in just 1–2 minutes, the ambiguity in her blank face and for some, resonance with Tina's inner state, induced others into their early survival attachment roles. When there is a blank face (Agazarian, 2015a, 2015b; Porges, 2011), our attunement is disrupted, our social engagement system shuts down, and we easily default to our own survival roles related to early attachment adaptations. In this state, we then project the perception from our survival roles onto the blank face (Agazarian, 2015a, 2015b). At the same time, the resonance circuitry in the leader and members is likely to have been responding to Tina's inner state, potentially touching their implicit memories embedded in their past adaptive roles (Badenoch, 2011; Iacoboni, 2009; Porges, 2011).

SCT methods with their emphasis on empathy, resonance, and attunement support what Porges (2011) calls a neuroception of safety (a felt sense below the level of conscious awareness), where our autonomic nervous system calms and social engagement can return. When we feel connected, our SEEKING system (the source of free-flowing curiosity and energy to move toward) comes online (Panksepp & Biven, 2012). As these capacities re-appeared, the group members began to expand their awareness beyond survival roles and explore what was happening. One group member started to notice he had gone into his "withdrawal" role and was not making eye contact with Tina. Another member noticed she felt her "one-up" role activated and was starting to stereotype Tina in a way that put Tina down. Tina joined the subgrouping exploration, noting that the faces of the other group members (reflecting their survival roles) initially stimulated her to go more deeply into her survival role where she disconnects from herself and others, hence her disconnected and "blank" face.

In contrast to this example, centring right at the beginning of group starts to build greater connection to the kind of apprehensive, right-centric experience that emerges when we feel safe. We are more attuned to the sensory, intuitive, oriented to the present moment, often without words, with a felt sense of settling into ourselves. As members move from this more centred person system to the inter-person system by coming into roving eye contact with each other, it is often apparent that the group and its members are in their social engagement systems, where eye contact is relaxed and open, faces are mobile as the striated facial muscles relax, and breathing naturally deepens. Porges (2011) describes the social engagement system as an exploratory assessment process where we look to see if the other is there for contact and test it out by seeing and sensing if their face is responding to ours. SCT sees this as our curious explorer role. Though done primarily at the implicit level, it is almost as if we are thinking, "Does Tina respond when I make eye contact with her and if yes, I can approach more and relax more" only at a much more rapid rate than language. This is a very rapid interchange of checking, offering and response that enables us to both test and establish the level of safety that provides an alternative to a series of survival role inductions. Supporting this social engagement function in one another in the here-and-now is essential to providing a critically important alternative to our default survivor roles that replicate our past adaptations and maintain us in fear activation. Once centred and present as members, the group begins subgrouping.

Functional subgrouping

Functional subgrouping is the heart of an SCT group. It enables a group to work with its inevitable human differences with less likelihood of activating the FEAR system (Panksepp & Biven, 2012) and awakening old survival roles with implicit right-centric activation. Instead, when subgrouping, members learn to engage and develop here-and-now connection using their social right lateralized brains rather than their right lateralized brains being caught up in a fear response. By first joining on similarities, functional sub-grouping facilitates differences becoming resources for development rather than as threats. As human beings, we are wired to respond very quickly if we perceive danger. Ledoux (1998) has borrowed a well-known analogy from Eastern culture: Walking in the woods, we encounter a piece of rope shaped like a snake and our split-second protective reaction is to run (flight) or kill the snake (fight) or freeze while we quickly assess what to do next. Typically, areas of our anterior cingulate and parts of our orbital frontal cortex activate to reassess our quick response to the perceived threat, inhibiting our faster amygdala firing pattern, a kind of top-down regulation.

SCT sees differences as potentially "threatening" to what we know already, our stability so to speak, as the process of integrating differences requires us to "de-stabilize" before we can integrate. In addition, drawing from Porges (2011), when our safety feels challenged, we may find it difficult to remain in connection with the person we experience as "different". Because our neuro-ception of safety supports and is supported by maintaining connection, we can feel as though our very survival is threatened by these differences, potentially leading to amygdala activation and implicit engagement of past adaptive roles. Functional subgrouping addresses the challenges differences introduce by first joining on similarities, which lowers fear activation, before exploring small differences within the similar subgroup. The group then makes room for larger differences to be explored in a separate subgroup with those who feel similarly about the difference. This creates a secure context for exploring with others in a climate of similarity, allowing the social engagement system to activate, enabling small differences to be explored without reacting to them as a threat. In time, the whole group integrates as each subgroup discovers similarities in what was initially different.

The basics of functional subgrouping

In functional subgrouping, group members start by reflecting the person who has spoken, in empathy, attunement, and resonance, and then building, by adding a similarity of their own. This begins with one person speaking and when he or she is finished, the person looks around the group in roving eye contact and says, "Anyone else?" The "next talker" reflects the heart of the "first talker" and then adds something similar. SCT recognizes that similarities more easily cross boundaries within and between group members and that when differences are perceived as too different, boundaries close for protection. Joining on a similarity develops a subgroup system (inter-person) that takes us beyond just ourselves (inner-person system). When joining, our social brains facilitate resonance and responsiveness with others, rather than vigilance and fear activation. This contains and organizes the flow of our feelings and apprehensive knowing.

For example, Bob, an older member, began talking about how vulnerable he felt with the recent ISIS-linked shooting in California, attributing his feeling to his age:

BOB: I have been feeling very vulnerable and am having a hard time even going grocery shopping without feeling scared. [Looking around and making roving eye contact with the group.] Anyone else?

JENNY: [Looking at Bob, making eye contact with him and watching his face to see if he feels understood as she reflects him.] So Bob, you feel vulnerable, even going to shop.

BOB: [Nodding and face relaxing as he is joined, evidence of social engagement activation and lowering of the sympathetic activation that had been apparent in his initial voice tone.] Yes!

JENNY: I have been feeling that way too. Like the only place I feel safe is at home.

After successfully reflecting Bob, Jenny shifts from focusing on him to reconnecting with herself (which at this point is a different self after connecting to and understanding Bob). She then built with her own similarity, thus introducing small differences.

Making eye contact and reflecting the heart of the talker's message activates the social engagement system in both members, evidenced here by the facial relaxation and voice tone. Reflecting someone requires using our own somatosensory system enabling "we-centric" dimensions by "reusing part of the same neural circuits underpinning our first-person experience of the same emotion" (Ammaniti & Gallese, 2014, p. 15). This mirroring system enables reflection to be more than a mere repetition of words by resonating with and capturing the prosody and rhythm of the speaker.

When groups are first learning to reflect the person they are joining, the words may initially be more like a rote paraphrase. Over time, members develop in their capacity to empathize and resonate with each other, their social resonance circuits become more available, and they learn to reflect the heart of the other person's message including the speaker's feeling, tone and tempo. The goal of reflecting is to make sure that the original speaker feels understood and to build reality-testing as talkers are encouraged to "correct" if they do not feel understood. This builds the member system (the inter-person system) in the group and develops the circuitry of both social brains. With this process, we are building a system norm of working to understand each other, which also isomorphically develops this neural capacity in each person so that it is available in their life contexts. This process replicates the R-L-R process where we resonate and then translate our felt resonance in words that lets us find out if we understood the other. In this process of reflecting and activating social engagement in the group context, members relax and become more open to exploring their experience and curious about themselves and others, making person, member and group development more possible.

SCT has long maintained that subgrouping builds emergent systems enabling the members of the subgroup to explore in ways they cannot on their own. As members subgroup together, they establish a secure here-and-now attachment among themselves, which becomes an alternative to being drawn into past adaptive survival roles. We can think of subgrouping as enabling here-and-now R-L-R adaptations, or in SCT language, present role adaptations, where members are building "we-systems". This kind of joining is supported by the research of Uri Hasson and his colleagues (Hasson, Ghazanfar, Galantucci, Garrod, & Keysers, 2012; Stephens, Silbert, & Hasson, 2010). Their work in laboratory experiments on communication has shown that when listeners and speakers become emotionally engaged, their brains become coupled with parallel neural firing patterns, enabling new joint behaviours that neither individual would do alone. When communication concludes, these brain coupling effects disappear.

Functional subgrouping in the here-and-now

Drawing from the SCT construct of isomorphy (similar in structure and function), the group leader listened to group members' voices as belonging not only to their experience of going to the grocery, but also as voices for the group's here-and-now experience. The leader then encouraged the group to explore how they might be "locking their doors" in the group itself, keeping parts of themselves from being present. The members subgrouped together and, drawing on both right-centric apprehensive experience and left-centric observation, identified the past adaptive survival roles they felt in themselves. Initially, they identified what SCT calls social survival roles (e.g. "have to be interesting to contribute", "not relevant"). Later the earlier attachment survival roles emerged (e.g. "Bad me"). As subgrouping deepened, the flow made space for all the individual differences that resonated with the group members. By the end of the meeting, the group was quite moved as it understood through its exploration that the alternative to the old survival roles was learning to work "with" and "together" to manage the fear that was aroused in the culture, impacting each person.

Functional subgrouping to integrate differences

Functional subgrouping is a conflict resolution method that enables groups to more easily integrate differences. Returning to our example, after a pause in the work that Jenny and Bob were doing, Ellen came in; following the subgrouping structure, she asked if there was room for a difference. The group supported her to bring it in.

ELLEN: I am just angry, I am angry at ISIS and I am angry that you two are letting yourself get scared. I am really angry. Anyone else?

MARK: [Reflecting her before speaking about his own feelings.] So you are really angry!

ELLEN: [Nodding.] Yes! You got me.

MARK: Me, too. I am angry about feeling frightened.

THERAPIST: [Hearing and feeling Mark's shift toward left-centric explanation of his anger and away from right-centric apprehensive experience.] This subgroup right now is at the fork-in-the-road between exploring your anger or explaining it. Explaining takes us to what we know already and exploring opens us to the unknown. Are you going to stay in the angry subgroup and explore your anger or when there is room, start a different subgroup to explore the impulse to explain?

MARK: I am staying in anger and now I am angry at you [therapist], too. Anyone else?

ELLEN: Yes, you are staying with your anger and you are angry at our leader too. [Mark nods.] I feel big and strong in my anger, I will not be pushed around. Anyone else?

MARK: You feel big, strong and won't be pushed around. [Ellen, smiling: "Yes!"] Yes, I feel planted, no one can push me over and my energy is hot with lots of power, feels great. Anyone else?

ELLEN: You are planted now with hot energy and power and you feel great! [Mark nodding.] My strength is starting to feel like hot energy too. And my feet are growing roots as you say planted.

As the subgroup explores apprehensively, it connects to the underlying life force energy in anger and free aggression. With the subgroup support, the group is able to contain the two human pulls that are activated when we feel threatened, to fight or flee, both part of our neurobiology. As Mark and Ellen subgrouped together, they both began integrating small differences sparked by the other. Over time, the two subgroups integrate into the group-as-a-whole with room to explore both human responses, fight (Ellen and Mark) and flight (Bob and Jenny).

Psychobiological regulation: Functional subgrouping as an alternative to attachment survival roles

The steps in functional subgrouping are reminiscent of the imitation infants and babies do that strengthens their mirroring circuits (Iacoboni, 2009). Similarly, functional subgrouping appears to replicate what Cozolino (2014) describes as the developmental process in children for expanding their capacity for emotional regulation, a strongly right brain function: "As children and caretakers move in and out of attunement, the cycle of joining, separating, and reuniting becomes the central aspect of developing psycho-biological regulation" (p. 64). Reflecting and joining stimulates our mirror-ing circuits and separating and reuniting enables the subgrouping system to integrate differences.

Functional subgrouping introduces a communication pattern that develops the social brains of the group and its members. Members learn first to empa-thize, attune, and resonate with others and with themselves. They do this first in a series of resonant pairs where the listener reflects and joins the speaker, then separating and reconnecting to themselves and adding their build into the flow of a subgroup or at times, the group-as-a-whole. Sub-grouping entails helping others to reflect us accurately (similar enough), attuning to our own bodies to be sure we feel heard, and then being able to let the other know what they missed (likely what was too different or unex-pected). When we do this, we are modifying our early adaptations rather than repeating them in the present and stimulating a repetition of the past. Our past adaptive survival roles are important to us as they keep us in a familiar stability, yet they also keep us more related to the past than to the present where new relational patterns can emerge. For example, we can revisit the earlier subgrouping example in a more developed group that had moved beyond the flight/fight subphase and was working more with the intimacy phase attachment roles. The work focuses on shifting from past adaptive survival roles to the member role (present adaptive) supported by the process of functional subgrouping.

BOB: I have been feeling very vulnerable and am having a hard time even going grocery shopping without feeling scared. [Looking around and making roving eye contact with the group.] Anyone else?

JENNY: [Looking down and talking softly.] So Bob, you don't like shopping anymore.

BOB: [Now looking down and quiet.]

THERAPIST: [Drawing on her understanding of the process and her felt sense of Bob's shift toward withdrawal.] Remember, Bob, your subgroup role right now is to hang in and help Jenny get you. It takes both of you hang-ing in to understand and be understood.

BOB: [Looking up again.] OK, almost withdrew instead.

THERAPIST: Yes, that is your old role.

BOB: [In eye contact with the therapist.] Yes, could just feel it happening, that pull to withdraw, and not wanting to look up is like not getting out of my car, not feeling safe. Whew. [Deep breathing, then turning to Jenny.] So Jenny, not exactly what you said. It's more that I feel vulnerable. It's a strong FEELING. I just notice this feeling more when I go shopping or out in public. Or this time when you didn't get me! Yes, that's it!

JENNY: It's not just shopping. It's also anywhere in public.

THERAPIST: Remember, Jenny, your job is to get the heart of Bob, more about his feelings than the facts.

BOB: Whew. [Sighing.] Still not really what I am saying. The most important part is I feel vulnerable right now. It doesn't matter where I am. I WANT TO KNOW [voice louder] that you get how I am feeling.

JENNY: Yes, I feel it more now. [In eye contact.] You feel vulnerable now when I don't get you.

BOB: [Face relaxing and smiling.] You got me!

JENNY: [Also smiling.]

THERAPIST: Jenny, remember when you are ready to let go of Bob and reconnect to yourself to see what you are going to add to the subgroup.

With encouragement from the therapist, Bob stayed steadfast to make sure he was understood well enough and discovered he felt more connected to himself and to Jenny in this process. He is learning to build an alternative inter-person role in the present for when he is not understood. His past survival role, learned within his family system, was to "let it go", withdraw, and live in his experience of alienation where he implicitly believes he will never be understood, and of course, when he is in his "withdrawal" role, he is not understood. These implicit patterns are strong, and when we live them, we often confirm that this is indeed the only reality possible for us.

Jenny also was working to come out of her old survival role that she has called "won't feel" where she focuses on facts and ignores feelings, hers and others. This dissociation from feeling was protective for living in a family that did not have the developed capacity to attune to each other. Neither Bob nor Jenny had early relationships that supported the development of this social circuitry, so in this focused work together, supported by the presence of the therapist and the security the norms of functional subgrouping establish, they are practicing new relational patterns that will develop the necessary neural connections for this to become an alternative way of relating in the world. This is a good illustration of how the structure of functional subgrouping, replicating the early process of developing what Cozolino (2014) calls psychobiological regulation, enables group members to start to inhabit present adaptive roles that then develop and enhance their social brain functioning.

From the very first meeting, functional subgrouping begins to build secure attachment patterns and self-correcting systems that enable both right brain exploration of our human experience as well as left-centric reality-testing with the other person to find out when we have understood them. Rather than repeating ingrained survivor roles, the group members practice repairing the mis-attunements in the reflections in the here-and-now context. Interestingly, Tronick's (2007) research shows that "good enough" attachment relationships are only attuned about one third of the time and that what discriminates good enough attachment is whether or not the mis-attunements are repaired in the mother–baby system. Increasingly, SCT is recognizing that the functional sub-grouping pattern has a strong potential for modifying not only our right brain function (integrating the orbitofrontal and medial prefrontal cortex, anterior cingulate, insula, and limbic system) but also correcting misperceptions in reality related to past adaptive roles. In this way, the circuitry of secure attachment takes the place of the neural patterns that keep us repeating early survivor attachment and social roles.

As functional subgrouping is the heart of systems-centred groups, SCT leaders work actively to establish the norms for this process. In addition, guided by theory and an emphasis on working in attunement and empathy with the person, SCT leaders teach the group to weaken restraining forces that orient to survival at the expense of development in order to free the inherent driving forces (life force energy and exploratory drive) that enable living human systems not only to survive but also to develop and transform. To this end, SCT leaders introduce phase-specific skills that facilitate the group weakening its restraining forces. Several of these are described below as they also relate to developing more balance in right and left hemisphere function and integration.

Undoing distractions

After centring, members are encouraged to undo any distractions that are keeping their energy out of the group (a restraining force for working in the here-and-now) by bringing in facts first and feelings second. This structure helps the person cross the boundary from outside to the inside group experience and to deepen their apprehensive connection to themselves. This process starts by discriminating comprehensive (facts) and apprehensive (feelings) experience. Frequently, the first rendition of "facts" is full of opinions or speculations, and provides the group a context to do useful left-centric work in discriminating stories from observable facts. This discrimination is quite important as it enables the group to build a reality-oriented context in which the group can use left brain attending for collecting data and checking reality. This then supports exploring feelings about difficult or satisfying realities. This is very different than using left brain constructions to speculate that then generate right brain implicit experience, which then pre-empts our relating to and exploring our emotional responses as they are emerging in response to what is happening in the moment. This process of discrimination also lays the foundation for integration of right and left brain processing as the two hemispheres collaborate.

In the distraction exercise, once the "facts" are reality-oriented, members are asked how they feel in the here-and-now moment about the facts of their distraction. This draws in right-centric processes as they access their feelings and then from this connection to their feelings, they make eye contact with each group member so that others can hold it with them. This enables the member to cross the boundary from the outside, comprehensive content and instead be supported in apprehension of the emotions that are emerging in this moment.

THERAPIST: What feeling or feelings do you want to bring into the group so you can bring your emotional self here and we can hold your feelings with you?

SALLY: Deep sadness.

THERAPIST: Connect as fully as you can to your sadness and then look around and make eye contact with each of us from your sad feeling so that we can hold it with you.

SALLY: [Looks around slowly, face changes, at first more tearful and then more relaxed.]

THERAPIST: Check and see if you are now more here, less here, or the same.

Very often, other group members report feeling more present as they make eye contact and open to the "distracted" member's feeling. Asking the person who was distracted to see if she feels more here, less here, or the same combines right-centric apprehensive awareness with the reality-testing left-centric function of observing the data to report and share with the group what is happening right now (feeling more present, less present, or the same).

Working in the context of the phases of system development

As mentioned earlier, SCT work is guided by its theoretical map of the phases of system development in which each phase is defined as a set of driving and restraining forces. SCT systematically weakens the restraining forces relevant for the group's phase which releases the driving forces for development. This attention to the phase context makes it more likely that SCT leaders are attuned to the group's phase conflicts.

Drawing from Bennis and Shepard (1956) and Bion (1961), SCT conceptualizes three phases of system development (Agazarian, 1997). The first is the Authority phase, where the major restraining forces are our social survival roles. Specifically, the group in this phase weakens their restraining forces of anxiety, tension, depression, outrage, social roles and role locks (like dominant or submissive), and the role locks that defend against our hatred of authority. Functional subgrouping in this phase is an important driving force for building a self-correcting, attuned system that lowers the human tendency to react to differences as threats. Instead subgrouping establishes a climate for exploring by discriminating and integrating differences, differences in the apparently similar and similarities in the apparently different, utilizing the resources of both hemispheres.

The Intimacy phase follows, where the major restraining forces are our attachment survival roles. As discussed earlier, the steps in functional subgrouping mirror the early developmental process for establishing attachment patterns and emotional regulation. It may very well be that exploring the steps in subgrouping in the Intimacy phase allows us to modify our attachment roles (McCluskey, 2002) in the same way that marriage to a securely attached partner does (A. N. Schore, personal communication, October 2012).

In the third phase of Work, SCT weakens the major restraining force of inner-person survival roles in order to support our inter-person roles that connect us to the group as our larger context for development and transformation. The major driving forces are learning to see the big picture, recognizing one's reactions as information about the group, and using this information to contribute what the context needs rather than responding from an old survival solution. This helps maintain a more expanded right-centric focus on connection and context rather than collapsing back toward the more narrow focus of our individual fears.

The fork-in-the-road between exploring versus explaining

SCT's "fork-in-the-road" between explaining or enacting (restraining forces) versus exploring is introduced early in the authority phase. It weakens the restraining forces that block exploring which enables more access to here-and-now right-centric group experience. Explaining takes the path to the known (grounded in left brain attending), enacting moves us into relational patterns fuelled by past survival roles (arising from right-centric implicit memories), while exploring opens the path into the unknown (right-centric attending to what is emerging in the here-and-now). In the second subgrouping example between Jenny and Bob described above, their exchange took the group into right brain exploring where they discovered their social brain resources. They recognized that the alternative to old survival roles was exploring the ISIS threats and the threat arousal "together" in a new way. With the leader helping them recognize survival roles that were surfacing and other group members supporting them, Bob and Jenny were each able to choose a different response. Even later, in an email exchange, members wrote of how the sense of "together" and "with" had stayed with them. Both at the level of the responses themselves and the emerging process, Jenny, Bob, and the group-as-a-whole were having disconfirming experiences (Ecker et al., 2012) that began to rewire the social circuitry into patterns that will support these kinds of collaborative endeavours in daily life. It is only in the here-and-now that we can develop present adaptive roles that enable us to contribute as members and that ultimately help us transform our inner-person past adaptive roles.

Undoing anxiety

SCT also introduces a skill for undoing anxiety (a predictable flight response) which is a restraining force in the authority phase. Any new group context is unknown, so our protective system is adaptively primed to be alert for threat and neuroception of danger. Very often, when this activation occurs, we accommodate by formulating left brain explanations in an attempt to relieve the distress of the right brain neuroception; however, this top-down thinking often creates further anxiety.

SCT groups undo anxiety whenever it occurs, and, typically, anxiety is undone in a subgroup with others who are also anxious. Asking those who are anxious to look around at each other in roving eye contact and to work together starts to activate right brain social circuits. In the subgroup context of similarity to similarity, anxiety begins to abate as the anxious members realize they are not alone and start to connect to others who feel similarly as social baseline theory (Beckes & Coan, 2011) suggests. In SCT, this is the shift from inner-person to inter-person, increasing our resources for regulation as we connect to the similarity in the other. As the neuroception of danger decreases, the preferred state of ventral vagal activation becomes available and the social engagement system is more likely to come online.

The subgroup is then asked to talk together about how they know they are anxious: "I feel uneasy, anyone else?" "I'm uneasy too and feel like butterflies in my belly, anyone else?" "Yes, and my hands are sweaty, anyone else?" The leader then introduces the idea that anxiety usually has one of three sources: from a *thought* that is making them anxious, a *feeling* or *bodily sensation* they are anxious about having, or *being at the edge of the unknown* where all human beings feel apprehensive (Agazarian, 1997). These questions start to activate what SCT calls the observer role where the group members are shifting from their apprehensive awareness of anxiety to more left brain function to collect data about its source. For those whose anxiety is coming from a thought, most commonly a negative prediction (e.g. I am thinking I will not like this group and it won't help me), they are encouraged to centre and turn on their researcher to find out if they actually believe they can tell the future. Mostly, the answer is no,[1] and the anxiety decreases. The final step is to ask the subgroup members: "How do you feel for yourselves that because of our brain's tendency to try to anticipate the future to prepare for danger, you have become anxious by a thought you do not actually believe?" A person might respond in many ways, from compassion to shame or even self-judgment, and the therapist works with whatever the answer is to help the person come into a feeling relationship with themselves.

It is an essential step to begin to feel for one's own human challenges. Compassion for our human struggles shifts us away from the left brain restraining force of negative predictions relating to fears of not being able to control the future. This leads to more integration of the driving forces in the left-centric observer role with right-centric feelings of connection with one's emotional self and often with others over this human challenge. The change from the left-centric protection of trying to control, which isolates us in the left hemisphere, to our right-centric knowing and right–left–right integration also moves us into the realm where co-regulation with others is more available to us. The subgroup members are then asked:

> Open up to your feeling and see what you now know as you connect to your feeling. Notice you are now connected to yourself in a very different way than when you were thinking thoughts that made you anxious. When you *can* choose, which kind of connection to yourself will help you and the group best meet its goals?

This work in undoing anxiety starts to modify what Hawkins and Blakeslee (2004) term "invariant representations" (largely left brain negative predictions) that reinforce the survival roles that once enabled us to adapt usefully and at the same time prevent us from developing present adaptations. Finding out how we feel for ourselves activates our right-centric explorer role. Connecting to this feeling for ourselves strengthens our here-and-now apprehensive connection, more related to right brain structures and function. When we have an apprehensive experience that is disconfirming and different from the past, our implicit memories can start to modify and the habitual comprehensive pattern that maintains the survival roles linked to early implicit memories can also begin to shift. Having undone the anxiety for themselves and the group, the subgroup can now experiment with activating curiosity and shift to finding out what it was in the present that they each moved away from by going to thoughts about the future.

The subgroup whose anxiety is coming from a sensation or feeling that is unfamiliar is also asked to be curious about how they are responding to this unknown sensation with anxiety instead of curiosity. Shifting to curiosity together lowers anxiety. Similarly, with those who are anxious at the edge of the unknown, SCT normalizes this kind of anxiety as the inevitable human challenge of relating to uncertainty. Noticing that we as human beings are uncomfortable when we open to not knowing makes more room for being in the unknown. Lastly, those who are in the unknown are asked to experiment to see if turning on their curiosity makes the unknown more bearable. Almost always, it does.

Introducing the compassion protocol

The compassion protocol ("how do you feel for yourself?") is integrated not only into the work of undoing anxiety, but used in all work in SCT groups. Importantly, this question is introduced by normalizing, legitimizing, de-pathologizing, and universalizing the myriad of realities that relate to the human brains we all have in our current state of evolution. This protocol is used throughout SCT work to re-establish a compassionate relationship with one's self (and by extension, with others) which often helps us develop more right–left–right integration in attunement with and an appreciation of how our past adaptive survivor roles helped us with the care-givers we had. When we are able to do this rather than criticizing ourselves, we create a different context with ourselves and with others for exploring and discovering.

Training SCT therapists and leaders

This chapter has highlighted key aspects of SCT group psychotherapy to illustrate how SCT groups work to develop right brain attending and better integration between right and left brain function. These same principles and methods are used in SCT training of therapists to develop the capacity for attunement, resonance, and empathy that is essential for therapists. This extensive training enables SCT therapists to internalize both right-centric embodied knowledge of the process and clarity about the left-centric maps used to guide the emerging group experience, isomorphic with what SCT therapy groups learn as well.

To this end, SCT training is highly experiential and members work in ongoing training groups to learn to subgroup with empathy and attunement and to apply the SCT methods with themselves before applying them with others. This enables the use of SCT methods and structure from an integration within one's inner-person and in attunement and empathy with others at the inter-person system level, essential for therapy that is meant to develop and enhance social brain function. It is only at the intermediate level of training where there is sufficient capacity for right-centric attunement, resonance, and empathy (which emerges from right–left–right integration) as well as left brain integration of SCT theory that trainees begin to apply SCT with others.

The example below is of an advanced SCT training group. Its goal was setting criteria for assessing each other's competency as SCT practitioners and then using their criteria to assess each other's work samples and readiness to practice with others, a context that can easily awaken past adaptive survival roles. The group was in the process of assessing each other's resources in order to divide work tasks. Michele, a member in this advanced training group, found herself in an old inner-person survival role, one in which she experienced herself as incompetent and in which she saw herself as having no resources. Her pain in this role was apparent to the whole group. Her face was tense and strained, and she mostly looked down, avoiding eye contact. In this role, she only had access to right-centric experience of difficult implicit memories, none of which was yet explicit. She also had very little if any access to her left brain function so that she could not reality-test the perceptions that these implicit memories brought with them. She was unable to center and activate curiosity, often useful steps to shift out of an old survival role adaptation. In her past adaptive survival role, she felt alienated and different. While this past role adaptation had provided an initial solution for the inevitable failures in attunement and resonance she had experienced early in her life, it now dominated her perception of the here-and-now. In this role, she only relied on herself and even though she felt significant pain and despair in her role, it protected her from disappointments with others or their disappointment in her. Repeated words from the leaders and group members failed to reach her. It was only when she was asked to look around and make eye contact, and discover as she looked who would be a resource for her in the upcoming task, that she was able to find someone she felt could be there for her. The relief was palpable as the group had been glued to her and feeling helpless about how to reach her. As her eyes met the eyes of others and then settled with Dawn's, Michele's body relaxed and her breath deepened along with the rest of the group. She was no longer alone and that changed everything. This right brain nonverbal attunement and activation of social engagement provided resonance across her survivor role boundary which had been closed to protect and safeguard her. This was a very moving moment in the group. It also provided an innovative model for the group to use their right brain nonverbal knowing as they did their work of assessment. Because of the felt sense of the connection between Michele and Dawn, the whole group was able to shift from just left brain criteria devoid of relational and contextual knowing to include and integrate right brain criteria, which deepened and enriched the group's work. This was isomorphic with their assessment task as SCT work requires this kind of right–left–right integration.

Summary

The beginnings of SCT emerged first from right-centric images that flowed through Yvonne Agazarian as she grappled with understanding groups and their dynamics, leading her over many years of work to develop a left-centric map to guide both right- and left-centric exploration and integration. SCT therapists hold both ways of attending as they empathize, resonate, and attune to the group and its members while also seeing the group through the lens of SCT theory. Integrating their right- and left-centric knowing enables SCT therapists to influence group norms to support the group exploring their inner-person system (with curiosity about both its past adaptive roles and the present), inter-person system (developing here-and-now adaptive roles in functional subgrouping), and the group-as-a-whole (ever-emerging transformation of norms). As SCT groups develop by discriminating and integrating differences, the emergent moment-to-moment experience develops our social brains.

With the social engagement that happens in subgrouping, as we are understood and understand the other, our social brains transform. This process provides the attunement, resonance, and empathy. This then enables differences that disconfirm implicit experiences to be gradually integrated and reduces the dominance of old survival roles. Further, functional subgrouping offers stronger co-regulation (inter-person) that enables the group-as-a-whole to continue to transform its norms for our ever-expanding experience of integrating differences in ever-more complex transformations.

Acknowledgement

Much appreciation to Rich Armington for his careful reading and feedback as we were writing this.

Note

1   For those who say yes, the follow-up question, "Do you believe 100% that you can tell the future this time?" The answers may range from 50% to 1%, almost always there is some lack of certainty. Members are then asked if there is any way to know if this is the 1% time or the 99% (Agazarian, 1997).

References

Agazarian, Y. M. (1997). *Systems-centered therapy for groups.* New York, NY: Guilford Press. Re-printed in paperback (2004). London, UK: Karnac Books.

Agazarian, Y. M. (2011). *Systems-centered core skills: SCT foundation manual 2011.* Philadelphia, PA: Systems-Centered Training and Research Institute.

Agazarian, Y. M. (2012). Systems-centered group psychotherapy: Putting theory into practice. *International Journal of Group Psychotherapy, 62*(2), 171–195. doi:10.1521/ijgp.2012.62.2.171

Agazarian, Y. M. (2015a). De-personalizing "personalizing". *Systems-Centered News, 23*(1), 4–6.

Agazarian, Y. M. (2015b). Our person-as-a-system revisited. *Systems-Centered News, 23*(1), 7–13.

Agazarian, Y. M. (2015c). Using the role system map. Introduction: Mapping role systems. *Systems-Centered News, 23*(2), 5–8.

Agazarian, Y. M., & Gantt, S. P. (2000). *Autobiography of a theory: Developing a theory of living human systems and its systems-centered practice.* London, UK: Jessica Kingsley.

Ammaniti, M., & Gallese, V. (2014). *The birth of intersubjectivity: Psychodynamics, neurobiology, and the self.* New York, NY: Norton.

Badenoch, B. (2011). *The brain-savvy therapist's workbook.* New York, NY: Norton.

Beckes, L., & Coan, J. A. (2011). Social baseline theory: The role of social proximity in emotion and economy of action. *Social and Personality Psychology Compass, 5*(12), 976–988. doi:10.1080/10926771.2013.813882

Bennis, W. G., & Shepard, H. A. (1956). A theory of group development. *Human Relations, 9*(4), 415–437.

Bion, W. R. (1961). *Experiences in groups.* London, UK: Tavistock.

Burlingame, G., Strauss, B., & Joyce, A. S. (2013). Change mechanisms and effectiveness of small group treatments. In M. J. Lambert (Ed.), *Bergin and Garfield's handbook of psychotherapy and behavior change* (6th ed., pp. 640–689). Hoboken, NJ: Wiley.

Cozolino, L. (2014). *The neuroscience of human relationships: Attachment and the developing social brain.* New York, NY: Norton.

Ecker, B., Ticic, R., & Hulley, L. (2012). *Unlocking the emotional brain: Eliminating symptoms at their root using memory reconsolidation.* New York, NY: Routledge.

Fredrickson, B. L., Grewen, K. M., Coffey, K. A., Algoe, S. B., Firestine, A. M., Arevalo, J. M. G., ... Cole, S. W. (2013). A functional genomic perspective on human well-being. *Proceedings of the National Academy of Sciences.* Early edition publication. doi: 10.1073/pnas.1305419110.

Gantt, S. P., & Agazarian, Y. M. (2010). Developing the group mind through functional subgrouping: Linking systems-centered training (SCT) and interpersonal neurobiology. *International Journal of Group Psychotherapy, 60*(4), 515–544. doi:10.1521/ijgp.2010.60.4.515

Gantt, S. P., & Agazarian, Y. M. (2013). Developing the group mind through functional subgrouping: Linking systems-centred training (SCT) and interpersonal neurobiology. In S. P. Gantt & B. Badenoch (Eds.), *The interpersonal neurobiology of group psychotherapy and group process* (pp. 73–102). London, UK: Karnac Books.

Gantt, S. P., & Agazarian, Y. M. (2017). *Systems-centered Group Therapy. International Journal of Group Psychotherapy, 67*(sup1), S60–S70. doi:10.1080/00207284.2016.1218768

Greenberg, L. S. (2007). Emotion coming of age. *Clinical Psychology Science and Practice, 14,* 414–421.

Hasson, U., Ghazanfar, A. A., Galantucci, B., Garrod, S., & Keysers, C. (2012). Brain-to-brain coupling: A mechanism for creating and sharing a social world. *Trends in Cognitive Sciences, 16*(2), 114–121. doi:10.1016/j.tics.2011.12.007

Hawkins, J., & Blakeslee, S. (2004). *On intelligence: How a new understanding of the brain will lead to the creation of truly intelligent machines.* New York, NY: Times Books.

Hebb, D. O. (1949). *The organization of behavior: A neuropsychological theory.* New York, NY: Wiley.

Iacoboni, M. (2009). Imitation, empathy, and mirror neurons. *Annual Review of Psychology, 60,* 653–670. doi:10.1146/annurev.psych.60.110707.163604

Ledoux, J. (1998). *The emotional brain: The mysterious underpinnings of emotional life.* New York, NY: Simon & Schuster.

McCluskey, U. (2002). The dynamics of attachment and systems-centered group psychotherapy. *Group Dynamics: Theory, Research and Practice, 6*(2), 131–142. doi:10.1037/1089-2699.6.2.131

McGilchrist, I. (2009). *The master and his emissary: The divided brain and the making of the western world.* New Haven, CT: Yale University Press.

Panksepp, J., & Biven, L. (2012). *The archaeology of mind: Neuroevolutionary origins of human emotions.* New York, NY: Norton.

Porges, S. W. (1995). Orienting in a defensive world: Mammalian modifications of our evolutionary heritage: A polyvagal theory. *Psychophysiology, 32*(4), 301–318.

Porges, S. W. (2011). *The polyvagal theory: Neurophysiological foundations of emotions, attachment, communication, and self-regulation.* New York, NY: Norton.

Schore, A. N. (2010). The right brain implicit self: A central mechanism of the psychotherapy change process. In J. Petrucelli (Ed.), *Knowing, not-knowing and sort-of-knowing: Psychoanalysis and the experience of uncertainty* (pp. 177–202). London, UK: Karnac Books.

Schore, A. N. (2012). *The science of the art of psychotherapy.* New York, NY: Norton.

Siegel, D. J. (2012). *The developing mind: How relationships and the brain interact to shape who we are* (2nd ed.). New York, NY: Guilford Press.

Stephens, G. J., Silbert, L. J., & Hasson, U. (2010). Speaker–listener neural coupling underlies successful communication. *Proceedings of the National Academy of Sciences (PNAS), 107*(32), 14425–14430. doi:10.1073/pnas.1008662107

Tronick, E. (2007). *The neurobehavioral and social-emotional development of infants and children.* New York, NY: Norton.

Chapter 6

Going beyond sucking stones

Connection and emergent meaning in life and in therapy

Barbara Dowds

> Daily, I attach less value to the intellect ... But it is to the intellect we must look all the same to establish the inferiority of the intellect ... It may hold only second place in the hierarchy of virtues but only it is capable of proclaiming that instinct has to occupy the first.
>
> (Proust, 1988, p. 3, 8)

How we view and engage with the world and the other is always an ethical and political question – in other words a question about relatedness. The philosopher David Michael Levin described the qualities of the left-brain's gaze before it was possible to ascribe it to the left hemisphere (LH):

> The present world is a world of science and technology whose political economy ... is organized around ideologies of mastery and domination. ... This world calls forth, simultaneously, ... an ontology and a vision, a way of seeing beings and their Being ... confrontationally, by a sharply and narrowly focused, raylike gaze. ... The object of vision is (to be) isolated and abstracted from its surrounding world, and of course, is (to be) perfectly illuminated. ... [T]he gaze most adequate to our ontology, is therefore (supposed to be) a disinterested and dispassionate gaze – the masterful, well-disciplined gaze of "the rational Man".
>
> (Levin, 1988, pp. 207–208)

This "raylike gaze" (LH narrow focus) is both cause and consequence of the patriarchal will to power, Levin declares trenchantly. But there is another way: the subject of perception does not have to be the grasping ego, but can be, instead, a bodily felt awareness, a vision of the heart. These are qualities that the Jungian Robert Johnson attributes to the feminine and which bring:

> *meaning* into life: relatedness to other human beings, the ability to soften power with love, awareness of our inner feelings and values, respect for

our earthly environment, a delight in earth's beauty, and the introspective quest for inner wisdom.

(Johnson, 1983, p. 19, italics added)

This is the mode of attention that can now be attributed to the right hemisphere (RH) of the brain. All human beings have a divided nature – what I have called the scientist and the poet with respect to the kind of attention we bring to the world (Dowds, 2014, ch. 3). In his magnum opus *The Master and His Emissary*, Iain McGilchrist has argued that the divided selves of our experience can be attributed to the quite distinct functions of the two hemispheres. He recognises that the neuroscience may turn out to be more complex, but even if his model is just a metaphor, it reflects what writers have described through the ages (2010, pp. 461–462). According to McGilchrist, the two sides of the brain have two different ways of relating to the world: the left is detached, objectifying, atomistic, abstract, analytical, narrowly focused and deals with the known, the non-living and impersonal; the right is direct, holistic, intuitive, empathic, broadly focused and deals with the unknown, the living and personal. The left hemisphere is associated with the conscious mind and the right with the unconscious, and it is through the right cortex and limbic system that we connect to our embodied experience (Schore, 2010). We need the left hemisphere for language and the right for nonverbal aspects of communication (Cozolino, 2010). Whether we are motivated primarily by love or power depends on which hemisphere is in charge or the "master" to use McGilchrist's term. The consequences of the hegemony of the left hemisphere spreads from personal relationships to our politics, societies and our stewardship of the earth; and, crucially, LH dominance empties life of meaning: the nihilism Levin points to in his subtitle. Our sources of meaning in RH experience, along with their relevance to psychotherapy, will be explored in this chapter.

In our right minds? Meaning, values and connection

Purpose and connection

In an era when meaning is being drained from experience by the technological, bureaucratic and instrumentalising forces of late modernity, it is vital to ask how we derive existential meaning in life and how this understanding can be transferred into the therapy room. One thing is clear: meaning is not to be found by left-brain questioning or analysis. He who asks the question about meaning is already disengaged from life and thus has lost meaning; he is thinking about meaning with his left hemisphere rather than experiencing life with his embodied right hemisphere. As Freud cannily observed: "The moment a man questions the meaning and value of life, he is sick" (1960, p. 436). The self-referentiality of the more or less cut-off left brain is inherently meaningless. "The more we rely on the left hemisphere alone, the more self-conscious we become; the intuitive, unconscious unspoken elements of experience are relatively discounted, and the interpreter [left brain] begins to interpret – itself" (McGilchrist, 2010, p. 399). The end point of this process is solipsism and madness: Beckett's Molloy with his sticky, obsessive thinking – alone, sucking stones and mechanically transferring them between his pockets. Calculating how to be certain that he won't suck the same one of the sixteen stones as last time is the only shred of "meaning" left to him (Beckett, 1979, p. 64).

If we connect with our deepest longings, we can intuit (RH) that we already have a place in the wider scheme of things, and it is this recognition that gives us a sense of purpose and therefore meaning, according to the existential therapist Emmy van Deurzen (1997). This implies that meaning is neither volitional (LH) nor an individual matter. Indeed Viktor Frankl warned that obsession with self-expression and self-actualisation prevents us finding genuine meaning, and indeed is a sign that the individual hasn't yet found his true purpose (cited in Yalom, 1980, p. 439). This is a shot across the bows of those in the human potential movement who believed that salvation could be found in self-actualisation, or indeed in the Jungian project of individuation. Such an ascent of the hierarchy of needs is all very well, but it is not the end of the road. Most of those who got caught up in the ideals of the 1960s and 70s soon found that the me-project, while initially exciting and liberating, was ultimately empty unless it was followed by a return to the wider world. Indeed, says Frankl, we become self-preoccupied only when we have missed our life's meaning. This phenomenon is evident today, when a sense of political powerlessness has caused people to turn to narcissistic obsessions with their own appearance, health or the way they are perceived by others. Because we are relational beings, ultimately meaning comes from connection – to the world and each other. A meaningful life must therefore contain an ethical dimension: meaning is about values, and thus trans-individual, argues the philosopher John Cottingham (2003). This is not a prescriptive or normative argument, but merely a descriptive statement of fact. We *are* connected, and if we ruthlessly pursue our own projects at the expense of our responsibilities to other human beings, we become fragmented and isolated – and therefore deny our own needs as well as those of others. So this can be read as both a self-focused (individual) and an ethical (collective) argument.

So meaning derives from connection, which is a right-hemisphere capability (Schore, 2003, 2010). It also requires that we follow our deepest beliefs and values. As we grow and develop, we create a "map that contains what the world itself does not: value, meaning, significance" (Thompson, 2009, p. 82). Therefore, beliefs and identity are formed in our interaction with the world (Dowds, 2010b). But this process is implicit. Beliefs and values are not rationally and consciously chosen by left-hemisphere argument, as the theologian Graham Ward has cogently demonstrated. Rather, our beliefs involve "deeper layers of embodied engagement and reaction" where we are touched "imaginatively, affectively and existentially" (Ward, 2014, p. 10). They are subliminal, automatic responses that govern how we perceive, interpret and behave. They are laid down in implicit or right-hemisphere memory. Because we are not consciously aware of them, they come to light only when triggered by accident. This might be when somebody makes a statement which strikes me as astonishing or outrageous because it is so contrary to my belief system. Or I may find myself taking a course of action in a new situation that I could not have predicted.

Frankl (1971) proposed there are three kinds of values or categories of meaning. Creative values concern accomplishing and giving to the world (a process involving both hemispheres), which thus expands one's identity. Experiential values involve being open and receptive to nature, art, love and other encounters in the world and therefore is a right-brain function (McGilchrist, 2010). Finally, attitudinal values manifest in one's stance towards limitation and suffering and are associated with the right hemisphere because they involve embodied connection to oneself and the other (Schore, 2010). So we may get meaning from helping others, delighting in the innocence of children, the beauty of nature, belief in God, excelling in a chosen field, participating in a great project or conducting ourselves honourably under difficult circumstances. But underlying all of these sources of meaning is a sense of *connection* to a great web of being in which we experience ourselves as part of something: a cause, a community, the natural world, God or the cosmos.

Attention, receptiveness and spirituality

Accordingly, existential meaning relies on experiencing our connection – to self, other and the world. The consequence of that connection can be active or receptive. We may act from a sense of purpose that comes from our implicit beliefs and values that emerge within a state of connection. But unless we are also receptive to the nourishment the world has to offer, we can burn out from good works and lose our sense of connection. The capacity for receptiveness to the world's gifts – what Frankl called experiential values – depends on the kind of broad, diffuse and holistic attention that is characteristic of the right hemisphere and is destroyed by the intense focus and analytic atomisation of the left (Dowds, 2014). Implicit values and relationship as well as emotionally suffused, embodied experiencing all rely on the right hemisphere of the brain. To repeat: like beliefs and values, meaning is not volitional, but emergent. It is not a LH, top-down concept, but a RH, bottom-up felt sense. It is the sense of queasiness in our stomachs when we see an animal mistreated; it is the heart-expanding joy of Proust's Marcel when the taste of the madeleine brings the magic of childhood flooding back. In our Western LH society we are alienated from the body and emotions and we have a reduced capacity for embodied relationship and for connection in a broader sense – to other sentient beings or the natural environment. Despair and meaninglessness are products of living in a LH world with its empathy-less, mechanistic, interpreted view of self and other.

Our spiritual drive arises from a longing to retrieve our experience of connection to the ground of our being through a sense of unity between subject and object (Levin, 1988, p. 219). Both our ontogeny and phylogeny have their origins in non-dual experience, and it is only modern adult man who has the detached and defined ego structure that Freud and most of modern psychotherapy insist is the healthy state. Levin, on the other hand, argues that the "oceanic" experience, with its "wisdom of interconnectedness and wholeness, [must be] brought back … and appropriately integrated into present living" (1988, p. 218). We need this unification of subject and object "for the deconstruction of structures of experience reified under the influence of our prevailing metaphysics" (ibid., p. 219). What Levin is calling for is – without the neuroscience – what McGilchrist argues for in *The Master and His Emissary*: a recognition and reinstatement of RH experience and values in a world that is dominated by LH ideology.

Understandably, however, spirituality is difficult for Westerners. Literacy permits us to classify and generalise and move away from the concrete present into abstraction, points out David Hay. Along with the loss of the here-and-now, we have much less sense of being part of community. Literate religious societies counteracted this problem with sophisticated practices of contemplative prayer or meditation. But these practices have now been largely abandoned, so we are left with "a disembodied, theoretical consciousness of the self, withdrawn from engagement in the surrounding environment" (Hay, 2006, p. 194). However, the old religious practices are open to criticism, and John Heron accuses the established religions, East and West, of pursuing "a detached, ascensional spirituality at the expense of human bodies, senses, sexuality, generativity and the earth itself" (1998, p. 5). In a sustained feminist attack, Heron charges the ascent model with viewing "spirit exclusively in terms of consciousness, emptiness and form to the exclusion of spirit as life, fullness and process" (ibid., p. 4). Transcendent spirituality is detached, hierarchical and is often associated with the ideology of the patriarchy, whereas a non-institutional, immanent spirituality oriented towards wholeness and the body emerges from more feminine experience and values. We are again talking here about left-brain abstraction and alienation versus right brain concreteness, holism, embodiment and relationship. The transcendent model is all about overcoming our human embodiment to dissolve the ego, the immanent model about temporary merger between the embodied self and the environment. The soul traditions such as shamanism, the work of Jungians such as Thomas Moore, ecopsychology, or Proustian-type epiphanies may all be considered as part of immanent spirituality.

Indeed, we may have had an in-dwelling spirituality for most of our evolutionary history as wandering nomads or hunter-gatherers, and transcendent spirituality may have been a response to the stress of settling in sedentary farming communities, alleges Morris Berman (2000) (see Dowds, 2010a for a summary of Berman's evidence for this position).

Immanent spirituality may involve moments of "regression" where we temporarily let go of the ego and re-experience a state of merger with the world around us. The capacity to enter such a state depends, not on struggle to overcome ourselves, but on a softening of the will and an opening to being receptive to our environment. In a challenge to Wilber's hierarchical model of spirituality, in particular his insistence on a distinction between prepersonal and transpersonal stages, Michael Washburn conceives of regression in the service of transcendence (1998). The ecopsychologist Anita Barrows (1995) has re-envisioned childhood development: not only as *separation from* mother to form an independent and isolated ego, but equally as *moving towards* a widened sense of oneness with the world. She argues that developmental theory needs to depathologise merger and take account of *both* of our two opposing tendencies: the movement towards shape and coherence and equally the tendency to yield and dissolve.

> Allowing ourselves such [temporary] merger is what will heal our loneliness, boredom and addiction. This is what will give our lives meaning and make it impossible for us to continue to view the world as separate and objectified, ours to use and abuse. If we do not heal this split, neither human beings nor the earth can thrive, or arguably, survive.
>
> (Dowds, 2014, p. 43)

To summarise: meaning is an *embodied experience of connection* with self, other, the universe, creativity, vision, beauty, indeed anything that matters at an extra-egoic level. It emerges most profoundly from dissolution of the subject–object divide that connects us with our ground of being.

Primordial connection

Our capacity for meaning relies on having experienced adequate connection at the earliest stage of our lives: "The degree to which we feel received, loved and welcomed into the world makes up the cornerstone of our identity. When our capacity for connection is in place, we experience a right to be" (Heller & LaPierre, 2012, p. 126). By contrast, early damage to this capacity for connection engenders a sense of existential futility. According to the neuroaffective relational model of child development, the key need in the first stage in life is to feel connected. Trauma in the womb or during the first six months of life will impair the connection with one's own body and emotions as well as with other people – all right-hemisphere functions. This need is distinct from and *precedes* the later needs for attunement, trust, autonomy and love. Those whose capacity for connection has been damaged try to manage their despair by actively searching for meaning in positive or negative ways – through drug addiction, living in the world of ideas or through spiritual exploration.

Whether ontogenetically (developmentally) or phylogenetically, connection precedes relationship. Connection is primordial: it is the foetus in his body-experience of being received into life, his connection to the ground of being. It is the experience that the universe is friendly. If all goes well, this permits a state of harmony within what Frank Lake (1986, p. 37) called "the womb of the spirit". Proust may have been talking about the adult losing touch with this early connectedness when he said "the true paradises are the paradises that we have lost" (1996, p. 222). However there are some situations where adults are graced with a transcendence of the subject–object divide that recovers this sense of connection: in spiritual experience (Washburn's "dynamic ground"), as a mother in a state of primary maternal preoccupation, or when our boundaries melt during the early stages of being in love. Erikson (1968) maintained that adults in reaching towards the unitive trance in spiritual experience are trying to recapture the early bond with mother. But in fact we are trying to recapture an even earlier state that is not created by, but if we are fortunate, can be maintained by a holding, non-impinging mother.

If it is relationships that heal us, why are they so problematic for virtually everyone? I would suggest that, while relationships are essential to surviving and thriving, they also present a challenge to our sense of connection – to ourselves and the environment, to what Winnicott (1984, 1990) described as our "going-on-being". If we are fortunate enough to have a non-impinging mother, our connection to the world can remain relatively undisturbed; child and mother can enter into a mutual experience of reverie. As Winnicott put it, we can experience being alone in the presence of another. This non-demanding holding creates a capacity for impulse-free peace and silence: for being-ness. Out of this comfortable formlessness, the infant's spontaneous gestures emerge.

If mother is "good enough" rather than unattainably perfect, her moments of misattunement induct the infant into a growing awareness that mother is different from him, and he begins to develop a theory of mind and a more or less separate ego. While, at these moments, going-on-being is challenged by the presence of what is now the other, in a good-enough facilitative environment we can hold on to our connection to the ground of being. By contrast, the consistently unattuned and impinging other is always experienced as an attack on our sense of primordial connection. But, if we are fortunate in our mothering, we will be able to survive later unattuned and even competitive or hostile interactions. However, if we don't have this early foundation of connection, other people will always be problematic. This is not just because of the intrinsic difficulty of dealing with them: for those coming from a childhood of intrusive caregiving, it is impossible to retain the feeling of primordial connection (to world or self) in another's presence. The fundamental question, for the body psychotherapist Nick Totton, is: "how can I breathe and relate to someone at the same time?" (2003, p. 100).

Meaningful doing must emerge out of a place of being-ness:

> The experience of doing in the absence of a secure sense of being degenerates into a meaningless succession of mere activities (as in the obsessional's meaningless repetition of the same thought, word or act), not performed for their own proper purpose but as a futile effort to "keep oneself in being", to manufacture a sense of "being" one does not possess.
>
> (Guntrip, 1992, p. 254)

Could there be a clearer description of the psychodynamics of Beckett's Molloy sucking stones, or indeed of the boredom and addiction widespread in modern society (see Dowds, 2014, ch. 2)? Meaningless doing also includes doing in which the ego is invested (because it is important for our self-esteem) but which is addictive: we cannot stop even when we know we are stressed or exhausted. This leads to much of the depression and anxiety we see among the privileged classes in the developed world. Unfortunately, a good start in life may no longer be sufficient to allow us to maintain connection while coping with the "ego-logical" (Levin, 1988), spiritual malaise of our society, alienated by an excess of urbanisation, globalisation, speed and technologically generated disembodiment. So there may also be clients cut off from connection, less because of early experiences, than because of later disconnection due to a toxic (but increasingly "normal") lifestyle.

Thus, feeling connected is not an optional extra, a luxury for the person who has everything, or a spiritual add-on after we have done the "real" therapy of ego-strengthening. It is the foundational and primordial ground of our being out of which healthy relationship and engagement with society emerge.

Therapy and connection

> ... our face and the face of the gods look out in the same direction and are at one; how then should we approach the gods from the front?
>
> (Rilke, 1988, p. 264)

Receptive connection in therapy

What can we say about therapy with the client whose sense of connection has been compromised in the womb/early infancy, or later in life? The therapist has to replicate a benign universe, a womb of the spirit, where the client can breathe freely and enter a state of reverie in the presence of the therapist. The therapist has to be a trans-egoic holding figure, like the non-impinging mother. The client who has been traumatised in the womb or as a baby requires trauma work of the kind described by Heller and LaPierre (2012), who work both bottom-up (calming the nervous system) and top-down (on the relationship) to heal combined relationship and event trauma. But this is far too large a subject for this chapter. Rather, I want to consider how to work with clients whose connection has been damaged or lost by intrusive relationships, or by an overly demanding life in a LH world.

Here are some "dos" and "don'ts" of such work. Don't instrumentalise, confront, impinge, analyse, interpret or insist upon a defended egoic relationship. Western therapy's inability to see connection is criticised by Levin – speaking specifically about Gestalt therapists, but this could equally apply to any ego-bound therapy: "Their experience of the figure-ground differentiation is governed by a gaze which is not yet prepared to receive, and be responsive to, the presencing of the ground as ground" (Levin, 1988, p. 208). The therapist's "dos" that might allow the client to presence this ground – to enter into a state of connection – include: embodiment, empathy, process and slowness. Contact with the therapist should be secondary; the purpose of the relationship is to hold the client so that she can connect with her own ground of being. This could be the sort of relationship where therapist and client sit side-by-side, only sometimes turning to look at each other. As Rilke (1993, p. 45) said, "love … consists in this, that two solitudes protect and border and salute each other". While Saint-Exupéry (2012, p. 195) is describing a state of non-confronting entrainment when he states: "Love does not consist in gazing *at* each other, but in looking outward together in the same direction" (italics added). The therapist would join the client in reverie, but of course also be ready to gently shift to intersubjective relating in response to the client seeking contact. There may be moments of mutuality, but like epiphanies they cannot be sustained. What I am advocating offers an intersubjective relationship (right hemisphere to right) rather than a subject–object relationship (therapist's left to client's right hemisphere), open to eye contact but not demanding it normatively.

Heller writes of a client with the frozen and locked-on eye contact indicative of intense anxiety and sometimes dissociation. He points out the paradox that by forcing eye contact, this client was *less* connected with him and with *herself*. Heller encouraged her to look away and only make eye contact with him when she could maintain connection to herself at the same time. In this way he helped her to regulate her relational anxiety (Heller & LaPierre, 2012, p. 162). There is, as everyone knows but few admit, some anxiety in all relationships, and face-to-face therapy can exacerbate this and keep the client from connecting with herself (also see Totton quote above). Indeed I may have lost a young client because the contact with me through play was so overwhelming for her that she lost her fragile connection to herself. It is naïve to believe that all clients will "find themselves" through full-on relatedness. Indeed the power of connecting through silence was highlighted for me with a stressed male client from an impoverished and chaotic background who repeatedly entered into a state of reverie where the only sound was the ticking of the clock. On one occasion, his tranquillity was broken by the noise of a vacuum cleaner in the corridor outside; his devastation (bursting into tears followed by rage) at the destruction of his going-on-being dramatised for me the healing power of beingness.

Some readers may be alarmed at allowing clients to enter such "regressed" states. But, we can become hypnotised by linear, temporal metaphors. For, like Heller's work, such states should be viewed not so much as moving back in time as moving down into depth: as bottom-up repair of the nervous system, or in Washburn's terms as regression in the service of transcendence. Like Barrows, we may ask about the adult client, not what is he losing but what *more* is he creating by merging with his dynamic ground? Merger with the ground as an adult incorporates and integrates a great deal more than for an infant. While such reverie may look like regression, it is not – in the sense of losing one's adult ego. It is very different from the re-living of a traumatic incident, where the individual experiences themselves as the age at which the traumatic event occurred. Such true regression may be re-traumatising if not processed properly, whereas reverie is in itself healing, replenishing, nourishing and expanding. Reverie may form part of a therapy session, but is never the whole thing. It is like the meditative slow movement in a piece of music sandwiched between two fast movements. The first fast movement is a transition from normal consciousness into merger, and the second, a way of integrating the slow movement/state of connection with self into a boundaried ego. Neither the listener nor the client is left in the vulnerable state of merger.

Ideally we can learn to access such states of spiritual/nervous system repair and emergent meaning to strengthen us before returning to the fray of life. However, many clients who most need to go there will judge it as too soft, too feminine, too helpless a place, or they just won't see the point. For them, much of the work in therapy would be to help them see beyond the limited and limiting worldview and disembodied analysis of the left hemisphere. Some others have too little ego and under-developed adult motivation, responsibility or commitments; for them immanent spiritual experience could become a dangerous addiction. One size never fits all. However in the current stage of evolution of our society, there is little awareness or tolerance of being-ness or connection. "Western metaphysics ... sees only the separation, and not also the connecting", alleges Levin (1988, p. 206). The repressed inevitably bursts forth in an extreme and unhealthy way as in drug or alcohol addiction.

Active connection in therapy

I have proposed that what provides a foundation of healing and ultimate state of primordial meaning in therapy is the ability of the client to enter into the state of connection to the ground of (their) being. However the process does not stop here. The client also needs to relate more actively to the world and other people. To learn to live creatively in the Winnicottian sense, we must act and relate while retaining a connection to our ground of beingness (see quote from Guntrip). There must be a balance between the client maintaining connection to their ground and emerging out of it to develop an ego that is flexible enough to both protect the self and let in the other. This requires a RH to RH relationship between client and therapist (as recommended by Allan Schore, 2010), one that is neither fusional nor a competition between two impenetrable egos.

Two extracts from literature exemplify the difference between the left and right hemispheres in terms of interpersonal relating:

> They really as it went on *saw* each other at the game; she knowing he tried to keep her in tune with his conception, and he knowing she thus knew it. Add that he again knew she knew, and yet that nothing was spoiled by it, and we get a fair impression of the line they found most completely workable.
>
> (Henry James, 1997, p. 349)

> Her voice had sunk very low: there was a dread upon her of presuming too far, and of speaking as if she herself were perfection addressing error. She was too much preoccupied with her own anxiety, to be aware that Rosamond was trembling too; and filled with the need to express pitying fellowship rather than rebuke, she put her hands on Rosamond's, and said with more agitated rapidity – "I know, I know that the feeling may be very dear – it has taken hold of us unawares – it is so hard, it may seem like death to part with it – and we are weak – I am weak –"
>
> (George Eliot, 1973, p. 728)

In the Henry James passage, we see the two characters, clever as psychopaths at reading each other, and each manipulating the other, but agreeing to the "game". This is a closed LH system where nothing new, creative or meaningful can emerge. The goal is pragmatic – a "workable" compromise between two monads. George Eliot, on the other hand, portrays RH genuine empathic emotional engagement. This is an open-ended and mutual exploratory process where knowledge of the other is incomplete, a synergic system where meaning is embedded in the awareness, attunement and honesty of the relationship.

RH to RH relating implies a subject to subject connection, the experience of embodiment in both partners, and an open-ended, exploratory process-orientation (moving towards what is new). In short this is the same kind of intersubjective relationship as has been observed between attuned mothers and their infants. The self is constituted in childhood within a facilitating, holding environment of attuned attention, empathic mirroring and energetic resonance/rhythmic entrainment between caregiver and infant (see the work of Winnicott, Stern, Trevarthen and others). Intersubjectivity relies not on left-brain egoic attention, but on right-brain embodied awareness: a pre-articulate and primordial aspect of the mind. Attuned mirroring enables the child – among other things – to experience himself proprioceptively, which gradually coheres into an embodied identity. Likewise the regulation of the child's affect emerges from the embodied relationship, with mother initially providing soothing or stimulation from the outside before the child can develop its own capacity for affect regulation (Gerhardt, 2015; Schore, 2003). Affect regulation depends on the right hemisphere and its top-down connections between the right cortex, limbic system and autonomic nervous system and endocrine system that regulate the body's physiology (Carroll, 2005; Schore, 2003, 2010).

But there are, of course, differences between mother-child and therapist-client relating. Infants are closer to being blank slates than adults. The right hemisphere grows before the left, and significant early infant development happens before the left hemisphere puts on a growth spurt in the middle of the second year. Furthermore, the corpus callosum matures slowly, even past the age of ten, so that the two hemispheres function relatively autonomously throughout childhood (Cozolino, 2010). The adult client, on the other hand, is likely to have a LH concept of self and may judge himself harshly as malfunctioning machine rather than feeling compassion for himself as a suffering sentient being. Adult clients often have anxious and inflexible relational styles and have built up defences and LH reflections, abstractions and confabulations. So the therapist, more than the mother, has to cope with the inherent conflict between the left and right hemispheres of the brain, with the left frequently repressing information provided by the right (Carroll, 2005). This may emerge as incongruence (mismatch between words and feelings, or words and actions), or a complete dismissal or unawareness of RH functions. While the unproblematically connected infant actively seeks relationship – initially anyway, until or unless something goes wrong in the attachment process – many clients have a highly compromised capacity or willingness to relate. So therapy is (in some ways) more challenging than child-rearing. But the only reparative relationship will necessarily be empathic and intersubjective, and the only reparative therapy will be experiential, embodied and process-oriented.

Hemisphere dominance in different therapy orientations

The body psychotherapist Malcolm Brown (1979) asserts that:

> The only cure for neurosis is the capacity for allowing one's core regions of being to become totally involved with those of another

human being. This will lead to all manner of short-circuiting, misperception, and misunderstanding ... Yet it is precisely the capacity to tolerate this ... that is indispensable to solidifying and eventually integrating all levels of feeling and cognition ...

In the practical part of this chapter I want to examine how different therapy orientations fare with regard to such an intersubjective and embodied relationship. But I also want to acknowledge from the beginning that the individual therapist in a LH approach may transcend its limitations and engage in a RH relationship. Likewise, some therapists in the more RH modalities may fail to live up to the philosophy of their approach.

Subject–object relationship

Schools of therapy that call for the therapist's left hemisphere to treat the client as an object to be fixed include: CBT (change the irrational thoughts or phobic behaviour); classical psychoanalysis (interpret the products of the client's unconscious and analyse the transference); and the more aggressive Fritz Perls school of Gestalt (make the client more authentic by attending to his incongruence; embarrass him into trying out experiments). In viewing the person as a machine with broken parts or a text full of prefabricated meanings, CBT and classical psychoanalysis empty life of meaning, whereas authentic meaning is always fresh and dynamic. If either client or therapist has everything worked out in advance, nothing new and spontaneous can emerge. The central aim of Gestalt therapy is to make "contact" with ourselves and our environment, but this is a goal-oriented, narrow-focused, boundaried and essentially separating contact – or better collision – of one independent monad with another, not an intersubjective field of mutually created potential. The contact resembles a ping-pong match and the inner process of the client becomes a defensive prediction and warding off of the therapist's next challenge, similar to the Henry James "game" quoted earlier. It is undoubtedly true that many clients – especially women – are in a state of confluence and are more attuned to the needs of others than themselves. These people do need to firm up their boundaries and get in touch with their own impulses and libido (though in supposedly ego-building Gestalt they may simply become compliant clients defensively playing the Gestalt game). However, there are equally many clients who need to soften boundaries and find their interdependence, though perhaps first going through an initial stage of strengthening the ego into a flexible *process* to replace a rigid and defended *structure*.

CBT and psychoanalysis largely ignore the body whereas Gestalt pays it a lot of attention. However, it tends to view the body as an object to be observed or manipulated, not as a living body to be experienced by the client or empathically related to by the therapist. These three approaches are usually goal-oriented and prescriptive (normative) with the therapist providing holding and direction, but not engaging in the relationship as one subject to another.

A particularly egregious example of LH interpretation in the absence of RH empathic attunement comes from extracts of two sessions of a schizophrenic patient with Wilfred Bion (1967, p. 28).

PATIENT: I picked a tiny piece of skin from my face and feel quite empty.
ANALYST: The tiny piece of skin is your penis, which you have torn out, and all your insides have come with it.
PATIENT: I do not understand ... penis ... only syllables and now it has no meaning.

Next session

PATIENT: I cannot find any interesting food.
ANALYST: You feel it has all been eaten up.
PATIENT: I do not feel able to buy any new clothes and my socks are a mess of holes.
ANALYST: By picking out the tiny piece of skin yesterday you injured yourself so badly you cannot even buy clothes; you are empty and have nothing to buy them with.
PATIENT: Although they are full of holes they constrict my foot.
ANALYST: Not only did you tear out your own penis but also mine. So today there is no interesting food — only a hole, a sock. But even this sock is made of a mass of holes, all of which you made and which have joined together to constrict, or swallow and injure, your foot.

As Thomas Verny observed: "It is difficult to imagine what the patient could say that could tell Bion anything he does not think he knows, ... or that his interpretations reduce any sense to total nonsense" (1994, pp. 163–165). This "dialogue" (actually two independent monologues) makes it clear just how *irrational* the supposedly rational left brain can be when it is coming from a disembodied and decontextualised belief system — in this case, the certainty that the patient's words illustrate splitting in the formation of symbols or the tired psychoanalytic conviction that everything is about sex. This is LH confabulation: "finding plausible, but bogus explanations for the evidence that does not fit its version of events" (McGilchrist, 2010, p. 234). As long as an argument is internally consistent, the left hemisphere is happy; the facts can be sacrificed in order to preserve the theory. The right hemisphere with its inherent common sense (underpinned by connection to our body/emotional responses and the perception and understanding of context) is flabbergasted, and also threatened if a delusional version of reality is accepted by all around as in "The Emperor's New Clothes".

Indeed such isolated left-brain interpretations cut off from the embodied experience of the right generate a mental process similar to that of schizophrenic patients, argues McGilchrist (2010) following on from the observations of Louis Sass. The so-called patient above sounds a good deal saner than his analyst, and it is telling that he feels that Bion has actually destroyed meaning.

Classical psychoanalysis claims to work with the unconscious of the client, but it is usually the left brain of the therapist analysing the products (dreams, images, impulses, fantasies) of the client's right brain and translating them into a LH interpretation: "where id was there ego shall be". The client's feelings and experiences or their reaching out towards relationship are subjected to the cold, detached and dissecting left hemisphere of the analyst in a way that can only be damaging. Even when the interpretation is correct and the client feels understood, their own self-discovery has been hijacked. Even more important is the implicit message underlying the interpretation: "see how clever I am"; "I am satisfied that you conform so well to the theory"; "I am anxious that you see how hard I am working on your behalf". The only time when interpretation can heal is if it conveys the message: "I really see you ... and accept you". Jung understood all too well the reductionist and abusive dangers of left brain categorising, analysis and confabulation when applied to the soul or to the individuation process in therapy:

> Understanding is a terribly binding power, a veritable soul murder ...
> The core of the individual is a mystery of life which dies when it is
> grasped ... The threatening and dangerous thing ... is that the individual
> appears to be understood.
>
> (Jung, 1992)

Subject–subject relationship

The therapy orientations that engage in subject-to-subject relating include the intersubjective wing in psychoanalytic psychotherapy and most humanistic therapies, including person-centred therapy, body psychotherapy and the less aggressive Laura Perls school of Gestalt. The humanistic therapies are all experiential, process-oriented and embodied, either explicitly or implicitly.

Person-centred therapy aims to provide the core conditions of empathy, unconditional positive regard and congruence. Transference is regarded as "a fiction, invented and maintained by the therapist to protect himself from the consequences of his own behaviour" (Shlien, 1984, p. 153). Here the relationship is understood to be co-created in present time, although entrenched, inflexible patterns are, of course, understood as emerging from past experience. The therapist *engages* in the relationship RH to RH, and current understanding of the person-centred relationship is that it is an intersubjective "*encounter* between the therapist and client, rather than the *provision* of a particular set of conditions *for* the client" (Mearns & Cooper, 2005, p. 9). The potential of PCT depends on the individual therapist's capacity to be present to the fullness of their own RH experience and to hold the tension between authenticity and being empathic and accepting. At its worst, some PCT practitioners substitute the demanding core conditions of Rogers with a phony niceness, or they fail to mirror accurately because of ignorance of developmental psychology. While Rogers was aware of the "estrangement of conscious man from his directional organismic processes" (1963, pp. 20–21), PCT, unlike Gestalt, didn't directly engage with the body until some practitioners started incorporating Gendlin's focusing into the work. This involves getting in touch with the felt sense of an experience in the body, often in the stomach or chest (Gendlin, 1996) and leads to an awareness of the distinction between the ego (left brain) and body (right brain-mediated) responses and hence the discovery of organismic truth.

Most of the diverse therapies linked under the humanistic umbrella combine Rogers' core conditions with a variety of creative, process-oriented techniques. In this group, I would include the tendency in Gestalt following Laura Perls who was deeply influenced by Martin Buber (Clarkson, 1989) as well as body psychotherapy (much of which evolved from Gestalt) and many of the creative therapies using art, drama, dance, and voice work. These vary in the degree of body involvement with art therapy at one pole and the body psychotherapies at the other end of the scale.

Right-hemisphere therapy in practice

A variety of examples from different therapy orientations will serve to illustrate therapy that is intersubjective, embodied and process-oriented. Here is Michael Eigen who, despite his analytic orientation, is not on the outside analysing. He is right there in the middle of the relationship and aware – to an almost paranoid degree – of the unstated in the relationship:

> Our palms were warm, moist sexual organs. They met across an abyss and returned to an abyss. They were shooting stars that exploded on contact and sent shivers through me. … I became attached to these handshakes and Cynthia could withhold them to punish me. We reached a point when I never knew whether she would extend her hand. I was at her mercy. When she touched my hand, I felt confirmed and when she left without a sign, I assumed the session failed. … Sometimes I extended my hand first and she responded with happiness and relief. When I did this, she could also make me feel that I breached a trust, that I had gone too far or not far enough. Her touch was forgiving and promising, yet also accusing, as if I had done something wrong, or not right enough, and my extended hand was a sign of it.
>
> (Eigen, 1992, p. 69)

I laughed out loud at Eigen's honesty, vulnerability and engagement. If you didn't know the context, you could mistake it for a description of a tormented, anxiously attached love affair of the Proustian variety. This is the stripped reality of relating to other people inside or outside the therapy room, though admittedly as an after-the-fact reflection by just one partner in the relationship.

Process thinking holds the goal lightly and never loses sight of the holistic context; therefore it allows something else to emerge and is synergic. For example, as a therapist, I may enter into a role-play with the LH intention of helping a defensive client resolve a relationship problem, but as she laughs at my attempts to "become" her husband, the initial intention metamorphoses into the relational process of the right brain, in laughing play and a warm feeling between us. If I insist on my LH-generated and goal-directed *objective* – however creative (RH) the *method* – the client may or may not achieve some clarity. But if I allow the RH relational process to take over, something more important occurs: our relationship deepens and we move from a problem-focus to play and possible synergy. Play is pleasure and doesn't need a purpose – indeed it is by definition not goal-oriented – but it can be justified even in LH utilitarian terms by being creative and producing unknown outcomes.

There is no shortage of RH approaches such as work with images and art, psychodrama and non-interpretive dreamwork. But will the client be willing to go there? Will they feel it is a waste of time, that it will shame them ("I'm no good at drawing") or make them feel even more anxious? This will probably be the case if the therapist stays firmly and safely in the left brain where nothing unexpected will throw them off balance. If the therapist sits watching with a cold LH eye, it will take a confident or dangerously compliant client to move into the unknown. The therapist must join them in movement, play a role themselves, share their images or body reactions, and generally take some risks themselves – though without insisting or taking over the space. The attitude is one of receptivity to what emerges in the intersubjective space.

Schore argues that we must relate to the client with the right hemisphere and allow ourselves to experience their projections as if they are part of ourselves (2003, p. 84). We can then take on the parental role of regulating the affect which the young child – and the inadequately mothered adult – is incapable of doing for himself. Another analyst, Lawrence Hedges, stresses the necessity of touch for very early developmental arrest "when physical contact with the maternal body was the only way that the infant mind could be effectively contacted". He argues that touch must be offered "at the exact moment that the internalized rupture in contact is activated", but views the touch not as a soothing re-parenting per se, but as "a physically concrete, empathically timed, interpretive response on the analyst's part" (Hedges, 1994, p. 294). One wonders if Hedges would still insist, more than twenty years later, that touch is only "interpretive" rather than constituting the actual reparative therapy: sensitively timed touch as affect regulation.

We must go to body therapists for therapy in which the movements, rhythms and voice timbre of two beings in relationship are at least as important as the words. As Margaret Landale describes it, embodied psychotherapy is not just about looking and listening; rather it must foreground the flow of present-time contact between two bodies sensing and resonating, breathing and moving with one another (Landale, 2002). An example of such a somatic conversation comes from the Developmental Somatic psychotherapist, Ruella Frank (2005). Her training and research led her to understand that infant movement patterns which underlie adult processes are primary supports for contacting self and the environment. Frank worked with a woman whose adult daughter had died in an accident a few months earlier. Jenny described a dream of a suitcase which Ruella invited her to imagine unpacking. She asks her to be aware of her small body movements as she does so and to exaggerate them. Jenny can't touch the lining of the case and eventually Ruella offers herself as container by placing her feet on either side of Jenny's, giving her a boundary to press into. Jenny cries out "Please don't leave me" and sobs. She moves towards Ruella and they embrace as Jenny weeps. Later she notices that her breathing has lost its usual gasping. She was able to link this and not feeling the lining of the suitcase to her mother being hospitalised during her infancy and being critical and distant when she returned: the unknown repressed spontaneously emerged in an embodied and exploratory relational process. It is impossible to do justice to the entire case study in so little space, but this gives some flavour of working with the right hemisphere: relationship attuned to body movements and imagery. The work above was fast, and after only two five-day blocks of sessions, Jenny felt she had accomplished what she wanted to do and could complete her mourning with friends, family and colleagues.

One final example of right hemisphere work is the exploration of a dream within a group setting. Mary had a dream of walking down a shadowy street alongside spiky railings at the edge of a park at night. She realised that she was being stalked by a man whose face was shaded. When she speeded up, so did he; when she slowed down, he did too. Suddenly, he speeded up and raised his arm to strike her. She woke, her heart pounding with terror. In a re-enactment within the group, we created the street using high backed chairs to simulate the fence. Mary chose a large man within the group to play the attacker and re-experienced the dream, remembering some forgotten details as she did so. Then came the most important part of the psychodrama: I invited her to act the part of the attacker while another woman in the group played Mary. She was very reluctant to play a violent man, as he represented everything that was opposed to her strongly Christian view of life. But, encouraged by other group members who had found their psychodramas transformative, she eventually agreed – "as an experiment". She donned the face-shading man's hat and we played the scene several times. On each occasion she entered more fully into the part. By the end she revealed – with no prompting on my part – that her fear had evaporated. Her body moved differently now, striding with more power. I refrained from making the left-brain observation that she had briefly inhabited her shadow: such labelling would have collapsed a powerful *experience* into a cliched *concept*. However, I was confident that – since she knew her Jung – Mary would realise this herself, now or later. There are other avenues that could be explored here, both as part of the drama and part of understanding it, but I hope the point is made. No amount of LH analysis of the dream would have given Mary the insight and transformative shift that inhabiting the energy of the assailant gave her in experiencing the emotions with her embodied right hemisphere. Somatic experience is as different from a mental concept as the painting of a pipe is from a pipe. It seems fair to conclude that analysis is a left-hemisphere mediated defence against experiencing the endlessly shifting and unpredictable process of the present moment.

Conclusion

The underlying, but largely implicit, agenda in psychotherapy is the creation of meaning. This emerges, as I contend, from connection – to self, other and the world. I argue that the primary goal of therapy should be to facilitate, not relationship, but the client's state of connection to their ground of being; thus therapy is inherently a spiritual practice. Active doing and relating in therapy is only meaningful if it emerges out of this ground. Only right-hemisphere therapy – experiential, embodied, empathic and intersubjective – can help the client access this state of connection.

References

Barrows, A. (1995). The ecopsychology of child development. In T. Roszak, M. Gomes, & A. Kanner (Eds.), *Ecopsychology: Restoring the Earth, Healing the Mind* (pp. 101–110). San Francisco, CA: Sierra Club Books.

Berman, M. (2000). *Wandering God: A Study in Nomadic Spirituality*. New York: SUNY.

Beckett, S. (1979). *The Beckett Trilogy: Molloy, Malone Dies, The Unnamable*, trans. S. Beckett and P. Bowles, London: Picador.

Bion, W. R. (1967). *Second Thoughts: Selected Papers in Psycho-Analysis*. London: William Heinemann.

Brown, M. (1979). Beyond Janov: The healing touch. *Journal of Humanistic Psychology*, *19*, 69–89.

Carroll, R. (2005). Neuroscience and the "law of the self". In N. Totton (Ed.), *New Dimensions in Body Psychotherapy* (pp. 13–29). Maidenhead, UK: Open University Press.

Clarkson, P. (1989). *Gestalt Counselling in Action*. London: Sage.

Cottingham, J. (2003). *On the Meaning of Life*. Abingdon, UK: Routledge.

Cozolino, L. (2010). *The Neuroscience of Psychotherapy* (2nd ed.). New York: W.W. Norton.

Dowds, B. (2010a). The evolution of human consciousness and spirituality. *Inside Out*, *61*, 20–29.

Dowds, B. (2010b). Filling in the spaces: Finding meaning in a meaningless world. *Inside Out, 62*, 30–40.

Dowds, B. (2014). *Beyond the Frustrated Self: Overcoming Avoidant Patterns and Opening to Life*. London: Karnac.

Eigen, M. (1992). *Coming through the Whirlwind: Case Studies in Psychotherapy*. Wilmette, IL: Chiron.

Eliot, G. (1973). *Middlemarch*. London: Pan.

Erikson, E. (1968). The development of ritualization. In D. Cutler (Ed.), *The Religious Situation* (pp. 711–733). Boston, MA: Beacon.

Frank, R. (2005). Developmental somatic psychotherapy. In N. Totton (Ed.), *New Dimensions in Body Psychotherapy* (pp. 115–127). Maidenhead, UK: Open University Press.

Frankl, V. (1971). *Will to Meaning: Foundations and Applications of Logotherapy*. London: Souvenir Press.

Freud, S. (1960). Letter to Marie Bonaparte of 13 August 1937. In *Letters of Sigmund Freud* (Trans. T. & J. Stern). New York: Basic Books.

Gendlin, E. (1996). *Focusing-Oriented Psychotherapy*. New York: Guilford Press.

Gerhardt, S. (2015). *Why Love Matters: How Affection Shapes a Baby"s Brain* (2nd ed.). London: Routledge.

Guntrip, H. (1992). *Schizoid Phenomena, Object Relations and the Self*. London: Karnac.

Hay, D. (2006). *Something There: The Biology of the Human Spirit*. London: Darton, Longman and Todd.

Hedges, L. (1994). *Search of the Lost Mother of Infancy*. Northvale, NJ: Jason Aronson.

Heller, L. and LaPierre, A. (2012). *Healing Developmental Trauma*. Berkeley, CA: North Atlantic Books.

Heron, J. (1998). *Sacred Science: Person-Centred Inquiry into the Spiritual and the Subtle*. Ross-on-Wye, UK: PCCS Books.

James, H. (1997). *The Wings of the Dove*. London: Everyman.

Johnson, R. (1983). *The Psychology of Romantic Love*. London: Penguin.

Jung, C. (1992). *Letter 1915 to Hans Schmidt. Letters Vol.1*. London: Routledge.

Lake, F. (1986). *Clinical theology: A theological and psychiatric basis to clinical pastoral care*. Darton, Longman & Todd.

Landale, M. (2002). The use of imagery in body-oriented psychotherapy. In T. Staunton (Ed.), *Body Psychotherapy: Advancing Theory in Therapy*. Hove, UK: Brunner-Routledge.

Levin, D. M. (1988). *The Opening of Vision: Nihilism and the Postmodern Situation*. New York: Routledge.

McGilchrist, I. (2010). *The Master and His Emissary: The Divided Brain and the Making of the Western World*. New Haven, CT: Yale University Press.

Mearns, D. and Cooper, D. (2005). *Working at Relational Depth in Counselling and Psychotherapy*. London: Sage.

Proust, M. (1988). *Against Sainte-Beuve* (Trans. J. Sturrock). London: Penguin.

Proust, M. (1996). *In Search of Lost Time, Vol. VI: Time Regained* (Trans. A. Mayor & T. Kilmartin). London: Vintage.

Rilke, R. M. (1988). *Selected Letters: 1902–1926* (Trans. R. Hull). London: Quartet Books.

Rilke, R. M. (1993). *Letters to a Young Poet* (Trans. H. Norton). New York: W.W. Norton.

Rogers, C. (1963). The actualizing tendency in relation to "motives" and to consciousness. In M. Jones (Ed.), *Nebraska Symposium on Motivation* (pp. 1–24). Lincoln, NE: University of Nebraska Press.

Saint-Exupéry, A. de (2012). *The Airman"s Odyssey* (Trans. L. Galantiere & S. Gilbert). Orlando, FL: Houghton Mifflin Harcourt.

Schore, A. (2003). *Affect Regulation and the Repair of the Self*. New York: Norton.

Schore, A. (2010). The right brain implicit self. In J. Petrucelli (Ed.), *Knowing, Not-Knowing and Sort-of-Knowing: Psychoanalysis and the Experience of Uncertainty* (pp. 177–202). London: Karnac.

Shlien, J. (1984). A countertheory of transference. In R. Levant & J. Shlien (Eds.), *Client-Centred Therapy and the Person-Centred Approach* (pp. 153–181). New York: Praeger.

Thompson, M. (2009). *Me*. Stocksfield, UK: Acumen.

Totton, N. (2003). *Body Psychotherapy: An Introduction*. Maidenhead, UK: Open University Press.

Van Deurzen-Smith, E. (1997). *Everyday Mysteries: Existential Dimensions of Psychotherapy*. London: Routledge.

Verny, T. (1994). Working with pre- and perinatal material in psychotherapy. *Pre- and Perinatal Psychology Journal, 8*(3), 161–186.

Ward, G. (2014). *Unbelievable: Why We Believe and Why We Don"t*. London: I.B. Tauris.

Washburn, M. (1998). The pre/trans fallacy reconsidered. In D. Rothberg & S. Kelly (Eds.), *Ken Wilber in Dialogue: Conversations with Leading Transpersonal Thinkers* (pp. 62–83). Wheaton, IL: Quest Books.

Winnicott, D. W. (1984). *Through Paediatrics to Psychoanalysis*. London: Karnac.

Winnicott, D. W. (1990). *The Maturational Processes and the Facilitating Environment*. London: Karnac.

Yalom, I. (1980). *Existential Psychotherapy*. New York: Basic Books.

Chapter 7

A right-brain dissociative model for right-brain disorders

Dissociation vs repression in borderline and other severe psychopathologies of early traumatic origin

Clara Mucci

From repression to dissociation, a new neuropsychoanalytic model for psychopathology

My main contention in this chapter is that there is a clear divide in psychopathologies between those based on the structure of dissociation deriving from early relational trauma (as attachment studies and neuroscientific research have consistently indicated) and those psychopathologies rooted in repression, as indicated by Freud, from the time of *Studies on Hysteria* (1895) onward.

This structural differentiation requires a new psychoanalytic theoretical model of psychopathology which profitably considers and makes use of neuroscientific research, especially on the development and deficits of the right hemisphere, in connection with the study of the neurobiological effects of different levels of relational[1] traumatizations, occurring in different moments of growth.

This developmental psychoanalytic-neuroscientific model would account for the complex interpersonal interactions necessary to create healthy personalities and will also take into consideration the deficits in the interaction that might epigenetically influence development. In this interaction, illness is to be understood as the combination of biological vulnerabilities with traumatic exchanges, starting from attachment, where there is a lack of subsequent relational repair.

Pathologies that have at their roots repression of unconscious conflicts, as indicated by Freud, are typical of a neurotic structure, which in my view implies a not so early interpersonal traumatization, while pathologies based on dissociation indicate an earlier and more severe kind of traumatization, determining pathologies of "borderline" nature; I am using the term "borderline"[2] here to indicate a peculiar and more severe organization of personality structure than the neurotic one, in the sense described by Otto Kernberg, as encompassing all kinds of personality disorders (borderline proper, narcissistic, schizoid, hystrionic and paranoid personality disorders, Kernberg, 1975).

Borderline pathologies are to be considered pre-Oedipal and the problematic impasse in development of which they are a sign takes place much earlier on in the subject's development, in comparison with neurotic developments, i.e. they originate from the difficulties encountered in the lack of attunement and constant re-pair between caregiver and child that would be necessary for optimal growth, from the first moments of interaction, which influence epigenetically the development of the brain of the child, starting from the right hemisphere that is particularly involved in child-rearing, especially in the first two years of life. This impact is particularly strong in critical or sensitive periods, which are periods of exuberant neuronal growth.

As has been widely illustrated, especially by Allan Schore in his decades of interdisciplinary research and in the "paradigm shift" he has consistently proposed, (Schore, 1994, 2003a, 2003b; see also Cozolino, 2002; Siegel, 1999), the first neuropsychological development starts from the right brain activity of the caregiver in connection with the right hemisphere of the child, which develops first. In fact, the right hemisphere has a higher rate of growth during the first 18 months of life, paralleling the development of sensory and motor capabilities (Chiron et al., 1997).

The right brain has more connections with the limbic system and the amygdala (Gainotti, 2000), and the right is dominant in the attachment process, controlling implicitly emotion, bodily experience between self and other, and autonomic processes, affecting future capacities for affect regulation, social cognition and mentalization.

The medial prefrontal cortex, fundamental for attachment, is the area that links the brainstem to the amygdala and the limbic system and therefore connects the superior areas of the brain. The orbitofrontal, ventromedial right hemisphere is recognised as the seat of the system of attachment (LeDoux, 2003; Schore, 1994, 2003a, 2003b), that will become the basis of the regulatory system of stress and affectivity. During this period, the development of the left hemisphere is slowed (Gould, 1997 in Cozolino, 2002).

Consistent data has been provided about the affective-emotional implicit connections derived from this dual right brain activity between caregiver and child during the first two years of life, a connection that creates an imprinting for future sense of self, future social relational disposition and empathic capacity, especially until the second half of the second year of life, when the left brain becomes more stimulated by the interaction with a "third term" in the maternal dyad, opening to the maturation of symbolic and language processes[3] (Schore, 2016).

It is maintained that the human limbic system myelinates in the first year and a half and the early-maturing right hemisphere (Schore, 1994), deeply connected into the limbic system, undergoes a growth spurt at this time, so that attachment communications specifically impact limbic and cortical areas of the developing right brain (Cozolino, 2002; Siegel, 1999; Henry, 1993;

Schore, 1994, 2000). Developmental neurobiological studies also show evidence of "lateralization of negative emotional production to the right hemisphere in infants as young as 12 months of age" and "a developmental enhancement of right hemisphere control of negative emotional expression" by 24 months (Schuetze & Reid, 2005, p. 207); Howard and Reggia confirm that "earlier maturation of the right hemisphere is supported by both anatomical and imaging experience" (Howard & Reggia, 2007, p. 112).

At 4 months, a child when shown female faces shows an increase of activation in his/her EEG in prefrontal right areas and at 5 months the right brain responds to female faces. At 6 months children show lateralization with special activation of fronto-temporal areas when they see their mother rather than a stranger. The same right activation is involved in audioprosodic, visuo-tactile and gestural communication.

The visual-facial attachment communications between mother and child, which are fundamental for establishing the pattern of attachment development, are based on implicit right hemisphere interactions. This data will have relevance for future therapeutic exchanges, as Schore has also cogently argued in his more recent studies (see Schore, 2012).[4] The development of the capacity to efficiently process information from faces requires visual input to the right, not the left hemisphere, during infancy (Schore, 2010). As early as two months of age – a critical period for synaptic connections in the developing occipital cortex which is modified by visual experience – infants show right hemispheric activation when exposed to a woman's face (Tzourio-Mazoyer et al., 2002). The maternal visual facial auditory prosodic communication focuses on the exchanges of the two right hemispheres of the dyad. Ranote et al. (2004) show that in mothers looking at videos of their own 4–8 month old infants there is an activation of the right anterior inferior temporal cortex and right occipital gyrus; viewing their own infants also activates the amygdala, which is usually activated both by unpleasant, fearful emotions but also by the processing of happy expressions of facial emotion. Noriuchi, Kikuchi, and Senoo (2008), analysing mothers viewing two videos of their 16 month old infants looking at their mothers smiling joyfully in the first video and looking anxious in the other, show activation of right inferior gyrus (associated with recognising infant's facial expression) and right orbitofrontal cortex, playing an important part in the reward system, receiving ascending dopamine projections from the ventral tegmental area (VTA); anterior cingulate and periaqueductal gray (PAG) are involved, as is the insula, fundamental in interoceptive perception of emotional states and in pleasant feelings of touch of a "limbic" empathic emotional quality between self and other (Schore, 2016).

The right brain connection between the two involved in the interaction therefore determines the emotional well-being of the child or the basic affective and emotional dysfunctions that will be responsible, if left unrepaired, for subsequent disorders, because of the disruption of the entire psychobiological development, due to cortisol in excess, derived from hyper-arousal. This is one of the possible consequences of early relational trauma, which disrupts the HPA axis regulation, influencing all the other psychobiological parameters (as epigenetic research with rodents and other animals has clearly shown, see Hofer, 1984; Meaney, 2001; Suomi, 1991), with release of noradrenaline, playing a fundamental role for the regulation of neurobiological development.

Various studies now show evidence of how the child's secretion of stress hormones in response to lack of repair in misattunement with the mother might even determine neuronal death in fundamental limbic and cortico-limbic circuits responsible for affect regulation (Karr-Morse & Wiley, 1997; Perry, 1997; Schore, 2016). On the contrary, secure attachment and acquired self-regulation are determining factors towards what we now term resilience and are the best protection against future traumatizations, both natural and man-made.

In humans, early relational traumatization and active abuse, in the presence of dysfunctions in the family, are seen in connection with a higher percentage of the development of psychological and physical illness, as the ACE research has convincingly argued (Felitti et al., 1998). An entire series of psychological and psychosomatic or conversion disorders are now being considered of traumatic and/or dissociative origin, in contrast with Freud's repression model (Harricharan et al., 2016; Kozlovska, 2005; Kozlowska, 2007; Roelofs, Keijsers, Hoogduin, Naring, & Moene, 2002).[5]

The psychopathogenic effect derives not only from attachment trauma, causing insecure or disorganised attachment (Liotti, 2012, 2013; Schore, 1994, 2003a, 2003b, 2012, 2014, 2016) but also from psychological trauma stemming from actual abuse, maltreatment, violence, severe emotional deprivation, or incest taking place over the years (Ferenczi, 1932a, 1932b; Mucci, 2013).

In *Beyond Individual and Collective Trauma* (2013) I have therefore distinguished between a first level of traumatization (due to lack of attunement between caregiver and child, with dysregulation of the neurobiological parameters and consequent hyperarousal and/or dissociation, as shown by Schore, 1994), and a second level of active abuse, severe deprivation, maltreatment or incest, with similar psychobiological consequences, and in addition the possible effect of cumulation. For instance, incest might cumulate its traumatic effects with secure or insecure attachment, leading to different consequences, also in conjunction with other psychobiological vulnerabilities. Secure attachment provides a protective base in the face of future traumatization of both man-made or catastrophic origin, while insecure and/or disorganised attachment does not constitute a protection and a base for resilience; on the contrary it creates the bases for cumulative trauma (the term has notoriously been used first by Masud Kahn, 1963, then by Grubrich-Simitis, 1981, among others).

As Schore wrote in his *The Science of the Art of Psychotherapy*, we need to acknowledge and clinically practice a paradigm shift in psychoanalytic models of psychopathology from "Oedipal repression to pre-Oedipal dissociation" (Schore, 2012, p. 126).

Freud's model of psychopathology

Freud has notoriously implied a repression model even for pathologies that we would now consider of a more severe, non-neurotic origin and would situate within the borderline spectrum of pathology, from severe hysterical cases to borderline and narcissistic, to the extreme limit of perversion and psychosis.

A model of psychopathology based on dissociation caused by severe traumatization was already available at the time of Freud's investigation (for a discussion of this model see Lingiardi & Mucci, 2014; Mucci, 2013, 2016), and this type of dissociation was considered the cause of illness by such contemporaries as Pierre Janet (Janet, 1889) and by Sandor Ferenczi (Ferenczi, 1932a) who spoke of "fragmentation of the soul" in connection with relational trauma and abuse (Mucci, 2013, 2014). A psychodynamic concept of dissociation may have been implied by Freud as early as the end of the nineteenth century; in fact, in *Studies on Hysteria,* reporting the case of Miss Lucy, he used the concept of "splitting of consciousness", when he said:

> The actual traumatic moment, then, is the one at which *the incompatibility forces itself upon the ego and at which the latter decides on the repudiation of the incompatible idea. That idea is not annihilated by a repudiation of this kind, but merely repressed into the unconscious* ... The splitting of consciousness in these cases of acquired hysteria is accordingly a deliberate and intentional one. At least one is often introduced by an act of volition; for the actual outcome is something different from what the subject intended. What he wanted was to do away with an idea, as though it had never appeared, but all he succeeds in doing is to isolate it psychically.
>
> (Breuer & Freud, 1895, p. 123, my emphasis)

As is clear in this passage, Freud understood this defense as "intentional and deliberate", therefore as partially conscious and he finally conflated the psychodynamic of "splitting of consciousness" with that of repression. The "deliberate and intentional" aspect of repression is pointed out at the very beginning of the text: "It was a question of things which the patient wished to forget, and *therefore intentionally repressed from his conscious thought and inhibited and suppressed*" (ibid., 1895, p. 10, my emphasis).

In contemporary psychotraumatic theory, we understand "splitting of consciousness" and dissociation as an earlier and more severe primary defense mechanism (see also Putnam, 2001; van der Hart Njenhuis & Steele, 2006;

van der Kolk, 1994; van der Kolk & McFarlane, 1996): dissociation is certainly neither "deliberate and intentional", nor closer to the conscious spectrum and in fact manifests itself in a continuum of severity, up to the level of actual confusion between reality and unreality, as in psychosis.

But why did Freud leave us with a repression model for hysteric illness, which he understood first as originating in "seduction" trauma (trauma due to sexual abuse, as in *Studies on Hysteria*) and then, after the renunciation of his "neurotica", (see letter to Fliess, 21 September 1897), when he came to believe that his patients had not actually been abused, as they claimed), as a mixture of intrapsychic and fantasmatic sexual conflicts, typical of hysteria?

Privileging a model that viewed the repression of unacceptable feelings and thoughts as the major cause of psychoneurosis, Freud opened the road to a "psychoanalysis" – as opposed to Janet's "psychological analysis" or to the traumatogenic path to illness illustrated by Ferenczi in the same years (Borgogno, 2004; Bonomi, 2006, 2015; Ferenczi, 1932a) – which privileged intrapsychic conflicts and fantasmatic organization onto the actual event and onto the intersubjective real traumatic experience. In the psychoanalytic model we received from Freud, the libido system and the drive theory were to prevail over the relational, intersubjective early experiences of the subject, in contrast to what Ferenczi and Janet were already claiming when they stressed the pathogenic value of interpersonal trauma. As a consequence, the construction of the entire Oedipal hierarchy (implying a more mature subject, whose intrapsychic world is taken into a symbolic triadic structure, around pre-school years) was to prevail over the pre-Oedipal, dyadic aspects of the caregiver-younger child relation. As Bowlby clearly objected in his work, stressing, in opposition to the Psychoanalytic Society, the correlation between the reality of child-rearing conditions, actual deprivations, loss and traumatizations, and future illness, and as Renè Spitz (1945) and Selma Fraiberg (1982) subsequently demonstrated in their work on abused and severely deprived children, we can now confirm that without those basic right-brain, limbic based, unconscious-implicit maternal exchanges, there is no healthy, mature, independent and prosocial subject.

Pre-Oedipal self, right brain development and maternal dyads

Judging from his large body of writings, it would seem that Freud had difficulties in actually acknowledging the place and role of the mother in the development of the human subject, recognizing the value and impact of maternal child-rearing or, as we would say now, of right hemisphere function, a deficiency that subsequent infant research and psychoanalytic studies of mother and child with an interpersonal and relational basis have been called upon to repair (starting from Margaret Mahler, Edith Jacobson, W. R. Fairbairn, Winnicott, Stern, to Beebe and Tronick, to Lichtenberg, up to Fonagy & Target).

In contrast to Freud's one person and intrapsychic psychological model, a dyadic (for the first year and a half, at least) and triadic and intersubjective model of development has been formulated which has been increasingly validated by contemporary research, including neuroscientific studies on the social formation of self in relation with an other, leading up to what has been termed the "two-person Unconscious" (Lyons-Ruth, 1999).

Following Allan Schore, we could say that the dyadic, bodily based right brain maternal function (played out potentially by ANY subject but traditionally played by women in the majority of known cultures, so that the very term "caregiver" in my mind equates with a female figure since in the majority of cases it is a woman who plays the maternal, right-brain emotional function on which attachment and future life cycles and encounters are based) is at the roots of the "birth of the subject", since the right brain and the limbic system are the basis of future emotional development (including empathy, connectedness and intimacy) on which superior frontal functions are grounded, and from which develops the capacity for agency, intentionality, choice, volition, and prosocial behavior, including a moral and ethical commitment for a proper consideration of the relationship between self and other and the value of community and connectedness (Mucci, 2013).[6]

This implicit Self system encoded in the right brain that evolves in the interaction with a primary caregiver develops through preverbal and bodily stages and signals of communication in interaction with a caring caregiver; the mother, Schore writes,

> is thus a regulator of arousal (van der Kolk & Fisler, 1994) and the transfer of affect between mother and child is thus mediated by right-hemisphere-to-right-hemisphere arousal-regulating transactions … During spontaneous right brain-to-right brain visual-facial, auditory-prosodic, and tactile-proprioceptive emotionally charged attachment communications, the sensitive, psychobiologically attuned caregiver regulates, at an implicit level, the infant's states of arousal.
>
> These events are inscribed in implicit procedural memory in the early developing right hemisphere that is specialized for the processing of visuospatial information (Galin, 1974). But the right cerebral cortex is also dominant for "implicit" learning (Hugdahl, 1995), an adaptive process that underlies all emotional phenomena, including those at the core of the therapeutic relationship.
>
> (Schore, 2003b, p. 222)

This implicit relational core is at the basis of what we now understand as Un-conscious, meaning what is implicit and non-conscious but nonetheless directs and implicitly guides self-esteem, and an overall sense of value and meaning. This overall emotional and subsequently cognitive estimation of the safety or unsafety of the environment is an exquisite endowment of the right brain (see McGilchrist, 2009, 2015), which is dominant in the first year of life.

In fact, it is possible to say with Schore that at the end of the first year of life the right lateralized cortical-subcortical circuits imprint, in the implicit procedural memory, an internal working model of attachment which encodes strategies of affect regulation that non-consciously guide the individual in future interpersonal exchanges. The connection of the limbic system with the orbitofrontal areas is a subsequent step in the development of the healthy mature human subject, and precisely what is hampered in borderline pathologies characterised by deficit in affect regulation and in the connection between orbitofrontal areas and the limbic system.

The Self in formation therefore is directly influenced by this dual right brain process. Reformulating Lyons-Ruth's fascinating relational concept of the "two person unconscious" (Lyons-Ruth, 1999), neurobiologically this dual reciprocal mechanism of implicit encoding and exchanges implicitly forms the unconscious of the subject in development, and consequently opens the relational world and creates the social, ethical and moral dimension in the child, or, on the contrary, in case of interrelational trauma, it contributes to the ruinous and violent disruption of positive subjective and relational experience as has happened to subjects who present violent and/or antisocial behaviour, or other severe psychopathologies such as personality disorders and psychosis. This view of the formation of the self is particularly dependent upon right-hemisphere function and has been described at length by Russell Meares, who also presents a dissociative model of borderline personality disorders (see Meares, 2012, p. 296).

It is also this "two person unconscious" (or two right hemispheres in connection, we could say) that helps explain why the interpersonal relational therapeutic practice based on the right brain that Schore has consistently proposed and so cogently and creatively illustrated in the last few years is particularly effective for these cases (Schore, 2012).

The right brain maternal (in the sense of care-giving) system has been shown as decisive for life and nurturing at all levels of existence: as Myron Hofer writes in his epigenetic research on families of rodents, the mother works as the "hidden regulator" (1984), and it does not need to be a biological mother to play that role and "do the job"; it could be in fact an adoptive mother or even a researcher playing the nurturing role (of feeding and regularly licking the pups), with the due rhythm and constancy and dedication: this right brain function can in fact be played by anybody who plays the care-giving role with due commitment, constancy and care; this is turn recalls the special right brain capacity for empathic attunement, emotional presence (or embodied-testimony, as I like to call it) and practice that is required in psychotherapy.

From these bodily right-brain imprints the traces of internalised representations of the relationship are created, something we can assimilate to the

IWMs as explained by Bowlby (1969). These IWMs encode the memory of the first sensory and emotional traces regulated by the amygdala, so that these bodily imprints and implicit memory constitute what we can consider the relational un-conscious of the child (Schore, 2016; Schore & Schore, 2008), stored mostly in the right brain and in the bodily sensory receptivity. Relevant to intergenerational transmission, these traces include not only the child's developing Self but also the embodied memories of the implicit relational Self of the caregiver, through the two limbic systems in connection.

Since the attachment system is reactivated by the caring system, this emotional right brain connection becomes a basic transfer of unconscious (implicit) relational material between caregiver and child. This is particularly important for the transmission of trauma between parent and child: the transfer happens through split, dissociated parts, non-conscious preverbal communication between the two, even in "silent exchanges" (Mucci, 2013). This means that we do not need actual abuse and active violence to create split parts in the child, since if the first generation has been severely traumatized and no elaboration or reparation has taken place, the traumatization will be carried through to the future generations, in a cycle of repetition that affects the mind-brain-body self in relation (for the intergenerational transmission, with particularly severe effects in the third generation, see Laub & Auerhahn, 1984; Laub & Lee, 2003; Mucci, 2008, 2013).

Going back to Freud's concept of repression, clearly a rewriting of the model is called for, since repression is a defense activated by a more mature subject or by a less damaged parent, while the majority of more severe, borderline disorders are based on dissociation and are of traumatic origin (of relational trauma stemming from three possible sources: early relational trauma, taking place in the first two years, due to the caregiver's incapacity to act as regulator of the neurobiological systems of the child; abuse, maltreatment, severe deprivation, incest; or unresolved trauma of the parent being transferred implicitly through the limbic right brain connection between the two in the relation).

Therefore I totally agree with what Allan Schore had already cogently suggested over ten years ago:

> current neurobiology suggests that repression is a developmentally more advanced left brain defense against affects like anxiety that are represented at the cortical level of the right brain, but the earlier-appearing and more primitive dissociation is a defense against traumatic affects like terror that are stored subcortically in the right brain.
>
> *This neurobiological conceptualization indicates that Freud's idea about trauma must be reassessed (van der Kolk, Weisaeth, & Van Der Hart, 1996) and that the concept of dissociation must be reincorporated into theoretical and clinical psychoanalysis. It is now clear that dissociation represents the most primitive defense against traumatic affective states and that it must be addressed in the treatment of*

severe psychopathologies (Putnam, 2001; Schore, 1994, 1997; van der Kolk, van der Hart, & Marmar, 1996).

(Schore, 2003b, p. 246)

I would like therefore to refer the reader to a dissociative model that was present at the time of Freud's speculations, Ferenczi's model, but was strongly opposed precisely for reasons not too different from those that had caused the intentional "repression" of Freud's "neurotica" in 1897. I think the time is ripe not only for a revision of the model as a dual paradigm (between two beings in relationship) based on implicit relational psychobio-logical imprintings – finally giving the mother, or the caregiver's right brain function, its due – but also to recognise the devastating effects of traumatisa-tion in families, in societies, and in the world at large. A different concept of the Un-conscious (as non-repressed, implicit, relational and of earlier for-mation) also stems from this paradigm shift as Allan Schore (2014) and Mauro Mancia (2006) have argued.

Ferenczi's "fragmentation"of the soul: a dissociative model of trauma and abuse, the internalisation of the persecutor, and present neuroscientific explanation of parasympathetic dissociation

For Ferenczi, the extent and impact of child abuse was greatly underesti-mated by the contemporary culture, while in his view it resulted in "frag-mentation" of the psyche for the young child (not an infant, but a developing child and adolescent), a concept we can assimilate to the pre-sent neurobiological concept of dissociation.

Here is Ferenczi, with the famous entry on "Fragmentation" in his *Clin-ical Diary* (1932a, p. 39), on 21 February 1932:

> A child is the victim of overwhelming aggression, which results in "giving up the ghost" … with the firm conviction that this self-abandonment (fainting) means death. However, it is precisely this complete relaxation induced by self-abandonment that may create more favorable conditions for him to endure the violence. … Therefore someone who has "given up the ghost" survives this death physically and with a part of his energy begins to live again; he even succeeds in reestablishing unity with the pre-traumatic personality, although this is usually accompanied by memory lapses and retroactive amnesia of varying duration. But this amnesic piece is actually a part of the person, who is still "dead", or exists permanently in the agony of anxiety. The task of the analysis is to remove this split.

The extraordinary accuracy of this description of the dissociative traumatic reaction resulting even in a fainting of the body, a freezing response, has been confirmed by neurophysiological findings, as in the research by Stephen Porges (2011), or the vagal response leading to blunting and analgesia (compatible with the "shrinking of conscious experience" as described by Janet). More than a defense, and certainly not an intentional or even partially intentional defense, the neurophysiology of trauma describes a collapse of mental and psychical resources as a response to the external overwhelming experience. It is not merely an intrapsychic defense at work.

The extreme defensive metabolic (parasympathetic) shutdown has been described by Schore in recent times as follows:

> The dissociative metabolic shutdown state is a primary regulatory process, used throughout the life-span, in which the stressed individual passively disengages in order to conserve energies, foster survival by the risky posture of "feigning death", and allow the restitution of depleted resources by immobility. In this passive hypometabolic state, heart rate, blood pressure, and respiration are decreased, while pain–numbing and blunting endogenous opiates are elevated. It is this energy-conserving parasympathetic (vagal) mechanism that mediates the "profound detachment" of dissociation.
>
> ("Foreword", to Bromberg, 2011, xvii)

In another revealing passage, extremely relevant for developments in psychoanalytic theory and in practice, on 25 March 1932 ("Psychic Bandage"), Ferenczi describes how the traumatic overwhelming experience leaves a permanent mark, and results in a splitting in the personality, and ultimately in a change in the victim's behavior:

> From the moment when bitter experience teaches us to lose faith in the benevolence of the environment, *a permanent split in the personality occurs.*... Actual trauma is experienced by children in situations where no immediate remedy is provided and where adaptation, that is, a change in their own behavior, is forced on them – *the first step towards establishing the differentiation between inner and outer world, subject and object. From then on, neither subjective nor objective experience alone will be perceived as an integral emotional unit* [...].
>
> (Ferenczi, 1932a, p. 69, emphasis mine)

Trauma brought about by human agency disrupts the internal emotional cohesion and representation of both self and other in the child and results in a permanent cognitive distortion, in which not only he/she is in doubt about who is guilty of the abuse (and usually decides, in order to keep the bond with the other, that he/she is bad and guilty, therefore the victim internalises the persecutor's aggressiveness and also the split sense of guilt of the persecutor), but eventually might even doubt the reality of what has happened. This often happens in connection with an environment which is totally unsupportive or in which the child is even accused of making up false realities (what Ferenczi acknowledges as vicarious traumatisation, Ferenczi, 1932a).

In interpersonal trauma happening slowly and repeatedly in the family, such as abuse or incest, according to Ferenczi, the negative traces of an external, relational overwhelming experience become internalised, intrapsychic, and negatively condition/effect future relationships with the outside world, through the mechanism of the internalisation of the aggressiveness and the split guilt of the aggressor (Ferenczi, 1932a, 1932b). In the relevance attributed to real events and real child rearing conditions, Ferenczi is closer to what Bowlby would explain years later in contrast with the psychoanalytic views of his time, for instance against Melanie Klein's idea of the intrapsychic world of the infant as innately full of aggressiveness and anxiety. The ostracism that struck Bowlby at the hands of the psychoanalytic community of his day has been totally reconsidered in the last few decades, leading to a revision or a "rapprochement" between psychoanalysis and attachment.

The psychobiological relational base of the IWMs as described by Bowlby has now been widely accepted as a biosocial intersubjective template for the formation of the future intrapsychic and interpersonal representations of self and other and subsequent behavior, starting from such views as Winnicott's acknowledgement of the simple fact that "there is no such thing as a child", since in psychopathology a child is understood only in relation with his/her caregiver. A similar view created misunderstanding and conflicts between Bowlby and Melanie Klein, who was for some time his supervisor and "prohibited" Bowlby from actually seeing his young three-year-old patient together with his own caregiver. We now understand the entire developmental process (and possible future pathology) as stemming from the interrelational process at the basis of life, growth and maturity, starting precisely with "two amygdalas in relation" as Schore has highlighted in his work, and mostly involving the right hemisphere.

In connection with traumatic memory, it is the amygdala that maintains and stores the implicit emotional meaning and the affect of the event, even before hippocampus maturation (between the second and the third year) can encode the actual explicit meaning of the event.[7] The implicit encoding system based on amygdala (and mostly right amygdala) circuits precedes the explicit hippocampal encoding and defines the peculiar "written on the body" quality of traumatic memories, often retrieved on the basis of smell, visual triggers, unexpected sensory arousal, and visceral bodily sensations. The symbolic-subsymbolic differentiation as exemplified by Wilma Bucci (1997) bears connections with the implicit-explicit system, being the explicit hippocampal encoding linked to language label retrievement. To go from subsymbolic (nonverbal) activation, expressed in and by the body through sensory, somatic and visceral components of emotional schemas or affects, we need to pass to symbolic representation, first through imagery (right brain based) and then through the linguistic and narrational, with the intervention of the left brain for the secondary revision, so that the connection is from limbic, subcortical, (and mainly right) to cortical and mainly left, with the final integration of both hemispheres.

This implicit encoding of amygdala based interrelations constitutes the "implicit nucleus of the self" as described by Schore. For the traumatised child it becomes encoded in a split, pathological nucleus of a representation of self and other as victim/persecutor and as persecutor/victim, a dyad that will remain active in distorted and painful future encounters with others, as is clear in the formation of the dyads that borderline patients represent and re-enact in therapy sessions in the model of TFP (transferenced focused psychotherapy) as devised by Otto Kernberg (Clarkin, Yeomans, & Kernberg, 2007). These dyads represent in the sessions the way in which traumatic experiences implicitly encoded through the right brain connections of the two subjects in relation (caregiver and child; abuser and child) return in the here and now of the therapy and re-present how psychopathology has been developmentally and relationally created (Mucci, 2013, 2016).

This is coherent with what Ferenczi stressed as early as 1932 in his trauma theory and clinical implications: the child will very likely internalise the aggressiveness and the dissociated sense of guilt of the persecutor. This internalisation of aggressiveness with dissociation of unbearable emotions and memories constitutes the pathological core of severe personality disorders and other severe psychopathologies, as is clear in borderline pathologies in which a clear victim-persecutor dyad is being enacted in therapeutic as well as in all other relationships.

Notoriously the dispute between Freud and Ferenczi resulted in Freud's prohibiting Ferenczi from presenting his paper on "Confusion of tongues between adult and child" to the Wiesbaden Congress in 1932, and the fracture between the two was never repaired.

"Unrepressed unconscious" as implicit memory and right brain process

Interestingly, some 20 years after *Studies on Hysteria*, in *On Metapsychology* (first published in 1915), in the Preface to the chapter on "The unconscious", Freud gave a definition of repression and simultaneously stated that "the repressed does not cover everything that is unconscious":

> We have learnt from psychoanalysis that the essence of the process of repression lies, not in putting an end to, in annihilating, the idea which represents an instinct, but in preventing it from becoming conscious. When this happens we say of the idea that it is in a state of being "unconscious", and we can produce good evidence *to show that even*

when it is unconscious it can produce effects, even including some which finally reach consciousness … *Everything that is repressed must remain unconscious;* but let us state at the very outset that *the repressed does not cover everything that is unconscious. The unconscious has the wider compass: the repressed is a part of the unconscious.*

(Freud, 1915, p. 166, my emphasis)

For Freud, the repressed is what has undergone repression but does not define all that is un-conscious to us or separated from consciousness and not at conscious reach.

This interesting definition of a wider un-conscious that is not all repressed has given way to a series of intriguing explanations as to what is un-conscious and repressed in mental life and what is un-conscious and not repressed. This is certainly in coherence with the "modern attachment theory" as formulated by Schore (Schore, 2012, 2014) and with all the models that see the right brain as dominant for affective, emotional – conscious and less conscious – and social life (Cozolino, 2014; Siegel, 1999) and for the capacity to develop and experience empathy.

There is an un-conscious life that is repressed (involving higher brain order faculties and depending on more mature brain capacities, and the development of the hippocampus) that is coincident with repressive processes as described by Freud as at work in neurotic subjects, and an un-conscious functioning as the amygdala-based encoding and affective imprinting that forms implicit bodily memories. This is what Mauro Mancia in his 2006 work had termed "unrepressed unconscious" which enabled him to indicate the right brain (in correspondence with Schore, distinct from other pathways) as the site of implicit memory (Schore, 2016; see also Mucci, 2016).

I think we can trace a convincing link between Schore's definition of the un-conscious as basically right-brain implicit memory processes based on amygdala encoding and the unrepressed unconscious as in Mancia's definition. For Mancia, the unrepressed unconscious or implicit memory is located in the posterior temporo-parieto-occipital associative cortical areas of the right hemisphere.

This unrepressed unconscious explains the kind of traumatic traces that, since the child was too young for hippocampus encoding (therefore, before the second or third year of life), are actually emotional and bodily memories stored in the limbic system, of amygdala encoding, therefore reactivated by bodily triggers and not pertaining to declarative memory. These are the unrepressed but early memories of amygdala encoding that can be reactivated in therapy through the right brain participation of the attuned therapist and, through the mechanism of enactment, projective identification and dissociation itself, can be brought from nonverbal, sub-symbolic form, to symbolic and verbal expression (this is in fact the path of psychotherapy).

Pre-Oedipal dissociation and borderline traumatic structure

Otto Kernberg clearly defines borderline personality disorders as based on splitting (not repression, nor dissociation) and as a pre-Oedipal organisation.

In the definition of borderline organisation, Kernberg notoriously defines "splitting" (following the Kleinian model) as the structural base of self-other defenses for these pathological expressions, leading to what he terms "dyads" in the representation of the internal/external psychic world. These dyads as representations of self and other, formed in primary relationships and exchanges with caregivers, are consistently repeated in the here and now of the sessions and the resolution of the difficulties presented by the patient consists in the integration of the split parts and identifications, achieved through painstaking and laborious observation in the therapeutic process of how they shape further relationships and emotional and cognitive processes linked to those internal representations.

Only partially recognising the traumatic origin of the disorder, Kernberg does not attribute splitting processes and imprinted implicit representational models of self and other to attachment models and developmental trauma, even though there is more and more consistent neuroscientific evidence that early relational trauma and especially disorganised attachment might be responsible for the dissociative structure.

The link between disorganised attachment and subsequent dissociative structure and dissociation-based pathology has been pointed out by Giovanni Liotti in his theoretical model (2013) and by Peter Fonagy and his research group (Fonagy, Gergely, Jurist, & Target, 2002). As already noted, a dissociative model for borderline pathology has been proposed by Russell Meares in his seminal work (Meares, 2012); he has also linked this model to a therapeutic process that privileges integration of self-other representations of traumatic origin with a conversational model.

Traumatic origin of severe mental disorders

Although at present we lack conclusive research evidence for the actual development of "borderline" disorders (in the wider sense of a structure as implied by Kernberg) or "personality disorders" (as in manuals such as DSM or ICD or PDM) as a result of disorganised attachment, nonetheless the early traumatic origin of these disorders was proposed as early as 2003 by Schore on the basis of a wide interdisciplinary work correlating infant research, neuroscientific brain development and neuroimmunopsychological studies with developmental research and various psychoanalytic models, and has been connected with the typical dysregulation that follows early relational trauma.

In an optimal mother–child connection, secure attachment results in connecting right amygdala and all limbic system functioning (starting with the
right hemisphere, which through the connections with the limbic and subcortical regions, is dominant in the processing, expressing and regulation of
emotional information; Porges, Doussard-Roosevelt, & Maiti, 1994) with
the orbitofrontal areas so that affect regulation is established and, from being
external, it slowly becomes an acquired internal system of functioning.

On the contrary, in a child who constantly experiences fear in attachment
processes with a traumatising parent (because the latter is incapable of synto-
nisation or because actively threatening and abusive), the right brain activation increases sympathetic reactions, increasing heart beat frequency, blood
pressure and breathing or even crying and screaming (responses of the
ANS). Terror in the child in hyperaroused state is mediated by the sympathetic system through the secretion of corticotropin releasing factor (CRF),
the major brain hormone of stress, inducing in turn catecolamin activation,
so that the levels of adrenaline, noradrenaline and dopamine increase creating
a hypermetabolic state in the developing brain and body. When the hyperaroused state continues the child might detach from the world through dissociative forms (depersonalisation, derealisation, numbing, total passivity, and
restricted affect). This metabolic shutdown state, which includes heart decel-
eration, is a primary regulatory process that can be explained as the neurophysiological response activated to save energy and survive in any future
situation, a parasympathetic form of "feigning death", as described by Ferenczi in the already quoted passage. This form of early relational trauma as
described by Schore is experienced as a psychic catastrophe (Bion, 1962) and
becomes the "flight when there is no flight" (Putnam, 2001).

The neurobiological mechanism of disorganisation of attachment, with its
clear connection with the right hemisphere, has been explained by Schore as
follows:

> the infant is matching the rhythmic structures of the mother's dysregu-
> lated arousal states. This synchronization is registered in the firing pat-
> terns of the stress–sensitive corticolimbic regions of the right brain,
> dominant for the human stress response and survival (Wittling &
> Schweiger, 1993). These right hemispheric structures are in a critical
> period of growth during the early stages of human development
> (Allman, Watson, Tetreault, & Hakeem, 2005; Bogolepova & Malo-
> feeva, 2001; Chiron et al., 1997; Schore, 1994).
>
> (Foreword to Bromberg, 2011, p. xviii)

The traumatic etiopathology of borderline disorders from disorganisation of
attachment in combination with specific vulnerabilities has not yet been
accepted as definitively established; nonetheless, a large body of research suggests that:

- disorganised attachment in the presence of factors of vulnerability and no reparatory elements predisposes to the instabilities and the dysregulation that characterise borderline disorders (Barone, 2003; Fonagy et al., 1996; Liotti, 2013; Liotti & Farina, 2011; Patrick, Hobson, Castle, Howard, & Maughan, 1994; Schore, 2012);
- abuse and especially sexual abuse and incest have been identified as a cause for the kind of dysfunctional response to images of self and other and destructiveness and impulsivity in several areas which seem to be some of the major dimensions of the painful condition of borderline disorders.

Clinicians and researchers such as Zanarini and colleagues (1989) and Gabbard (2014), who have a great clinical expertise with personality disorders, all testify to the high percentage of abuse (and sexual abuse especially) in patients who have been diagnosed as borderline (in combination with other etiopathogenic elements). Otto Kernberg as well has acknowledged "the prevalence of physical and sexual abuse in the history of patients with severe personality disorders" (Clarkin, Yeomans, & Kernberg, 1999, p. 245); van der Kolk (1994, 2014) and Pat Ogden (Ogden, Minton, & Pain, 2006) identify in affective dysregulation and in dissociation the major cause of the pathology.

On abuse as etiopathogenesis for borderline disorders, stressing the link between early trauma, neurobiological alteration of the right brain and severe psychological and psychiatric disorders, Schore has written very conclusively:

> It is now well established that early childhood abuse specifically alters lateralised limbic system maturation, producing neurobiological alterations that act as a biological substrate for a variety of psychiatric consequences, including affective instability, inefficient stress tolerance, memory impairment, and dissociative disturbances.
>
> (Schore, 2002 Foreword to Bromberg, 2011, xx)

As early as 1994, Allan Schore had already indicated the interval between 12 and 18 months (following Gergely, 1992) as the period of formation of splitting defenses in the child:

> Importantly, due to the later maturation of the parasympathetic nervous system and the resultant cognitive advances of the late practicing period, the child's atttempts to defensively cope with the stress inducing mother are more complex. With the additional maturation of the ANS, the child can now lock into two distinct, nonoverlapping dissociated psychobiological states of existence. According to Kernberg (1975), a major structural characteristic of the borderline condition is the utilization of

the splitting defenses that allow for the presence of mutually dissociated or split off states. *It is now thought that the cognitive preconditions for defensive splitting become established by the time the infant is between 12 to 18 months old* (Gergely, 1992). [The same phase of the possible development of a borderline disorder if there is a relational trauma.] Its function may be to avoid external stimuli that could precipitate an unregulated hyperaroused or hypoaroused state.

(Schore, 1994, p. 420, emphasis mine)

In regard to the link between disorganised attachment and the development of borderline disorders, several authors underline how the personality of an individual is the result of the continuous interactions between genetically inherited traits and the relational intersubjective experiences from his/her environment (Schore, 2012; Siegel, 1999).

Not all researchers agree on the dissociative base of personality disorders (see the review by Scalabrini, Cavicchioli, Fossati, & Maffei, 2016), but dissociation is at the basis of the formation of the split in personality, both affectively and cognitively.

In severe personality disorders, lack of emotional regulation, with dissociation, projective identification and primitive defenses, couples with the internal impossibility of a soothing object to which to return when the child is imbalanced and overwhelmed, because of very poor attachment experiences or even neglect, maltreatment and abuse protracted over a long time. Self-regulating strategies are not able to prevent the child from going from hyperactivity to extreme hypoactivity of the orbitofrontal cortex and of the amygdala, so that an internal void is accompanied by internal chaos and constant turmoil. Right parietal and frontal regions reveal deficits in these patients.

Psychotherapy with traumatised patients needs to be restructured accordingly as is made clear by what Schore writes (2012) about attachment trauma patients (whom he defines as personality disorder patients):

The patient brings into treatment an enduring imprint of attachment trauma: an impaired capacity to regulate stressful affect and an overreliance on the affect-deadening defense of pathological dissociation [and many others]. Under relational stress this affect dysregulation deficit is characterologically expressed in a tendency toward low-threshold, high-intensity, emotional reactions followed by slow return to baseline. Highs and lows are too extreme, too prolonged, or too rapidly cycled and unpredictable. Patients with histories of attachment trauma (i.e. personality disorders) thus contain unconscious insecure working models that automatically trigger right brain stress responses at low thresholds of ruptures of the therapeutic alliance. In addition to their hypersensitivity to even low levels of interpersonal threat (narcissist injuries), they also frequently experience enduring states of high-intensity negative affect and defensively dissociate at lower levels of stressful arousal.

(2012, p. 164)

Interestingly, and in connection with Schore's findings, van der Kolk (2014) has observed a strong lateralisation of the activity of the right brain when traumatic memories are reactivated, in addition to a striking reduction of activity of the Broca area in the left hemisphere, the area notoriously involved in language and verbalisation of meaningful experiences. This would seem to suggest that there is indeed a possibility for attributing new meaning to the traumatic events, restructuring the brain activity in a way that is more balanced and that deactivates the excessive response of the limbic system, while giving more possibility of cortical awareness and explicit verbalisation.

In my experience, very often borderline pathologies stem from a cumulative effect between early relational trauma (with traumatisation happening between 12–18 months for borderline, after 18 months for narcissistic disorders and earlier more severe traumatisation, between 4–9 months for antisocial behavior with amygdala cell death) and further relational traumatisations in the family.

In Schore's terms,

> dissociation thus reflects the inability of the right brain cortical subcortical implicit self system to recognise and process the perception of external stimuli (exteroceptive information coming from the relational environment) and on a moment-to-moment basis integrate them with internal stimuli (interoceptive information from the body, somatic markers, the "felt experience"). This failure of integration of the higher right hemisphere with the lower right brain system and disconnection of the central nervous system from the autonomic system induces an instant collapse of both subjectivity and intersubjectivity. Stressful affects, especially those associated with emotional pain, are thus not experienced in consciousness (Bromberg "not-me" self-states).
>
> (Schore, Introduction, p. xxiii, in Bromberg, 2011)

We can simply hint here at the consequences that this paradigm shift from repression to dissociation, from pre-Oedipal to Oedipal, bear for psychotherapy of severe disorders. Moreover, following Bromberg's illuminating insights on the treatment of pathologies of a traumatic and dissociative nature, we should also remember that "repression as a defense is responsive to anxiety – a negative but regulable affect that signals the potential emergence into consciousness of mental contents that may create unpleasant, but bearable intrapsychic conflict" (Bromberg, 2011, p. 49) and "dissociation as a defense is responsive to trauma – the chaotic, convulsive flooding by unregulatable affect that takes over the mind, threatening the stability of self-hood and sometimes sanity" (ibid.).

Bromberg (2011) also highlights how in dissociation the usual link between symbolic and subsymbolic communication (in Bucci's terms) has been interrupted, which results in a disconnection between higher right cortical (symbolic) and lower right subcortical (subsymbolic) implicit self systems.

Implicit traumatic memories are therefore encoded and encrypted in the right brain, in connection with amygdala activation more than cortical awareness. A psychotherapy that is fine-tuned between patient and therapist through the right brain ("the biological substrate of the human unconscious", in Schore's terms), allows dissociative moments, enactments, and projective identification to return in the right hemispheric exchanges of the therapy. Enactments and projective identification are the major forms of expression of not-me dissociated parts. Enactments in particular according to Schore should be understood as: "bodily based communications of dissociated affects transmitted and received through right brain-to-right brain channels" (Schore, 2012, p. 162). This is always a process that takes place at the regulatory boundaries of relationships, through the right hemispheres of the two selves in relation, going from right to left and then to right again.

Affect regulation therapy is linked to intersubjectvity and implicit-procedural processes. In the words of Schore, "enactments are right brain-to-right brain transference-countertransference communications, interactions occurring between the patient's relational unconscious and the therapist's relational unconscious" (Schore, 2012).

From Freud's univocal and intrapsychic perception (that corresponded to a one-sided therapeutic process supposedly characterised by neutrality but which according to Ferenczi was actually nothing more than hypocrisy and coldness), we have now arrived at an intersubjective, relational unconscious that is right-brain based. To conclude with Schore, "enactments, common in psychotherapy with borderline patients, potentially allow for the reorganisation of cortical (orbitofrontal), subcortical (amygdala) connectivity" (2012, p. 175).

Notes

1 I stress "relational" here because I think we should distinguish between traumatizations brought about by human agency and traumatizations attributable to natural causes, such as earthquakes or tsunamis, for instance. There is a great difference between the impact of trauma caused by human action (not only related to attachment and to abuse but also to many other forms of violence such as rape, war, genocide), and trauma of a natural origin such as earthquake or typhoon: children can develop dissociation after a traumatic event caused by human action, especially if connected to a caregiver, while they do not develop dissociation after an earthquake or a typhoon; this fundamental difference is due to the importance of caregiving in human development. I want to stress that this difference has been undervalued and

disregarded in the categories of PTSD in the DSM, even the most recent one, DSM-5. A more appropriate categorization should include this difference and possibly acknowledge categories such as "PTSD complex" (not present in DSM-5, but proposed by Herman and van der Kolk in the past) and "developmental trauma disorder" (as proposed by van der Kolk in 2011; see van der Kolk, 2014).

2   Therefore by "borderline" I intend a structural organization as defined by Kernberg and not the kind of personality disorder defined "borderline" by the DSM-5.

3   It is of course essential to point out, as McGilchrist among others reminds us, that for future brain activities both right and left hemispheres are active participants (McGilchrist, 2009) but the first two years of life see the right brain developing faster and therefore determining epigenetically most of the future emotional and social or interrelational life for the growing subject.

4   For this reason, in severe pathologies such as borderline disorders the use of the couch is not recommended in therapy because patients profit much more deeply from visual-facial interrelationships that have complex hormonal and neuroendocrinological correlates which inscribe relational and intersubjective models.

5   I want to express my gratitude to Allan Schore for having pointed out these articles to me.

6   For connectedness I mean the ability to value and understand and promote actual relatedness with a capacity for empathy, testimony and prosocial behavior that are particularly important for highly traumatized societies like our own (see especially the fourth chapter of *Beyond Individual and Collective Trauma*, 2013, "Going beyond trauma: mourning, connectedness, creativity, and the practice of forgiveness").

7   Therefore, memories in the first and second year are implicit and are dependent on amygdala activation. It is only within a re-established relation of security that past wounds can be healed. Through the medial prefrontal cortex, the amygdala with its emotional content links itself to areas of the cortex in order to inscribe a different sense of the symbolic and representational Self. At the same time, it is precisely the medial prefrontal cortex that links the brainstem to the amygdala and the limbic system and so to the superior areas of the brain.

8   I would like to express my gratitude to Dr Ludovica Della Penna for helping me with the bibliography.

References[8]

Allman, J. M., Watson, K. K., Tetreault, N. A., & Hakeem, A. Y. (2005). Intuition and autism: A possible role for Von Economo neurons. *Trends in Cognitive Sciences*, *9*(8), 367–373.

Barone, L. (2003). Developmental protective and risk factors in borderline personality disorder: A study using the Adult Attachment Interview. *Attachment & Human Development*, *5*(1), 64–77.

Bion, W. (1962). A theory of thinking. *The International Journal of Psycho-analysis*, *43*, 306.

Bogolepova, I. N., & Malofeeva, L. I. (2001). Characteristics of the development of speechareas 44 and 45 in the left and right hemisphere of the human brain in early post-natal ontogenesis. *Neuroscience and Behavioral Physiology*, *31*, 349–354.

Bonomi, C. (2006). (A Cura Di), *Sandor Ferenczi E La Psicoanalisi Contemporanea*. Borla, Roma.

Bonomi, C. (2015). *The Cut and the Building of Psychoanalysis. Vol. I Sigmund Freud and Emma Eckstein*. Lonodn and New York: Routledge.

Borgogno, F. (2004). (A Cura Di), *Ferenczi Oggi*. Bollati Boringhieri, Torino.

Bowlby, J. (1969). *Attachment and Loss. Vol. 1: Attachment.* New York: Basic Books.

Breuer, J., & Freud, S. (1895). *Studies on Hysteria.* Trans. and ed. J. Strachey. London, Hogarth Press, 1955.

Bromberg, P. M. (2011). *The Shadow of the Tsunami.* New York: Routledge.

Bucci, W. (1997). Symptoms and symbols: A multiple code theory of somatization. *Psychoanalytic Inquiry, 17*(2), 151–172.

Chiron, C., Jambaque, I., Nabbout, R., Lounes, R., Syrota, A., & Dulac, O. (1997). The right brain hemisphere is dominant in human infants. *Brain, 120,* 1057–1065.

Clarkin, J. F., Yeomans, F., & Kernberg, O. F. (1999). *Transference-focused Psychodynamic Therapy for Borderline Personality Disorder Patients.* New York: John Wiley & Sons.

Clarkin, J. F., Yeomans, F. E., & Kernberg, O. F. (2007). *Psychotherapy for Borderline Personality: Focusing on Object Relations.* Washington, DC: American Psychiatric Publications.

Cozolino, L. (2002). *The Neuroscience of Psychotherapy: Building and Rebuilding the Human Brain (Norton Series on Interpersonal Neurobiology).* New York: WW Norton & Company.

Cozolino, L. (2014). *The Neuroscience of Human Relationships: Attachment and the Developing Social Brain (Norton Series on Interpersonal Neurobiology).* New York: W. W. Norton & Company.

Felitti, V. J., Anda, R. F., Nordenberg, D., Williamson, D. F., Spitz, A. M., Edwards, V., … Marks, J. S. (1998). Relationship of childhood abuse and household dysfunction to many of the leading causes of death in adults: The Adverse Childhood Experiences (ACE) Study. *American Journal of Preventive Medicine, 14*(4), 245–258.

Ferenczi, S. (1932a). *The Clinical Diary of Sandor Ferenczi.* (ED. E. Dupont). Cambridge, MA, and London: Harvard University Press, 1998.

Ferenczi, S. (1932b). Confusion of the tongue between adults and the child (the language of tenderness and the language of [sexual] passion) (Trans. J. M. Masson & I. Loring), Appendix C. In J. M. Masson (Ed.), *The Assault on Truth: Freud's Suppression of the Seduction Theory.* New York: Random House, 1984.

Fonagy, P., Gergely, G., Jurist, E. L., & Target, M. (2002). *Affect Regulation, Mentalization and the Development of the Self.* London: Karnac Books.

Fonagy, P., Leigh, T., Steele, M., Steele, H., Kennedy, R., Mattoon, G., … Gerber, A. (1996). The relation of attachment status, psychiatric classification, and response to psychotherapy. *Journal of Consulting and Clinical Psychology, 64*(1), 22.

Fraiberg, S. (1982). Pathological defenses in infancy. *Psychoanalytical Quarterly, 51,* 612–635.

Freud, S. (1915). *The unconscious. S. E., 14.* London: Hogarth Press.

Freud, S. (1963). *General Psychological Theory: Papers on Metapsychology; with an Introduction by the Editor Philip Rieff.* New York: Collier Books.

Freud, S. (1966). Letter 79 extracts from the Fliess papers. In *The Standard Edition of the Complete Psychological Works of Sigmund Freud, Volume I (1886–1899): Pre-Psycho-Analytic Publications and Unpublished Drafts* (pp. 272–273). London: Hograth Press.

Gabbard, G. O. (2014). *Psychodynamic Psychiatry in Clinical Practice.* Washington, DC: American Psychiatric Publication.

Gainotti, G. (2000). What the locus of brain lesion tells us about the nature of the cognitive defect underlying category-specific disorders: A review. *Cortex*, *36*(4), 539–559.

Galin, D. (1974). Implications for psychiatry of left and right cerebral specialization: A neurophysiological context for unconscious processes. *Archives of General Psychiatry*, *31*(4), 572–583.

Gergely, G. (1992). Developmental reconstructions: Infancy from the point of view of psychoanalysis and developmental psychology. *Psychoanalysis & Contemporary Thought*, *15*(1), 3–15.

Grubrich-Simitis, I. (1981). Extreme traumatization as cumulative trauma: Psychoanalytic investigations of the effects of concentration camp experiences on survivors and their children. *The Psychoanalytic Study of the Child*, *36*(1), 415–450.

Harricharan, S., Rabellino, D., Frewen, P. A., Densmore, M., Theberge, J., McKinnon, M. C., ... Lanius, R. A. (2016, December). fMRI functional connectvity of the periaqueductal gray in PTSD and its dissociative subtype. *Brain and Behavior*, *6*(12), e00579.

Henry, J. P. (1993). Psychological and physiological responses to stress: The right hemisphere and the hypothalamo-pituitary-adrenal axis, an inquiry into problems of human bonding. *Integrative Physiological and Behavioral Science*, *28*(4), 369–387.

Hofer, M. A. (1984). Relatioships as regulations: A psychobiological perspective on bereavement. *Psychosomatic Medicine*, *46*, 183–197.

Howard, M. F., & Reggia, J. A. (2007). A theory of the visual system biology underlying development of spatial frequency lateralization. *Brain and Cognition*, *64*(2), 111–123.

Hugdahl, K. (1995), Classical conditioning and implicit learning: The right hemisphere hypothesis.

Janet, P. (1889). *L'Automatisme Psychologique. Essai De Psychologie Expérimentale Sur Les Formes Inférieures De L'activité Humaine*. Paris: L'Harmattan.

Karr-Morse, R., & Wiley, M. S. (1997). *Ghosts from the Nursery: Tracing the Roots of Violence*. New York: Atlantic Monthly Press.

Kendler, K. S., & Eaves, L. J. (1986). Models for the joint effect of genotype and environment on liability to psychiatric illness. *The American Journal of Psychiatry*, *143*(3), 279–289.

Kernberg, O. F. (1975). *Borderline Conditions and Pathological Narcissism*. New York: Aronson.

Klein, M. (1956). *A study of envy and gratitude the selected Melanie Klein*, New York: The Free Press. 211–229.

Kozlovska, K. (2005). Healing the disembodied mind: Contemporary models of conversion disorder. *Harvard Review of Psychiatry*, *13*, 1–13.

Kozlowska, K. (2007). The developmental origins of conversion disorders. *Clinical Child Psychology and Psychiatry*, *12*(4), 487–510.

Laub, D., & Auerhahn, N. C. (1984). Reverberations of genocide: Its expression in the conscious and unconscious of post-Holocaust generations. In *Psychoanalytic Reflections on the Holocaust* (pp. 151–167). Denver, CO: Holocaust Awareness Institute Center for Judaic Studies, University of Denver.

Laub, D., & Lee, S. (2003). Thanatos and massive psychic trauma: The impact of the death instinct on knowing, remembering, and forgetting. *Journal of the American Psychoanalytic Association*, *51*(2), 433–463.

LeDoux, J. E. (2003). *Synaptic Self: How Our Brains Become Who We Are*. London: Penguin.

Lingiardi, V., & Mucci, C. (2014). Da Janet a Bromberg, passando per Ferenczi. *Psichiatria e psicoterapia, 33*(1).

Liotti, G. (2012). Disorganized attachment and the therapeutic relationship with people in shattered states. In J. Yellin & K. White (Eds.), *Shattered States: Disorganised Attachment and Its Repair* (pp. 127–156). London: Karnac.

Liotti, G. (2013). Disorganised attachment in the pathogenesis and the psychotherapy of borderline personality disorder. In Adam N. Danquah & K. Berry, (Eds.), *Attachment Theory in Adult Mental Health: A Guide to Clinical Practice* (pp. 135–150). London and New York: Routledge.

Liotti, G., & Farina, B. (2011). *Sviluppi Traumatici. Eziopatogenesi, Clinica E Terapia Della Dimensione Dissociativa*. Milano: Cortina.

Lyons-Ruth, K. (1999). The two person unconscious: Intersubjective dialogue, enactive relational representation, and the emergence of the new forms of relational organization. In L. Aron & A. Harris (Eds.), *Relational Psychoanalysis*. Hillsdale: Analytic Press, 2005.

Mancia, M. (2006). Implicit memory and early unrepressed unconscious: Their role in the therapeutic process. In G. Craparo & C. Mucci (Eds.) (2016), *Unrepressed Unconscious, Implicit Memory and Clinical Work* (pp. 27–54). London: Karnac Books.

McGilchrist, I. (2009). *The Master and His Emissary: The Divided Brain and the Making of the Western World*. New Haven, CT: Yale University Press.

McGilchrist, I. (2015). Divine Understanding and the Divided Brain. Chapter 10 In J. Clansen & N. Levy (Eds.), *Handbook of Neuroethics* (pp. 1583–1601). Dordrecht: Springer.

Meaney, M. J. (2001). Maternal care, gene expression, and the transmission of individual differences in stress reactivity across generations. *Annual Review of Neuroscience, 24*(1), 1161–1192.

Meares, R. (2012). *Borderline Personality Disorder and the Conversational Model: A Clinician's Manual*. New York: WW Norton & Company.

Mucci, C. (2008). *Il Dolore Estremo: Il Trauma Da Freud Alla Shoah*. Roma: Borla.

Mucci, C. (2013). *Beyond Individual and Collective Trauma: Intergenerational Transmission, Psychoanalytic Treatment, and the Dynamics of Forgiveness*. London: Karnac Books.

Mucci, C. (2014). Trauma, healing and the reconstruction of truth. *American Journal of Psychoanalysis, 74*, 31–47.

Mucci, C. (2016). Implicit memory, unrepressed unconscious, and trauma theory: The turn of the screw between contemporary psychoanalysis and neuroscience. In G. Craparo & C. Mucci (Eds.), *Unrepressed Unconscious, Implicit Memory, and Clinical Work* (pp. 99–129). London: Karnac Books.

Noriuchi, M., Kikuchi, Y., & Senoo, A. (2008). The functional neuroanatomy of maternal love: Mother's response to infant's attachment behaviors. *Biological Psychiatry, 63*(4), 415–423.

Ogden, P., Minton, K., & Pain, C. (2006). *Trauma and the Body: A Sensorimotor Approach to Psychotherapy*. New York: WW Norton & Company.

Patrick, M., Hobson, R. P., Castle, D., Howard, R., & Maughan, B. (1994). Personality disorder and the mental representation of early social experience. *Development and Psychopathology, 6*(02), 375–388.

Perry, B. D. (1997). Maltreated children: Experience. New York: Norton.

Porges, S. (2011). *The Polyvagal Theory: Neurophysiological Foundations of Emotions, Attachment, Communication, Self-Regulation*. New York: W.W. Norton.

Porges, S. W., Doussard-Roosevelt, J. A., & Maiti, A. K. (1994). Vagal tone and the physiological regulation of emotion. *Monographs of the Society for Research in Child Development*, 59(2–3), 167–186.

Putnam. (2001). *Dissociation in Children and Adolescents*. New York: The Guilford Press.

Ranote, S., Elliott, R., Abel, K. M., Mitchell, R., Deakin, J. F. W., & Appleby, L. (2004). The neural basis of maternal responsiveness to infants: An fMRI study. *Neuroreport*, 15(11), 1825–1829.

Roelofs, K., Keijsers, G. P. J., Hoogduin, K. A. L., Naring, G. W. B., & Moene, F. C. (2002). Childhood abuse in patients with conversion disorder. *American Journal of Psychiatry*, 159, 1908–1913.

Scalabrini, A., Cavicchioli, M., Fossati, A., & Maffei, C. (2016). The extent of dissociation in borderline personality disorder: A meta-analytic review. *Journal of Trauma & Dissociation*, 18(4), 522–543.

Schore, A. N. (1994). *Affect Regulation and the Origin of the Self: The Neurobiology of Emotional Development*. Mahwah, NJ: Erlbaum.

Schore, A. N. (1997). Early organization of the nonlinear right brain and development of a predisposition to psychiatric disorders. *Development and Psychopathology*, 9(04), 595–631.

Schore, A. N. (2000). Attachment and the regulation of the right brain. *Attachment & Human Development*, 2(1), 23–47.

Schore, A. N. (2002). Dysregulation of the right brain: A fundamental mechanism of traumatic attachment and the psychopathogenesis of posttraumatic stress disorder. *Australian and New Zealand Journal of Psychiatry*, 36(1), 9–30.

Schore, A. N. (2003a). *Affect Regulation and Disorders of the Self*. New York: Norton.

Schore, A. N. (2003b). *Affect Regulation and the Repair of the Self*. New York: Norton.

Schore, A. N. (2010). Relational trauma and the developing right brain: The neurobiology of broken attachment bonds. In Baradon (Ed.), *Relational Trauma in Infancy. Psychoanalytic Attachment and Neuropsychological Contributions to Parent-infant Psychotherapy* (pp. 19–47). London and New York: Routledge.

Schore, A. N. (2012). *The Science of the Art of Psychotherapy*. New York: Norton.

Schore, A. N. (2014). The right brain is dominant in psychotherapy. *Psychotherapy*, 51(3), 388.

Schore, A. N. (2016). The right brain implicit self: A central mechanism of the psychotherapy change process. Chapter In G. Craparo & C. Mucci (Eds.), *Unrepressed Unconscious, Implicit Memory, and Clinical Work*. London:: Karnac Books.

Schore, J. R., & Schore, A. N. (2008). Modern attachment theory: The central role of affect regulation in development and treatment. *Clinical Social Work Journal*, 36(1), 9–20.

Schuetze, P., & Reid, H. (2005). Emotional lateralisation in the second year of life: Evidence from oral asymmetries. *Laterality: Asymmetries of Body, Brain, and Cognition*, 10(3), 207–217.

Siegel, D. J. (1999). *The Developing Mind: Toward a Neurobiology of Interpersonal Experience*. New York: Guilford Press.

Spitz, R. (1945). Hospitalism- an inquiry into the genesis of psychiatric conditions in early childhood. *Psychoanalytic Studies of the Child*, *1*, 53–74.

Suomi, S. J. (1991). Early stress and adult emotional reactivity in rhesus monkeys. *The Childhood Environment and Adult Disease*, *156*, 171–183.

Tzourio-Mazoyer, N., De Schonen, S., Crivello, F., Reutter, B., Aujard, Y., & Mazoyer, B. (2002). Neural correlates of woman face processing by 2-month-old infants. *Neuroimage*, *15*(2), 454–461.

van der Hart Njenhuis, E. R. S., & Steele, K. (2006). *The Haunted Self: Structural Dissociation and the Treatment of Chronic Traumatization.* New York: Norton.

van der Kolk, B. (2014). *The Body Keeps the Score.* New York, NY: Viking.

van der Kolk, B. A. (1994). The body keeps the score: Memory and evolving psycho-biology of post-traumatic stress. *Harvard Review of Psychiatry*, *1*, 253–265.

van der Kolk, B. A., & Fisler, R. E. (1994). Childhood abuse and neglect and loss of self-regulation. *Bulletin of the Menninger Clinic*, *58*, 145–168.

van der Kolk, B. A., van der Hart, O., & Marmar, C. R. (1996). *Dissociation and Information Processing in Posttraumatic Stress Disorder* (pp. 303–327). New York: Guilford Press.

van der Kolk, B. A. & McFarlane, A. C. (1996). The black hole of trauma. In B. A. van der Kolk, A. C. McFarlane, & L. Weisaeth (Eds.), *Traumatic Stress: The Effects of Overwhelming Experience on Mind, Body, and Society* (pp. 3–23). New York: Guilford.

van der Kolk, B. A., McFarlane, A. C., & Weisaeth, L. (Eds.), (1996). *History of Trauma in Psychiatry* (pp. 47–74). New York: Guilford Press.

Wittling, W., & Schweiger, E. (1993). Neuroendocrine brain asymmetry and physical complaints. *Neuropsychologia*, *31*(6), 591–608.

Zanarini, M. C., Gunderson, J. G., Marino, M. F., Schwartz, E. O., & Frankenburg, F. R. (1989). Childhood experiences of borderline patients. *Comprehensive Psychiatry*, *30*(1), 18–25.

Chapter 8

Growing, living and being rightly

Darcia Narvaez

Sometimes it is hard to remember, but humans are creatures of the earth and dependent on the earth. There is no way around it. But too many human beings lately have had a tendency to forget what that means. As creatures of the earth, there are certain ways of growing that are better than others. There are certain ways of being that are better than others. There are certain ways of living that are better than others. Truly. Interestingly, they all seem to be rooted in proper right hemisphere development and functioning.

Ways of growing

During the first few months and years of life, the functions of the right hemisphere (RH) are established, with further development through childhood. But the roots for RH development are established during the highly sensitive first years of life. These are sensitive years because human beings are born highly immature compared to other animals (9–18 months early) with the establishment and shaping of many systems set to occur after birth.

Humans evolved with a particular nest for their young, like all animals have. The human nest (Evolved Development Niche; EDN) is intensive and includes a soothing birth, lots of affectionate touch and no negative touch or coercion; warm responsive care of needs and cues with little imposed stress; self-directed free play with multi-aged mates; positive social support for child and mother from the community; multiple adult responsive caregivers. Each EDN characteristic has been related to human health and well-being (Narvaez, 2014; Narvaez et al., 2016; Narvaez et al., 2013; Narvaez et al., 2014).

But we focus here on right hemisphere functioning. All EDN components influence right hemisphere development. When the early nest is provided, the RH grows well because it is scheduled to grow dominantly during these early years. Physiologically, scheduled growth requires a supportive environment, one that provides "limbic resonance—a symphony of mutual exchange and internal adaptation whereby two mammals become attuned to each other's inner states" (Lewis, Amini, & Lannon, 2000, p. 63). Dysynchrony must be repaired, first the parent and then the child eventually learning herself to do this in social relations. Toxic stress (like extensive distress crying or isolation) must be avoided so as to not derail normal development toward wellbeing. Scheduled growth also requires the proper establishment of layers of functions that underlie later layers (e.g., gene expression, neurotransmitter number and capacity).

Psychologically the RH dominance of developmental focus in the first years is related to the social knowhow being co-constructed with caregivers, implicit relational knowledge upon which lifelong social relations are constructed. This knowledge includes "vitality contours" of getting along with others in the micro-moments of being (Stern, 2010)—when to share eye gaze, how to enter and leave interactions, and so on, through a communicative musicality (Trevarthen, 1999). When early life goes well and vitality contours are well rehearsed (as in species typical development), this forms the basis for the relational attunement that undergirds compassionate morality (Narvaez, 2016).

Whether discussing physiology or psychology, development is a dynamic shaping of embodiment. The growth and development of the child occurs within a creative nexus of interaction, "an unbounded and continually unfolding field of relations" (Ingold, 2011, p. xvi), intertwining the physical, psychological and cultural. The child develops a relational pathway through the world, "a movement along a way of life" (Ingold, 2011, p. 146). RH capacities for self-governance and empathy are grown through experience of those very things.

RH functioning includes self-governance since arousal is lateralized to the right hemisphere (Schore, 2003a). For example, when the RH-governed vagus nerve is properly tuned up by responsive care in early life, the individual is able to socialize without distress and become intimate with others in the ways of the culture (Porges, 2011). Right hemisphere capacities also influence what are termed executive functions, which include not only self-control but foresight, and empathy, all highly influenced by experience in the first year but which take several decades to mature.

Most of who we are is founded on implicit social knowledge/patterns/ habits established in the first years of life. These are virtually impossible to change except with extensive longterm effort. So it matters what those implicit foundations are. Unfortunately, most of the time in most families in the USA, the EDN is not fully provided. In fact, Lewis et al. (2000, p. 225) describe the USA as "an extended experiment in the effects of depriving people of what they crave most."

What happens without the EDN, in conditions of undercare? Undercare undermines RH development. When one undercares for a baby, she does not fully develop social capacities for "moving with" others and natural processes. Instead, there is awkward neurobiology and sociality. Undercare builds up aversive feeling and stress reactivity at multiple physiological levels ("all the way down"). In this case, stress response systems are geared up to be hyper-reactive, as it is toxically stressful to not receive EDN-consistent care. When the stress response is activated, cortisol floods the system, shifting focus to survival while dissolving synapses. Instead of the socially calming hormones of oxytocin, serotonin or prolactin, the individual spends life in a state of dread. As a result of these underdevelopments, the individual's social relations are more likely to be governed by primitive survival systems—fear, panic, rage (plus greed, hoarding, dominance and rivalry) (Panksepp, 1998).

When early life does not go well, the child can be stressed and socially dysynchronous, leading to more stress and a preference for being alone. The child can become an empty shell with a psyche divorced from soma, intellectualizing life or controlling others to alleviate anxiety. Flexible, relational attunement was not learned so the social world seems impenetrable, requiring a set of external rules for behaving because the natural mode of learning implicit relational knowledge did not get established properly.[1]

Ways of being

What seeds sprout in the early months and years under inherited conditions? Seeds for receptive intelligence, which includes emotional intelligence but also receptivity to other-than-human, a bigger picture of relations. Those without these capacities ridicule them as "women's intuition" or "superstition" or worse. An illustration of the types of capacities the right hemisphere has is provided by Jill Bolte Taylor, neuroanatomist. These would typically be nurtured by early life experience consistent with the EDN, during the period when the brain's right-hemisphere comes on line. [NOTE: The right hemisphere tends to process, filter and act on the world nonverbally, whereas the left hemisphere tends to house the areas of the brain related to verbal processing and expression.] Bolte Taylor (2008) described the sudden and unexpected right-hemisphere dominance she experienced after having a stroke in her left cerebral hemisphere:

> Our right hemisphere is designed to remember things as they relate to one another. Borders between specific entities are softened, and complex mental collages can be recalled in their entirety as combinations of images, kinesthetic, and physiology. To the right mind, no time exists other than the present moment, and each moment is vibrant with sensation ... the moment of *now* is timeless and abundant ... The present moment is a time when everything and everyone are connected together as *one*. As a result, our right mind perceives each of us as equal members of the human family. It identifies our similarities and recognizes our relationship with this marvelous planet, which sustains our life. It perceives the big picture, how everything is related, and how we all

join together to make up the whole. Our ability to be empathic, to walk in the shoes of another and feel their feelings, is a product of our right frontal cortex.

(Taylor, 2008, pp. 30–31)

Some of the capacities that Bolte Taylor identified—dominant sensation of the present moment, of the big picture and relationships, and of energy—are often not given attention in a science-y worldview that attends primarily to the physically measurable, isolated and controlled. But she correctly identified these characteristics as fundamental to our morality, at least the morality of connection and compassion. (Detached from right hemispheric functioning, morality can be turned into one of utilitarian cold logic—dangerous to living systems.)

The relationally attuned morality that Bolte Taylor evokes develops from the proper development and use of RH capacities. I call it an *engagement mindset*. It is receptive to the other as an equal, as a partner in co-constructing the present encounter. Its characteristics are flexible attunement, beholding the other as they are (and not according to self-protective filters), playful appreciation and resonance with the other.

Engagement ethics are more obviously present among foraging communities, representative of the majority of humanity's history (e.g., Ingold, 2011; Wolff, 2001). Societies that stay in physical contact with their infants and children in the manner of the EDN, are more likely to be peaceful societies (Prescott, 1996). EDN experiences within a community led to sociality allowing for peaceful cooperation even with shifting membership among groups (e.g., Dentan, 1968; Hill et al., 2011). One could postulate that the range of personality differences are much greater in "civilized" nations (towards the pathological and antisocial), as a result of modern childrearing practices that have degraded the early nest, which gives psychologists much more to do.

Ways of living

Proper right hemisphere development allows full communication systems to be seeded, including with other-than-humans (e.g., animals, plants). One can see how early seeds sprout into sensibilities for the common good, a sense of oneness or Common Self with all entities, undergirding a cooperative orientation to getting along with the natural world. In fact, these capacities are apparent in societies that provide the EDN and live close to the earth. Integrated Right Hemisphere living is different from what we see around us in civilized societies. Instead of being caught in intellect and intellectualizing, the heartmind guides life. The flourishing individual demonstrates more receptive relational emotions than self-protective ones–this extends beyond the familiar ingroup to outgroup humans and nonhuman entities. A sense of connection to the Whole and its mystery is always present. This is a right hemisphere orientation.

Flourishing societies live within a balanced biodiversity. A flourishing society is one that lives with the earth where non humans are considered partners, not adversaries, where relational responsibility to all Life is fundamental. We can see this in traditional Native American community practices. The community uses ritual and story to maintain a sense of connection to the Whole, to tap into the oceanic energies and discern appropriate action. Human beings are "formed by this mystery, touched by it, shaped by it, breathed into by it, and are part of its constant song" (Windeagle and Rainbow Hawk, 2003, p. 67). The maintenance of harmony and a sense of sacredness toward all life are central to living life well. The society raises well their young, empowering their freedom to follow their unique spirits and contributions to the Whole. The individual is generative in the context of flourishing for All. Narratives and understandings are within the scope of earthly living. Humans live optimally when they live the earth-balanced life.

These societies have an implicit sense of the living earth. Western science more recently has been uncovering this same knowledge (Mancuso & Viola, 2015). For example, plants have the five senses that we have identified in ourselves: sight, hearing, touch, smell, taste. But they have 15 other senses, like gauging humidity in soil, sense gravity or chemical gradients. Though we are told that humans are the species that dominate planet earth, over 99% of the biomass on the earth is made up of highly intelligent plants.

Misguided ways

What happens when those who missed the early nest, the underdeveloped, grow up? I'm starting to think that the bossy children are showing an underdevelopment of vitality contours. They learned instead to try to control things because they did not learn to go with the micro-social flow. These impulses for control occur so early in processing that it's hard to realize they were shaped by early social patterns of interaction.

On the personal level, we can see moral shrinkage. Undercare forms wedges between whom a child could become and what they end up becoming. Each aspect of the nest that is missing may form a wedge against trusting the self and others. Undercare and coercion go hand in hand. Undercare leads to certain lacks of intelligence, requiring external rules and coercion to figure out how to get along, since the normal course of development was interrupted and undermined. Morality becomes rooted in self protectionism which emerges from undercare in babyhood (left alone, left crying). The individual is left with a materialistic morality, needing rules and laws to feel safe, with an inability to accept mystery and oneness.

On the societal level, cultural narratives influence which type of moral system is accessed frequently—protectionism or relational attunement? The individual is shaped and guided by living in and practicing the culture's ways. Misdeveloped people run the world according to enhanced (conditioned up by early experience) primitive survival systems that emphasize fear, greed, territoriality, submission to authority and assume to be normal primitive lust and rage. Extremists tend to emphasize security.

On the political level, Iain McGilchrist (2009) points out how the Western world has suppressed the wisdom of the right hemisphere and instead is governed by the bureaucratic/scientific mode of the left hemisphere (which prefers static dead things and absolute control). In societies governed by this Western mindset, individual self-control and grounded sociality are underdeveloped and so must rely on external braces throughout life such as ideologies, many of which endanger other humans and particularly the more-than-human world.

David Korten (2015) identified the dominant narrative as the Sacred Money and Markets story. The emphasis is on monetary wealth (at the expense of every other kind of wealth such as social or ecological; Narvaez, 2016). The economically wealthiest nation in the world, the USA is socially impoverished and has become a self protectionist society, with a glorified control of nature, children, minorities and other nations.

We can go further. Underdevelopment of the RH leads to adults with a "taboo on tenderness", a brittle, tough-mindedness that pervades the society they create, as in the USA (Suttie, 1935/1988). The result is a macho society that extends across fields and domains (dominator society; Eisler, 2013). What does a macho society look like?

- Parenting is less about tenderness and support than about control (e.g., forcing baby into independence through isolation and sleep training, teaching baby to ignore feelings and needs).
- Schooling uses top down methods of inculcating the highest moral values of obedience and submission, including "drill and kill" and other forms of punishment, especially to those considered to be in lower echelons of society.
- Stories about history emphasize dominance and necessary violence against a threatening world.
- Science becomes competitive and intellectualized, narrow and limited in focus, and dangerous to Life (see Medin & Bang, 2014). Theories (e.g., evolutionary theory) emphasize competition instead of cooperation as the dominant characteristic of nature (most characteristics are conserved from generation to generation; see Margulis, 1998; Weiss & Buchanan, 2009).
- The society rationalizes and creates environments to support staying apart from others, avoiding intimacy, avoiding the immersion in the interpersonal dance of relationship, which requires heartsense, attention and surrender.
- Avoidantly-attached persons become dominant. They are underdeveloped in interpersonal perception, social interpretation and action skills (which normally make social life fun and relatively easy). For the avoidantly attached, the physical sciences are much easier than psychology.

Warrior culture, though in the past a temporary shift for males, becomes a permanent way of life of shutting down empathy, care, and relational attunement. Unfortunately in the USA today, such people are considered normal and are given vast amounts of power (Derber, 2013). It is considered to be normal to be divorced from earth-care, restless and self-absorbed. Instead of honoring and meeting human basic needs, power of the few impairs the wellbeing of the many. Social poverty increases because those in charge have limited capacities or concern for egalitarian sociality.

Getting back to rightliness

Early experience influences which emotion systems are most accessible and sensitive periods can influence how chronically accessible particular emotion systems are. Moral landscapes shift based on the emotion systems that are activated. If we have learned from a young age to be self-protective, as we grow we elaborate on this position and make it into a moral theory (like Ayn Rand did; Weiss, 2012).

Humanity's recent focus on self-protection and self-promotion are due in part to the lack of attachment to earth systems. Humans have separated themselves from the earth in the last millennia, considering themselves separate from nature. Our "species isolation" fuels a sense of supremacy and difference (Berry, 1988; Jensen, 2016; Mander, 1991). What do we do to return ourselves to living as earth creatures, as one species among many in community?

Humanity needs to restore lost capacities, specifically those of the right hemisphere. Their loss occurs primarily in cultures dominated by civilized child raising practices and ways of thinking. First, we need to provide the evolved developmental niche to children and help them develop ecological attachment to their landscape. This will take efforts at the policy and institutional levels (see Narvaez et al., 2013). We return to the child raising practices that fully nurture human capacities. Second, we return to an intuitive grasp of a living earth knitted together with our scientific awareness of living systems. We nurture our ecological attachment to a particular landscape for which we are responsible (*this* tree, *that* river). We design our lives with the earth in mind, using our whole minds.

Note

1 There are interventions, such as therapy, that can revamp the brain in terms of self-regulation and social functioning.

References

Berry, T. (1988). *The dream of the earth*. San Francisco, CA: Sierra Club Books.
Dentan, R. K. (1968). *The Semai: A nonviolent people of Malaya*. New York, NY: Harcourt Brace College Publishers.

Derber, C. (2013). *Sociopathic society.* Boulder, CO: Paradigm Press.

Eisler, R. (2013). Protecting the majority of humanity: Toward an integrated approach to crimes against present and future generations. In M.-C. C. Segger & S. Jodoin (Eds.), *Sustainable development, international criminal justice, and treaty implementation* (pp. 305–326). Cambridge, UK: Cambridge University Press.

Hill, K. R., Walker, R. S., Božičević, M., Eder, J., Headland, T., Hewlett, B., & Wood, B. (2011). Co-residence patterns in hunter-gatherer societies show unique human social structure. *Science, 331*(6022), 1286–1289. doi:10.1126/science.1199071

Ingold, T. (2011). *The perception of the environment: Essays on livelihood, dwelling and skill.* London: Routledge.

Jensen, D. (2016). *The myth of human supremacy.* New York: Seven Stories Press.

Korten, D. (2015). *Change the story, change the future.* Oakland, CA: Berrett-Koehler Publishers, Inc.

Lewis, T., Amini, F., & Lannon, R. (2000). *A general theory of love.* New York, NY: Vintage.

Mancuso, S., & Viola, A. (2015). *Brilliant green: The surprising history and science of plant intelligence.* Washington, DC: Island Press.

Mander, J. (1991). *In the absence of the sacred: The failure of technology and the survival of the Indian nations.* New York: Random House.

Margulis, L. (1998). *Symbiotic planet: A new look at evolution.* Amherst, MA: Sciencewriters.

McGilchrist, I. (2009). *The master and his emissary: The divided brain and the making of the western world.* New Haven, CT: Yale University Press.

Medin, D., & Bang, M. (2014). *Who's asking: Native science, Western science, and science education.* Cambridge, MA: MIT Press.

Narvaez, D. (2014). *Neurobiology and the development of human morality: Evolution, culture and wisdom.* New York, NY: W.W. Norton.

Narvaez, D. (2016). *Embodied morality: Protectionism, engagement and imagination.* New York, NY: Palgrave-Macmillan.

Narvaez, D., Braungart-Rieker, J., Miller, L., Gettler, L., & Hastings, P. (Eds.). (2016). *Contexts for young child flourishing: Evolution, family and society.* New York, NY: Oxford University Press.

Narvaez, D., Panksepp, J., Schore, A., & Gleason, T. (Eds.). (2013). *Evolution, early experience and human development: From research to practice and policy.* New York, NY: Oxford University Press.

Narvaez, D., Valentino, K., McKenna, J., Fuentes, A., & Gray, P. (Eds.). (2014). *Ancestral landscapes in human evolution: Culture, childrearing and social wellbeing.* New York, NY: Oxford University Press.

Panksepp, J. (1998). *Affective neuroscience: The foundations of human and animal emotions.* Oxford: Oxford University Press.

Porges, S. W. (2011). *The polyvagal theory: Neurophsiological foundations of emotions, attachment, communication, self-regulation.* New York: W.W. Norton.

Prescott, J. W. (1996). The origins of human love and violence. *Pre- and Perinatal Psychology Journal, 10*(3), 143–188.

Schore, A. N. (2003a). *Affect dysregulation & disorders of the self.* New York, NY: Norton.

Stern, D. (2010). *Forms of vitality: Exploring dynamic experience in psychology, the arts, psychotherapy, and development.* New York: Oxford University Press.

Suttie, I. (1935/1988). *The origins of love and hate.* London: Free Association Books.

Taylor, J. B. (2008). *My stroke of insight.* New York: Viking Press.

Trevarthen, C. (1999). Musicality and the intrinsic motive pulse: Evidence from human psychobiology and infant communication. *Musicae Scientiae, Special Issue,* 157–213.

Weiss, G. (2012). *Ayn Rand Nation: The hidden struggle for America's soul.* New York: Macmillan.

Weiss, K. M., & Buchanan, A. V. (2009). *The mermaid's tale: Four billion yers of cooperation in the making of living things.* Cambridge, MA: Harvard University Press.

Windeagle, & Rainbow Hawk. (2003). *Heart seeds: A message from the ancestors.* Edina, MN: Beaver's Pond Press.

Wolff, R. (2001). *Original wisdom.* Inner Traditions, Rochester Vermont.

Chapter 9

The therapeutic purpose of right-hemispheric language

Russell Meares

We are made of words. Most authorities agree that the human mind, the kind of consciousness unique to our species, cannot emerge without the use of language. Psychotherapy is concerned with the making and remaking of mind, by the use of words, in those whom this experience is stunted, distorted, or in some other way, unsatisfactory. This chapter is about the therapeutic significance of the *form* of language, of the way in which words are put together so as to create expressive patterns which "fit" similar patterns presented by the patient. These expressions are not framed in the propositional speech of the left hemisphere. Rather, the therapist uses a different kind of language which has a "picturing" effect. Its creation depends upon the right hemisphere.

Two modes of expression

It is not any kind of language that is necessary to the emergence of human consciousness. Other primates also have the capacity for speech of a kind (Cheney & Seyfarth, 1990). It is a language of signs. In this case, words have a "pointing" function. They indicate, for example, the approach of a leopard and what action to take. An additional mode of speech is needed to facilitate the appearance of human consciousness. In pure form, it has qualities shared by some kinds of poetry, for example, that of Emily Dickinson. It is not entirely oxymoronic to say that it is a right hemisphere language.

John Hughlings Jackson had been among the first to recognise that everyday "propositional" or syntactical speech is usually governed by left-hemispheric function. Severe damage to that side of the brain may render the patient mute. He also discovered that a mute subject, having an apparently speechless right hemisphere, is capable of a limited, non-propositional speech, which is brief, condensed, and triggered by emotion and song. He also made the very interesting observation that patients who were not able to speak to the nursing staff or to Jackson himself, could sometimes do so in a familial or intimate context. One man, for example, said to his wife, although otherwise speechless, "God bless you my dear" (Jackson, 1866, p. 124).

Jackson noted that: "There are two modes of expression, one emotional and the other intellectual. By one we show what we feel, and by the other we tell what we think" (Jackson, 1866, p. 121). It is the system which is to do with the feeling that makes us human (Meares, 2016a). Jackson's formulation gives it a right-hemispheric basis. The main thrust of this chapter concerns the damage to this system by relational trauma and a proposal about the form of therapeutic relationship and conversation that might be helpful in its restoration.

Symbols and culture

Humans have a remarkable capacity, peculiar to the species. Like other creatures we can discern patterns in what the environment presents to us. However, unlike other creatures, we can create representations of our experience. Most importantly we can represent not only that which we discern but also that which we cannot see, e.g. feelings. Representations taken from the outer world can be used to represent the inner. We can use symbols. This invention allowed us to create the vast and complex system of culture, in which we live and which, in part, creates us. Without such a capacity we are, as Clifford Geertz put it; "incomplete and unfinished animals" (Geertz, 1973, pp. 48–49). Culture is the cardinal identifying feature of the human species (Cassirer, 1944; Geertz, 1973). It is understood here as a system of symbolically mediated behaviours shared by a particular society and transmitted intergenerationally by symbolic means. Cultural transmission is distinguished from behaviours learnt by simple mimesis, which chimpanzees can achieve (McGrew, 1992).

Whereas other primates can use only signs, humans have a language which depends upon both signs and symbols. Different kinds of linguistic interplay involve different proportions of one in relation to the other. I. A. Richards remarked on "the contrast between discourse which primarily *points* and discourse which in one way or another, in some degree *depicts*" (Richards, 1976, p. 119). Depicting depends upon the "shaping" function of the right hemisphere.

The two themes of pointing and shaping reflect different kinds of consciousness. They have distinct but interwoven developmental trajectories (Meares, 2016b). Both emerge in the context of different forms of play with the caregivers. We may metaphorically conceive early development as going on in two experiential spaces, or playrooms, having their own necessary characteristics. However, the developmental strand relating to depiction is the more vulnerable to disruption. It is the "fragile *spielraum*" or "playspace" (Meares, 1990, 1993, 2005). Since it is more recent in evolutionary history than the "pointing" trajectory, it is more easily overthrown by trauma. This idea follows the Jacksonian proposal that those functions which are latest to appear in evolution and development are the first to be lost following insult to the brain-mind system. The "pointing" theme, leading to intentional consciousness (Tomasello, 2000), is relatively robust.

We should suppose, then, that those who have suffered "relational trauma" will manifest a form of language, or more particularly, conversation, which is largely asymbolic. This supposition leads to a brief consideration of the notion of symbol.

Analogy and metaphor

A fundamental distinction separates signs, which animals can use, and symbols. A cloud may be a sign of rain. It "points" to that possibility. A symbol, as remarked previously, depicts. The same image can be used as either a sign or a symbol. It can also be both together, as Shakespeare often demonstrated.

The archetypal symbol is a metaphor. It is a re-presentation of some entity or state. As a depiction, it is typically visual. "The test of a true metaphor", wrote the essayist Joseph Addison, "is whether or not there is sufficient detail for it to be painted" (cited by Geary, 2012, p. 48). Cicero also noted that although all senses may be used in the creation of metaphor, "metaphors drawn from the sense of sight are much more vivid, virtually placing within the range of our mental vision objects not actually visible to our sight" (cited by Geary, 2012, p. 49).

Both these writers conceive metaphors as an aspect of a picturing function. Cicero limits metaphoric representation to that which cannot be seen. This is an important limitation not always adhered to. A similarity between one entity in the sensible world and another, should, in my view, not be called metaphor. Rather, it is an analogy. This point, apparently merely academic, is germane to the understanding of human consciousness developed here.

This distinction is evident where when we consider (again) the figurative use of the cloud image. A cloud can "picture" various kinds of mental states, such as creative thought, when as yet unformed clouds of ideas shift and drift, shaping and reshaping in the mind. Joseph Conrad gives an extended example of this metaphor when, as he said,

> My thought goes wandering through great spaces filled with vague forms. Everything is still chaos, but, slowly ghosts are transformed into living flesh, floating vapours become solid, and – who knows? – perhaps something will be born from the encounter with the indistinct ideas.
>
> (Conrad, 1894, p. 330)

Clouds may also depict an obscured or confused consciousness; or a darkening of mood; or a state of threat and impending doom. John Piper, in his role as war artist during the blitz of the early 1940s, was asked to paint, as a record, a series of buildings important to the national heritage. They were portrayed under the shadow of ominous cloud (Birne, 2017). The king, after viewing an exhibition of these paintings, said to the artist: "You seem to have had terrible luck with your weather, Mr Piper" (Birne, 2017 pp. 20–21).

On the other hand, to call a liquid "cloudy" is not to speak metaphorically but analogically. Both the liquid and the cloud are elements of the visible. An analogue is a thing or entity which has the same "shape" in proportion as another thing.

Additionally, an analogue of something may be another thing with which it shares a particular quality. An example used by Dedre Gentner, an authority on the nature of analogue, is the similarity between a reservoir and a battery, both having the capacity for storage (Gentner & Jeziorski, 1993). There is a "correspondence between two things because of a third element they are considered to share" (McArthur, 1992).

Despite their difference, metaphor and analogy have the same structure. The difference, however, is important, as intimated by Caroline Spurgeon in introducing a discussion of Shakespeare's imagery; "I incline to the belief that analogy – likeness between dissimilar things – which is the fact underlying the possibility and reality of metaphor, holds within it the secret of the universe" (Spurgeon, 1935, p. 6). Although these words are written with the licence of a literary critic, they convey the gist of my argument, which is that the use of analogy is a necessary precursor to the discovery of symbols, and so, to the birth of human consciousness. Both analogy and metaphor depend upon right hemisphere function (Brownell et al., 1990; Bryan, 1988; Winner & Gardner, 1977). The right hemisphere is concerned with pattern recognition, shape and shaping, and a grasp of Gestalt (McGilchrist, 2009, p. 48). We should expect, following the Jacksonian principle mentioned previously, that the use of symbols, which appears late in evolutionary history, would be lost or impaired in those who have suffered relational trauma. It would also be predicted that the neurological systems necessary to their employment would be relatively inactivated, presumably impairing their maturation. In short, a hypothesis is suggested that those suffering the effects of relational trauma will show a deficiency in certain elements of right hemisphere function. This hypothesis gains some support from a series of studies which form a background to this chapter.

Chronicles, scripts and narrative

This account arises out of studies of borderline patients (e.g. Meares, 1993/ 2005, 2000, 2012; Meares et al., 2012; Meares, Stevenson, & Comerford, 1999) and an attempt to find a method of treatment for these people, previously considered "unanalysable" (e.g. Korner et al., 2006; Meares, Stevenson, & Comerford, 1999; Stevenson & Meares, 1992). They are now known, through multiple studies, beginning with the work of Herman, Perry, and van der Kolk (1989), to have suffered various kinds of abuse, typically repetitive.

The development of an approach to the treatment for these traumatised subjects, which has more general application, has been in collaboration with my friend and mentor, the late Robert Hobson (1920–1999). He launched the project with a paper in 1971 and gave it its name, the Conversational Model, in 1985. This chapter is a further contribution to the evolution of the model.

Our studies suggested that, although many kinds of conversations occur with traumatised people, those having the style of a "chronicle", interspersed with the intrusions of a traumatic "script", appear to be typical (Meares, 1998). The chronicle is a catalogue of recent events, symptoms and problems in relationships. The affect is either dull or negative, made up, in the usual case, of a largely undifferentiated state of distress. The expression lacks evidence of the more complex emotions that are characteristic of higher order consciousness. Complex feelings do not appear in conventional lists of "affects". These feelings include, for example, states that are "bittersweet". They might be called "little emotions" (Meares, 2016c). The language of the chronicle reflects a thought process that is literal, concrete, and hyposymbolic.

The intrusion of the "script" of unconscious traumatic memories introduces a different system into the therapeutic conversation. It is a complicated problem, involving issues such as dissociation, the discussion of which would take us beyond the scope of this article. It can be found elsewhere (e.g. Meares, 1999, 2000, 2012). The script can be conceived as the memorial record of repeated impacts of the trauma system upon a developing self.

The focus of this article is upon the chronicle, which I believe to be the outcome of a deficiency, a failure of caregivers to provide appropriate responses to the child's presentations. The therapeutic direction is towards a conversational narrative in which the right brain axis of symbolic depiction is co-ordinated with left brain, linear and syntactical "social speech" (Vygotsky, 1962).

Trauma and disintegration

Although the two conditions reflected in chronicles and scripts are different, they share a state of disintegration which can be demonstrated linguistically (e.g. Butt et al., 2014, 2010; Meares et al., 2005a). That of the chronicle is manifest most clearly in relational terms (Meares, 2017). Superficially, because a syntactical structure is maintained, it does not seem to be disintegrated. It can be understood as a disintegration of right brain origin. It differs from the disintegration in schizophrenia, which may be due to a failure of the lateralisation of language functions (Mitchell & Crow, 2005).

Disintegration is perhaps *the* central pathology induced by relational trauma. It manifests a failure to develop a co-ordination among the elements of the brain/mind system necessary to the emergence of self. For Jackson, self *is* co-ordination. "Le moi", he said, quoting his follower, Ribot, with approval, "est une co-ordination" (Jackson, 1867, p. 82).

This disconnectedness among brain elements in borderline patients has been shown in our studies, in two main, and quite fundamental ways. Both were concerned with the central nervous system's processing of a simple stimulus. In both cases, the data showed that brain systems which normally operate together no longer do so. In the earlier study, co-ordination between sympathetic and parasympathetic systems was impaired. Usually activity of one waxes as the other wanes. In the traumatised patients, this inverse relation was lost (Horvath, Friedman, & Meares, 1980). The para-sympathetic system seemed to be particularly affected, consistent with Porges "polyvagal theory" (Porges, 2011).

In the more recent study, we investigated the brain's processing of a strange, or "odd", stimulus in borderline patients. This process depends upon the co-ordination of two main neural networks. One has a mainly pre-frontal distribution while the other depends on a mainly parietal network. In a control group of patients, the electrical output of the two networks was linked, producing a single waveform in the ERP (event-related potential). In borderline patients, however, the two outputs were not co-ordinated and the onset times of activity in the two networks was no longer correlated. A double peaked waveform was evoked (Meares, 2012; Meares et al., 2005b).

Jacksonian theory predicts the disconnectedness among brain systems shown in these studies. It also predicts that, together with such higher order disintegration, goes a failure of higher order inhibition. In the second study, it was possible to examine this prediction. The part of the P3 (an ERP com-ponent elicited in the process of decision-making) that is generated by the largely prefrontal network, called P3a, is an index of inhibition. A failure of inhibition is reflected in a P3a having an abnormally large amplitude. This was found in the borderline patients (Meares, 2012; Meares et al., 2005b). The finding may help to explain, at least in part, the emotional dysregulation that is a main feature of the borderline syndrome.

A second finding in this study has a more specific implication for the design of a therapeutic method. The P3a enlargement was confined to the right hemisphere. The difference between the readings in the two hemi-spheres was shown with unexpected clarity. The left hemisphere readings in the patient groups did not differ significantly (Meares, 2012; Meares, Schore, & Melkonian, 2011).

In summary, these various observations lead to a view that the emergence of self is underpinned by the parallel and interwoven development of two maturational themes, each dependent on neurological systems largely associ-ated with one or other of the hemispheres. Relational trauma damages this development. The right side is particularly vulnerable. The effects of the traumatic impacts are evident in language and deficiencies of right-hemispheric function. The outstanding pathology is one of disintegration. The chief clinical problem is a stunted experience of self.

Development of self

In order to build a schema for the development of self we need to define what it is we are trying to depict. The definition of this experience has proved elusive. However, some kind of "consensus" is becoming apparent at least in the view of E. O Wilson. Speaking of it in the broadest sense, "mind is a stream of conscious and unconscious experience" (Wilson, 1999, p. 119). This is the core of William James's description, which is now being used by neuroscientists such as Damasio (2012, p. 7) and Edelman (1992) to structure their thinking on the subject. James is now being restored to his role as the culture-hero he once was, after years of neglect during the twentieth century.

James's "self", apparently simple, is quite complex. It has a structure. A main feature is connectedness. "Thoughts connected as we feel them to be connected are *what we mean* by 'personal selves'" (1892, pp. 153–154). In this way, it is as if the opposite of dissociation. As Ogawa and colleagues put it; "Self, in fact, refers to the integration and organisation of diverse aspects of experience, and dissociation can be identified as the failure to integrate experience" (Ogawa et al., 1997, p. 856).

Secondly, self is double. James spoke of the duplex self. The experience of his famous "stream" is made of a unified experience in which are abstractly distinguished two poles, of knower and known, subject and object. Doubleness is a feature of self as Hughlings Jackson also found. There is, however, a fundamental doubleness that James did not explore. It is the essential structure of the symbol. The achievement of symbol use is the hallmark of the appearance of human, or higher order consciousness, as it is manifest in the creations of culture (Cassirer, 1944; Geertz, 1973). The metaphor is two things at the same time, e.g. a shape in the sky and a state of mind. I am proposing that the origin of this doubleness of the human mind is a special form of conversation between child and caregiver, typically the mother (Meares, 2016a). This proposal follows that of Vygotsky.

Lev Vygotsky (1896–1934) was a brilliant Russian psychologist who died young and who was little known in the Anglosphere until the end of the twentieth century. His most important discoveries were in the field of child development and language. He was particularly concerned with the development of the functions making up higher order consciousness. He preceded authorities such as Edelman and Wolf Singer in maintaining that, although earlier types of consciousness, referred to as "primary" (Edelman, 1992) or "phenomenal" (Singer, 2001), can be conceived as evolving and developing largely without the help of the human environment, higher order consciousness, the human self, cannot. Humans have evolved and developed in the context of two environments, one non-human the other human. As Clifford Geertz put it, "man determined, if unwittingly, the culminating stages of his own biological destiny. Quite literally, though quite inadvertently, he created himself" (Geertz, 1973, pp. 48–49).

The contribution of the human environment, both Edelman and Singer agree, is through the use of language (Edelman, 2004, p. 101; Singer, 2001, p. 123). Neither can describe what kind of language this might be. Singer, however, does speak of "early interactions between caregivers and babies" (Singer, 2001, p. 125). Vygotsky gives us a way of characterising these interactions.

Vygotsky's basic "law", if we can characterise it thus, is articulated in a lecture entitled "The Problem of the Environment". He states:

> The child's higher psychological functions, his higher attributes which are specific to humans, originally manifest themselves as forms of the child's collective behaviour, as a form of co-operation with other people, and it is only afterward that they become the individual functions of the child himself.
>
> (Vygotsky, 1935, p. 353)

He was saying that the form of the activity going on between the caregiver and child structurally resembles the function that will become internal.

He enlarges this statement somewhat in introducing the concept of culture, implying that with the achievement of higher order consciousness the child becomes a cultural creature, able to participate in, and even help create in some way, however small, the immense project in which our lives are lived. He wrote:

> Any function in the child's cultural development appears twice, or on two planes. First it appears on the social plane, and then on the psychological plane. First it appears between people as an interpsychological category and then within the child as an intrapsychological category. This is equally true with regard to voluntary attention, logical memory, the formation of concepts, and the development of volition.
>
> (Vygotsky, 1978, p. 163)

Self is not a single function like attention, memory, concept formation, or volition. It is all these things at once, as a single coherence. One might say its function *is* coherence and connectedness. The form of relatedness with the clinical caregiver, or caregivers, is, then, one of connection. This is a simple word but the activity of connection is complex and not easy to describe. First of all, it is *not* like the linkages between train carriages. As James said of self; "It is nothing jointed. It flows" (James, 1890, I, p. 239). The connection is of the kind that is manifest in the game the mothers play with their babies which Colwyn Trevarthen called a "proto-conversation" (Trevarthen, 1974).

The development of self begins at birth or earlier. The mother talks to her baby, and then answers in return, speaking for the child as if they are having a conversation (Kaye, 1982). She is pretending. She is setting up a doubleness which I believe is the first form of the symbol. This conversational game quickly develops so that at about 2–3 months the baby now takes part in a to-and-fro patterning of vocalisation, facial expressions, and body movements which has a structure resembling mature conversation. This is proto-conversation.

The mother's part in this play is to give a "picture" of the baby's immediate expression in the melodic contours of her voice, and in her face and body. If it connects, it creates an instant enlivenment in the baby which, after a series of interactions, may escalate to the expression of what looks like joy. Her picturing is analogical, made of connecting "shapes".

The manner of connection is difficult to characterise. The descriptors of it, researchers such as Brazelton, Stern, Beebe and others, often use the term synchrony. However, as Malloch and Trevarthen (2009) have discovered, the description is not quite apt. Their study concerned the musical patterns made by the mothers and babies voices. A responding pattern was not a mirror nor repetitive. The connections more nearly resembled the structure of harmony. This is consistent with descriptive terms such as "rhythmic coupling" (Stern, 2001) and "timing" (Beebe et al., 1985).

What is important in this connection is a feeling resembling that experienced in a certain kind of dance, in which the expressive patterns of the partners, although not quite the same, "fit" each other in such a way that the other is felt as part of one's experience. It may bring with it an elation, similar to the baby's "joy".

The proto-conversation, evidence collated by Allan Schore (Schore, 2003, 2005) suggests, is as if "a conversation between two right brains" (Meares, Schore, & Melkonian, 2011).

The proto-conversation predicts, and is a necessary precursor to, the next step in the right-hemispheric theme of the development of self. Piaget called it symbolic play, but it is better termed proto-symbolic or analogical play. In this game, a child plays by herself, as if oblivious of others. She chatters as she plays, using what Vygotsky called "inner speech" (Vygotsky, 1962). It has a construction quite different from "social speech", which, in the usual case, is left hemisphere generated. "Social speech" is syntactical, directed towards communication with others and has a goal. It "points" to something. "Inner speech" does not point. Rather, it participates in a "picturing". The language is condensed, abbreviated, and asyntactical. The subjects of sentences are often omitted. Vygotsky called it a language of predicates (1962). Although there can be no such thing in pure terms, "inner speech" is right-hemispheric language.

This rather odd language is "used not for communication with others or for adaptive purposes. Rather, it *seems necessary to the representation of a personal reality*" (Meares, 1993, p. 44; 2005, p. 38). It will be further discussed later on.

Another main feature of proto-symbolic play is relational. The child seems to have partly internalised its necessary predecessor of the proto-conversation, as Vygotsky might have predicted. Not only has she appropriated the mother's analogical mode of expression, she has also "taken in" the relational experience of proto-conversation. As she chatters, she seems to be talking not only to herself but to someone else as well, who is, as it were, part of herself. Piaget, in a beautiful description of this state, called it a "life of union" (Piaget, 1959, p. 243).

The left hemisphere theme of development is going on in parallel with the right. Each theme depends upon a characteristic relational structure. Piaget's "life of union" defines the right-hemispheric relationship. The left is more clearly dyadic, with a distinct difference between subject and object. Its characteristic activity is one of shared "pointing".

The left-hemispheric development evolves through the child coming up against the world, in this way discovering its "otherness". The child's "me" develops a relation to "not-me". Since it's difficult to avoid grappling with the world, this developmental strand is, as remarked earlier, robust. The "pointing" pathway is laid down later than the other. An example of its beginning is provided by the story of Alice who is about 7 or 8 months old (Meares, 2016a). She has recently learnt properly to play the good-bye game. Before this, she waved her fingers at her own face. In doing this she was demonstrating a cardinal feature of the psychic life of the normal developing child before about 7 months. At this stage, infants seem to conceive (as compared to perceive) others as part of themselves. There is not much difference between "your world" and "my world". Rather, there is only one world, the personal, in which "how you see me" is much the same as "how I see you". In the last few weeks a great change has come about in Alice's development, indicated by the turning of her hand through 180° in playing the good-bye game. Michael Tomasello (2000) would call it a "revolution". Alice now takes the first step on the path towards the discovery of "otherness". Sitting on her grandmother's lap they gaze together at something that is "other". It is the night sky, seen through a window. "Look!" exclaims her grandma, pointing to the sky, "stars!"

About a month later, the grandmother is carrying Alice as she walks outside in the night. Once again, she points at the sky saying, "Look! Stars!" Almost in unison, Alice throws up her arm in a parallel pointing gesture. Shared "pointing", to repeat Tomasello's contention, is a major step towards the formation of intentional consciousness. A month later, Alice points alone.

A couple of years later, she is playing the "no" game [not all parents treat this as a game]. It shows others, and confirms for herself, that she is her own entity different from others.

At about the age of 4, the two developmental pathways become co-ordinated to form the double experience of self, a state in which there is both "inner" and "outer", each zone conceived as distinct, but, at the same time experienced as part of unity (Meares & Orlay, 1988) The two language forms are integrated in ordinary conversation. The syntactical, linear form of social or logical speech, which "points", becomes the vehicle for the symbolic mode, the asyntactical, non-linear inner or analogical kind of language which "depicts" (Meares, 1993, 2005). Symbols now appear. The child's use of analogy merges into metaphor, and verbal representations are no longer dependent on the objects used to make them.

Roman Jakobson and the similarity disorder

Observations reported in the previous two sections help to pinpoint the main disturbance brought about by relational trauma. They suggest a scenario in which those subjected to relational trauma have been deprived of the relationship necessary to the emergence of the analogical/symbolising stream of development. This leads to a deficiency of right-hemispheric function. The deficiency can be understood as the result of insufficient activation of specific right-hemispheric systems necessary to their maturation. An essential feature of this activation, the developmental schema suggests, is a certain kind of conversation that is like a "conversation between two right brains", conducted by means of a specific kind of language. A major thrust of a therapy generative of self will be this type, based on principles derived from developmental data. In order to consider how this kind of method can be instituted, we need to examine further the nature of right hemisphere language.

The great Russian linguist, Roman Jakobson (1987), distinguished between two axes of language, one paradigmatic, the other syntagmatic. In the former, one entity can be *substituted* for another, not found in the present. The latter, on the other hand, goes on in the present, involving the *combination* of entities either simultaneously or in succession. These axes correspond to the analogical/symbolic and logical/syntactical systems, spoken of so far. Jakobson considered, as James had done, that these systems "hang together" (James, 1905, p. 107) by relations of similarity and contiguity respectively. The typical trope of the similarity/analogical axis is the metaphor; that of the contiguity/logical axis is metonym. Jakobson went beyond James in building his story on the observations of Hughlings Jackson, thus locating the basis of the two systems in different hemispheres.

The nature of the right-hemispheric language is gained in two main ways. Vygotsky's studies of children, in whom the co-ordination between right brain and the left brains is not yet properly made, is one way to investigate the matter. Jakobson found another. He studied disturbances of speech produced by damage to one or other hemisphere. He structured his inquiry around the themes of similarity/metaphor and contiguity/metonym exploring what he called "similarity aphasia" and "contiguity aphasia".

In discussing the patternings of this disorder, Jakobson made the point that, in normal circumstances, the two systems do not work alternatively but are interwoven and co-ordinated. "In normal verbal behaviour," he wrote "both processes are continually operative but careful observation will reveal that under the influence of a cultural pattern, personality, and verbal style, preference is given to one of the processes or the other" (Jakobson, 1987, p. 110). He gives an example of a simple test designed to show this preference. Subjects are told to say the first thing that comes into their heads on being confronted with a particular noun, for example the word "hut" (Jakobson, 1987, p. 110). The "similarity" preference elicits such words as (i) cabin and hovel, and (ii) den and burrow. The category (i) is an analogue. Category (ii) verges towards metaphor.

Metonymic responses to "hut" might be "thatch" or "litter". In metonym, a part of a thing is used to represent it, or the thing itself is a part of something larger, of which it is an index [e.g. White House for presidential administration].

Jakobson's data concerning a "similarity aphasia" gives an elaborated picture of the chronicle. It is essentially a description of hypertrophy of left-hemispheric, propositional speech. It is highly context dependent. Jakobson remarks that "words with an inherent reference to the context, such as pronouns and pronominal adverbs, and words serving merely to construct the context, such as connectives and auxiliaries, are particularly prone to survive" (Jakobson, 1987, p. 101). This observation is supported by those of Brownell and colleagues who found that patients with right-hemispheric damage show an excessive use of the pronoun "I" relative to controls (Brownell et al., 1992).

These patients are trapped within context. Their verbal operations are "guided by spatial or temporal contiguity rather than similarity" (Jakobson, 1987, p. 104), resembling the "stimulus entrapment" (Meares, 1993, 1997) of the chronically traumatised. This condition, however, is exaggerated by right-hemispheric damage. For example, "the sentence 'it rains' cannot be produced unless the utterer sees that is it actually raining" (Jakobson, 1987, p. 101).

Jakobson described a further entrapment which is of therapeutic relevance. These patients, not being able to use similarity, cannot move from a particular word to its synonym. The patient has an "idiolect" which becomes the "sole linguistic reality" (Jakobson, p. 104). He or she cannot participate in the co-creation of a shared form of language which becomes a means of connection with others. The subject is essentially an isolate.

Jakobson's (1987) analysis, which is strictly linguistic, can be supplemented by more recent findings regarding those with right-hemispheric stroke. An example comes from Davis and colleagues (1997). In this study patients with right hemisphere strokes were compared with controls in the performance of a number of tasks including the telling of a story depicted in the three successive cartoons. This is the story as described by a control subject:

> A lady is walking along the street nicely dressed with a little dog, and she encounters a car with a whole bunch of guys standing around watching the repairmen repair the car. Next one, the lady is repairing the car. The repairman is holding the dog. The rest of the guys are standing around laughing except for the old guy who's not too happy about, with a chauvinist attitude about her fixing the car. The last picture she's got the car all fixed. She waves goodbye to the happy guy inside the car. The rest of the guys are standing around, say "I'll be darned about that".
>
> (Davis, O'Neil-Pirozzi, & Coon, 1997, p. 207)

Here are two examples from subjects' with right hemisphere stroke:

> Well, they had troubles with their car. In the second one, the girl tried to help repair it. In the last one, they seemed to give directions, seemed to be the girl walking the dog.
>
> (Davis, O'Neil-Pirozzi, & Coon, 1997, p. 204)

> A car became disabled, and then a bunch of people came around the car. And they were trying to diagnose what the problem with the engine was. So they lift the hood, and they were looking in the engine. And then apparently whatever was wrong was fixed, because then the car drove off.
>
> (Davis, O'Neil-Pirozzi, & Coon, 1997, p. 202)

A striking feature of these responses is their impersonal nature. They are affectless, leaving out the initial derision of the group of men and then their amazement. In the second patient's response, the girl, who is the "heroine" of the story, is omitted. A sense of the "personal" is the first feature James gives in listing the characteristics of the "stream of thought" (James, 1890, I, p. 225). McGilchrist presents evidence suggesting the experience of the personal depends upon the right hemisphere (McGilchrist, 2009, p. 54).

A second feature of the pathological responses was a subtle kind of disintegration. They had a superficial integration in that they maintained some syntactical cohesion indicated by a method derived from Halliday (1985). The disintegration was of a higher order. They could tell the story only in its bits, with no overarching view. They could not construct a proper narrative. Furthermore, they could not discern the irony that was the point of the story. The investigators concluded that this was the outstanding feature of their subjects' disorder. Irony, like metaphor, depends upon a juxtaposition of two realities. Those with right-hemispheric damage are without the capacity for this doubling of consciousness.

Jakobson compared the deficit produced by right brain damage to dysfunction of the left. This is a state which is agrammatical or, as Jackson would put it, non-propositional. "As might be expected, words endowed with purely grammatical functioning like conjunctions, prepositions, pronouns and adverbs disappear first, giving rise to the so-called telegraphic style". Thus the "kernel subject word ... is the least destructible" (p. 106). Jakobson concluded his thesis with the observation that the distinction between the two forms of language is manifest in the verbal arts in the difference between prose and poetry. A consideration of a certain kind of poetry gives a further illustration of the nature of right-hemispheric language.

The revolution of Emily Dickinson

Not long after Darwin's main publication, another little known revolutionary was at work in an American country town. She was developing a new mode of expressive patterning. In an extraordinary year of creative activity, 1862, Emily Dickinson wrote a poem a day. One of these poems was used by the neuroscientist Gerald Edelman (2004) as an epigraph to his book "Wider than the Sky" in which he summarised his neural model of self. Here is the poem:

> The Brain – is wider than the Sky –
> For – put them side by side –
> The one the other will contain
> With ease – and You – beside –
> The Brain is deeper than the sea –
> For – hold them – Blue to Blue –
> The one the other will absorb –
> As sponges – Buckets – do
> The Brain is just the weight of God –
> For – Heft them – Pound for Pound –
> And they will differ – if they do –
> As Syllable from Sound –

Edelman used the poem because it resonated with his aim "to develop a view of consciousness as a product of evolution rather than Cartesian substance" (Edelman, 2004, p. 2). As Dickinson's poem makes clear, he was by no means a pioneer of such a view which is implicit, for example, in Hughlings Jackson's formulation of the neural basis of self (Jackson, 1867) and William James's various considerations of the nature of consciousness. It is remarkable that Dickinson, a young woman living in a secluded existence, and far from the intellectual capitals, could have developed such a view before them. It is even more remarkable considering the religious atmosphere of her time and the context of her life.

She was part of a community of puritan descent, in which at times, the faith was expressed with evangelical fervour. It would have been hard to resist the fundamental belief, held in every culture that has been studied, and persisting in western culture at least from the time of Plato, that human existence is made of two parts; one part the body and the other "an animating, separable, surviving entity, the vehicle of individual personal existence" (Tyler, 1871, ii, p. 85), variously called soul, psyche, spirit, or mind.

The doctrine of duality was not Descartes' alone. It lay at the heart of the Christian orthodoxy of Emily Dickinson's era. Edward Tyler, the founder of cultural anthropology, remarked that "the conception of the human soul is, as to its most essential nature, continuous from the philosophy" of the hunter gatherer and pre-Christian culture "to that of the modern professor of theology" (ii, p. 85). Tyler's work was published in 1871, nine years after Dickinson's poem. In a few lines, she was demolishing a theory of mind and soul which had persisted for thousands of years.

Her poem is more complex and modern than simply proclaiming an equivalence between brain and mind. She was putting forward a more subtle idea. Both, it is implied, are material. Those states of mind that are "Wider than the Sky", in which we can wander the vast spaces of imagination, memory, of spiritual contemplation, are of the brain. So is God. They have the same "weight" – "The brain is just the weight of God". God is a human construct.

Nevertheless, although brain and mind are aspects of the same thing, they are distinguishable, as "syllable from sound". The sound is what we hear, the experience, while the syllable is the structure that forms the sound.

The revolutionary content of this poem is couched in equally revolutionary form. It is a new kind of poetic language, of great purity, in which the contaminations of prose, and the left hemisphere style of thought, are stripped away. Words extraneous to the "kernel subject" are omitted. The strange system of punctuation creates a prosodic effect which is a cardinal feature of right hemisphere function. It is not unlike the language of protosymbolic play which Vygotsky saw as a precursor to "inner speech". He had described it as "an entirely separate speech function. Its main distinguishing trait is its peculiar syntax. Compared with internal speech, inner speech appears disconnected and incomplete" (Vygotsky, 1962, p. 139). It reflects "thinking in pure meaning" (Vygotsky, 1962, p. 49).

The form of this poem resembles proto-symbolic play in another way, of great importance. The poem implies a relationship. The apparently inconsequential words "you" and "beside" suggests an aspect of the nature of the mind which is beyond anything expressed by Edelman in his attempt to discover the basis of human consciousness. She was saying that it contains a relationship, a "you". She also intimates something of the feeling and structure of this relationship with the word "beside". The "you" is as if by one's side. Some may argue that "beside" meant "as well", and that she chose the word because it rhymed. However, Dickinson was precise in her use of language. I believe the word is a condensation of both meanings.

Vygotsky noted that condensation is a characteristic of inner speech. "The senses of different words flow into one another – literally 'influence' one another – so that the earlier ones are contained in, and modify the later ones" (1962, p. 147). He called it an "influx of sense".

A background to Dickinson's extraordinary burst of creativity between 1860 and 1863, during which she wrote 663 poems (Gordon, 2010, p. 93), was in a strange relationship with someone she called "Master". She wrote three letters to him between 1858 and 1862. A two-line poem, written, perhaps, in 1860 intimates his presence in her mind:

> Least rivers – docile to some sea.
> My Caspian – thee

Who her Caspian was is unknown. The three letters may never have been posted. The letters she had received during her lifetime were destroyed on her instructions, by her sister.

The Master letters suggest that the personage to whom she wrote had some basis in fact, perhaps an infrequent married visitor to the Dickinson home (Franklin, 1986). The reality, however, was largely taken over by the poet's creation of an imaginary figure who may have resembled the one with whom she communicated when she was sixteen who was then called God (Habegger, 2001, p. 168), and in whose vastness she wished to dwell, as if a stream into the Caspian. The tone of these letters suggests that Dickinson's poetry at this time was written in an atmosphere of intimacy. This possibility resonates with Jackson's observations suggesting that the right hemisphere underpins intimate relatedness. I am suggesting that it is in such an atmosphere that the form of consciousness peculiar to humanity develops. It is an early relationship in which the other was felt "beside", in a position in which "you" and "I" sit side by side, gazing at a world, the experience of which is shared (Meares, 1983). This leads us to a brief consideration of the nature of therapeutic conversation in the case of those whose development of self has been disrupted and impeded.

Analogical connectedness

The words designed to bring forth the emergence of self are used in a particular manner in a kind of play, a verbal interplay. It is truly a conversation and not a series of verbal actions and reactions, as in a debate or a certain kind of dialogue. These are public exchanges. That which is concerned with the potentiation of self has the quality of embryonic "innerness". It reflects a relationship which William James called "intimate", a word having a restricted meaning in this discussion. It refers to a condition in which, "when two terms are *similar*, their very nature enters into the relation" (James, 1905, p. 109). The purpose of this relation is to create externally, between two people, a connectedness which will lead to the appearance of the cardinal features of self. Such a hypothesis is "testable", as we shall see.

The relationship of similarity is analogical. The therapist creates an expression having a "shape" that resembles the patient's expression. The resemblance extends beyond a presentation of the patient's "meaning" to include a similarity in the lexicon and verbal structuring of the patient's presentation. Here is an example.

A woman starts her session in a tiny, timid, voice: "Here I am", she says. "Here you are", replies the therapist, in a warm and welcoming tone. They both laugh. The patient starts again, in a stronger, more confident voice, beginning a prolonged anecdote.

The therapist's response appears unremarkable, even banal. Yet it is both skilful and effective. She provides a re-patterning of the words presented to her, creating a resemblance which is larger than the presentation and amplified by her affective tone. Most importantly, she provides the starting point in a movement towards connection.

This session, discussed in more detail elsewhere (Meares, 2017), can only be considered here in the briefest way. The patient R., is a 30-year-old unmarried woman, who has been living for years on the edge of suicide, enduring a barely expressible pain of living. She has had multiple hospital admissions and emergency department visits. Treatment from a series of therapists has yielded little benefit other than keeping her alive. There have been no suicide attempts during her current therapy of one year's duration.

Her background has two most salient features. First, she is beautiful. People stop her in the street to ask if she is a ballerina. Second, she has suffered a severe disturbance in early development. Her mother was afflicted with a paranoid illness during her child's early life. As is well known, the behaviour of paranoid subjects includes a misreading of social signals. Such misreadings give a "shock" to their recipient. There is a startling, even frightening disconnect between the recipient's immediate experience and the paranoid "picturing" of it. This is the situation which produces disorganised attachment. R. had no history of abuse but this early background was traumatic, creating a series of "impingements" (Winnicott, 1965). The responses of the unwell mother would, for much of the time, have failed to "connect with the child's immediate reality and so seem to come from 'outside'", having an effect on the child "rather like that of a loud noise", as a shock (Stevenson & Meares, 1992, p. 358).

Following the opening, the therapist worked consistently towards finding a connection and a sense of "fit" with her patient, using both creativity and discipline in her "picturing capacity". In this process, the "picture" may be a small analogy, perhaps the tone of voice or a bodily posture. The typical form of verbal analogy/metaphor is not always applicable.

The therapeutic conversation comes to be dominated by the theme of beauty. At one point, for example, R. asks: "What happens when people aren't telling me that I have a gorgeous figure, my hair's beautiful? What happens then?" She is caught in a kind of addiction. She constantly seeks, and usually gains, admiration for her beauty. In such a circumstance, her chronic state of fragmentation and anxiety is in part relieved. Her behaviour presumably resembles that of early life. A hypothetical developmental scenario is suggested of a mother burdened by troubling thoughts, unable to attend properly to her child. When, however, she notices she has a beautiful child she feels better and responds. The bond between them is restored. The consequence is that the child, over and over again, works towards gaining the positive feeling of calm and relief that comes with admiration of her beauty.

Soon after this, R. speaks of her despair about a minor, and temporary, facial blemish – a pimple. The therapist knows she is expected to resonate with the despair but knows also that she cannot. It would be fake. It was as if she were caught between two impossible choices, as if in a trap. She felt almost dissociated. She had discovered, through her own experience, what had not been evident in the therapy until that moment. Her dilemma resembled that of her patient, who repeatedly finds herself in situations involving contradictory imperatives.

She made a bland reply which avoided the issue. R., sensed the loss of connection. A slow, controlling voice began. R. was now on the slide to suicide. A crisis had arisen. An unconscious traumatic memory system, different to that relating to beauty, had been triggered. It was presumably related to the earliest and most fundamental disconnections between her and her mother, which precipitated a state of personal annihilation and profound emptiness which is difficult for the adult mind to comprehend and express.

The therapist now made an attempt to describe, in feeling tones and influenced by her own sense of entrapment, her patient's dilemma. They were now both as if side by side gazing at an invisible screen on which the outlines of a "picture" might begin to appear (Meares, 1983). She concluded, her voice rising: "It's such a vice!" a vice being a mechanism which holds in its jaws something so tightly that it is unable to move.

With excitement verging on triumph, R. replied: "Yeah, that's right! That's my life. What part of my life is not a vice?" She went on to describe a fluctuating sense of constriction in living which is the source of her "destiny" in suicide:

> I think ultimately, ultimately, when the walls close in on one so much, that's the way to go. Because if you can't move, you can't breathe, there's nowhere to turn. That's why people do that, and it actually makes sense to me. It does, it doesn't feel like a foolish idea.

She reflects on her situation in a way which had not been possible earlier, remarking on other therapists being misled by the "glamour thing". She said to her therapist: "I think you think people can love me for, you know, not the beauty". She is mentalising. A little while later, an autobiographical memory appears. Reflection, mentalising, and autobiographical memory are cardinal indices of self. Their emergence in the therapeutic conversation followed the therapist's contribution to it of a depicting analogue/metaphor which had the effect of connection with R.'s immediate experience. The hypothesis stated earlier in this section is supported.

The transformation that was affected in this session exemplifies "the therapeutic purpose of right-hemispheric language". This kind of language is analogical/metaphoric having the quality of "picturing". It tends to be brief and condensed. Very often the sentence lacks a subject. The language is used in a particular kind of relationship which can be seen as triadic. Both partners gaze towards a third thing, the "picture" or image which both partners are creating, an example being the "vice". The image is not static, but moving, having a developing course. The conversation is emotionally toned. A successful, and generative conversation has a patterning in which each partner responds to the other in the manner of harmony, a new and different piece of the pattern "fitting" the one before.

References

Beebe, B., Jaffe, J., Feldstein, S., Mays, K., & Alson, D. (1985). Interpersonal Timing: The application of an adult dialogue model to mother-infant vocal and kinesic interations. In T. Field (Ed.), *Infant Social Perception*. New York: Ablex.

Birne, E. (2017). Just a way of having fun. *London Review of Books*. 30 March, pp. 20–21.

Brownell, H., Carroll, J., Rehak, A., & Wingfield, A. (1992). The use of pronoun anaphora and speaker mood in the interpretation of conversational utterances by right hemisphere brain damaged patients. *Brain and Language, 43*: 121–141.

Brownell, H. H., Simon, T. L., Bihrle, A. M., Potter, H., . H., & Gardner, H. (1990). Appreciation of metaphoric alternative word meanings by left and right brain-damaged patients. *Neuropsychologia, 28*(4): 375–383.

Bryan, K. L. (1988). Assessment of language disorders after right hemispheric damage. *British Journal of Disorders of Communication, 23*(2): 115–125.

Butt, D., Henderson-Brooks, C., Moore, A., & Eyal, A. (2014). Motivated selection in verbal art, verbal science and psychotherapy. In Y. Fang & J. Webster (Eds.), *Developing Systemic Functional Linguistics: Theory and Application* (pp. 295–318). Sheffield, UK: Equinox.

Butt, D., Moore, A., Henderson-Brooks, C., Meares, R., & Haliburn, J. (2010). Dissociation, relatedness and cohesive harmony: A linguistic measure of degrees of "fragmentation"? *Linguistic and Human Sciences, 3.3*(2007): 263–293.

Cassirer, E. (1944). *An Essay on Man: An Introduction to a Philosophy of Human Culture.* New Haven and London: Yale University Press, Paperback, 1972.

Cheney, D., & Seyfarth, R. (1990). *How Monkeys See the World: Inside the Mind of Another Species*. Chicago, IL: Chicago University Press.

Conrad, J. (1894). Letter to marguerite poradowska. In F. Karl (Ed.), *Joseph Conrad: The Three Lives* (p. 330). London: Faber, 1979.

Damasio, A. (2012). *Self Comes to Mind*. London: Vintage, Random House.

Davis, G. A., O'Neil-Pirozzi, T., & Coon, M. (1997). Referential cohesion and logical coherence of narration after right hemisphere stroke. *Brain and Language, 56*: 183–210.

Edelman, G. (1992). *Bright Air, Brilliant Fire: On the Matter of Mind*. New York: Basic Books.

Edelman, G. (2004). *Wider Than The Sky*. London: Penguin.

Franklin, R. W. (Ed) (1986). *The Master Letters of Emily Dickinson*. Amherst: Amherst College Press.

Geary, J. (2012). *I Is Another: The Secret Life of Metaphor and How It Shapes the Way We See the World*. New York: Harper Perennial.

Geertz, C. (1973). *The Interpretation of Culture: Selected Essays*. New York: Basic Books.

Gentner, D., & Jeziorski, M. (1993). The shift from metaphor to analogy in. In W. Science & A. Ortony (Eds.), *Metaphor and Thought* (2nd edn, pp. 447–449). Cambridge: Cambridge University Press.

Gordon, L. (2010). *Lives like Loaded Guns: Emily Dickinson and Her Family Feuds*. London: Virago.

Habegger, A. (2001). *My Wars are Laid Away in Books: The Life of Emily Dickinson*. New York: Random House.

Halliday, M. A. K. (1985). *An Introduction to Functional Grammar*. London: Arnold.

Herman, J., Perry, J., & van der Kolk, B. (1989). Childhood trauma in borderline disorder. *American Journal of Psychiatry, 146*: 490–495.

Hobson, R. F. (1971). Imagination and amplification in Psychotherapy. *Journal of Analytical Psychology, 16*: 79–105.

Hobson, R. F. (1985). *Forms of Feeling: The Heart of Psychotherapy*. London: Tavistock.

Horvath, T., Friedman, J., & Meares, R. (1980). Attention in hysteria: A study of Janet's hypothesis by means of habituation and arousal measures. *American Journal of Psychiatry, 137*: 217–220.

Jackson, J. H. (1866). Notes on the physiology and pathology of language. In J. Taylor (Ed.), *Selected Writings of John Hughlings Jackson* (Vol. 11, pp. 121–128). New York: Basic Books, 1958.

Jackson, J. H. (1867). Remarks on the evolution and dissolution of the nervous system. In J. Taylor (Ed.), *Selected Writings of John Hughlings Jackson* (Vol. 11, pp. 76–91). New York: Basic Books, 1958.

Jakobson, R. (1987). Two aspects of language and two types of aphasic disturbances. In K. Pomorska & S. Rudy (Eds.), *Language in Literature* (Chap. 8, pp. 95–120). Cambridge MA and London: Belknap/Howard University Press.

James, W. (1890). *Principles of Psychology* (Vols 1–2). New York: Holt.

James, W. (1892). *Psychology: Briefer Course*. London: Macmillian.

James, W. (1905). The thing and its relations. In W. James (Ed.), *Essays in Radical Empiricism* (pp. 92–122). London: Longman's, Green and Co.

Kaye, K. (1982). *The Mental and Social Life of Babies*. Chicago, IL: Chicago University Press.

Korner, A., Gerull, F., Meares, R., & Stevenson, J. (2006). Borderline personality treated with the conversational model: A replication study. *Comprehensive Psychiatry, 47*: 406–411.

Malloch, S., & Trevarthen, C. (Eds.) (2009). *Communicative Musicality: Exploring the Basis of Human Companionship*. Oxford: Oxford University Press.

McArthur, T. (1992). *The Oxford Companion to the English Language*. Oxford: Oxford University Press.

McGilchrist, I. (2009). *The Master and His Emissary: The Divided Brain and the Making of the Western World*. New Haven and London: Yale University Press.

McGrew, W. (1992). *Chimpanzee Material Culture*. Cambridge: Cambridge University Press.

Meares, R. (1983). Keats and the "impersonal" therapist: A note on empathy and the therapeutic screen. *Psychiatry, 46*: 73–82.

Meares, R. (1990). The fragile speilraum; an approach to transmuting internalisation. In A. Goldberg (Ed.), *The Realities of Transference: Progress in Self Psychology* (Vol. 6, pp. 69–89). Hillsdale, NJ: Analytical Press.

Meares, R. (1993). *The Metaphor of Play: Disruption and Restoration in the Borderline Experience*. Northvale, NJ: Jason Aronson.

Meares, R. (1997). Stimulus entrapment: On a common basis of somatisation. *Psychoanalytic Inquiry, 17*(2): 223–234.

Meares, R. (1998). The self in conversation: On narratives, chronicles and scripts. *Psychoanalytic Dialogues, 8*: 875–891.

Meares, R. (1999). The Contribution of Hughlings Jackson to an understanding of dissociation. *American Journal of Psychiatry, 156*: 1850–1855.

Meares, R. (2000). *Intimacy and Alienation: Memory, Trauma and Personal Being*. London: Routledge.

Meares, R. (2005). *The Metaphor of Play: Origin and Breakdown of Personal Being, Revised and Enlarged Edition*. London: Routledge.

Meares, R. (2012). *A Dissociation Model of Borderline Personality Disorder*. New York: W. W. Norton.

Meares, R. (2016a). *The Poet's Voice in the Making of Mind*. London: Routledge.

Meares, R. (2016b). Pointing and depicting. In R. Meares (Ed.), *The Poet's Voice in the Making of Mind* (pp. 93–100). London: Routledge.

Meares, R. (2016c). Little emotions. In R. Meares (Ed.), *The Poet's Voice in the Making of Mind* (pp. 67–84). London: Routledge.

Meares, R. (2017). Conversational play in the treatment of narcissism. In S. Doering, H. P. Hartmann & O. Kernberg (Eds.), *Narzissmus* (2nd edn). Stuttgart: Schattauer (in press).

Meares, R., Bendit, N., Hailburn, J., Korner, A., Mears, D., & Butt, D. (2012). *Borderline Personality Disorder and the Conversational Model: A Clinicians Manual*. New York: W. W. Norton.

Meares, R., Butt, D., Henderson-Brooks, C., & Samir, H. (2005a). A poetics of change. *Psychoanalytic Dialogues, 15*: 661–680.

Meares, R., Melkonian, D., Gordon, E., & Williams, L. (2005b). Distinct Pattern of P3a event-related potential in borderline personality disorder. *NeuroReport, 16*: 289–293.

Meares, R., & Orlay, W. (1988). On self-boundary: A study of the development of the concept of secrecy. *British Journal Medical Psychology, 61*: 305–316.

Meares, R., Schore, A., & Melkonian, D. (2011). Is borderline personality a particularly right hemisphere disorder? A study of P3a using a single trial analysis. *Australian and New Zealand Journal of Psychiatry, 45*: 131–139.

Meares, R., Stevenson, J., & Comerford, A. (1999). Psychotherapy with borderline patients: I. A comparison between treated and untreated cohorts. *Australian and New Zealand Journal of Psychiatry*, *33*: 467–472.

Mitchell, R. L. C., & Crow, T. J. (2005). Right hemisphere language functions and schizophrenia: The forgotten hemisphere? *Brain*, *128*: 963–978.

Ogawa, J. R., Sroufe, L. A., Weinfield, N. S., Carlson, E. A., & Egeland, B. (1997). Development and the fragmented self: Longitudinal study of dissociative symptomatology in a nonclinical sample. *Development and Psychopathology*, *9*: 855–879.

Piaget, J. (1959). *The Language and Thought of the Child* (3rd edn). London: Routledge and Kegan Paul.

Porges, S. (2011). *The Polyvagal Theory*. New York, NY: W. W. Norton.

Richards, I. A. (1976). *Complementarities: Uncollected Essays*. Manchester, UK: Carcanet.

Schore, A. N. (2003). *Affect Regulation and Disorders of the Self*. New York: Norton.

Schore, A. N. (2005). Back to basics: Attachment, affect regulation and the developing right brain: Linking developmental neuroscience to paediatrics. *Paediatrics in Review*, *26*: 204–217.

Singer, W. (2001). Consciousness and the binding problem. *Annals of New York Academy of Sciences*, *929*: 123–146.

Spurgeon, C. (1935). *Shakespeare: Imagery and What It Tells Us*. Cambridge: Cambridge University Press.

Stern, D. (2001). Face-to-face play: Its temporal structure as predictor of sono-affective development. In J. Jaffe, B. Beebe, S. Feldstein, C. Crown & M. Jasnon (Eds.), *Monographs of the Society for Research in Child Development* (2001/06/29 end, Vol. 66, pp. 144–149). Oxford and Boston, MA: Blackwell.

Stevenson, J., & Meares, R. (1992). An outcome study of psychotherapy for patients with borderline personality disorder. *American Journal of Psychiatry*, *149*(3): 358–362.

Tomasello, M. (2000). *The Cultural Origin of Human Cognition*. Cambridge MA: Harvard University Press, paperback edition.

Trevarthen, C. (1974). Conversation with a two month old. *New Scientist*, *62*: 230–235.

Tyler, E. B. (1871). *Primitive Culture: Part II*. London: John Murray, Reprinted, New York: Harper, 1958.

Vygotsky, L. S. (1935). The Problem of the Environment. In R. Van der Veer & J. Walsiner (Eds.), *The Vygotsky Reader* (pp. 338–354). Oxford: Blackwell, 1994.

Vygotsky, L. S. (1962). *Thought and Language*. E. Hanfmann and G. Vakar (trans and eds). Cambridge, MA: MIT Press.

Vygotsky, L. S. (1978). *Mind in Society: The Development of Higher Psychological Processes*. Cambridge, MA: Harvard University Press.

Wilson, E. O. (1999). *Consilience: The Unity of Knowledge*. London: Abacus/Little, Brown and Co.

Winner, E., & Gardner, H. (1977). The comprehension of metaphor in brain-damaged patients. *Brain*, *100*: 717–729.

Winnicott, D. W. (1965). *The Maturational Processes and the Facilitating Environment*. New York: International Universities Press.

Chapter 10

The formation of two types of contexts by the brain hemispheres as a basis for a new approach to the mechanisms of psychotherapy

Vadim S. Rotenberg

The investigation of brain asymmetry has developed in two different directions. On the one hand, neurologists for a century and a half collected data of the role of local brain structures of both hemispheres in the realization of some definite mental and behavioural functions. This direction of investigation is now equipped with modern methods of brain investigation such as positron emission tomography and fMRI (see Craik et al., 1999).

The investigations performed on epileptic patients with bisected brains also brought much unexpected data. It was shown that in these patients, even in right-handed subjects, the right hand could not copy simple geometric figures and was unable to build simple constructions of child bricks, while the left hand performed all these tasks easily. With closed eyes, the patient could not recognize even quite familiar objects with the right hand, while the left hand did this immediately. If the information was presented to the left visual field (right hemisphere) the subject's behaviour was relevant to the content of this information, but the subject was unable to explain the reasons for his/her behaviour. Moreover, patients with bisected brains periodically demonstrated the behavioural signs of inner motivational conflict which was not realized. Thus, one patient complained that he volitionally embraced his wife with his right hand (managed by the left hemisphere), and at the same time unexpectedly pushed her away with his left hand – a story which in another condition in subjects with undivided brains might immediately bring a psychodynamic interpretation.

The first attempts to interpret the data of investigations performed on these patients were superficial and ignored the possible relationships of this data to essential psychological functions. The most popular assumption proposed that brain hemispheres deal with different types of information: the left hemisphere processes special signs like those present in natural and artificial languages, while the right hemisphere processes the natural nonverbal information such as images, melodies, and intonations of voice, and is responsible for orientation in space and within the subject's own body. This concept seemed to be confirmed by the outcomes of the organic damages of left and right brain hemispheres. For instance, damage to the left temporal lobe is accompanied by motor and sensory aphasia while damage to the right parietal lobe is associated with disorientation in space.

However, further investigations have shown that both hemispheres are able to deal with any kind of information (see Rotenberg, 1993). More reasonable is the concept of Gordon (1978) and Zaidel (1984), according to which the main function of the left hemisphere is the consequential analysis of any information, verbal as well as nonverbal, while the function of the right hemisphere is the simultaneous "grasping" of all elements of information in a holistic way. Such formation of the holistic image determines the comprehension of the object or event just before its consequential analysis.

However, what is really grasped in a holistic way by the right hemisphere? The answer to this question requires the consideration of some philosophical aspects. The objective world that we deal with in our everyday life contains not only objects, subjects, and events. More important are the numerous *interrelationships* between these objects, subjects and events, both real and potential. It is precisely these interrelationships that make the objective world so vivid, rich, and dynamic. These interrelationships may be cooperative, complimentary, or contradictive. The left and right hemispheres differ according to the way they process these interrelationships. The left hemisphere extracts a few of them in order to split reality into simple elements and fragments, and to analyse them in an ordered and consequential way. In contrast, the right hemisphere grasps all interrelationships simultaneously and builds a holistic gestalt of objects or combinations of objects. The more frontal is the brain structure, the more complicated are its functions and the more prominent is the difference between the left and right sides of the brain. Thus, both occipital lobes are responsible for simple visual sensation (simple light flashes, colour, simple shapes) but the right hemisphere has an advantage in processing the comparison of holistic units – for instance, in recognizing whether two images are equal or if one displays a mirror of another (Funnell, Corballis, & Gazzaniga, 1999).

The right temporal lobe is responsible for the perception of single objects (Belyi, 1988) and for the recognition of words as united gestalts, while the left temporal lobe is responsible for the recognition of the word as a combination of single letters. The phonemic, syntactic, and grammatical organization of speech are functions of the left temporal lobe, and this part of the brain is responsible for the discrimination of single components of speech and its hierarchy. Due to this function we are able to understand the difference between the expressions: "Peter was beating Alex" and "Peter was beaten by Alex".

The right temporal lobe is responsible for the discrimination of vocal intonations, and for the discrimination of the voices of different genders – this discrimination is based on the holistic gestalt of the voice. The relevant understanding of poetry depends on the frontal part of the right temporal lobe. The right hemisphere produces more associations on single verbal stimuli in comparison to the left one, including also very distant, indirect associations (Chernigovskaya & Deglin, 1986; Chiarello, 1998). The right temporal lobe assimilates holistic melodies while the left temporal lobe is sensitive to the definite patterns in music such as rhythm.

The right parietal lobe is responsible for the perception of groups of objects (such as pictures with a narrative of simple scenes) while the left parietal lobe is responsible for the calculation of objects and for the fragmentation of reality (Belyi, 1988). The performance of strict and precise movement is under the competence of the left parietal lobe, while the coordination of different movements that determine the harmony of motor behaviour is regulated by the right parietal lobe. The frontal part of the left parietal lobe is responsible for the direction of attention towards definite single objects while the symmetrical part of the right hemisphere is responsible for the attention toward broad unrestricted space. The left hemisphere accepts information only from the right visual field, while the frontal structures of the right hemisphere collect information from both visual fields (Corbetta, Kincade, & Shulman, 2002; Heilman, Watson, & Valenstein, 2003; Weintraub & Mesulam, 1987). As a result, damage to the frontal part of the right hemisphere can lead to the disappearance or neglect of the left part of the space (left side neglect) while damage to the left hemisphere does not cause the disappearance of the right part of the space. It is the right hemisphere that determines the alteration of attention when some rare and unexpected stimulus suddenly appears (Downar et al., 2002).

The right prefrontal area is responsible for the recognition of complicated images such as human faces while the right parietal lobe recognizes emotional expressions (Schore, 2003; Wager et al., 2003). We are convinced by emotional nonverbal expression only when all the components of this expression (mimic, hand movements, etc.) are forming in a holistic gestalt. At the same time, the language of deaf and dumb persons is a function of the left temporal lobe, although it is a nonverbal language, because every single sign in this language has to be understood according to its precise and unambiguous meaning.

If the left hemisphere is damaged in the early stage of maturation, the right hemisphere can compensate its verbal functions. Moreover, the partial restoration of speech perception after the left temporal insult in adults also depends on the compensatory contribution of the right hemisphere. However, if the right hemisphere is damaged in the early stage of maturation the left hemisphere is unable to compensate the deficiency in space orientation. This means that the right hemisphere has some advantages in comparison to the left one even in the early stages of human ontogenesis (Saugstad, 1998).

The contribution of both hemispheres to memory is also different (Rotenberg & Weinberg, 1999). The right hemisphere is responsible for episodic memory, the memory of personally-relevant events, and this memory is based on the strong collaboration between the right hemisphere and the limbic system (Markowitsch, 1995). This depends on numerous interrelationships between single events which make this memory both rich and also resistant to local damage of the brain. The left hemisphere is responsible for declarative memory, based on single linear interconnections between memory units. It is like a combination of numerous more or less independent single networks.

By taking into consideration all of the above-mentioned data, it is possible to conclude that the common function of all of the structures of the right hemisphere is to apprehend and deliver the holistic approach to the world based on the simultaneous grasping of numerous interrelationships between its features and synthesis of these features. The opposite approach, which contains the division of reality into simple elements and its analysis according to definite algorithms, characterizes the left hemisphere structures and achieves its highest level in the left frontal lobe. Frontal "left-hemispheric" logical ways of thinking organize any relevant sign material (whether symbolic or iconic) so as to create a strictly ordered and unambiguously understood monosemantic context. This context only uses a few definite connections between the multiform objects, phenomena, and events in order to avoid any internal contradictions. By forming this monosemantic context the subject builds a pragmatically convenient but simplified model of reality (including the reality of human social relationships) that can be consciously recognized. The monosemantic context is based on:

1. Unambiguous understanding of people communicating through both natural and artificial languages
2. Probability forecasting and expectations
3. Cause-and-effect relationships
4. Categorization
5. The temporal vector

Here are two simple illustrations of how this monosemantic context works:

a. Most words in the dictionary have a number of different meanings; however, in a sentence (if it is not a poem), a particular word usually only has one definite meaning. This happens because in the sentence most of the single word's potential relationships with other words and notions (absent in this sentence) are cut off.
b. The so-called "Kuleshov effect" in cinema, which is when the same human face is perceived subjectively as displaying differing or opposite emotional expressions depending on the context (such as when surrounded by plates or food, or when seen near a coffin).

The frontal lobe of the left hemisphere is responsible for the formation of the self-concept, enabling the subject to separate himself/herself from the world, for conscious self-realization, and for the ability to perceive oneself as an object with different and distinct characteristics. Verbal communication and logical ways of thinking and consciousness have usually been considered by psychologists to be the highest mental functions, and consequently the frontal lobe of the left hemisphere for a long period had a reputation of being the most highly developed part of the brain.

At the same time, the functional meaning of the symmetrical right part of the brain – the right frontal lobe – remained largely unknown and ambiguous until very recently.

However, during the last few decades data has been collected suggesting that the fronto-orbital part of the right hemisphere is responsible for the very complicated mental functions that characterize only humans. These functions include:

1. Empathy (Shamai-Tsoori et al., 2003).
2. Sense of humour (Winner & Gardner, 1977).
3. The understanding of metaphor (Wapner, Hamby, & Gardner, 1981).
4. Theory of mind – the ability to understand how other people understand you in the process of communication (Platek et al., 2004).
5. Creativity (Rotenberg, 1993).

Finally, frontal and fronto-orbital parts of the right hemisphere are responsible for holistic self-recognition (Decety & Chaminade, 2003) and for the formation of the Self-image (Craik et al., 1999; Decety & Sommerville, 2003; Keenan et al., 2001, 2000). Right hemisphere lesions disrupt the sense of self (self-feeling), self-recognition and ego boundaries.

Self-image is an integrative and holistic self-presentation not divided into parts and components. It cannot be totally consciously realized, being polydimensional and too complex to be represented in a monosemantic way. In fact its formation is based on numerous interrelationships between the subject and his/her significant others, not only those who are surrounding him/her in the present but also those who appeared in his/her life in the past, starting from early childhood. It also includes the relationships between the subject and different cultural domains, such as the impressions evoked by literature, art, cinema and so on. Damage to the temporo-parietal cortex of the right hemisphere causes Cotard syndrome – a feeling that the subject does not exist (see Pearn & Gardner-Thorpe, 2002).

Self-image is richer than the idea of self-concept; it includes self-concept as a part of it and is the most important characteristic of the subject that determines the choice of behavioural attitudes and alternatives in complicated and contradictory situations, and is strongly related to the psychological defence mechanisms (see later). Many years ago I proposed that this very important psychological structure (no less important than consciousness and human speech) is localized in the right hemisphere (Rotenberg, 1982).

How to integrate, on the theoretical level, all of the above-mentioned highest functions of the frontal part of the right hemisphere? I suggest that in contrast to the formation of the monosemantic context by the left frontal lobe, the function of the right frontal lobe is the formation of the polysemantic context. In this context the individual facets of images interact with each other on many semantic planes simultaneously, and the whole is not determined by its single components: all specific features of the whole are determined only by interrelationships of these components.

The holistic entity of the right hemisphere activity forms the polysemantic entity only after the formation of the monosemantic context and only in contrast to this context. Here are some illustrations of the polysemantic context:

1. Dreaming. The verbal reports of dreams are usually less impressive and have less meaning than the vivid images of dreams themselves, not only for others who are listening to these reports, but also for the subject himself/herself, because the impression evoked by dreams is caused by numerous (and often contradictory) interrelationships between dream images that cannot be comprehensively expressed in the verbal report, which follows the rules of the monosemantic context.
2. Creative works of art, poetry etc.
3. Emotional expression and its recognition (Adolphs et al., 1994) – for example, where the subject cannot explain in words without substantial failure why he/she loves somebody.

Due to the activity of the frontal part of the right hemisphere, fuzzy categories such as "near", "far", "beautiful" are subjectively understandable but it is difficult to explain them verbally. This nonverbal, implicit form of understanding was alluded to by St Augustine in his well-known observation about the nature of time: "What, then, is time? If no one asks me, I know; if I want to explain it to the questioner, I do not know" (Augustine, 2002, p. 260). The knowledge he is speaking about is the right hemisphere knowledge.

The same regularity characterizes the difference between self-image and self-concept. The subject might for example describe himself/herself verbally in details (self-concept), yet something substantial about what makes the subject unique (self-image) would be lost. The subject's statement, "I can't accept this proposition yet I do not know why", reflects the interference of self-image. Thus on a conscious level Raskolnikov (in Dostoyevsky's *Crime and Punishment*) declares that it is reasonable to kill the old woman who makes a profit at the expense of poor people, and that he is ready to do it. However, when he starts to kill the woman he seems in an altered state and not to understand what he is doing (as if in a dream), and after the act he is confused and unable to overcome a powerful feeling of guilt. This is the voice of his self-image, which is not convinced by the rationalization of his self-concept.

It is necessary to take into consideration that "holistic" is not synonymous with "polysemantic". All the previously described structures of the right hemisphere are concerned with grasping reality in a holistic way, but the formation of the polysemantic context is the function only of the right frontal lobe, as an attempt to overcome the restriction of the monosemantic context created by the left frontal lobe, and only in front of this monose-mantic context. For the right hemisphere by itself, this dichotomy between mono- and polysemy has no sense.

The difference between the two hemispheres also displays itself in their psychophysiology. The estimation of brain hemisphere physiological activity was based for a long period exclusively on the EEG dynamic. As it was con-sidered by many investigators, the percentage of the EEG alpha-waves ("alpha-index") reflects the level of non-specific cortical activation caused by brainstem reticular formation. It was a negative correlation between the alpha-index and the degree of involvement of the corresponding cortical area in mental activity (Wertheim, 1974). However, there are many excep-tions. For instance, the alpha-index sometimes increases during the successful solution of creative tasks performed by creative persons (Martindale, 1975; Whitton, 1978). Such increases in alpha activity are especially strong in the right hemisphere, which is crucial for creative solutions (Ornstein, 1972). In altered states of consciousness caused by meditation, the alpha-index and alpha-wave amplitude are also increased especially in the right hemisphere, in comparison with the ordinary state of consciousness, while there are physiological evidences of the functional activation of the right hemisphere during meditation as well as in other altered states of consciousness (Hirai, 1974; Ornstein, 1972). This means that the increased physiological activation which is important for solving logical left-hemispheric tasks and for finding cause-and-effect relationships is not obligatory for right hemisphere functions and may even destroy them.

In an attempt to solve and overcome these contradictions, Professor V. Arshavsky and I (see Rotenberg & Arshavsky, 1991) have performed psycho-physiological investigations comparing the alpha-index and the so-called spatial synchronization of brain bio-potentials under functional loads addressed predominantly either to the right or to the left hemisphere (see also the correlative analysis of the first EEG derivative, Livanov, 1972). Spa-tial synchronization manifests itself in the number of correlations between brain biopotentials recorded on different points of the scalp (brain cortex). Spatial synchronization reflects the value of the statistical interactions between these spatially disparate points. The increase in spatial synchroniza-tion of brain biopotentials reflects the contribution of definite cerebral mechanisms in the functional system which ensure the performance of the corresponding functions. There are no differences in the amount of spatial synchronization between the two hemispheres during quiet, relaxed wakefulness but the difference becomes obvious when the subject is involved in particular mental activity, and spatial synchronization increases in the right or in the left hemisphere according to the quality of the task.

In order to analyse the dynamic of spatial synchronization we used a special electronic machine which has the capacity to compare the first EEG derivatives in different brain areas and to count the EEG correlations and select the most pronounced correlations in the right and left hemisphere. The alpha-index was calculated in every functional state every sixty seconds. Mental tasks were displayed to the subjects by tachistoscope and included arithmetic tasks, whose difficulty more or less correlated according to the age of the subject. The subject had to solve these tasks during the subsequent sixty seconds. This functional load was according to our proposition addressed to the left hemisphere.

The other task included pictures of landscapes, which the subject had to remember after a short exposition and then describe in detail after imagining them for sixty seconds. This task was presumably addressed predominantly to the right hemisphere. EEG was recorded during both tasks.

Every task was exposed to the subject's left visual field, right visual field, and on the mid-line. When the task was exposed to the visual field opposite to the presumed essence of the task (for instance, when the arithmetic task was exposed to the left visual field – i.e. to the right hemisphere) there were no definite alterations in spatial synchronization. This suggests that the right hemisphere was not actually involved in the solution of the task.

We investigated 117 females and 932 males, ranging in age from 6 to 55. All subjects were right handed.

Analysis of the spatial correlations determined the division of all subjects into three groups:

1. Subjects with functional dominance of the right hemisphere during the imagining of the landscape displayed a high spatial correlation (0.7) between brain potentials in the right hemisphere. During the arithmetic task, these subjects did not manifest an increase of spatial synchronization in either the right or in the left hemisphere.
2. Subjects with functional left hemisphere dominance manifested high correlations of brain biopotentials in the left hemisphere during the arithmetic task presentation. During the process of imagining the landscape these correlations did not increase in either the left or the right hemisphere.
3. Subjects with an equilibrium of hemisphere functions displayed an increase of biopotentials correlations in the right hemisphere during the imaginative activity and also in the left hemisphere during counting.

In subjects of the first group, the alpha-index was reduced in the left hemisphere not only during the arithmetic task solution but even during the rest
period before the task performance. The arithmetic produced a decrease of
alpha-index in both hemispheres, while the imaginative activity did not produce a suppression of alpha-index in comparison to the initial level either in
the left or right hemisphere. In the second group, the arithmetic task performance was not accompanied by a pronounced diminution of the alpha-
index in either the left or right hemisphere, although in the left hemisphere
it had a small tendency to reduce. During imaginative activity the alpha
index reduced in both hemispheres.

The group with functional dominance of the left hemisphere included
more members with an increased level of anxiety and depression and some
psychosomatic disorders (heart ischemia, blood hypertension, peptic ulcer
etc.). It was a sign that less prominent right hemisphere skills may predispose
subjects to neurotic and psychosomatic disorders.

The most prominent decrease of the alpha-index took place during the
arithmetic task performance in subjects with functional dominance of the
right hemisphere. In persons with functional dominance of the left hemisphere, the process of imaginative activity (which is not insignificant for
them) caused a greater physiological activity than the arithmetic task solution. Nevertheless, the arithmetic task solution also caused a small reduction
of the alpha-index. Only the imaginative activity in subjects with right
hemisphere dominance was unaccompanied by additional cortical activation,
which corresponds to the above-mentioned data that creativity and altered
states of consciousness characterized by the functional domination of the
right hemisphere are accompanied by a high alpha-index, which means less
physiological activation of the brain.

The reduction of the alpha-index is pronounced in the condition
which produces dissociation between initial brain capacity and the essence
of the task that had to be solved. We suggested that this activation
reflects the general effort to compensate the relative functional insufficiency of the hemisphere capability in the process of task solution. The
processing style that displays itself in spatial synchronization and general
arousal (unspecific activation of the brain system) are supplemental to
each other.

It seems reasonable to suggest that the additional non-specific activation is
especially necessary for the restriction of the "entropy" of the information.
The production of the monosemantic context by the left hemisphere especially requires such a restriction of "entropy" for the definite and highly
ordered organization of information, and if the brain is not sufficiently prepared for such functioning it requires additional efforts and activation to
stimulate such skills. The polysemantic context is more free and more flexible and does not require additional efforts in subjects with high right-
hemisphere skills (such as creative persons) because the polysemantic context

is oriented not on the restriction of connections and interrelationships between "facets" of information but on its broadness and vividness.

Effective brain hemisphere function, including organization of polysemantic context, does not require the additional activation of the brain which is necessary for the concentration on concrete and restricted relationships in order to analyse the complicated reality. Moreover, such activation cannot compensate the functional insufficiency of polysemantic right hemispheric thinking, which requires an opposite state with a broad view, and for this reason the additional activation of brain structures cannot help patients with mental and psychosomatic diseases that are characterized by deficient image thinking. Additional activation of the brain in subjects with a domination of left hemisphere functions in the process of the solution of right hemisphere tasks demonstrate the insufficient effort of the brain to overcome its restriction and to solve tasks in the relevant way. Polysemantic context and a holistic view requires and determines both "entropy" and "freedom".

Additional brain activation is relevant for the construction of the monosemantic context, but is often used as an attempt to solve tasks for which the brain is initially not prepared, because these tasks need right hemisphere functions and the attempts to displace them by the left hemisphere can lead to the opposite outcome. However, subjects often display a tendency to use skills they already have.

Of course, the "entropy" of image thinking is only a metaphor. It is very specific in nature and it does not mean that this form of thinking is chaotic. Image thinking seems to be disorganized only if we try to compare the rules of its organization with those responsible for the organization of the monosemantic context. Organization of the polysemantic context is based, from my point of view, on the mechanism that makes different probabilities subjectively equivalent. As a result, the most probable combinations or consequences of events (most probable from the logical point of view) have no advantages in the subject's mentality in comparison with formally less probable combinations. Due to the disregard of distinctions between different probabilities, the right hemisphere mode of thinking seems to be "entropic" and does not need the additional activation which is needed for the restriction of connections between objects and events and for the organization of the definite forecast.

The functional insufficiency of the right hemisphere mode of thinking can lead to the hyperactivation of the brain during task solutions in an attempt to compensate this insufficiency using those skills that they already have. Subjects with such insufficiency of image thinking adopt the long-lasting experience of exploiting their left hemisphere mechanisms during the engagement in any difficult task and display the "hyperarousal" state.

The different functions of the left and right frontal lobe can help explain some phenomena in social psychology. In the investigations performed under the supervision of Prof. J. Kuhl (Baumann, Kuhl, & Kazen, 2005) it was shown that even a very simple activation of the left hemisphere (by using physical exercises performed with the right hand) determines in healthy subjects the "infiltration" in the consciousness of the suggestions of the authority ("boss"), and these suggestions are mistakenly estimated by the subject as his/her own voluntary choice. By activation of the right hemisphere such infiltration is blocked. This infiltration differs from the real voluntary integration of the suggestion because it is accepted on the formal, although conscious, level, and may at the same time cause rejection on the unconscious level, although this rejection is suppressed and repressed. It is possible to suggest that the inability to perceive the holistic picture of reality caused by hyperactivation of the left frontal lobe leaves the person unprotected in front of the suggestion. This can be a mechanism of the manipulation of consciousness of "left-hemispheric" subjects which is regularly performed by mass-media. These data correspond with data of the same group of scientists which suggest that in subjects with an activated left hemisphere motives of affiliation and emotional attachment are less prominent than motives of social domination, while the opposite happens with activation of the right hemisphere. The concept of social hierarchy is especially important for the left hemisphere.

Our general statements have been confirmed by discoveries of the ontogenesis of brain laterality and the maturation of the brain (see Saugstad, 1998; Schore, 2003). The first two years after birth is characterized by domination of the right hemisphere. This displays itself in the ability to discriminate the mother's voice from any other sounds and the mother's face from any other objects, and to encode, according to intonation of the voice and facial expression, the mother's attitudes towards the child. Already on the fourth day after birth, the child is able to recognize the mother's voice. Generally speaking, the domination of the right hemisphere (the early development of the right occipital, temporal, and parietal lobes) determines the ability of the child to grasp reality as a holistic entity before any detailed analysis is available, to feel himself/herself as being an integrated part of the world, and to form a general attitude towards the environment, such as whether it requires approaching or avoiding. Such decisions are essential for adaptation and even for survival.

Interestingly, it is a system with a positive feedback: the neuronal connections (networks) in the right hemisphere develop through the process of emotional relationships with the mother and under its influence (Schore, 2001). The initial verbal communication skills appear between 18 and 24 months, when the right hemisphere still dominates, and for this reason it is not surprising that after early damage of the left hemisphere the right hemisphere is able to take responsibility for verbal communication. Parents use speech in the process of communicating with the child: the intonations and global sense of the speech has to be recognized and it is the right hemisphere that displays the necessary predisposition to grasp these. This remains largely reliable even in adulthood, after functional left hemispherectomy (Trudeau et al., 2003). These early skills of the right hemisphere in processing verbal material have long-lasting consequences: I have proposed (Rotenberg, 2001) that the inner speech of adults represents the organization of verbal material according to the rules of the polysemantic context. This corresponds with Vygotsky's idea that the inner word (the basis of inner speech) represents, on the one hand, a precise and definite meaning of the object (as a conditional sign), while also incorporating numerous senses of other, previous and consequent, words, thus tremendously enlarging the boards of its own meaning. This is actually a metaphor for the polysematic network of the senses. The translation of inner speech into communicative speech means a translation from right hemispheric polysemantic context to left hemispheric monosemantic context.

After the second or third year of life, the left hemisphere starts developing more actively than the right. In the school years, the left hemisphere starts to dominate (especially in Western societies). It is not only the development of language but also the development of a specific left hemisphere way of thinking that determines the distinguishing of self from social environment. The final point of this development is the maturation of the left frontal lobe and the formation of the self-concept and the conscious model of reality. This is very important for a person's adaptation in society, and for volitional behaviour, but the domination of the left frontal lobe also has some serious disadvantages: it encourages a feeling of the subject's separation from the world, and can sometimes lead to a sense of actual opposition to the world. This also brings a feeling of disintegration, as if the world is divided into numerous fragments and details. In order to feel themselves comfortable, and to be successfully integrated into the polydimensional world, a person on this level has to overcome the restrictions of monosemantic context. Subjects require a new step, a new level of integration that is different from the initial and relatively primitive integration in the world typical of early childhood when a subject still had no experience of the separation of self from the world. This new level of integration is based on the function of the right frontal lobe, which is the last structure of the brain to be matured.

There is also a difference in brain maturation between genders. In women, the maturation of the left hemisphere starts earlier and the final maturation of both frontal lobes achieves its highest point earlier than in men. In men, the maturation of the right frontal lobe is delayed in comparison to women (Saugstad, 1998).

In the context of the above-mentioned statements, it is possible to give a new interpretation of the Biblical story concerning the eating of the fruit in the garden of Eden, which of course was why Adam was exiled from Paradise. The idea that Adam was punished simply because he did this without permission and prematurely is not very convincing because, according to the text, Adam's initiative and decision was one that was apparently already known and foreseen by God. Adam was in many ways in Paradise in the condition of childhood: he did not separate himself from the environment, as happens in childhood. His every intention was immediately carried out in action, exactly how it happens in children when they are not restricted in their activity. Such a condition if prolonged has no chance to change or develop by itself.

My explanation is the following one. Adam was in a childish paradise without self-consciousness, without the ability to analyse the environment and to separate himself from it. This corresponds to the initial domination of the right hemisphere. For further maturation it is necessary to make the next step. After eating the fruit, Adam starts to realize himself and finds himself in front of a real world with all its contrasts, contradictions, and conflicts. He finds himself different from Eve and in a new relationship with her: he also discovers that they are both nude (which means having a critical view of himself and his partner). He finds his holistic world is broken in pieces, as it happens when the logical-analytical approach dominates. Thus, by eating the fruit (presented to him by Eve – i.e. by the gender that is characterized through earlier left brain maturation), Adam has pushed himself away from the childish Paradise where everything was in harmony, in order to became adult and to perceive and analyse the reality and himself in a proper way. It was an unavoidable step of maturation. However, to find himself in a decomposed world in which he is not integrated is very stressful. The subject requires a new integration that corresponds to the creativity and to the polysemantic view of the world that overcomes the restriction of the purely analytical view. To come to this new level of integration requires a lot of effort. Thus, this Biblical story can be seen as corresponding to the modern view of brain maturation.

The longer the process of maturation in a structure in ontogenesis, the higher the level of function that can be achieved by this structure. The delay in the maturation of the right frontal lobe presents an advantage in the development of the polysemantic way of thinking – one illustrated, for example, in the level of creative skills. However, this long maturation can have also some negative consequences: the longer the period of maturation, the longer the period of increased vulnerability of the structure, which is sensitive to any type of damage – infection, physical and psychological trauma, and so on. Thus, the longer process of maturation of the brain in men may explain the relatively higher number of serious mental disorders such as schizophrenia. Even subtle damage of the right frontal lobe during stress before its final maturation may disturb the integration of the subject in the world and the formation of effective defence mechanisms.

In this context, it is important to first of all determine the main function of these defence mechanisms. It is unlikely that these are primarily to prevent the realization of negative emotional feelings. This would be maladaptive since that subject has to cope with many events that cause such feelings and have ample opportunity to generate them. Rather, I suggest that the task of the defence mechanisms is to prevent the disintegration of the self and of goal-oriented holistic behaviour, and for these reasons they prevent the realization only of that information which may cause such disintegration. However, by accepting this view we are not avoiding the well-known paradox of how defence mechanisms which are functioning out of the subject's consciousness are also protecting that consciousness and taking into consideration its needs. I suggest that the concept of self-image localized in the right frontal lobe can solve this paradox. As I have already stressed, it belongs to the kingdom of the unconscious but at the same time incorporates, among other things, conscious attitudes (self-concept is a part of the self-image – that is, is integrated in the self-image which is the highest instance of personality). Thus it represents consciousness in the domain of unconsciousness. On the other hand, the right hemisphere pays attention to both sides of space and collects all information and all possible interrelationships between different facets of information (Weintraub & Mesulam, 1987). Moreover, the right hemisphere has an advantage in the speed of its information processing (see Schweinberger & Sommer, 1991). Thus, self-image is able to grasp and to estimate information on the unconscious level before its realization, and to decide what is relevant for consciousness and what is not. The latter is not allowed to enter consciousness (by mean of repression).

Perceptual defence (denial) is another mechanism. At first glance, it is also paradoxical in its nature: in order to increase the threshold of perception for any inappropriate information and not to allow this information to be accepted by the brain, the latter has to decide what information has to be blocked, so it has to be somewhere informed about this information. This paradox may be one of the reasons why this defence was denied by some authors or mixed with repression by others. However, it is possible to give a reasonable explanation for this mechanism. The brain estimates all information in the context of its previously-formed model of reality, with expectations based on prior experience. The brain is able to use probability forecasting in order to predict whether the present information that is not destructive by itself can be followed (and was previously statistically significant followed) by the dangerous information that the subject has to be protected from. Thus, the relatively neutral information in the particular context may be estimated as a sign to increase the perceptual threshold.

One clinical case confirms this theoretical assumption. I remember on one occasion speaking with a friend who was known as being very anxious and vulnerable to health problems. He was worrying at that time about a small furuncle on his face and asked me whether I supposed it could be dangerous. In a psychotherapeutic way I explained to him that it was not a problem at all, and that it was quite enough to simply use iodine for few days. However, on this occasion another person heard our conversation and he interfered with the following message: "Don't be so sure! Once my friend had a similar furuncle, it increased, an inflammation developed, a blood-poisoning appeared, and he died from encephalitis." I was really shocked by this sudden comment and became so confused that I reacted in a stupid way: "What are you saying? He died? That's incredible!" And suddenly my friend asked me with great surprise: "Who died? Why you are talking about death? Did somebody mention death?" It was obvious that he'd missed the most terrible part of the message. But how? My friend had approached me with his worries, being sure that I would calm him down as usual. When another person, a stranger, started his speech with the attention eliciting phrase, "Don't be so sure" etc., and afterwards started to tell the story, it was felt as yet another sign that something inappropriate was coming to frustrate my friend. According to this sign, his perceptual threshold increased and he actually missed the most frightening part of the story. However, when I opened my mouth and started to respond, the perceptual threshold immediately dropped, because from me, according to previous experience, he expected only positive information. And suddenly he heard my confused reaction: "He died?" being at that moment unprotected by perceptual defence.

This suggests that, first of all, the perceptual defence really exists – if it would be a repression, my own sentence would be also repressed. Secondly, this defence is not perfect: if the (monosemantic) context does not contain relatively neutral but predictive information, the subject is not protected enough. On the other hand, the information that is really not predictive can on occasion be estimated as a signal one, and as a result the perceptual defence can be activated and the subject can lose some important information that does not require defence.

The role of the right frontal lobe in the formation of self-image, in the relevant integration in the polydimensional world by means of the polysemantic way of thinking, and in defence mechanisms, can explain the development of mental and psychosomatic diseases in subjects with deficiency of the right frontal lobe function. The subject with such deficiency can find himself/herself unprotected in front of a complicated and contradictory reality.

The main mental and psychosomatic diseases are characterized by right hemisphere dysfunction. In schizophrenia, such dysfunction represents itself in the deficiency of the following functions: perception of facial emotional expression (Borod et al., 1993); visuospatial task performance (Gabrovska-Johnson et al., 2003); ability to grasp global forms; clumsy behaviour; general deficiency and the disintegration of self-image (Rotenberg, 1994); affective blunting; lack of empathy; and inability to create a polydimensional picture of the world.

Depression is also characterized by deficient right frontal functions (Bench et al., 1992; Rotenberg, 2004): inability to interpret nonverbal information (facial expression, voice prosody, gestures), poor face recognition, less vivid imagery, lack of dream reports, lack of cognitive flexibility. A common factor in mental and psychosomatic disorders is alexithymia, which can also be seen as a sign of right hemisphere deficiency (Rotenberg, 1995).

Thus, the main task of psychotherapy is the restoration of the patient's right frontal lobe skills, the polysemantic way of thinking. It is a commonplace that the basis of any form of psychotherapy is the emotional empathy between the psychotherapist and the client. Speaking in our terms, this empathy is the first thread that restores the violated, vivid, and polysemantic relationships between the client and the world. For this reason, the scale of the psychotherapist's personality has to be at least as high as the scale of the personality of the client. Although the concrete forms are less important than this basis, it is possible to show that very different forms of psychotherapy have common roots related to right frontal lobe functions: art therapy, dance therapy, and music therapy, for example, all activate right hemisphere skills and creativity. Altered states of consciousness very often used in psychotherapy, such as meditation, yoga, and hypnosis, are activating the same structures of the brain (Ornstein, 1972; Rotenberg & Arshavsky, 1995). According to Ammon, positive social energy in the process of group therapy is actually based on the vivid net of polysemantic interrelationships between group members (see Rotenberg, 1995). Even in classical psychoanalysis the analytical intervention by itself is secondary, while dream reports and free associations directly stimulate and develop right hemisphere skills. I suggest that this is more important than the analytical interpretation of dreams and associations. It is not an accident that from session to session in psychoanalysis, as well as in other forms of psychotherapy, both the length of dream reports and the number of free associations increases, and it is a sign of the success of psychotherapy. It is important for the mental health restoration in itself, no matter how correct are the interpretations presented by the therapist. I have come to the conclusion that the classical statement of psychoanalysis: "Cure through the realization of complexes and repressed wishes" has to be replaced by another statement: "Realization of the complexes and previously repressed wishes through the cure based on the activation of the polysemantic way of thinking. And, as result, the reintegration of the subject in the polydimensional world." Only after this reintegration is achieved, step by step, does the subject not require more repression for the protection of self-image and integrative holistic behaviour, and as a result the subject can realize some problems that previously paralysed him/her.

Some data of the psychophysiological predispositions vs. outcomes of psychotherapy confirm the above-mentioned physiological entropy of right frontal brain activity. Moscovitch et al. (2011) investigated regional EEG activity in patients with social anxiety disorders (SAD) before and after cognitive behavioural therapy. These patients shifted from greater relative right frontal brain activity (according to alpha-rhythm) in the resting state before treatment to greater left resting frontal brain activity just after treatment. In some other investigations (Barnhofer et al., 2007; Davidson et al., 2003) it was also shown that frontal EEG asymmetry is sensitive to the effect of therapy. This means that the emotional tension in socially anxious subjects determines right frontal brain activity. According to Moscovitch et al., pretreatment frontal alpha EEG asymmetry (less right-sided or more left-sided activity that is typical for healthy subjects during rest) was associated with more prominent reduction in social anxiety after treatment.

According to the above-mentioned suggestion (Rotenberg & Arshavsky, 1991), the relative increase of physiological activation of the right frontal lobe may reflect the functional insufficiency of this structure in patients with mental disorders. The weak skill of this structure may explain the low effect of any types of psychotherapy, including cognitive behavioural therapy, because in the process of any type of psychotherapy the emotional contact and empathic relationships with the patient is very important. It is sometimes not mentioned that without this empathic interrelationship between patient and psychotherapist any attempt of the rational analysis of the client's problems and of the patient's reorientation on the new view of his/her situation may not be sufficiently successful.

However, there can also be another explanation. Some authors (see Moscovitch et al.) suggest that the predictive relation between increased relative left hemisphere activity at pretreatment and enhanced response in behavioural therapy might reflect superior left-sided verbal processing abilities which support the core verbal therapeutic techniques used in cognitive behavioural therapy. Brody et al. (1998) reported that patients with OCD (obsessive-compulsive disorder) with a higher pretreatment level of activity in their left orbital frontal cortex responded best to behavioural therapy. This means that in addition to the role of the functionally sufficient right hemisphere in the process of psychotherapy the possible role of the left hemisphere has also to be taken into consideration.

I once got a letter from someone who was familiar with my publications on the important role of the emotional relationship between the psychotherapist and client in the process of psychotherapy, and decided to share with me his own experience and to put my attention on the ignored aspect of the problem — on the possible role of the left hemisphere in the process of the restoration of normal emotional states.

This person was for a long time in a state of frustration and emotional stress, had lost his creativity, and suffered from melancholia. At that moment he had nobody to apply to for help and emotional support — neither professional psychotherapists nor friends and relatives were able to really listen to him. But then he got the idea from someone to write down for himself everything that he felt and all the thoughts that came to his mind in this terrible emotional state. He started to transfer his unclear and confused feelings into an organized text, and suddenly felt improvement. Of course, this method is oriented predominantly in the left hemispheric analytical way of thinking. What happens during the process of such activity?

Subjects in the state of stress, for instance caused by inner motivational conflict, become helpless in front of the complicated and polysemantic world of their own emotional experiences and relationships and are unable to integrate themselves in this world. Their right hemisphere, which is creating their self-image, is not functioning well enough to integrate the self-image into the image of the world. In order to solve this problem it is necessary to simplify the surrounding world artificially, and it is the left hemisphere that can do this. Of course it is an artificial solution, but at least it helps to decrease the emotional tension in subjects who do not have sufficient right-hemispheric skills.

References

Adolphs, B., Tranel, D., Damasio, H., Damasio, A. (1994). Impaired recognition of emotion in facial expressions following bilateral damage to the human amygdala. *Nature 372*:669–672.

Augustine. (2002). *Confessions*. R. S. Pine-Coffin (Trans.). London: Penguin.

Barnhofer, T., Duggan, D., Crane, C., Hepburn, S., Fennell, M., Williams, J. (2007). Effects of meditation on frontal alpha-asymmetry in previously suicidal individuals. *Neuroreport 18*:709–712.

Baumann, N., Kuhl, J., Kazen, M. (2005). Left-hemispheric activation and self-infiltration: Testing a neuropsychological model of internalization. *Motivation and Emotion 29*:135–163.

Belyi, B. (1988). The role of the right hemisphere in form perception and visual gnosis organization. *International Journal of Neuroscience 40*:167–180.

Bench, C., Friston, K., Brown, R., Scott, L., Frackowiak, R., Dolan, R. (1992). The anatomy of melancholia: Focal abnormalities of cerebral blood flow in major depression. *Psychology Medicine 22*:6Hl–6\5.

Borod, J., Martin, C., Alpert, M., Brozgold, A., Welkovitz, J. (1993). Perception of facial emotion in schizophrenic and right-brain damaged patients. *Journal of Nervous and Mental Diseases 181*:494–502.

Brody, A. L., Saxena, S., Schwartz, J. M., Stoessel, P. W., Maidment, K., Phelps, M. E., Baxter, L. R. (1998). FDG-PET predictors of response to behavioral therapy and pharmacotherapy in obsessive-compulsive disorder. *Psychiatry Research 84*:1–6.

Chernigovskaya, T. V., Deglin, V. L. (1986). Brain functional asymmetry and neural organization of linguistic competence. *Brain and Language 29*:\A\–\5i.

Chiarello, C. (1998). On codes of meaning and the meaning of codes: Semantic access and retrieval within and between hemispheres. In M. Beeman, C. Chiarello (eds.): *Right Hemisphere Language Comprehension: Perspective from Cognitive Neuroscience*; pp. 141–160. Mathwah, NJ: Erlbaum.

Corbetta, M., Kincade, J. M., Shulman, G. L. (2002). Neural systems for visual orienting and their relationships to spatial working memory. *Journal of Cognitive Neuroscience 14*:508–523.

Craik, F., Moroz, T., Moscovitch, M., Stuss, D., Winocur, G., Tulving, E., Kapur, S. (1999). In search of the self: A positron emission tomography study. *Psychological Science 10*:26–34.

Davidson, R. J., Kabat-Zinn, J., Schumacher, J., Rozenkranz, M., Muller, D., Santorelli, S. P., Urbanowski, F., Harrington, A., Bonus, K., Sheridan, J. F. (2003). Alterations in brain and immune function produced by mindfulness meditation. *Psychosomatic Medicine 65*:564–570.

Decety, J., Chaminade, T. (2003). When the self represents the other: A new cognitive neuroscience view on psychological identification. *Consciousness and Cognition* 12:577–596.

Decety, J., Sommerville, J. (2003). Shared representations between self and other: A social cognition neuroscience view. *Trends in Cognitive Science* 1:527.

Downar, J., Crawley, A., Mikulis, D., Davis, K. (2002). Cortical network sensitive to stimulus salience in a neutral behavioral context across multiple sensory modalities. *Journal of Neurophysiology* 87:615–620.

Funnell, M., Corballis, P., Gazzaniga, M. (1999). Deficit in perceptual matching in the left hemisphere of a callosotomy patient. *Neuropsychologic* 37:143–H54.

Gabrovska-Johnson, V., Scott, M., Jeffries, S., Thaker, N., Baldwin, R., Burns, A., Lewis, S., Deakin, J. (2003). Right hemisphere encephalopathy in elderly subjects with schizophrenia: Evidence from neuropsychological and brain imaging studies. *Psychopharmacology (Berlin)* 169:367–375.

Gordon, H. (1978). Left hemisphere dominance for rhythmic elements in dichotomically presented melodies. *Cortex* 14:58–70.

Heilman, K. M., Watson, R. T., Valenstein, E. (2003). Neglect and related disorders. In K. M. Heifman, E. Valenstein (eds.): *Clinical Neuropsychology*; pp. 296–346. London: Oxford University Press.

Hirai, T. (1974). *Psychophysiology of Zen*; p. 186. Tokyo: Igaku Shoin.

Keenan, J. P., Nelson, A., O'Connor, M., Pascual-Leone, A. (2001). Self-recognition and the right hemisphere. *Nature* 409:305.

Keenan, J. P., Wheeler, M., Gallup, G., Jr., Pascual-Leone, A. (2000). Self-recognition and the right prefrontal cortex. *Trends in Cognitive Sciences* 4:338–344.

Livanov, M. N. (1972). *The Space Organization of the Brain Processes*. (in Russian). Moscow: Nauka.

Markowitsch, H. (1995). Anatomical basis of memory disorders. In M. S. Gazzaniga (ed.): *Cognitive Neuroscience*; pp. 765–779. Cambridge, MA: MIT Press.

Martindale, C. (1975). What makes creative people different? *Psychology Today* 7:44.

Moscovitch, D. A., Santesso, D. L., Miskovic, V., McCabe, R. E., Antony, M. M., Schmidt, L. A. (2011). Frontal EEG asymmetry and symptom response to cognitive behavioral therapy in patients with social anxiety disorder. *Biological Psychology* 87:379–385.

Ornstein, R. (1972). *The Psychology of Consciousness*. San Francisco, CA: Freeman.

Pearn, J., Gardner-Thorpe, C. (2002). Jules Cotard (1840–1889). His life and the unique syndrome which bears his name. *Neurology* 58:1400–1403.

Platek, S., Keenan, J., Gallup, G., Jr., Mohamed, F. (2004). Where am I? The neurological correlates of self and other. *Brain Research Cognitive Brain Research* 19:114–122.

Rotenberg, V. S. (1982). Funktionale Dichotomie der Gehirnhemispheres und die Bedeutung der Such-aktivitat fur Physiologische und Psychopathologishe Processe. In G. Ammon (ed.): *Handbuch Der Dynamische Psychiatrie*. Vol. 2; 275–335. Munchen: Ernst Reinhardt.

Rotenberg, V. S. (1993). Richness against freedom: Two hemisphere functions and the problem of creativity. *European Journal For High Ability* 4:11–19.

Rotenberg, V. S. (1994). An integrative psychophysiological approach to brain hemisphere functions in schizophrenia. *Neuroscience and Biobehavioral Reviews* 18:487–495.

Rotenberg, V. S. (1995). Right hemisphere insufficiency and illness in the context of search activity concept. *Dynamic Psychiatry 150*(151):54–63.

Rotenberg, V. S. (2001). *Dreams, Hypnosis and Brain Activity.* Moscow: Center of Humanitarian Literature (in Russian).

Rotenberg, V. S. (2004). The peculiarity of the right-hemisphere function in depression: Solving the paradoxes. Progress. *Neuro-Psychopharmacology & Biological Psychiatry 28*:1–13.

Rotenberg, V. S., Arshavsky, V. V. (1991). Psychophysiology of Hemispheric Asymmetry. The "Entropy" of Right Hemisphere Activity. *Integrative Physiological and Behavioral Science 26*(3):183–188.

Rotenberg, V. S., Arshavsky, V. V. (1995). The "entropy" of right hemisphere activity and the restorative capacity of image thinking. *Journal of Mental Imagery 19*:151–160.

Rotenberg, V. S., Weinberg, I. (1999). Human memory, cerebral hemispheres, and the limbic system: A new approach. *Genetic, Social and General Psychology Monographs 125*:45–70.

Saugstad, L. F. (1998). Cerebral lateralization and rate of maturation. *International Journal of Psychophysiology 28*:37–62.

Schore, A. (2001). The effects of early relational trauma on right brain development, affect regulation, and infant mental health. *Infant Mental Health Journal 22*:201–226.

Schore, A. (2003). *Affect Regulation and the Repair of the Self.* New York, London: Norton.

Schweinberger, S. R., Sommer, W. (1991). Contributions in stimulus encoding and memory search to right hemisphere superiority in face recognition: Behavioral and electrophysiological evidence. *Neuropsychologia 29*:389–413.

Shamai-Tsoori, S. G., Tomer, R., Berger, B. D., Aharon-Peretz, J. (2003). Characterization of empathic deficits following prefrontal brain damage. The role of the right ventromedial prefrontal cortex. *Journal of Cognitive Neuroscience 15*:324–337.

Trudeau, N., Colozzo, P., Sylvestre, V., Ska, B. (2003). Language following functional left hemispherectomy in a bilingual teenager. *Brain and Cognition 53*:384–388.

Wager, T. D., Phan, K. L., Liberzon, I., Taylor, S. F. (2003). Valence, gender, and lateralization of functional brain anatomy in emotion: A meta-analysis of findings from neuroimaging. *Neuroimage 19*:513–531.

Wapner, W., Hamby, S., Gardner, H. (1981). The role of the right hemisphere in the apprehension of complex linguistic material. *Brain and Language 14*:15–33.

Weintraub, S., Mesulam, M. M. (1987). Right hemisphere dominance in spatial attention. *Archives of Neurology 44*:621–625.

Wertheim, A. H. (1974). Oculomotor control and occipital alpha activity. A Review and a hypothesis. *Acta Psychologica 88*:235–256.

Whitton, A. H. (1978). EEG frequency patterns associated with hallucinations in schizophrenics and "creativity" in normals. *Biology Psychiatry 13*:123–133.

Winner, E., Gardner, H. (1977). The comprehension of metaphor in brain damaged patients. *Brain 100*:717–729.

Zaidel, M. (1984). Les functions de l'hemisphere droit. *Recherone 15*:332–349.

Index

Printed in Great Britain
by Amazon

47665500R00172